P9-DCM-627

OFF TO THE RACES

OFF TO THE RACES

25 Years of Cycling Journalism

Samuel Abt

BOULDER, COLORADO

OFF TO THE RACES: 25 YEARS OF CYCLING JOURNALISM

Printed in the United States of America

10 9 8 7 6 5 4 3 2 1

Distributed in the United States and Canada by Publishers Group West

International Standard Book Number: 1-931382-06-9

Library of Congress Cataloging-in-Publication Data applied for.

VeloPress
1830 N. 55th Street
Boulder, Colorado 80301-2700 USA
303/440-0601; Fax 303/444-6788;
E-mail velopress@7dogs.com

To purchase additional copies of this book or other VeloPress books, call 800/234-8356 or visit us on the Web at velopress.com.

Cover design and interior design by Susie Alvarez Perry
Cover photo by Graham Watson. Milan–San Remo, Italy, 1991.

One more time, with love and respect,
this book is for my children, Claire, Phoebe and John.

It is better to be out than in. It is better to be on the lam than on the cover of Time *magazine.*

— Nelson Algren

Contents

PART THREE: RACES AND PLACES

Acknowledgments

DURING ALL THESE YEARS of going to bicycle races, I have been luckier than I deserved in my traveling companions, including Barbara Bell, Becky Rast, James Startt, Geoffrey Nicholson, Stephen Bierley, Graham Jones, Salvatore Zanca, Robert Zeller, Phil Liggett, John Wilcockson, David Walsh, Rupert Guinness, Mike Price, Steve Wood and Tim Maloney.

I also thank the fine editors who have worked with me at the *International Herald Tribune* and *The New York Times,* where many of these pieces first appeared.

Thanks also to Wyli Kao for her typing help and, once again, to Anne-Sophie Bolon for her computer wizardry.

Preface

1999

FOR THE FIRST FIVE YEARS after I moved to Paris from a job in New York in 1971, the only sports that still mattered to me were the ones I grew up playing and watching. Through blizzards of static I listened on a short-wave radio to the Armed Forces Network in Germany (France had expelled all American soldiers years before) as it broadcast baseball and football games from home. Television showed only soccer or rugby matches and the infrequent bicycle race—all of them incomprehensible sports, especially bicycle racing, which, in a phrase I liked to repeat then, was merely a bunch of guys pedaling in their underwear.

The person I liked to repeat that phrase to was the woman I was living with in Paris, an American also and one with many interests and even passions. They included, in no particular order, the cello, physics, anything Spanish, badminton, acoustics, me and bicycle racing. I was indifferent to most of these, with bicycle racing near the top of that list. When, for example, she invited me in 1974 to join her in watching the finish of the Tour de France at the Stade Municipale de Vincennes, in the east of Paris, I ostentatiously chose instead to spend the day with a friend in a forest west of Paris, hunting mushrooms. What made it ostentatious was that I had never looked for mushrooms before, as she well knew, and never did again. This other friend, male, and I found quite a few of the big, meaty kind that the French call *cèpes* and had them for dinner in a tasty omelet. That was the worst trade-off since Esau gave away his birthright for a mess of gruel; I realized, years later, that I had blown my chance to see not only the last finish of the Tour in the Vincennes velodrome—the race ended the next year, and ever since, on the Champs-Elysées—but also the last Tour won by Eddy Merckx.

I caught up with Merckx, or the shell he had become, in 1977. By then, in a feverish swirl of office politics, I had moved from being news editor of the *International Herald Tribune* to sports editor, a less-demanding job and one out of the line of fire. My roommate and I had married by then and had a son, and I decided, obliging fellow that I was and am, to show my wife a good time by assigning myself to cover a bicycle race and bringing her along. No point in starting at the bottom or even the middle: The first race I saw was the prologue to the 64th Tour de France, June 30, 1977, in the town of Fleurance in the southwest, my favorite part of France for eating, drinking and sightseeing. Off the family went, all expenses paid. So what if I had to justify the trip by writing about a bicycle race? That couldn't be too difficult, although uninteresting. Just a bunch of guys pedaling in their underwear.

As I write this, I am also looking at the clipping of my first article about the sport, in which I reported that Didi Thurau, a 22-year-old German, won the prologue (which I seem to have called "a trial sprint," whatever that meant) over Gerrie Knetemann, 26, a Dutchman, with Merckx, 33 (whom I described, accurately, as both a veteran and the people's choice). A possibly indifferent world learned from me that Knetemann's performance was no surprise since he was "a sprint specialist" and had no long-range future in the Tour but that Thurau's was a stunner and promised much since he was "considered to be of longer-lasting quality." Not that I was the one doing the considering. That was the counsel of Emile Besson, the correspondent of *l'Humanité Dimanche,* next to whom, by chance, I was sitting in the covered market that served as a press room for the 30 or 40—today 300 or 400—reporters with the Tour. A kindly man, now retired but still to be seen sometimes at Tour and team presentations, Besson took the time to instruct me that Thurau had already won that year the Tour of Andalusia in Spain and had finished second, to Knetemann, in the Grand Prix of Frankfurt. Those details stood out in my article, testimony to my intimate knowledge of the sport. When Thurau continued to hold the yellow jersey the next two weeks, my reputation was made to editors of both the *Herald Tribune* and *The New York Times,* which have published my work ever since. (My reputation was slightly unmade two weeks later after the climb to Chamonix, when Thurau lost the jersey to Bernard Thévenet, the eventual winner of that Tour, and I wrote that "this territory seems tailored for Lucien van Impe, last year's winner," but nobody should blame Besson for that bit of expertise. By then I considered myself so knowledgeable that I needed nobody's counsel. After all, I had been following the sport for a full two weeks.)

By then, also and of course, I was hooked. The color, the speed, the glorious scenery, the companionship, the pageantry, the sheer athletic skill of the riders, their availability and willingness to talk—all thrilled me then and still, after more than 20 years of watching and writing about the sport.

My second piece about the Tour was a portrait of Merckx: "When he mounted the starting ramp, the crowd pressed in, the cheers grew louder, the cameramen swarmed around and fathers lifted their small children for a look at Merckx in his final Tour de France." One of those fathers was me and one of those small children was my son John, then not quite nine months old. His mother lifted him for a look at Merckx, too. People remember that they saw Eddy Merckx in the Tour, even if only once. This is a sport that, for a lucky few, you have to see only once to love.

"WHY DO YOU ALWAYS REFER to the Tour de France as a bicycle race?" a vexed Lance Armstrong asked several years ago. "Why don't you just call it a race?" (For somebody who says he never reads about the sport in newspapers, he always seems to know what they say about it.)

I explained that many general readers simply did not know what the Tour de France is—or was in the days before Armstrong began winning the race and becoming a national figure. For that reason, I said, I never wrote about such technical matters as gear ratios or saddle heights, remembering that even my mother, my most devoted fan, told me she stopped reading whenever the word "kilometer" appeared. She didn't know what one was and didn't want to know.

Instead I have tried to write about the people in this sport of sacrifice and suffering, hoping "to see a world in a grain of sand," as William Blake put it in a somewhat different context. In selecting the articles for this book, I have grouped those people into the leaders, in my eyes, in the last 25 years and those back in the pack. The third part of the book is devoted to different races and the places where they have been staged, since I believe the general reader is interested in what a course looks like and in its cultural context. The selection was based mainly on which pieces gave me the greatest pleasure to reread.

The book was fun to put together and I thank Amy Sorrells, editor of VeloPress, and Theresa van Zante, managing editor, for their encouragement and labors while I did it. All these articles are as originally written although sometimes not as originally edited. Among the few changes have been corrections of my dreadful arithmetic in converting meters into feet and the removal of a rider's quote that I learned broke a heart. Also, I have usually removed the word "bicycle" before the word "race." (2002)

Part One

ATOP THE PODIUM

Introduction

NOT SPRING, NOT YET

1985

FAR UP THE ROAD, SPECTATORS HAD ALREADY JAMMED *the switchback curves of Alpe d'Huez. The police finally gave up trying to estimate the size of the crowd and could only say it was many more than the usual 300,000 to 400,000 who waited each year for the bicycle riders in the Tour de France to climb to the peak. This Sunday morning in July, while the sun burned off traces of fog in the valley and melted a bit of the glaciers permanently atop the French Alps, the crowd was waiting for one rider. "Allez, Simon," the banners said. But by then it was over.*

Far down the road, on the Chapelle-Blanche hill, precisely at kilometer 95 of the day's 223-kilometer stage, Pascal Simon had ended his race. The television motorcycle that had been hovering for a week let millions of Frenchmen watch as Simon tried to climb the hill, grimacing with the pain of a left shoulder blade broken in a fall. He had strength in one arm only, and his unbalanced bicycle wobbled; the other riders stood on their pedals and put their weight forward on their shoulders as they thrust, but Simon had to remain seated. Doctors had been taping his shoulder blade each day and treating it with heat, ice and laser beams, but Simon's pain was obvious as he labored up the hill. Sweat illuminated his face and darkened the back of his yellow jersey, the symbol that Simon led the Tour de France. Another rider might win an individual day's race, a stage, but there was no special jersey for this; only the leader in overall elapsed time of the three-week race wore the yellow jersey. In the rainbow of team colors, the yellow jersey was the one the crowds looked for.

Simon's mouth began to hang open as he gulped for breath. Then he coasted onto the shoulder of the road and made the bicycle racer's traditional gesture of surrender: He put his feet to the ground while the race continued and unpinned the cloth with his number on his back. "I'm very sad and very sorry," Simon said, "but the pain is too great." He turned his bicycle over to a mechanic for his Peugeot team and climbed into an ambulance to finish the trip to Alpe d'Huez.

He had been saying for a week that the pain was growing worse but that he did not want to quit while he was still wearing the yellow jersey. As he coasted out of the race, he was 11 minutes behind the day's front-runners and had lost the yellow jersey.

BERNARD VALLET TURNED PROFESSIONAL IN 1976, *the same year as Bernard Hinault. "One of us just took off and the other, I mean me, blew it," Vallet remembered years later. "My first year as a professional reassured me: good results in Paris-Nice, the National and the Dauphiné Libéré. I thought I was capable of having a pretty career. The next year I had a good Tour de France, but I had to improve to be a star and the trouble was that my health was bad. By the end of the season I was exhausted. It got worse. Then came the bad year, 1978, the catastrophic year. All kinds of health problems, including hepatitis. The doctors couldn't understand it. I didn't race in the Dauphiné or the Tour—a terrible blow, my worst memory. I even thought of quitting.*

"It was very difficult. When you win 36 bouquets a year and you've gotten into the habit, twice a week, of giving them to your mother and your friends, it's awful to race three and a half years and not bring home even one bouquet.

"Before this, I used to think of bicycling as something between a religion and a love, but then it became just a profession, a job. Now I take cycling as it comes. Everything goes well—terrific. Things don't go too well—that's okay too. Since I realized that I wasn't going to make it big, bicycling has changed for me. When you've put in 10 years with the pros, seen what you've seen, suffered what you've suffered, you can handle the rest of life. The hard knocks and the defeats—I don't care about them, because bicycling has taught me how to live.

"I don't regret anything, understand that. But I would have preferred starting as a pro without ambition. That would have been less difficult. It's hard to have a Mercedes at 18 and a jalopy at 35. I was at the top and I fell into obscurity."

"THE FIRST TIME I WAS INVITED *to travel with the Tour de France," said a French television personality, one of those people some teams bring along in their cars as official guests, "it was in the Pyrenees, and in the fog and rain we came to a spill of about 30 riders. They were lying all over the road. We drove on and a little while later we were having our lunch in the car—chicken, wine, strawberries—when some of the men in the crash went by and I saw them through the windows, covered with rain and with blood streaming down their faces. I was having lunch and I was embarrassed, so I rolled down the window and told one of them I was sorry. And he just said, 'It's okay, I'm used to it.'"*

THIS MORNING IN EARLY MARCH, Paris scents spring. Winter is not joyful here: When the gray months start in November, there is no sun, and the blue sky the Impressionists painted, darkened for decades by automobile exhaust fumes, turns gloomier still. An hour away from the great bowl that is Paris, in the bean fields of Arpajon or on the grape hills of Champagne, there may be snow. But in the city the rare snowfall melts quickly in the streets. It is cold but never cold enough for winter to assert itself. In Paris, winter is a negative season, and the cheerless months follow each other like doughboys in a World War I photograph, shuffling to the front as the mud sucks at their boots and the rain turns their greatcoats black.

Spring is another parade altogether, royal blue and starched tan, the golden braid and crimson piping of soldiers stepping smartly down the Champs-Elysées. Spring is a military band playing a march scored for cymbals. This March morning, when the forsythia is just beginning to open, there is music. From the Hôtel de Ville, the city hall, come the sounds of an accordion. A wind from the nearby Seine carries the tune around the plaza: the upbeat "Viva España," the traditional French introduction to anything Spanish. While a crowd of several hundred looks on, the Teka bicycle team rolls past wooden barriers and into the plaza. Far from base in sunny Valencia ("In my dreams, I hear you calling me"), the Spanish riders look cold. They wear long leggings and heavy jerseys, and in semblance of warmth have pulled their cloth caps low over their eyes, but not low enough to hide their expressions. They look dubious as they park their bicycles and file into the city hall.

The accordion turns to "La Vie en Rose" to welcome the next riders, the pink-shirted Système U team. Each of the 17 teams arrives to a song or even a medley, depending on how strung out are its riders, up to 10 a team. Each team wins a round of applause from the crowd, mostly businessmen and the obviously retired, many of them in the beret that only country people wear now. Paris draws them, in their old age, to live with the children who long ago left their native villages; the sons are in business suits, but the fathers still wear the beret or the distinctive Breton sweater. Soon the mayor will arrive and make a short speech on the outdoor podium, wishing all the riders well in the Paris-Nice race. He goes on a bit too long, but few in the audience begin drifting away for lunch. The riders also stay put. The speeches and ceremonial welcome are part of their job, like the compulsory round of handshaking with which the French worker warmly greets colleagues he has not seen for the 12 hours since he shook their hands to say good-bye. The music, the speeches, the standing around in the cold—all this a rite of spring.

During the winter the cycling columns of the daily sports newspaper *l'Equipe* have been full of gossip, for want of anything better: This rider is changing teams, that rider is planning a comeback; this *directeur sportif* is revealing his hopes for the coming season, that *directeur sportif* is already preparing his excuses. Some of the riders have spent a week in Senegal or Martinique, racing when not basking in the sun. The gossip is hospital food, nourishing but thin. Then the first crocus pushes through the snow. The Coop team has gathered in the Alps for an oxygenation stage—bicycle racers believe mightily in the power of clear air to reinvigorate the body—and will shortly start training on the road. Soon begin some of the innumerable and unimportant short races that are a specialty on the Riviera, the Côte d'Azur, in February. Along the coast from Monaco to Cannes and back in the hills, where a soft wind stirs, the riders will resume climbing and descending, leaning into curves shielded by palm trees.

Most of these races last a day, and the more important ones are called classics. They ease the riders into the longer races, the ones run in daily stages, of which Paris-Nice is always the year's first major one. In a half hour the riders will get back on their bicycles and pedal slowly to the suburbs, where they will begin their weeklong race to the Côte d'Azur. Down there the mimosa is in flower, and some afternoons it is already hot enough to raise the scent of lavender off the hills along the road. There are snowy mountain passes to cross first and sleet storms to endure, but the season has opened and spring is officially on the way. All through the bleak winter the bicycling magazines have published the classic photograph of professional racing: in soft focus in the foreground a field of poppies or bachelor's buttons or daffodils, and behind the flowers the riders in their short-sleeved jerseys. The yellow of Renault-Elf reflects the daffodils, the scarlet slashes of Skil-Sem highlight the poppies and the blue of La Redoute the bachelor's buttons.

Sitting upright and relaxed in the photograph, the riders are obviously on a flat stretch and nobody is yet trying to break away or otherwise disturb the torpor of a day in the country, cruising for seven or eight hours at a speed of 35 kilometers an hour, a bit over 20 miles an hour. Most of the riders are staring ahead, but a few are looking around, checking a rival's position or seeking a friend. Nobody is admiring the scenery, although some riders say that on a long and slow uphill they do notice the cows in the field or the roadside crops. It depends on the rider: A former farm boy will be interested in the height of the field corn, while a rider from the coal-mining north may just marvel at how small are the parcels of land into which a farm has been subdivided among sons. In the photograph some mouths are open and the conversation must be banal. Like workers anywhere, the riders say they discuss women and politics and their dumb employers.

At the Hôtel de Ville in Paris, the politicians' speeches have ended. The riders get on their bicycles and begin moving out. A cloud has come over the sun. In the next few weeks the newspapers and bicycle magazines will show race photographs of Jean-Luc Vandenbroucke, a Belgian rider, with hands swollen and frozen; of Jean-Claude Bagot, a French rider, heading on a breakaway into a wall of fog; of Stephen Roche, an Irish rider, grimacing with pain after a mountain finish under rain and sleet. Bernard Hinault, the French star, will report two fingers still partly frozen a week after a climb through the Massif Central. This morning in early March, Paris has scented spring, but first there are races to be run. The way to the mimosa on the Côte d'Azur is over mountain passes lined with snow. The time of year is not spring—not yet—but bicycle racing season.

Farewell, Eddy Merckx

1978

THE TOUR DE FRANCE BEGAN this morning with an Eddy Merckx team riding Eddy Merckx bicycles. In the hundreds of small towns through which the Tour will pass, a biography of Eddy Merckx in comic strips is for sale.

When the race ends on the Champs-Elysées in three weeks, sidewalk vendors will undoubtedly still be selling Eddy Merckx ceramic plates commemorating his five victories in the Tour, his three world records in the hour's race against the clock and his victories in almost every major race.

All the signs of Eddy Merckx are still there, but this morning in Leiden, the Netherlands, the Tour de France began without Eddy Merckx.

He is through as a racer, retired in May after 13 years as a professional, the greatest ever. But he is supposed to be a technical adviser to the team he helped assemble for his one last attempt to win the Tour for a record sixth time, and so he was expected at the start.

Merckx was with the team yesterday for the prologue. He was seen riding in a team car behind the cyclists, ready to offer support and advice. Those who saw him thought he looked anguished and despondent.

Members of his Belgian team C&A seemed embarrassed to have his absence noticed today. Joseph Bruyère, Merckx's faithful shadow for years, looked down at his feet and said, "I haven't seen him today. Perhaps he's not here."

A faraway look came into the face of another rider, Walter Planckaert, who later won the sprint finish into Brussels. Pressed on whether Merckx was expected, Planckaert said, "I don't know. That is all. I don't know." Other C&A riders remained silent.

Everybody, it appears, is feeling bad about Eddy Merckx, perhaps few more than Merckx himself.

Last year at this time, when it was evident that he was no longer winning races, Merckx was philosophical. "A day comes when the strength of youth declines," he said. "It's in the nature of things, and one submits to it even while still fighting to reach the limit."

Attempting to win his sixth Tour of the eight he contested, Merckx failed badly last year, finishing sixth after a crisis in the Alps that was officially described as food poisoning.

In truth, at age 33, Merckx was done. It took him a long year to realize it.

At first he broke with his former team in a disagreement about his role. Then he entered few races—none this season—blaming health problems. Each time he insisted that the race was unimportant—"another victory, more or less, is meaningless"—and that his only goal was to win the Tour de France and break the tie of five victories with Jacques Anquetil, the champion of the 1960s.

Finally, he announced his retirement. To become a team official and ride in the team car, he had to return his professional rider's license to the Belgian federation.

He assisted in one race, a spring semi-classic in the French Alps, and there were photographs of him standing through the open top of a car, framed by bicycles lashed to the roof, upside down. It was probably too easy to read this as a distress signal.

This morning, in Leiden, Raymond Poulidor, a rider in 14 Tours de France, was walking around, cheerful and buoyant, in the second year of his retirement. Poulidor was gracious, but then, in 14 years, he had never won the Tour de France.

The man who had, five times, and so badly wanted a sixth, was nowhere to be found.

Father and Son

1995

AS MOST FATHERS WOULD, Eddy Merckx offered his son a lift home from work. But Axel Merckx was delayed. "Work" was the Het Volk bicycle race through Flanders and, on a stretch of road made slippery by heavy rain, he had crashed.

Instead of a quick shower and massage before the drive with his father to the family home outside Brussels, Axel Merckx first had to spend time visiting the doctor for his Motorola team.

Now, as a masseur kneaded his body in a hotel room in Ghent, the younger Merckx lifted his bare legs. His shredded left knee had been cleaned and kept exposed to the air while a bloody bandage covered part of his left thigh.

"There was a small breakaway and I went after it," Axel Merckx explained. "It was during the cobblestones, and I went too fast and was surprised when we came to a sharp turn." He laughed with embarrassment. "And I crashed. It was stupid, my fault," he said, "but racing is like that."

Sitting on a bed in the hotel room, Eddy Merckx nodded at the sentiment. No need to tell him about racing. Between them, Merckx father and son, they have 446 victories in professional races and Eddy Merckx has 445 of them.

In his glorious career from 1965 through 1977, he won the Tour de France five times, the Giro d'Italia five times, the world championship road race three times and the Vuelta a España once. Hardly a classic escaped him—three victories in Paris-Roubaix, seven in Milan–San Remo, two in the Tour of Lombardy, five in Liège-Bastogne-Liège, two in the Tour of Flanders. He broke the record for the hour's ride against the clock in 1972.

Eddy Merckx, now a 49-year-old bicycle manufacturer in his native Belgium, was the greatest champion the sport has known. Because of his appetite for victories, he was nicknamed "The Cannibal."

In his second full season as a professional, the 22-year-old Axel Merckx has that sole victory, a daily stage in the 1992 professional-amateur Tour de l'Avenir that he won in a sprint finish as a member of the Belgian team. Although last year, which he spent with the Telekom team in Germany, was a washout, his results this season have been promising.

Despite the crash, he finished the Het Volk in a creditable 37th place. Earlier last month, he finished 11th overall in the Trophee Laigueglia in Italy. A few days before, as the season began, he finished sixth overall in the Tour of the Mediterranean after crossing the line seventh in the testing climb up Mont Faron and 10th in an even steeper but shorter ascent in Marseille.

His strength is climbing, he explained. His father's strength was climbing, time-trialing, grinding it out for hours on the road, even sprinting—the works.

Before he turned professional, the son knew intimately how hard the sport was even for somebody not named Merckx. But he is. In bicycle-crazy Belgium, everybody knows that he is the great Eddy's son and that, so far at least, he is not the second Eddy Merckx.

Usually sons of great fathers do not try to follow in their footsteps, so why had he? Because he likes the sport, he said. Because it suits him. He played soccer at first and was good at it but decided that he could be even better at racing bicycles, which he began to do in earnest when he was 16.

"I try to do my best," Axel Merckx said, shifting on the massage table from his back to his stomach. "We'll see, year after year, if I can improve. We'll see what kind of level I can reach."

His son most resembles him, Eddy Merckx said, in character, a word that racers use to describe dedication and will.

"He has a lot of character," the father said. "He has more character than me. In the winter I might have had some beers with friends but he doesn't. He likes to stay home and train a lot.

"Also he has good condition. Maybe not my power. He's very tall so maybe not the power now. But I think in a few years he will have more power."

Axel Merckx stands 6 foot 3 inches and weighs 160 pounds. His father is a shade over 6 feet and raced at about 165 pounds.

"At the beginning he played soccer but he always said it would be cycling, so . . . " Eddy Merckx said. "I hope he can be a good professional. It's important in life to do what you like to do, no?"

He had not discouraged his son's choice, Eddy Merckx continued. "No," he said, a long, drawn-out "No." He searched for more words. "It was difficult because to have a name like Merckx and coming after his father and being compared with the results of his father. And cyclists in Belgium always compare our results. But if he likes to do cycling, I don't see why I should say no."

Axel Merckx confirmed that it had been difficult.

"It was tough when I started in Belgium and all the guys were jealous," he said. "Now it's different. Some guys are still jealous, but I'm a professional now and do my job.

"Now, in a race like today, they don't look at me as the son of Eddy Merckx. They see me as another rider, just another guy, another competitor.

"But maybe the guys on small teams, because I'm in Motorola and they're in a little team, they say, 'Oh why is he there and why am I on a small team?'

"I think I've proved I deserve the place where I am," the younger Merckx said. "But the jealousy, it will always live. All my life."

He hinted that his year with the Telekom team had not been happy. "It was different there. I was the only foreigner on the team, the only Belgian on a whole team of Germans." He was also sick for part of the season.

Life is much better on the Motorola team, based in the United States, with which he entered the professional ranks late in 1993. "On this team there are 12 nationalities and everybody has to give a little of himself to create team morale. There's no stress here, just good feelings."

Surprisingly, both Merckx said that the father rarely offered advice about racing and that the son rarely requested it.

"Cycling has changed a lot since the time he was riding," Axel Merckx said. "And these races in Belgium, mostly I know them because I did them when I was an amateur."

Eddy Merckx echoed this, pointing out that even though he had won the Het Volk twice himself, "There's not much to tell him: Stay in front because it's all small roads and it's raining and it's dangerous. But he knows that. It's not his first year and he knows most of the races now.

"In the beginning I gave him coaching, helped train him. That's normal. But now cycling has changed so much, I can't tell him much."

If Axel Merckx had a son, would he encourage him to become a racer?

"I'd prefer not," Axel Merckx replied. "Because I know how hard it is. It may not be as hard for him as it was for me but the name will still be following him.

"But if he wants to do it and likes to do it—my parents gave me the opportunity so it's not possible that I say no to him." Wincing, he moved off the massage table and began to dress. The injured knee, he said, would not interfere with his racing schedule for March: the Tour of Murcia in Spain, followed by Tirreno-Adriatico in Italy and then perhaps the Milan–San Remo classic.

"One week or two for the knee to heal," he said. "For two, three days it's going to be hurting. It's not so bad."

From long experience, Eddy Merckx agreed.

"It's nothing serious," he said. "If that's all it is, it's nothing. That's part of cycling."

They began moving down the hotel corridor, heading for the car, going home. Eddy Merckx noticed that a sleeve of his son's jacket was dusty and, as most fathers would, reached over and brushed it off. Then his hand moved up and Eddy Merckx lovingly clapped Axel Merckx once, twice, three times on the back of the neck.

Honorary Frenchman

1984

LONG AGO, BUT ONLY A YEAR EARLIER, Joop Zoetemelk, a Dutchman, could never be written about in a French newspaper without being identified sooner or later in the story as Honorary Frenchman No. 1. He had earned this heartfelt title during the 1970s while he was riding and winning for French teams. His marriage to a Frenchwoman, with whom he opened a hotel in Meaux, near Paris, only added to his status. His strong-willed wife ran the hotel because, as everybody said, Zoetemelk cared only about cycling and had a head for nothing else.

This seriousness was celebrated. Every winter was devoted to training—daily jogging or cross-country cycling and skiing. "I can't stand inactivity," Zoetemelk liked to say. His form was so far ahead of other riders' that he excelled in spring races; he hated cold and rain, and so concentrated on races in the south of France.

In 1980 he joined the Raleigh team in the Netherlands but returned to France after a year, saying, "I quit mostly because I couldn't face starting the season in Belgium with the rain, the cold, the cobblestones. At my age, what I want are some nice little races in France, the Tour du Tarn or Tour de l'Aude, the Midi Libre, where I can get ready for the season peacefully."

Although he won some big races, Zoetemelk never seemed to care about the grand exploit, and his career was studded with triumphs in nice little races. He won the somewhat negligible Tour du Haut-Var three times and would have won a fourth time except that he'd had the bad luck to be misdirected down a side street near the finish and could not make up the lost time when he realized his mistake. His first victory in the Haut-Var came in 1973; his last, in 1983.

By then, Zoetemelk was often held up as an example to younger riders because he was 36 years old. Thus, according to Raymond Poulidor, his captain in the early 1970s: "Joop is, above all, a serious rider. He trains like a youngster no matter what the weather."

Or Louis Caput, another old-timer: "Joop proves that the modern theory that a rider is over the hill at 30 is false. When a champion declines it's because he no longer has the willpower to make the sacrifices that his job demands. He can still do it physically, but not in his heart."

Zoetemelk's attitude fit in well with the message that teams were sending their riders in the early 1980s. "Under the present economic conditions, everyone should realize that it's more and more difficult to find the money to keep a team going," said the manager of his Coop team, Jean-Pierre Danguillaume. "Zoetemelk has understood this. He couldn't set a finer example."

He could be courageous as well. In 1974, after a crash in the Midi Libre, a spinal infection nearly killed him. When he recovered, it was assumed he would stop riding, but he was back the next season.

In addition to his devotion to his work, Zoetemelk was celebrated for his caution. When he first became a professional in 1970, he was the butt of a joke that went, "Why is Zoetemelk always so pale?" The answer was, "Because he always rides in Merckx's shadow"— a reference to Merckx's charge that Zoetemelk was that most despised of riders, a wheel-sucker, the man who lets somebody else do the work and keeps his strength to zip by at the finish. Zoetemelk denied the charge, which died out. If he ever was a wheel-sucker, it must have been out of caution or timidity; nearly seven minutes ahead with one stage to go in the 1980 Tour de France, he could still say publicly, "Nothing is won yet, nothing can be won until we cross the finish line." Worse, he probably believed this.

Not often did Zoetemelk exceed himself. Bridging the Merckx and Hinault eras, he finished second in the Tour de France a record six times, in 1970, 1971, 1976, 1978, 1979 and 1982. He won just once, in 1980, when Bernard Hinault, leading at the halfway point, had to withdraw because of an initial attack of tendinitis in his right knee. The Dutchman's first bad year followed the Tour victory, and people began to wonder if Zoetemelk had grown too old. "Father Joop," Hinault had long called him, and not out of affection.

But Zoetemelk recovered in 1982, and then explained that the problem was that he had neglected his training during the previous winter.

"What killed me was all the demands on my time during the winter. You know me, I like it quiet, and all those receptions, banquets and personal appearances just wiped me out. By the time they were all over, I just wanted to stay at home, and so I neglected my training." No more mistakes: Back he went to the jogging, cross-country cycling and skiing, the winter training, the spring victories, the season designed to march in small steps toward the Tour de France.

Nobody ever accused Zoetemelk of bravado or panache. Asked in 1982, when things were going well for him again, if he thought he could win the Tour, he replied honestly, "No, there's no point dreaming. Finishing in the top five would be satisfying and a place on the podium more than honorable." He knew and accepted his limits, which could also be his strength.

"What knocks me out is Zoetemelk's intelligence in a race," said Luis Ocaña, the winner of the 1973 Tour. "He always works within his means, he decides on a goal and usually achieves it. Often it's second or third place, and that's just where he'll finish. He prefers not to throw himself into a decisive battle, but to fight his way slowly up the ladder. That's just the way he is."

Riding for Coop in the 1983 Tour de France, with Hinault sidelined, Zoetemelk was rated among a small group of favorites. When Coop scored an unexpected victory in the team time trial in the second stage, Kim Andersen took the yellow jersey, and Zoetemelk, second by a few seconds, seemed well-placed with attention focused on his teammate. But it became obvious after a few days that something was wrong. Zoetemelk was riding badly and seemed mournful. Soon it was announced that he had failed the drug test after the team time trial. His appeal had also failed. All this was known to him, but he had not said a word publicly.

What would people think?

As riders usually do, Zoetemelk denied taking illegal drugs and insisted the urine test had been wrong. Obviously demoralized, he finished the Tour 23rd overall, 47 minutes behind. Everybody expected him to end his protests, go home and probably retire. He'd had a long and moderately glorious career and, besides, who really cares about a doping charge?

For once, second place was not enough for Zoetemelk. Reversing his long habit of taking small steps, he startled the bicycling world by bringing a court suit to clear his name. Riders had protested before and some had written letters to the authorities, but few had sought legal redress.

Zoetemelk was strongly supported by his wife and by the Dutch cycling federation, but the name on the court suit was his. He sued the Tour organizers and was rebuffed legally. The case went from court to court, with medical experts offering contradictory findings.

Zoetemelk insisted that his body naturally produced an excess of hormones, which showed up in the urine test. More experts and counteropinions were needed, and then it was spring, with the case still not settled, and Zoetemelk had switched from the French Coop team to the new Kwantum team in the Netherlands.

Now, in newspaper articles, he was no longer Honorary Frenchman No. 1 but the Dutchman, sometimes the 37-year-old Dutchman. Why did so many reporters seem embarrassed to see Zoetemelk militant?

Interviewed in the spring of 1984, he was asked why exactly he was still racing. He replied, "I get asked that a lot. Since last year, I've been thinking only of the Tour, where I was the victim of an enormous injustice. It's become an obsession, and I won't have any peace until the race."

No happy endings: This was his Tour too many. He never had liked racing in the Pyrenees, in contrast to good placings in the Alps, and the stage from Pau was a disaster. Long after the main pack finished, while motorists fretted because the road was still closed to traffic to protect the stragglers, an ashen Zoetemelk rode in 19 minutes behind the winner. "It's all over for me," he said when he found his breath. "This is my last Tour."

Starting the day 18th overall, a bit more than four minutes behind Laurent Fignon, he fell to 64th place.

A few days later he confirmed the decision. "I'll finish my contract with Kwantum at the end of the year and stop racing," he said placidly. "It's become too tough. No more Tours."

He would make it to Paris, as he always did, finishing for the 14th time in 14 Tours. He ranked 30th, 1 hour 6 minutes 2 seconds behind, and then went home to spend his winter awaiting the court ruling. It still had not come by spring, when he was racing again for Kwantum but insisting that his days with the Tour de France were finished.

A Man of Character

1984

"THERE IS A SAYING HERE," Red Smith wrote from France in 1960, "that an army from Mars could invade France, the government could fall and even the recipe for sauce béarnaise be lost, but if it happened during the Tour de France, nobody would notice." In the years since this observation, governments—though not the Martians—have come and gone and the tarragon-flavored sauce has become available in any grocery store frozen, bottled and canned. But a few years ago the Tour began escaping Frenchmen's notice.

The trouble was that the French did not particularly like Bernard Hinault, a Breton who had by then won the Tour de France four times since his debut in 1978. Though widely respected, Hinault was no longer a national hero, a condition he shrugged off with the seeming coldness that cost him much of his public. "I race to win," he said, "not to please people." He succeeded at both. "I'm the one who rides," he insisted. "If somebody thinks he can do it better, let him get a bicycle."

Hinault's domination had reduced the uncertainty about the Tour's outcome to the point where he could say in 1982, "It's a race for second place," and nobody could disagree. The crowds came in diminished numbers and enthusiasm, and even in victory, Hinault was criticized. It was difficult to remember by then how fiery the love affair had been when it began.

After his first victory in the Tour, he was the great hope of French bicycling, if not all sports, so the stories about him found eager listeners. Raymond Poulidor, 14 times a rider in the Tour but never a winner, told one often in 1978, that first year: "One understood immediately that he had character and that neither Merckx nor Poulidor impressed him. He was afraid of nothing. One day, in the Midi Libre race, I believe, we had a start that went up a mountain. The evening before, Hinault had been hopelessly outdistanced and was, for all practical purposes, out of the race.

"But the next morning he started at full speed and stayed at the head of the pack 25 kilometers, going all out. Behind him we had our hands full to keep up. And then, having done it and showed us, he dropped out of the race. I realized then that we were going to have further dealings with him, that he was not an ordinary racer."

Or Raymond Martin, then riding with the Mercier team: "One time, when he was just starting, during a critérium in Châteaulin, all the big names were there. They were willing to cut me in on the sharing of the prizes, but not him. He got on their nerves too much. So Hinault got mad. He won the first five or six cash bonuses and, if this wasn't bad enough, made faces at the other riders when he swept by them. I told him to cool it, but he replied, 'I don't give a damn.' Totally relaxed. By the seventh or eighth lap, Eddy Merckx came up alongside him and said, 'Okay, you're in on the split, but stop your crap.'"

Luis Ocaña, the 1973 winner of the Tour de France, added to the budding legend: "I remember a stage in the Dauphiné Libéré—it must have been 1975 or 1976. Everybody was calm and the pack was rolling quietly when we got to a long hill. Hinault went to the front and began to ride like a madman. I moved up to him to make him understand that this wasn't on, that he should leave the rest of us in peace.

"Instead of calming down, he accelerated. I dropped back, but he just pushed on. The more everybody yelled at us from behind, the faster he went. He didn't care at all what everybody thought of him, this kid. I liked him at once."

As Poulidor did, the French call this "character," a trait they revere—up to a point.

In a few more years they had decided that the stories proved only that Hinault had too much character and the times called for something different. Ironically, in many ways Hinault was the Frenchman of the 1980s: practical, efficient and realistic—in short, a pragmatist, or trying hard to be one. Nowadays, nobody talks about *la gloire*, the cornerstone of de Gaullian France, but about inflation and budget deficits and the balance of trade. The franc has been a sick currency for most of the decade, and unemployment was nearly triple the 1 million figure that was once regarded as unacceptable. Projections showed that by 1985 one Frenchman in nine would be on welfare, unemployed or retired early. What the country needed in its heroes was bravado, gallantry, flare—panache.

Hinault was irritated with complaints that he had shown little panache, a quality the French have come to associate with Tour de France winners. "For me," Hinault said, "panache isn't worth anything. If I go all out in the mountains and then have nothing left the next few days and lose the Tour de France, who really won in the mountains? In the Tour, there are days when you have to know how to win, days when you have to know how to lose and days when you have to know how to help your opponent, the better to beat him tomorrow. I know all these."

He knows much more. Sitting in the living room of his modern, two-story stone house in Quessoy, a village in Brittany, he sounded like a Ministry of Trade official as he discussed the value of bicycle racing in relation to national exports. When Hinault's sponsor was Renault, the French car manufacturer, he raced periodically in such big foreign markets as Italy and Spain. He wanted badly to ride in the first Tour of America in 1982—a three-day race through Virginia and the District of Columbia—but could not get permission from the organizers of a simultaneous race in France that had first call on his services. As a pragmatist, he was peeved. "France is a country that needs exports," he explained, "and for Renault, this includes the car we are building in the United States. Appearing in a bicycle race is one way of advertising not only Renault but also Gitane," Hinault's secondary sponsor and Renault's bicycle-making subsidiary.

Hinault gave practiced answers to cycling questions but really came alive when he talked about what was occupying the thoughts of his countrymen. He grumped about unemployment benefits ("Everywhere in France now you see people begging for money and everywhere you see jobs begging for people") and taxes ("If I push the pedal five times, one is for me and my family and four are for the tax collector"). With an annual income estimated between $300,000 and $500,000, including salary, prizes, endorsements and bonuses, he is rare in cycling circles for having a professional business manager. Still, like everybody else, he brooded about his future. "For racing, nature gives you certain gifts, but for retirement, nature gives you nothing. It's up to you to arrange it. If I'm a failure in retiring, then my whole career will have meant nothing."

Hinault insisted he would retire in 1986 and he had already bought a farm—65 kilometers from Quessoy, but still in Brittany—where he intends to move with his wife and two small sons to raise dairy cattle and become, as he put it, a peasant. The son of a railroad worker in the nearby town of Yffiniac, he seems to many Frenchmen the definitive Breton, down to his Celtic dark good looks. However, most Frenchmen do not think of these as the chief Breton trait. Instead, "stubborn as a Breton" is a common epithet.

"People say that Bretons have a hard character, stubborn, even rude," said Martine Hinault as she waited for her husband to complete a training run over flat, windblown roads. "That's our reputation—aggressive and stubborn."

When he returned home, Hinault flopped onto the couch and politely differed. "I think it refers to people who are hard, who are able to endure bad climate, among other things. I think when people refer to the Breton character, they mean people who when they want something do their best to get it."

This definition was tidy and, in Hinault's case, the truth—but not the whole truth. Vividly remembered was the tantrum he threw in 1982 when, a beaten man, he dropped out of the one-day French championship and then, on nationwide television, blamed the public, the press and his fellow riders. The other riders kept a politic silence, but the public responded throughout the Tour de France with jeers and whistles. The press let loose with long-suppressed anger. "A small masterpiece of the hateful and the stupid," said *l'Equipe* of Hinault's petulance. "In the eyes of the general public, Bernard Hinault is revealed for what he is: a great champion but a small man."

"My nature isn't always to be prudent," said Hinault, responding to the editorial. "As everybody knows, I can sometimes be impulsive." He laughed at this statement of the obvious.

Another word usually attached to Hinault was *méchant,* literally meaning spiteful, nasty or malicious. French homes often have signs warning of a *chien méchant*, a vicious dog. In cycling, to be *méchant* is not to be all bad, as Hinault noted. "It's natural for a cyclist to be *méchant*," he said. "I can't understand how a racer cannot have this trait, at least a bit of it. All winners have it. People who like to fight, who like to win, they all have it. I think when you're going all out, it's impossible to do it with a smile. If you ever see me smiling during a race, you'll know I'm not really competing." Hinault's standard race photograph shows glaring, burning eyes and a set jaw. He resembles an animal on the scent and is, indeed, nicknamed for one—le Blaireau, the Badger.

Hinault rose from the couch and crossed the room to display a stuffed and mounted badger, teeth bared, that a fan had sent. "The nickname was given to me by another rider early in my career and it stuck. The badger is a strong animal, especially in relation to its small size, and he can make a lot of trouble if he's attacked. I think the nickname sort of reflects my own attitude: I can take a lot of blows without saying anything, but the next day I attack, and when I do, I can be very, very *méchant*." Hinault glared at the badger, then grinned.

A French bicycle fan was troubled a few years ago when he wrote a letter to *l'Equipe:* "We Frenchmen have Bernard Hinault and we don't have the right to complain about him. We should be proud of him. It's worth more to have several French victories of 5 or 6 minutes each than one French victory of 45 minutes every 15 years. If the winner of the Tour de France had been a foreigner, it would be the same Frenchmen who would be complaining."

Hinault agreed with the tactical sense of the letter, although not with the chauvinism. He welcomed the growing popularity of bicycling abroad and, while still with Renault, designated as his cycling heir a young American, Greg LeMond, who became his teammate in 1980. "It doesn't bother me at all that he's not French. If the French want to catch up to him, let them make the effort."

The pragmatist continued: "What good are legends?" he asked. "What good does it do if I win the Tour de France by 10 or 15 minutes instead of 6. I race to last, not to finish broken."

Hinault worries about lasting. "When I started in the Tour, in 1978, I showed a bit of the spirit of youth, superior physical strength. Now I'm more calculating, more a thinking rider. When I look around, I don't see many riders left who started with me."

Like being *méchant*, calculation can be a strength in a rider. "To win the Tour de France," Hinault explained, leaning forward to give his words weight, "you've got to do well in everything—be able to win in the mountains when you must, win a time trial, or at least do well.

It's enough to be a champion in one discipline if you're good enough in the others, a complete athlete. You can't win the Tour if you have any weaknesses." A strong climber, he had long excelled in time trials.

With four victories in the Tour de France, Hinault could equal the record of five shared by Jacques Anquetil and Eddy Merckx. Anquetil finished first in 1957 and 1961 through 1964, and Merckx in 1969 through 1972 and 1974. Hinault knew that his time was running out—he would turn 30 in November 1984. "Until the age of 30," he said, "I don't want to think about anything except bicycle riding, about winning. Starting at 30, I'll begin to think about other things, including my farm. I want to retire correctly, without bitterness, without feeling bad about leaving racing. After 30, I'll probably not be as competitive as I am now, and so my role will be to give the kids I ride with the best chance to win. I'll be more of a road captain, saying, 'This is the way you do this, this is the way you do that.'"

Hanging Up His Bicycle

1986

BERNARD HINAULT REMEMBERED his first race, on May 2, 1971: "I was 16 and a half years old. That morning, I told my mother, 'Tonight I'll bring you the winner's bouquet.' She didn't believe a word of it and I don't know why I said it, but I was so sure of myself and the promise was sincere, not a boast.

"I hadn't gone 100 meters when I realized that I really didn't know how to race. Weaving from left to right, I spent all my time and all my attention on trying not to have to ride in the pack because I was so afraid of falling. I rode behind them or in front of them or even far out on the side of the road.

"If a rider came anywhere near me, all I could think about was a collision. To feel more comfortable, I even rode on the grass, which isn't the best way to treat your bicycle. Ten times, 20 times, I should have fallen. But there's a god who looks out for innocents and, one circuit from the end, I was still in the race. I went to the head of the pack and when I spotted a small bump in the road that I had noticed earlier, I took off. Like a madman.

"I pumped away like that for a few hundred meters. When I turned around to look, there was nobody behind me except for one rider, the best youngster around. He was riding in his hometown and really wanted to win. A very strong sprinter, he had decided to wait for the last minute to put me away, but I didn't give him the chance. With a kilometer to go, I really went all out, with him right on my back wheel. Seven hundred meters later, he wasn't there and I had won my first race."

Hinault remembers his last race, on November 9, 1986, the one in which he went out a loser, smiling all the way. Ending his 12-year professional career, Hinault placed 14th in a field of 34 and for once did not sulk or glower. He accepted defeat with the same smile he wore most of the day. He also accepted another of his pet hates: the crush of photographers, reporters and fans that surrounded him at the finish line, thrusting cameras and microphones into his face, asking questions and slapping him on the back. The man who once said that for backslappers he would like to wear a jersey studded with thumbtacks, points facing outward, stood stoically as people thumped him.

At the end, with the crowd chanting "EE-no, EE-no" as he neared the last finish line of his career, everybody seemed to want just one more close look at le Blaireau, the Badger. Nearly all the 15,000 fans lining the half-mile cyclo-cross track in the town of Quessoy in his native Brittany rushed across the cow pasture and into the finish area for their final chance to see Hinault in competition.

He handled it with grace. Patiently he explained to the television cameras that he would always remember this "because of the joy I saw on the faces of the children in the crowd." Hinault thanked the spectators for encouraging him throughout the difficult race around a muddy track and for coming to tiny Quessoy to help him celebrate his retirement. He invited one and all to remain for dinner under a tent ("the second biggest in France," he bragged to a friend) and for a piece of his birthday cake. He said he appreciated their support from the first years when he was a teenager through the five Tours de France he had won.

And then, for the last time, he helped hang his racing bicycle on a rack. As he announced five years before, Hinault retired from racing on his 32nd birthday, November 14, 1986. The celebration, which he had helped plan for a year, was held all day on the preceding Sunday. "It's not a funeral procession," he announced, "but a big party."

Festivities included a long spin for nearly 2,000 cyclo-tourists who passed through the nearby town of Yffiniac where he was born and where his parents still live; a concert; fireworks; and a display of the many jerseys, plaques, pennants and ribbons he had won, including the discreet red buttonhole ribbon of a member of France's Legion of Honor. As a Breton bagpiper skirled a triumphant tune and hawkers pestered passersby with jerseys, magazines, caps and commemorative bottles of wine, Hinault circulated everywhere, smiling. The entire day, he said, was his way of thanking his fans and the press, and of saying good-bye.

A suspicious reporter asked him later if he really meant to stay retired. "Are you sure you won't be unretiring just in time for Paris-Nice?" the reporter asked, referring to the first major stage race of the spring.

"You won't trap me with that question," Hinault answered. "Everybody knows I won't be coming out of retirement until the Critérium International," the second major stage race of the spring. This time he grinned. Hinault made it plain that he meant to stay retired. He went out on top, ranked first among French athletes of the last 60 years in a magazine poll.

At a news conference, he ticked off the many ways he would fill his life. He serves three months of the year as a consultant to the Look sports equipment company. With a partner, he set up a company to manufacture and market educational wooden toys that children can assemble. He does a certain amount of public relations work and serves as a technical consultant to the Tour de France, spending one day a week in the organization's offices and the three full weeks with the race on the road.

Mostly, Hinault and his wife, Martine, and their two young sons will spend time together, living in the country. After his retirement, they moved to a cattle and wheat farm he bought some years earlier. "I love nature, I love animals," he said. "To watch your crops grow, to harvest them—that's the life. If I hadn't become a cyclist, I might have become a woodcutter." In truth, he admitted that he knew nearly nothing about farming; his father was a laborer on the railroad and Hinault studied at school to become a mechanic.

He will even continue to ride a bicycle, but not in competition. "I'm quitting before I'm fed up with cycling," he explained. "I've seen a lot of champions who tried to hang on too long, who just couldn't do it any longer but didn't know anything else to do. Not me. It's as important to me to succeed in my new life as it was in racing."

To hear Hinault tell it, he had no regrets. Was the man who won 52 time trials during his career sorry that he never tried to break the record for the hour's ride? Oh no, he said, never. When he was riding for Renault in 1979 or 1980, he continued, the team had talked about his attempting that feat and had even developed a special streamlined bicycle after tests in a wind tunnel. Hinault's interest, however, was not in records; what he liked to beat was not time, but people. (Asked as a 20-year-old rider in Paris-Nice what he thought of Eddy Merckx, the unawed Hinault answered, "He has two legs, like me.")

The feats he relished included the 140-kilometer breakaway in the 1979 Tour of Lombardy, the last race of the season, which gave him the victory points to squeeze by Giuseppe Saronni for the annual Super Prestige title. Or the day in the 1977 Dauphiné Libéré when he took a curve too tightly on a descent and went hurtling into a ravine, climbed back up, remounted and won that day's stage—as well as the multiday race itself. Or the way he recovered from an operation for tendinitis in his right knee in 1983, when the doctors gave him a 50-50 chance of ever racing again, and came back a year later to finish second in the Tour de France before capping his season with a fifth victory in the Grand Prix des Nations, a mammoth time trial.

Since he turned professional in 1975, he had won more than 250 races. Fifty feet from where Hinault spoke at his retirement party, in a wing of Quessoy's town hall, his fans were trooping through an exhibition of his many trophies and jerseys, including the rainbow-striped jersey of the world road-race champion that he donned in 1980. Pinned to a display board, it was surrounded by the final yellow jerseys that he won five times in the Tour de France, the pink jerseys he won three times in the Giro, the greenish-yellow jerseys he won twice in the Vuelta and the red-and-white-striped jersey he won in the Coors Classic in Colorado in 1986, his last victory. On display too were some of the first-place plaques he won in the Super Prestige, the unofficial world championship for professional riders, from 1979 through 1982, and in the Prestige, the unofficial championship for French riders, from 1976 through 1982 and again in 1984.

"*Adieu Blaireau et Merci*," read a fan's poster from the 1986 Tour. Would he miss competition? Hinault was asked. "Every day will be filled with competition now," he replied. "I've always been inspired by competition in sports and now I expect to be inspired by the competition of daily life. I don't think I'll be bored."

Wunderkind

1985

WHEN BERNARD HINAULT WAS FORCED to withdraw from the 1983 Tour de France because of tendinitis in his right knee, his Renault team was left with nobody resembling a leader. This might have disrupted other teams, but, aside from a few veterans, Renault without Hinault was a collection of young, zesty riders, some of them eager to see what they could do individually, and the withdrawal liberated them from all duties and devotions except to themselves. Nobody appreciated this more, or took better advantage of it, than Laurent Fignon.

Then approaching his 23rd birthday and riding in his first Tour de France, Fignon had served Hinault as a valorous lieutenant in the Giro d'Italia in 1982 and the Vuelta a España in 1983 but had not done much personally. He broke in well enough as a neophyte professional in 1982, winning the Critérium International, a prestigious spring race, but his first year was remembered mainly because of a mechanical accident. Riding in the Blois-Chaville race that fall, Fignon was on a breakaway, not 20 kilometers from the finish, seemingly certain of victory, and the shaft on a pedal broke, unbalancing him at full speed. He fell, of course, and the photograph of him sitting in the road, looking bewildered, with his bicycle lying behind him, was voted the best sports picture of the year.

Fignon began to realize his value the next year in the Vuelta. He was setting the pace on a steep climb when Hinault shouted to him to slow down, that he could not keep up. The incident was forgotten as Hinault went on to win the Vuelta and Fignon finished seventh, but he had gotten the first hint of his ascendancy and Hinault's decline. "That's where I realized that I really had the stuff for stage races," Fignon said later of that Vuelta. "I recuperated well, I ate well, I slept well. I felt just fine. So there were no physical problems. Psychologically, I said to myself that I could think a little better of my chances."

Two months later, when the Tour de France started, Fignon was overlooked in all predictions of a winner. For want of anybody better, the Renault team designated him and Marc Madiot as leaders. It was generally assumed that Renault was just along for the ride, a view that Madiot shared. "Without Hinault, we didn't expect much of ourselves, nothing more than to have somebody on the team in the first 15 finishers, maybe Fignon or me to win a stage or two, just to show that we were around." Fignon had a grander vision. "My goal was to get to Paris wearing the white jersey of the best first-year rider in the Tour and maybe to wear the yellow jersey for a day or two."

He was 13th overall until the Pyrenees, when he chose the right man to follow, Pascal Simon, and went by a lot of riders still waiting for the moment to move. It was then. Fignon finished seventh on the day and moved into second place overall behind Simon, 4 minutes 22 seconds back. The next day Simon fell and broke his left shoulder blade; a week later he quit, and Fignon took over the leader's jersey. He held it five more days, doing just well enough as his challengers eliminated one another, and was becoming a victor by default. Then, on the next to last stage, Fignon startled the pack by winning an individual time trial, his weakest discipline. "I got sick and tired of hearing everybody say that a Tour de France winner who doesn't win even one stage isn't a real champion," Fignon said. "So I wanted to show people something."

Afterward, when everybody was fussing over him, the blue-eyed, blond-haired young cyclist established a reputation for modesty and sweetness. "The yellow jersey did things for me," he said. "Everything I did in the mountains wouldn't have been possible without the jersey. Everybody was astonished by my performance in the mountains. Well, so was I." Or, "With a dream at the end of the road, it's possible to do some surprising things."

Probably he meant these guileless statements, but there is another, deeper side to Fignon. He is a rare sort of rider, middle class and educated, even having gone briefly to a provincial college, where he studied veterinary science. This, and his wearing of glasses, which few professional riders use, was enough to get him regarded as an intellectual, a charge he is bright enough to deny. "'Intellectual' is a pretty big word. I've been to school, but intellectual, that's a label, just a label. On a bicycle there are no academic degrees, there are just racers—good ones and less good ones."

Fignon is one of the good ones. "We don't really know his true limits," his *directeur sportif*, Cyrille Guimard, has said. "He doesn't either." Eddy Merckx had his word of praise: "Fignon inspires confidence, a pretty rider, obviously at ease." So did Jacques Anquetil: "His coolness and mastery astonished me. He's still got some things to learn about tactics, but with his punch he's going to become a super-champion."

Punch is what Fignon cares about. "I was only a middling amateur," he said, "and there certainly were classier riders. But did they have a fighting spirit? That's not so sure. That's my strength." About tactics he could be flip, saying, "There's nothing hard about it: Your teammates do the work during most of the stage and then the leader arrives to finish it off." By this time he was beginning to cash in on his Tour victory. He rode in 30 critériums and, after letting it be known that an Italian team was interested in him, negotiated a new two-year contract with Renault that nearly doubled his salary, to 18,000 francs a month (then about $2,000). "I don't want to shock anybody," he said, "but I really do race for money. A big victory means money."

It also means a walloping taste of the good life, invitations to celebrity ski resorts, disco parties and personal appearances at whatever chic cocktail party needed a champion bicycle rider. Flattered and fawned over and just turned 23, Fignon began to believe all the wonderful things people were telling him. "I got a little carried away," he admitted months afterward. "I got a little brusque with fans and reporters. Then I remembered a warning from Gerrie Knetemann, something the Dutch rider said to me while we were on vacation on Guadeloupe: 'When you become world champion—and I have been—you can get a swelled head, but it gets deflated pretty quickly.'

"I'll be honest," Fignon added, "it happened to me. But that's over with."

As he always does, Fignon learned. "Now I understand why Hinault could sometimes be so testy," he said. "It's not easy to separate the people who want to help you from those who don't. There's always somebody who's ready to exploit your name to make a little money for himself."

His relations with Hinault, polite when they both rode for Renault, became less so after Hinault left at the end of 1983. "We have good relations, but they're between competitors," Fignon said, and then let slip a hint of his resentment. "Bernard won everything, and when you said something to him, he answered, 'You haven't won four Tours de France, you haven't won this, you haven't won that.' Personally I don't tell people who ask me things, 'First win the Tour de France and then we'll talk.'"

He was also critical of Merckx, mainly because Merckx became critical of him, saying, "For me, Fignon is a playboy, nothing more. You don't prepare for a race by staying out and dancing until 4 o'clock in the morning." Fignon had a quick answer: "He gets on my nerves with all his talk about how much better and harder it was in his time. All he does is speak badly about today's riders. When I was suffering from sinusitis at the start of the season, he accused me of not doing my job. Let's not talk about Merckx."

By then Fignon was in Italy for the Giro, hoping to compensate for the bad spring he had in 1984. Sinusitis set back his training, especially during the cold and wet weather, conditions Fignon detests. He had a splendid Tour of Italy, finishing second to Francesco Moser only because the race was stolen from him. Moser, who set a record earlier in the year in Mexico for the hour's race against the clock, was a hero in Italy and all he needed to conclude his brilliant year, even in May, was the victory that had eluded him in 10 previous Giros. He got it with the help of the Italian organizers. Because of snow, they canceled the highest mountain stage, where Moser was certain to crack; they overlooked numerous pushes up hills by Moser fans and relatives and, in addition, prevented Guimard's car from approaching Fignon with advice. ("We don't ride in Italy to win," said Moreno

Argentin, the 1983 Italian champion, "but to make somebody else lose.") With all this, it was discovered that Fignon suffered from a condition called hypoglycemia, which resulted in a quick discharge of adrenaline that burned up his body sugar and produced a sudden weakness. Still, Fignon held the lead into the final day, a time trial; but Moser used the aerodynamic bicycle he took with him to Mexico City to break the record for the hour and picked up nearly four minutes, to win by a little over a minute.

Finishing second, Fignon showed not Hinault's defiance but a studied acceptance. Asked if the pressure of defending his 1983 victory in the Tour de France might make him crack in the 1984 race, he responded, "No way, not after what happened in the Giro. I'm armor plated now."

And so he was, alas. The Sunday before the 1984 Tour de France he rode in the French national championships and followed the pace of a teammate, Pascal Poisson. Near the end, with Poisson struggling, Fignon easily pulled away and won. What shocked many spectators was that when he passed Poisson, Fignon neither looked at him nor made any show of sympathy. A wave of the hand, a pat on the shoulder, a smile, a shouted word—there was more than enough time for any of these, but Fignon simply rode by.

At the Side of the Road

1993

THAT METEOR, THAT LIGHTNING BOLT Laurent Fignon had blazed out. Riding in a minor French race late in the summer of 1993, Fignon coasted to the side of the road halfway through and got off his bicycle for the last time as a professional. The authority for that was Fignon himself, and he could be believed.

Blazed out or burned out, how to decide? What could be said was that after a dozen years of majestic heights—two victories in the Tour de France, one in the Giro d'Italia, two in Milan–San Remo, a French national championship—and profound depths—a heel injury that cost him peak seasons, last-stage losses of both the Tour and the Giro, two positive drug findings—at age 33 Fignon had retired as a racer.

The Frenchman went out his own way, announcing beforehand that since he had no interest in competing in the world championships, the Grand Prix Ouest–France would be his farewell. He would have retired quietly, he said, but he owed it to his fans to be there.

That statement was pure Fignon: an arrogance that was almost touching in its naïveté. Or, if you wish, a naïveté that was almost dumbfounding in its arrogance. By the time he retired, nobody came to see just him. The rider ranked 201st in the world considered himself a fan attraction? The rider whose sole victory that year came in the Ruta Mexico in February? A two-page photograph in *Velo* magazine, the bible of bicycle racing in France, inadvertently said it all. There in the foreground was Fignon, the familiar ponytail, the familiar granny glasses, the familiar strained look, and there in the background were five fans—all looking down the road away from Fignon.

Besides the photograph and a brief text block, *Velo* had little else to say about his retirement. Not so long ago, a rider who recorded 76 victories in his career, including nine stage victories in the Tour de France, would have been given a proper sendoff of a long article, perhaps even a cover photograph and half a page of tributes.

He was not speaking publicly after his retirement and so, to know his thoughts, a fan had to look back to the interview he gave to *l'Equipe,* the daily sports newspaper, the day he quit. From the beginning of the interview, he was vintage Fignon, remote and brusque. Not for lack of trying was he voted the *citron* (lemon) prize for rudeness when he won the Giro in 1989.

Had it meant something to him to start his last race? the reporter from *l'Equipe* asked.

"Something?" Fignon repeated. "No, why should I have felt something?"

Not a heavy heart or sweaty palms?

"No. There was no reason for me to feel sad. I'm rather happy to retire. I decided on this many months ago and I started thinking about it two years ago. Since I signed with Gatorade [before the 1992 season], I knew I was joining my last team. Only the dead are sad and, as far as I'm concerned, don't talk about a burial but about the start of a new life. So don't be sad for me. What would have been sad was for me to continue, to keep quitting at the first feed zone, to finish a little like Eddy Merckx, who so badly ended his career."

You say you're fed up. With what?

"With everything. Fed up with cycling, with a world where all you see is the same people. With everything."

And what are your plans?

"I'm going to stay far away from the world of cycling next year, but I'll probably be back afterward, although I don't know in what capacity."

Do you fear that you'll be remembered more for your failures than your successes?

"Fear, no, I'm not afraid. People will remember whatever they want to. It won't mean anything to me."

Cold, defensive and ungrateful: Let us now praise famous men. Fignon won the Tour de France twice, in 1983 as a virtual unknown and in 1984 when everybody went gunning for him. A month after he lost the Giro in the final day's time trial, when Francesco Moser introduced his aerodynamic bicycle to overtake him, Fignon overpowered the field in the 1984 Tour, winning five stages. The victory was a demonstration of sheer dominance such as the pack witnesses only from a Merckx, an Hinault, an Indurain—and only in their prime.

And then, just 24 years old, he was struck down. An operation for tendinitis in his left heel sidelined him for most of 1985 and not for years afterward did he fully recover. In 1988, he won Milan–San Remo, and the next year he was back on top: first again in the Italian classic, first in the Giro and first in the Tour until the final day, when Greg LeMond beat him by 58 seconds in the time trial and by 8 seconds overall.

Everybody remembers the photograph of a spent Fignon slumped and weeping on the Champs-Elysées after he crossed the finish to find himself a runner-up. Few remember that he placed third in the fastest time trial in the long history of the Tour. What people forget now is that he went down fighting.

Fignon was always good at fighting—but often it was verbally and with rivals, the press and the fans. He mocked Bernard Hinault and LeMond, he struck photographers and refused to speak with reporters. At the end of his career, it seemed clear that Fignon really was fighting with himself.

He raged. Fignon was not so much a French rider as a Paris rider, and there is a clear distinction to be made here. French riders are generally well-mannered and soft-spoken, uncomplaining and accommodating. They win races but they are never winners in Fignon's class. They are formed young, burdened by the heavy satchel that all French schoolchildren wear on their shoulders to pack books, even to first grade. See, French society appears to be saying, we all have a weight to carry through life.

Once in a while, though, a French rider throws off the weight and expresses that most admired and most feared attitude: character. Hinault was famous for his character. "I race to win, not to please people," he often said.

Like Hinault, Fignon had an excess of character. Born just outside Paris and a longtime resident of the capital, he was the archetypal Parisian, indifferent to everybody but himself. When foreigners say the French are rude or self-serving, they rarely mean the French; they mean Parisians. Outside Paris, foreigners are startled to find the French can be kind and even unselfish.

Fignon took victories from teammates (the 1998 Tour of the European Community), chased them down (the 1989 world championship), treated them like hired hands and made few friends in the pack. He was respected and, at his peak, feared, but not admired. He was a Parisian to his fingertips and not many would miss him. He was also a champion, and the sport, especially in France, needs more riders like him.

THE LORD INDURAIN

1993

THIS WAS HOMECOMING DAY for Miguel Indurain. Only 48 hours ago he had won his second Tour de France and now he was returning to Spain, to Navarre Province, to his village of Villava. In the eight years since he had become a professional racer, Indurain had returned home many times but never quite like this: seated in the back of an open limousine as thousands cheered while he was driven from the airport to the Navarre Parliament.

The farmer's son from a pueblo had become a national hero, and Spain was offering him tribute once again. After Indurain's first victory in the Tour the year before—only the fourth for a Spaniard since the race began in 1903—he was welcomed home to a day and night of fiesta by 15,000 people, more than double the size of his village. This time the crowds were even larger, for he had won not only the Tour again but also the Giro d'Italia in the same year. In 1991 he returned in a helicopter before going to address the Navarre Parliament; in 1992 nothing less than a motorcade would do.

At the Parliament he was handed a microphone and, as a huge crowd chanted his name, he spoke simply. "My triumph is yours," he said. "I want to share it with you to thank you for all the passion you have always shown me." Indurain held out one of the yellow jerseys that he had won in the Tour. "I offer this yellow jersey, the symbol of my victory, to the president of our government. It belongs to all of you, too. Forever."

Homecoming day was just starting and, in the words of Cervantes, Indurain was "a king by [his] own fireside as much as any monarch on his throne." After lunch with his family at their farmhouse he went to the Pamplona apartment of his fiancée, Marisa Lopez de Goicoechea, to rest before returning to Villava early in the evening.

Indurain was back in the limousine as it traveled to the Plaza Miguel Indurain where a choir sang a hymn composed in his honor. Off he went to his boyhood church, as he had the year before, to pray and leave flowers at the statue of the Virgin of Rosario in thanks. The rest of the night was spent at a hall where fans celebrated him and his victory with wine, food and song. Throughout, although he was the center of attention, Indurain kept slipping into the crowd, toward the back, away from the clamor. His smile of pleasure hinted at a certain disbelief, although this might have been shyness.

In a chivalrous age Miguel Indurain would be the *parfait* knight: pure, serene, untroubled by second thoughts. He has won the Tour twice and there is no reason to doubt he can win it again. Ask him how many Tours he thinks he can win and he replies, "Several." But he doubts he can equal the record of five. "No," he said early in 1992, "because I give myself only four more years in the sport, five at the most. So I'd have to win every year or almost every year, and that seems impossible. I won my first Tour when I was 27, a little late."

He might have won a third Tour already but sacrificed his chances in 1990 for the sake of team strategy. He was uncomplaining. "Win or lose, I try to remain the same person," Indurain said after his first Tour victory. "I'm proud of what I've done in the Tour but you have to keep your perspective. It's just a bicycle race, after all."

Nobody can quite explain why he is so dominant. His *directeur sportif* with the Banesto team from Spain thinks the secret is his height. Indurain measures 1.88 meters (6 feet 2 inches) and 80 kilograms (176 pounds), both figures abnormally large for a star climber. "It's the length of his femur," his thighbone, says the *directeur sportif*, José-Miguel Echavarri. "Because of his build, his legs provide more power than other riders can generate." Opponents point to other physical gifts. "Indurain has a lung capacity of 6.9 liters and, if you have ever seen photos of him, you will have noticed how his stomach protrudes as he rides," wrote Allan Peiper of the Tulip team in *VeloNews*. "His lungs take up so much space in his torso that his intestinal tract is pushed out to give more room to his lungs to open fully."

Other rivals are not so scientific in their observations. "He's an extraterrestrial," declared Gianni Bugno after Indurain humiliated him, and the rest of the pack, in a time trial in the 1992 Tour. "I thought I was riding well, really strong, but I kept losing time to him every kilometer," complained Greg LeMond after the same time trial. "It was unreal and I can't explain it."

Indurain cannot either. Or, if he can, he chooses not to. After his easy victory in the 1992 Giro, he told how he hoped to win the Tour de France. The strategy was the same one he used in the Giro and it was simple: Stay with the best climbers in the mountains and pulverize them in the time trials.

"It's classic," said the American rider Andy Hampsten. "But it isn't easy. He makes it look easy."

He smiles a lot and acts friendly but relies on teammates and officials to translate his Spanish and flesh out his answers in interviews. His younger brother, Prudencio, who also rides, without distinction, for Banesto, often signs autographs for both of them.

His modesty extends even to competition. Echavarri explains it this way: "I've known only one other rider able to dominate the way Indurain does and that was Eddy Merckx. But Merckx was a robot and his force humiliated his opponents. Miguel is a lord. He's generous and respects his opponents." Echavarri named four riders who won stages in the 1992 Giro. "They know they won because Miguel held back and let them win. Two of them came around and thanked him afterward."

Indurain looks fast in a race. He does not sway on his bicycle as most others do toward the end of a long time trial and he usually climbs with his mouth closed, instead of open and gasping for breath. "Everybody tells me that I never look as if I'm suffering," he says. "But when I watch videotapes of a race, I always remember the pain I had to endure."

"His pants are never dirty because he never works up a sweat and has to wipe his hands on his pants," says Peiper. "He always looks like he's riding down the Champs-Elysées. His shorts are never dirty, his hat is always in the same position, there's never a hair out of place.

"That's because he never gets to the point where he has to sweat until he's up in the mountains. He's never really put under pressure till about 95 percent of us aren't there anymore."

Time Trial

1992

ANYBODY WONDERING WHERE the Tour de France's defending champion, Miguel Indurain, had been hiding for the last week got the answer: He was in a telephone booth changing into a racing jersey with a very big letter S on it.

Absolutely overpowering in the day's long time trial, Indurain finished more than three minutes ahead of the rest of the 179 remaining riders.

Until now there might have been some doubts about how strong and committed the Spaniard was as he sought his second successive victory in the race. No longer.

Riding 65 kilometers out of and back into Luxembourg, Indurain finished in 1 hour 19 minutes 31 seconds. The second-placed rider, Armand De las Cuevas of Indurain's Banesto team, was a flat three minutes behind.

After that it was sheer destruction.

Indurain gained 3:41 on Gianni Bugno, 4:04 on Greg LeMond, 4:10 on Stephen Roche and 5:26 on Claudio Chiappucci, to name his major challengers for overall victory when the Tour finishes July 26 in Paris.

Long minutes after Indurain finished came the second big surprise of the day. Pascal Lino, the young Frenchman in the yellow jersey, rode a superb race against the clock and finished fifth, retaining the symbol of leadership.

Overall, Lino is 1:27 ahead of Indurain in second place. Third is Jesper Skibby, a non-climbing Dane with TVM. Roche is fourth and LeMond fifth.

Very rarely does a rider crush his opponents so thoroughly in a long time trial. LeMond lost to Indurain by just eight seconds, for example, in the first time trial in last year's Tour. Excelling at every time check in the race, Indurain rode with his usual fluid grace and power, leaving his main rivals farther behind with each kilometer.

Yellow is definitely the color he has in mind as the Tour approaches the Alps this week. He climbs as well as he rides in time trials, but Lino does not.

Other than Lino, the race has now sorted itself out into the expected battle among the favorites, a group in which Indurain must rank by far the highest.

Until Monday this was not entirely apparent. Since the Tour left Spain, where it started July 4, Indurain had done little to defend the No. 1 he wears on his back.

LeMond, the American who has won the Tour three times, and Chiappucci were especially pesky in the last week, picking up time as part of a breakaway into Brussels. Bugno, more careful, had waited for the time trial. A lot of good it did them. LeMond is three minutes behind Indurain overall, Chiappucci 3:27 and Bugno 3:12.

Bugno, an Italian who rides for Gatorade and finished second in the last Tour, lost eight seconds to Indurain in the first two kilometers. By seven kilometers, that was up to 22 seconds.

Nor were things going much better for LeMond, who left two minutes after Bugno and four minutes after Indurain. At the seven-kilometer mark, he was five seconds down on Indurain.

Since Indurain was ahead of them and his times could be relayed, Bugno and LeMond knew what they had to do. Their problem was that they could not stay with the Spaniard. By kilometer 37, when the race turned right and headed away from the Moselle River and its traffic of barges and swans, Indurain led Bugno by more than two minutes and LeMond by a bit less.

From then on the Spaniard just kept getting stronger.

When he was about 400 meters from the finish, he caught and passed Laurent Fignon, a Frenchman with Gatorade, and the huge and noisy crowd gasped. Fignon had started six minutes before Indurain.

Lino did almost as well, catching his two-minute man, Jens Heppner, a German with Telekom, who was in second place before the start. He dropped to seventh.

In reality, it was a fine time trial for almost all the top-ranked riders, who finished near each other. For Indurain it was a superb time trial.

The course—mainly flat and straight except for a small climb and some gentle curves—called for little technical ability. What was demanded was strength, which Indurain had in abundance.

As usual, he rode with a look of unemotional determination, not even grimacing slightly when he left the paved highway and bumped onto cobblestones in the village of Ehnen, halfway through the course.

All sorts of equipment were in evidence for the time trial as riders varied their wheels, frames, saddles and handlebars, seeking an extra advantage. Most riders used a rear disc wheel but from then on it was anybody's choice.

The most cutting-edge rider was Chiappucci, who lost the decisive time trial to

LeMond in the 1990 Tour when the Italian showed up with a standard road bicycle. This time he had a natty aerodynamic helmet, aerodynamic bars, a disc wheel, power shifting and everything else except a horn and a kick stand. For all the good the gadgets did him against Indurain, Chiappucci should have added a motor.

Homecoming

1996

EL REY MIGUEL INDURAIN V came home a hero in the Tour de France.

After five consecutive victories in the race, the king will not be changing the number after his name to VI this year—Bjarne Riis has won the race, barring accident or illness before the finish in Paris. But that seemed to matter not at all to hundreds of thousands of Indurain's fans in Pamplona, the stage finish, and a similar number along the route from France into Spain.

"Miguel, Miguel, Miguel," thousands chanted as he rode through Villava, the town where he grew up, and then just down the road into Pamplona. In the grandstands they rose and applauded him.

Eight minutes behind in the daily stage, Indurain rode the final two kilometers through a corridor of drumming as his fellow Spaniards beat rhythmically on aluminum barriers and screamed his name.

Finally, looking drawn after the finish, he mounted the platform that is usually reserved for the day's winner and the overall leaders in three categories: the top climber, the points leader and the man in the yellow jersey, the No. 1.

That is the number Indurain is wearing in this Tour after his victory last year. His jersey is not the leaders' white with polka dots, green or yellow, however. He wears the white, red and blue colors of his Banesto team for the first time this late in the Tour since 1990.

Indurain tried to manage a smile for his adoring crowd. Then Riis, who finished second in the mountainous stage and leads by nearly four minutes, presented his bouquet to Indurain and raised the Spaniard's arm. Indurain waved, threw the flowers out into the horde and climbed slowly down the stairs and off the victors' platform.

Riis stayed on. The Dane, who rides for the Telekom team, led a long breakaway in the Pyrenees by eight riders that exploded the standings and left him seemingly invulnerable at the top.

Indurain is in 11th place, 15:36 behind, the lowest he has been in the Tour in this decade.

Just turned 32 on Tuesday, he must be wondering what has happened to his legs. They failed him again Wednesday, just as they did Tuesday and 10 days ago in the Alps. The man who has constructed his Tour victories out of overwhelming triumphs in long time trials and the ability to stay with the best climbers in the mountains is simply not up to the job in this Tour.

There will be another Tour next year and at least one fan is already looking ahead to it. A sign somewhere in the sweltering approach to Pamplona told the champion: "Miguel, Super 1997."

THE BIG QUESTION

1996

THAT WAS A SWELL PARTY they gave before the Paris-Tours bicycle race: bouncy music, good food, not-so-good wine but plenty of it, friends not seen since the end of the Tour de France two months ago. The only problem was the conversation. It was boring.

Nobody in the small world of bicycle racing wants to talk about anything these days except Miguel Indurain. Will he or won't he retire? Don't even try to talk about the ozone layer or the elections in Bosnia or what exactly is the European single currency. Indurain—is he gone or isn't he?—has become the sole topic of conversation.

"I turned off the saga a couple of weeks ago," said Neil Stephens, an Australian rider with the ONCE team in Spain, as he imitated a man—click!—switching off the television.

He is one of the few no longer paying attention. The Big Mig question dominated proceedings at the presentation of teams in Issy les Moulineaux, a Paris suburb, and at their hotels afterward.

There was no point in trying to find the one man who might have answered the question accurately—Indurain himself. He never rides in Paris-Tours, 244.5 kilometers of flat, windswept course. Nothing about this World Cup classic suits his strengths, so he stays home in Spain, training.

Not this year, though. He's in Spain, yes, but not training. He's down on the Costa del Sol with his wife, Marisa, and their infant son, Miguel Jr., taking in the sun.

The season will continue another month, including the world road race and time trial championships this week in Switzerland, but Indurain has nothing on his schedule except a series of exhibition races in Spain. Some people regard those races as his farewell to the countrymen who have cheered him through five successive victories in the Tour de France. Others think the races are just a nice gesture and, at $25,000 an appearance, a lucrative one.

After that? He's not saying. Indurain has an option year on his contract with the Banesto team, which pays him about $3.5 million annually, and has told anybody who asks that he does not yet know whether he will continue to race. He will decide in November, he says. And, if the answer is yes, he will also decide then which team he will represent next season.

After a dozen years with the same management under different sponsors' jerseys, he is so hurt and angry that he is willing to listen to other offers. The line forms to the left: ONCE, Banesto's main rival in Spain, started wooing him intensely last month during the Vuelta a España. The Vuelta is where all the talk about his possible retirement began. It was not a good race for Indurain, who knew it would not be a good race for him.

"My legs felt like blocks of wood," he said two weeks ago when he quit the Vuelta during a hard mountain stage. "It was impossible to breathe."

He had conferred with his Banesto team's doctor a couple of times during the stage before pulling off the road at the team's hotel 30 kilometers from the finish. Adios Vuelta.

"I had worse days in the last Tour de France," he said. "But the law of our sport is very hard and when you don't have good health, nothing good follows," he told the French newspaper *l'Equipe.*

"These things happen in sports," he added. "Bicycle racing, even when you're a professional, is only a sport. There are more serious things in life."

There went possibly his last attempt to win the only big Tour that has eluded him, the one in his own country. Five times the winner of the Tour de France and twice the winner of the Giro d'Italia, he has finished no better than second in the Vuelta.

Indurain had not even ridden in it the last few years, preferring to focus instead on the Tour de France in July and then the world championships in October. He did not intend to participate this season either, but was forced to by his team.

That was indignity No. 2, following the major humiliation of his career, 11th place in the last Tour and his dreadful 19th place on the stage into Pamplona, when hundreds of thousands of Spaniards turned out to see the local boy make good. When he finished more than eight minutes behind the winner in that stage, did his heart break in two or 22?

Next on the schedule were the Olympic Games, which, pleading exhaustion, he wanted to skip. Only an unpublicized appeal by Juan Antonio Samaranch, the Spaniard who heads the International Olympic Committee, and by King Juan Carlos of Spain persuaded Indurain to go to Atlanta, where he won the time trial.

People wrote then that Big Mig was back, not understanding that the results almost exactly duplicated the finish two weeks earlier in the Tour's last time trial, when Indurain finished second and Abraham Olano third to Jan Ullrich, a German with Telekom. With Ullrich absent in Atlanta, Indurain moved up to first and Olano, a Spaniard with Mapei, to second.

Then came the forced participation in the Vuelta. "In 12 years as a professional," he said, "it's the first time the team has imposed its wishes on mine, the first time the team has not let me decide my own program."

Indignity No. 3 preceded the start of the Vuelta when it became known that the Banesto team was trying to recruit for next season Olano, who looks like Indurain, often rides like him and, at 26, is six years younger than him.

Even if the Olano deal has not been signed, the implication was obvious: Banesto believed Indurain no longer could win the Tour de France and wanted another leader, in fact if not in name. Big Mig could spend his last season grooming his successor.

So Indurain is taking the rest of the year off, skipping the world championships, where he would have defended his title in the time trial and perhaps, after two second places, finally won the road race, his unspoken dream.

Will he or won't he retire? One guess is that he is too proud to quit so near what is for him the bottom.

An Outdoors Boy

1987

"I'M AN OUTDOORS BOY," GREG LEMOND SAID, and he is comfortable around guns.

He remembered that when he was a child in Lakewood, California, outside Los Angeles, his parents practiced trap and target shooting and won local and state medals. "My dad used to break 100 straight targets, my mom, too."

So LeMond grew up around guns. Shotguns, but not pistols, which he says he considers dangerous. "I feel safe around guns because I know how to handle them. I've taken hunters' safety courses and always been open-minded about guns except for pistols." He believes in gun control because, he continued, "as far as I'm concerned, pistols are for nothing except killing people. Anybody who registers a gun is in it for sport."

After his family moved to Lake Tahoe, Nevada, when he was 7 1/2 years old, LeMond began downhill skiing. They spent three years in Lake Tahoe, then moved to Washoe Valley, closer to Reno, in ranching country. There were a lot of quail around the property and when he was 11 or 12 years old, LeMond started hunting them. At the same time he started trapshooting, like his parents.

In addition to downhill skiing and trapshooting, his main sport was backpacking, which he did almost every weekend when he was 13. Before he took up cycling, he planned to spend the summer of 1975 walking at least part of the Muir Trail from Canada to Mexico, a one-month or two-month trip, mainly to stay in shape for skiing. Another favorite sport was fly fishing. A small stream filled with brook trout flowed behind his house and LeMond taught himself how to fly fish by practicing on the brook trout. He got to be pretty good at it, he admits, and now has started to teach his older son how to fish.

LeMond and his father practiced target shooting together once a week. "I really liked the sport and lifted bricks to build up my arm strength so I could hold the gun up," LeMond remembered. "When you shoot 100 targets, it takes quite a bit of arm power. It's funny to have started on the way to cycling like that because none of the muscles or reflexes you develop in target shooting or fishing help you at all in cycling. But those sports were one of the reasons I got into cycling."

The sport that got him directly involved with cycling was downhill skiing, which he practiced three times a week during the winter. Then he turned to freestyle skiing and was advised that the best training for the sport was bicycling. Came the winter of 1976 with no snow in Nevada and LeMond began racing his bicycle. After a couple of races, he never went back to skiing.

"After I got into cycling, for the first five or six years I worked so hard at it that I never did anything else. I was so into cycling that I didn't ski anymore, didn't hunt anymore, didn't fish anymore. Not until I turned professional at 19 and cycling became so much of a job did I go back to those sports as a release."

He likes to hunt pheasants but says that the best bird is quail because they are fast and demanding to shoot. "I've never hunted them with dogs but just walk up on them; quail, if they're not hunted all the time, they're a pretty nervous bird and they'll flush themselves. Same with pheasant, but a pheasant will sit, just sit, until it gets really nervous and then takes right off. Usually you have to wait, wait, wait and wait—and then they jump up. Once in a while they'll sit there and you practically step on them before they take off."

He hunted five or six days a year, usually with such close friends as Jeff Bradley, a cyclist, too. "It's a great way to get together. We usually stay at a motel—I used to be able to camp out all the time but I'm getting soft now. Spoiled or soft, I'm not sure which."

Quail and pheasant, but no big game. He tried that only once, when he was 14 years old and wanted to try deer hunting. Awakening at 4 A.M., he left home and walked two or three mountains alone, saw a buck, took a shot at it, missed and decided that he didn't really want to hunt deer. "Don't ask me why. I'm still not sure why I quit after one shot."

So, on April 20, 1987, when he was shot and almost killed while hunting with relatives, LeMond was an experienced hunter. An uncle of his lived in Lincoln, California, perhaps 45 minutes by car north of LeMond's former home in California, on land where LeMond often went quail hunting. The year before he had noted that there was wild turkey on the property, too. For the six weeks that LeMond was home while his hand, which was broken in a fall during an Italian race, healed, his uncle had been inviting him to go turkey hunting, but he had kept putting it off, saying, "I'll do it next week." Then it was almost time to go back to Europe, just three days left, so LeMond accepted. He invited Pat Blades, the husband of one of his two sisters, a building contractor who was supposed to build the LeMonds a house in Rancho Murieta, the enclave of luxury homes around a golf course where they were already living. Blades had gone shooting only once or twice before, LeMond said.

When he packed that morning for the hunt, LeMond brought his bicycle in the car, planning to hunt that morning, cycle home for the training and then go to his doctor in the afternoon to have the hard cast removed from his hand.

"We got up to the property about 7:30 A.M. and made almost no plans what we were going to do to get some turkey, just said, 'We'll head up there,' up a hill, about 300 yards from the house. It's a farm with rolling hills, lots of berry bushes and quail, lots of birds on it. We split up, with my uncle going to the left, my brother-in-law to the right. One other thing we said was, 'We'll walk slowly, real, real slow and sit and wait, then walk up farther and sit and wait to see if we can spot anything.' Just planned to sit there, watching.

"Now it's very difficult for me to remember exactly what happened but I remember Pat whistling, trying to figure out where we were. He wasn't sure of my location. Berry bushes are pretty high and, besides, we were camouflaged in army fatigues. In turkey hunting, you've got to be camouflaged or the birds will spot you. We had hats on, net masks—maybe my uncle didn't but some of the details are so vague now.

"I do remember hearing Pat whistle, trying to figure out where we were, and I didn't respond because I thought that if I could understand his whistle, surely the birds could understand it. Then he didn't whistle for a while. I remember sitting there and then getting up—I was going to stand up and see where everybody was.

"That's when I got shot.

"The movement did it. I think it was the standing—he saw that movement in the bushes and reacted to it.

"I was crouching and just starting to get up when I got shot. That's the only way I could get all the pellets where I got them. I have only two pellets in my backside and if I'd been standing straight up, I would've had more. I got it all in my back.

"At first I wasn't sure what happened. When somebody else is shooting at a target, when he's pointing the barrel at something, it sounds as if it's a distance away. But when Pat shot at me, it sounded as if my own gun had gone off. It felt that close even though he was 25 or 30 yards away. I'm sure it was that distance because any closer and I would have been dead.

"I could not figure out what had happened. My first sight that anything had happened was a finger, the ring finger on my left hand: I saw there was blood on it. I felt numbness. You go into shock instantly and don't really know what's going on. When I got shot, I tried talking but my right lung had collapsed and I could barely breathe.

"'Oh my God,' I thought, 'I've been shot.' And I said, or tried to say, 'Pat, Pat, I've been shot.'

"Then I started freaking out, I started panicking. Pat said, 'What happened? What happened?' and he was running down to me and saw me shot. At first he was calm. I was in such shock that I was saying, 'Oh my God, I'm going to die' and 'I won't be able to race anymore' and 'What's going to happen? We were going to build a house, we won't build it now.'

"Everything passes through your head. 'Oh my God, my life is going to end.'"

Blades went into shock himself. "I can understand," LeMond continues. "For one thing, he shoots his brother-in-law and then he starts realizing he was going to build my house, all the pressure was going to come down on him because he shot me, Greg LeMond, the cyclist. Once I calmed down and help came, I felt worse for Pat than for myself."

His uncle came running because he heard Blades screaming. In LeMond's account, he himself had to restore calm. "Here they're both screaming and yelling that I had to calm down. So I screamed back at them, 'Calm down, I'm going to die if you guys don't calm down.'" Then his uncle went and called 911 and asked for an ambulance. The two men tried to lift LeMond but the right side of his shoulder hurt so badly that he couldn't manage it.

Blades said, "It doesn't look so bad, there's a little blood coming out, it's going to be okay." But, LeMond said, "I felt as if I was losing everything, like I was going to pass out. I was in shock and I guess you just fall asleep or pass out. That's kind of reassuring. Sometimes you think if somebody's shot they're in so much pain. I was in very much pain but your body takes over, goes into shock and you really don't realize the pain you're in."

Finally he was shouldered to a truck, got in and sat there about 25 minutes, waiting for the ambulance. What nobody knew was that an ambulance, a fire truck and the police had reached the property but could not enter because a gate was locked. LeMond's uncle drove the truck to the gate, where LeMond was put on a stretcher. "All I could think was, 'If we drive in, we're never going to make it.'"

Just then a helicopter from the California Highway Patrol dropped down and LeMond was wheeled over. He started calming down and pain started setting in.

"Boy, was I lucky! The helicopter took 11 minutes to get to the hospital at University of California–Davis, which is a special trauma unit, specializing in gunshot wounds and other traumas and accidents. They've got a team of surgeons there full-time, ready for any kind of accident. An ambulance would have taken me to the nearest hospital. We would have gone to Roseville, a good 30-minute drive from there, a bumpy drive. And I could have died because it would have taken longer and I wouldn't have been in the right type of trauma hospital.

"Lucky? Here's how lucky I was: The helicopter didn't come because they heard it was Greg LeMond—it was pure chance. Scanning the radio, the CHP helicopter just happened to overhear that a guy had been shot—and that was me. They were debating between going to a car accident, a minor accident as it turned out, or coming to my shooting. They decided to come over to the shooting, and that saved my life. At UC–Davis, the doctor said I was within 20 minutes of bleeding to death."

When the copter reached UC–Davis, LeMond was rushed into the emergency room, where a nurse repeatedly asked his name and address. "I could barely talk, it was so much pain to talk because of my punctured lung. Now I believe they did it just to keep me conscious, to keep me alert, but then I started getting angry at having to repeat Greg—G-R-E-G—LeMond—L-E-M-O-N-D—745 Anilo Way, Rancho Murieta, California 95683. I could barely say it but I said it three or four times, gritted it out. Finally she asked me again and I said, 'Dammit, Greg LeMond, 745 Anilo Way, Rancho Murieta, California 95683, and don't ask it again!'

"I'm not sure whether this was before or after they put a chest tube in me. That was crucial because my lung had collapsed. They gave me a local anesthetic and put a chest tube in, just pushed it through. I remember arching my back, coming off the stretcher, in pain. It hurt so much! So damn much pain! They gave me something to calm me down but they couldn't give me any painkiller because they had to figure out everything that was wrong with my body.

"I remember going under and then waking up in the recovery room. No, I remember them sponging me down and cleaning me up in the prep room before they put me under for surgery. I went into surgery about 9:30 A.M. and came out at 2:30 P.M.—that's what my wife says—but I didn't come to until midnight."

LeMond's wife, Kathy, picks up the story: "When I walked into the recovery room, you groaned and I knew that somewhere deep down you knew I was there. It was terrible. I had gone into labor by then and they knew I had to go to my hospital but they said I could see Greg when he came out of surgery. I walked in but they weren't ready for me yet. People in recovery are bare naked, completely exposed, so they can see you and they had just lifted Greg up to change the sheets. Out of every single hole in his body he was dripping blood. It was just like a colander—blood was dripping out of you. I asked, 'Are you sure he's going to be all right? He has all these holes in him.'"

An ordeal of pain began the next day, when LeMond started having spasms.

His right shoulder was the most painful part of his body. He says he did not realize that his right arm, including the fingers, was numb until four days later. The tip of his left ring finger was shattered and the doctors did not learn it was broken until five days later.

"Their main concern was saving me, getting out the pellets. The doctors had to remove pellets from my liver, kidneys and intestines. I had seven removed from my arm and took some others out myself. About 30 are still there, two in my heart lining but most in my back or legs. The doctors say there is no danger in leaving them there."

Because of his pain, LeMond was getting morphine shots every four to six hours but they did not seem to be helping. Even an epidural needle that regulated the flow of morphine failed to relieve the pain. "In the trauma center at UC–Davis, 90 percent of the people there are from Folsom Prison or are drug addicts and most of them want drugs to feel good. I believed that most of the nurses there are conditioned to believe that maybe I just wanted morphine to feel good. I kept saying to one nurse, 'I don't believe this epidural is working, I'm in too much pain.' She asked, 'Is the pain between 1 and 10?' I said, 'It's a 12.' And they kept thinking I was joking. They said, 'We know you're not in that much pain if you can joke with us.'"

His wife's sister Mary is a doctor and she persuaded an anesthesiologist to come up from the emergency room at midnight and confirm that the epidural was not working. The anesthesiologist thought that perhaps the epidural had twisted or there was a block in the tube or in his spine. LeMond was put on a treatment where he administered morphine to himself.

"When I got that, it started helping. I still had incredible pain but the new treatment was just enough to take the severe edge off. I was crying I was in so much pain.

I've never been in that much pain in my life. I could not do anything. If I coughed, it would go on for 20 minutes because I couldn't control anything. Once the pain started to spasm up, it wouldn't relieve itself for so long.

"This went on for four or five days. I was in the hospital six days altogether; I might have stayed a couple more days but in that type of accident they want you to be as active as you can. Also, I don't believe the doctor and nurses understood the severity of my accident. They thought I was lazy, that I didn't want to get up. They didn't understand that for me to go to urinate 10 feet away—to me that was like riding a mountain pass in the Tour de France. Harder!"

The pain persisted for three or four weeks after he came home, where his wife, mother and mother-in-law took care of him 24 hours a day. LeMond remembers sitting at home in a chair, shaking with pain, with sweat running down his face. He would pace in the bedroom and cry because it hurt so much.

"I spent four weeks going from my bed to a chair—no more than that."

Again his wife continues the story: "The accident made us realize that nothing is forever. That Monday I had just hung up the phone on Paul Köchli, the manager of Greg's team—we were leaving California for Europe on Wednesday, Greg was going to be racing on Friday. I called over to his aunt's house to tell him about the call and they're still out hunting. And two minutes after that the phone rings with word that he was shot.

"We didn't know if he'd ever ride his bike again, we didn't know if he was going to live, we didn't know anything.

"Two weeks before that, we were driving home one night and I said, 'You know, it's almost like we're too lucky. We've got too much. We have everything. Everything's good. We've got each other, we've got our son, everything's going to be perfect with Scott, we've got no money worries.'

"Everything was just fine. I mean everything just seemed too happy, too good. Not like this was meant to happen but in a way it's good that it happened. Now we appreciate everything. Since it happened we can justify it by saying we learned something from it: You've got to make every day count. We've learned to do everything we want to do."

Leaning forward in his chair, LeMond nodded in agreement. "That's exactly right. It's not as if I learned that I would never hunt during the season. There are lots of accidents hunting but there are statistically many more deaths in bike riding and it just makes you realize how fragile life is. Everything can be going perfectly and then suddenly, boom, you're dead!

"I'm sure a lot of European sports journalists would like to see me have my mind changed—now Greg won't be hunting anymore and he won't do golfing during the season, he'll just be riding his bike. But it's all more reason why I won't dedicate myself to nothing but ride my bike the next five years of my life. I want to be successful and do what it takes to make it in cycling.

"It's not as though I'm not dedicated; I train as well as anybody in the world. You've got to be dedicated if you've won the Tour de France, the world championship and the Super Prestige award by the time you're 25. But I have different priorities. The accident has made me realize that a healthy family is the most important thing to me.

"This accident gave me time to reorganize my life, reorganize and find out what's really important to me. Nothing's changed from what my philosophy was before but now it's been strengthened: I'm not willing to be like Eddy Mercx and devote my life 100 percent to cycling. That isn't the only priority.

"This accident has allowed me to spend so much more time with my family. Otherwise I would never have seen the birth of Scott, I would never have helped Geoffrey catch his first fish. I've spent a lot of time away from home for seven years, half the year out of a suitcase in a hotel, and now it's given me time to know and be with my family. We went on a vacation where, for the first time, I didn't give a darn what I ate, didn't worry about being in shape, didn't worry about cycling."

The Fastest Ever

1989

THE NIGHT BEFORE THE FINAL TIME TRIAL, reporters asked Paul Köchli if Greg LeMond could possibly make up the 50 seconds by which he trailed Laurent Fignon. As the former *directeur sportif* of La Vie Claire, Köchli knows LeMond and his abilities well. In addition, he is regarded as one of the finer minds in the sport, a master at training and strategy, a devotee of the computer in assessing a rider's performance. Köchli is also extremely fond of LeMond personally, which would have tended to affect his judgment.

"It's not possible," he said nevertheless. "One second a kilometer is possible. Two seconds a kilometer is impossible."

"I thought it was possible to win," LeMond insisted weeks later. "I thought it was possible," he repeated, "but it was a lot of time to make up."

He felt strong that Sunday in Versailles as a huge crowd lined the starting area on the Avenue de Paris to watch the 138 remaining riders in the 1989 Tour de France begin the time trial, a little over 24.5 kilometers to the finish on the Champs-Elysées.

The day started overcast before the summer sun burned the clouds off and left the sky a washed blue. By midafternoon the temperature was in the low 80s, hot for Paris, with a light wind tempering the heat. LeMond had slept well, eaten a big breakfast and lunch, and gone for a long warm-up ride; he was feeling confident. As he neared the start, many spectators yelled encouragement. He seemed not to hear them, except that every now and again he would smile back at a fan who shouted at him. Everything depended on this time trial, but the atmosphere was joyful, not tense. It was a Sunday in July, a holiday, the last weekend before August, when most Parisians traditionally depart on their month-long vacation.

Not since 1975 had the Tour ended with a time trial. Since that year, the surviving riders had entered Paris in a pack, made six passes up and down the Champs-Elysées and then sprinted wildly toward the final finish line. When the course had been announced in October 1988, no one would have guessed that the last stage would decide the race, but nearly everybody approved of the return to a final time trial. "It's fine being sucked along on a free ride down the Champs-Elysées," said Andy Hampsten, the 7-Eleven leader. "The greatest moment of the Tour always is arriving on the Champs-Elysées, just finishing the race. But arriving alone and not having to share the cheers is a wonderful reward for everybody."

There would be cheers for every rider, though interest centered on only two of them. The American would leave at 4:12 in the afternoon and the Frenchman at 4:14. They would be the last two off since in a time trial riders start in inverse order of standing. Those far behind in the standings had left a minute apart, but the leading 20 riders started two minutes apart.

With a 50-second lead, Fignon should have been feeling fine that morning, but he wasn't. When the riders had reached Paris by train the evening before, French television showed Fignon spitting at the cameras, striding away angrily from all questioners and appearing even more irritable than usual.

"You want a punch in the mouth?" he asked one cameraman. A few days before, he said later, he had begun to be troubled by saddle sores that had quickly infected his urinary system. On the next-to-last stage he had been unsure that he could even finish, so great was the discomfort. Unable to sit comfortably on the narrow saddle, he had to cut short his warm-up for the time trial because of the pain. He could not take any painkillers or most other medicine, of course, because of the long list of drugs forbidden as performance enhancers.

In contrast, LeMond was feeling good. The evening before, French television showed him smiling and relaxed, quite willing to chat with reporters on the train entering Paris. The contrast with Fignon's rudeness was striking.

The American's confidence carried over to the next morning. After finishing his warm-up ride, LeMond was sure he would do well. A month later, he recalled the feeling as he rested on a trainer's table while his *soigneur* and confidant, Otto Jacomé, kneaded his legs after a training session for the world championship road race in the Savoy region of France. Lying on his stomach with a towel knotted around his waist and a faraway look in his eyes, LeMond recalled the last morning of the Tour. "I told Otto, 'My legs are good. I'm going to have a very good day.'" Jacomé nodded, remembering that morning, too. Suddenly they were both far from the small, shabby hotel room in Aix les Bains and back in Versailles, with the royal palace as a backdrop to the Tour's simple platform and starting ramp.

On the platform, covered with a canopy against the hot July sun, LeMond reached down one last time to ritually check the shoes locked into his bicycle pedals. A clock showed that he would leave within seconds.

"Five," announced the timer in French.

"I was nervous," LeMond admitted.

"Four."

"I don't like doing time trials."

"Three."

"When I'm warming up, I say to myself, 'I don't know if I can do this again.'"

"Two."

"You think, 'Oh my God, I've got to push myself to the limit for the next 30 minutes or however long it is.'"

"One."

"But when I finish one, I've always liked it. I excel at them."

Then LeMond was rolling down the ramp, surging for 26 minutes 57 seconds through Viroflay, Chaville, Sèvres, Meudon and many of the other southwestern suburbs of Paris.

"I started extremely fast," he remembered. In a time trial a rider can judge how he is doing by how quickly he catches the rider who left before him—or how quickly he himself is caught by the rider who departs after him. Team officials driving behind the rider can shout out his time at the different points in the course, but for this last stage LeMond did not want to know.

After his ADR *directeur sportif* gave him his time at the five-kilometer sign, LeMond told him he didn't want any further information. Instead he emptied his head of all thought except riding as fast as he could. "I didn't think; I just rode," was the way he put. His strategy was an easy one since he had nothing to lose by going flat out from start to finish. He laughed lightly in recollection. "It was pretty simple, really."

Wearing an aerodynamic helmet and leaning on the Scott extensions on his handlebars, LeMond rode with his back bent and his head low but often bobbing. When he passed the Arc de Triomphe and turned down the Champs-Elysées with the finish in sight, he appeared to reach back and find the strength for one more long kick. "I rode as if my whole career depended on it," he said.

So strongly did he ride that when he crossed the finish line he did not feel spent. "It was weird. I felt I'd put less effort . . ." he began. "No, I put an all-out effort . . ." Again he broke off. "I almost felt when I crossed the line that I hadn't pushed myself enough." In fact, he went on, he felt that he could have ridden at the same pace for another 10 miles.

Then there began the wait for Fignon to finish. Standing in the middle of the Champs-Elysées in a crush of reporters, photographers and race officials, LeMond watched the Frenchman moving toward the Arc de Triomphe. Loudspeakers boomed out his time and an electronic clock near LeMond showed the widening deficit. Starting fast, Fignon had been so startled to hear his *directeur sportif*, Cyrille Guimard, shout at the five-kilometer mark that already he trailed LeMond by six seconds that he stopped pedaling for a moment and turned in astonishment to look at his team car. After 11.5 kilometers of the 24.5, LeMond led Fignon by 21 seconds and the gap kept rising; it was 24 seconds after 14 kilometers, 35 seconds after 18 kilometers and 45 seconds after 20 kilometers, when Fignon turned left at the Louvre and entered the Rue de Rivoli, then the Place de la Concorde and at last the Champs-Elysées.

Now the Frenchman shifted gears and began his descent away from the Arc de Triomphe. "All I could think of was how terrible it would be to lose by one second," LeMond remembered.

Fignon was still about 50 meters from the finish line when he lost the race. At that point the clock showed that he trailed LeMond by 50 seconds for the day and that their times for the full 2,025 miles of the Tour de France were equal—but Fignon still had 50 meters to ride.

While LeMond watched the final seconds, French television reporters gave him a set of earphones in an attempt to interview him, but the crowd noise prevented him from hearing their questions and from getting any information about his rival's time. Then, as it became clear that Fignon would not finish in time, LeMond began pumping the air with his fists, broke into a huge grin and punched one uppercut after another. Standing near him and holding his bicycle, Jacomé shouted, "You won it, Greg, you won it," as Fignon passed the line. Jacomé let out a whoop and went bounding up the avenue in joy, dragging the bicycle behind him.

Kathy LeMond was in tears. As she heard Bernard Hinault announce the final time, she shouted at her husband, "Eight seconds, Greg. You've got eight seconds less than Fignon." LeMond heard her voice and understood only some of her words, but by that time he already knew the result.

Almost lost in the turmoil was the fact that Fignon had not folded under pressure. He finished 58 seconds behind, good enough for third place on the day, but LeMond had won the stage and the Tour de France by 8 seconds. LeMond's speed of 54.5 kilometers an hour was the fastest ever for a winner of a stage in the Tour by nearly five kilometers an hour.

One Small Hole

1990

ONE AND ALL—riders, team officials, race organizers and journalists—agreed that the 1990 Tour had been decided. Refusing to tempt the fates, Greg LeMond was not claiming victory but simply saying, "If I don't fall, if I keep my form, if I continue riding like this . . ." While those were a lot of "ifs," who could doubt that he was at his best? Not even Bernard Hinault, who rarely missed a chance to snipe at LeMond in his column in *l'Equipe.*

Hinault thought that if an upset was going to develop, it would not be on the next stage in the Pyrenees, from Lourdes to Pau, even if it did pass over the Aubisque Peak, rated beyond category, and the Marie Blanque, rated first category.

Would the Aubisque blow the race open again? Hinault was asked. "I don't think so. Maybe the Aubisque will launch a rider who's trying to win the stage, but no more than that."

He thought even less of the Marie Blanque's potential to dynamite the Tour. "It's so far from the finish," he pointed out. The Marie Blanque lay at almost exactly the halfway point in the 150-kilometer stage. After that, the mountains were past.

In a feisty mood after his courageous climb to Luz Ardiden, Claudio Chiappucci had to admit that he didn't think much of his chances either.

"Greg LeMond told journalists that I was finished—well, that was my answer," the Italian said, referring to his strong climbing the day before in which he saved the yellow jersey by five seconds. "I wanted to show what kind of rider I am. For the first time in my life, I'm a leader and I wanted to prove that I can be a great leader, a true yellow jersey.

"I know that he's probably going to win the Tour, but he's got a great team and I don't. Five seconds on LeMond, that's not much, probably not enough. I know it. But LeMond better be sure of one thing: He'll have to come looking for me if he wants to find those five seconds."

What brave words Chiappucci spoke, and how true! What a sensible analysis Hinault presented, and how true! What a wonderful sport is bicycle racing, where true words and sensible analyses can be made to fall apart by the tiniest hole in a tire!

For 20 kilometers, LeMond lost control of the race during the 17th stage. Then he and his fellow Z riders rallied to prove the old adage that this is an individual sport practiced by teams.

At kilometer 77, about 800 meters from the Marie Blanque summit, the rear tire on LeMond's bicycle flatted. "It was my first flat of the year," he said, "and it couldn't have come at a worse time." He was at the front of the pack, chasing a distant breakaway, in a small group of leaders including Chiappucci, Gianni Bugno, Pedro Delgado and Miguel Indurain, Delgado's locomotive. The climb over the first of the day's two mountains, the 1,709-meter-high Aubisque, had gone without incident.

Two, three, four times Delgado attacked on the 1,035-meter climb up the Marie Blanque, and each time LeMond and Chiappucci caught him. And then LeMond had his flat.

He charged afterward that Chiappucci, seeing the flat, violated etiquette and attacked with Delgado. Chiappucci insisted that his attack toward the peak was part of a series of offensives begun by Delgado and denied that he had breached a code of conduct.

Many observers even wondered if, in an age of million-dollar contracts, there really was room in the sport for much etiquette. Attacks after a crash used to be considered a low thing to do and now they are not uncommon. More rare is the attack while riders are stopped at the side of the road to urinate, another violation of the rule in the old days but now just how Joel Pelier won the stage into Futuroscope in the 1988 Tour. In short, nobody gets overly upset anymore at an attack after a flat.

LeMond's anger had other causes: He was troubled by a deep saddle sore that, along with nervousness, was causing him to lose sleep, especially on the nights before the stages in the Pyrenees. It was an extremely hot and muggy day in a week of torrid weather and his feet had swollen and were paining him. Worse, he was without teammates in the lead group and his team car was far behind him, blocked in traffic on the narrow road.

"It was the first time I had no teammates with me to give me a wheel," LeMond related. "It was the first time the team car was so far behind. It was a lot of firsts."

Another first, or no worse than a second, was that Chiappucci was surrounded by four Carrera teammates. "We poured it on," confirmed Acacio da Silva. "It's the Tour and in the Tour you don't give an opponent any presents."

Far behind, LeMond was raging. "I waited, it seemed like hours," he said. Actually it was a little over a minute before Roger Legeay, the Z team's *directeur sportif*, pulled alongside his rider. While a mechanic replaced the rear wheel, two Z teammates, Eric Boyer and Jérôme Simon, arrived.

"We just couldn't keep up with Greg on the climb," Boyer said, "and we knew he was isolated. Jérôme and I said to each other, 'Let's get going. Greg is alone up there.' Then we heard spectators yelling at us, 'Hurry up, Greg has a flat.' When we reached Greg, he kept saying that he was very worried. That minute it took to get him going seemed like an hour to him. He thought he was losing the Tour. Greg kept saying, 'I've blown it, I've lost the race.'"

LeMond got back on his bicycle but had to stop again after 25 meters because the new wheel was rubbing the frame. This time he was given another bicycle and set out with Boyer and Simon behind him. Chiappucci was over the Marie Blanque and his lead was 1:07.

Far ahead in the breakaway of about 30 low-ranking riders were two other Z teammates, Gilbert Duclos-Lassalle and Atle Kvalsvoll. Using his car telephone, Legeay got in touch with his assistant, Serge Beucherie, who was covering the lead riders, and ordered that they stop and wait for LeMond. For Duclos, this was a heartbreaker since he was riding for the stage victory in his native region of France. "But, of course, it's part of my job," he said. "I'm nearly 36 years old and I'm going to win my first Tour with Greg. That's worth a chance at a stage victory."

Once over the peak, LeMond led the charge down it. He rode in a frenzy, a man both angry and, as he admitted, scared of losing. "I've never risked my life like that before and I hope I never have to again."

How fast was he going? Jean-François Pescheux, the Tour official who rides a motorcycle and relays time splits between breakaways and the pack, was awed. "I've never seen a descent that fast," he said as he sliced a zigzag with his right hand. "That was the road and LeMond never braked once. He took each curve at top speed. He must have been hitting 80 kilometers an hour. I thought he was crazy." Boyer would never be disloyal enough to question his leader's sanity, but he was shaking afterward. "We never touched the brakes," he confirmed, "and we couldn't keep up with Greg."

At the bottom, they linked up with Duclos-Lassalle and Kvalsvoll. Taking turns at the front, the five rode a mini-team time trial and soon were in sight of Chiappucci. After a 20-kilometer, 25-minute chase, LeMond was back with the leaders. They stayed together the rest of the way into Pau.

Good-bye to All That

1994

GREG LEMOND HAS TO SAY GOOD-BYE.

At age 33, the three-time winner of the Tour de France and the greatest bicycle road racer ever produced in the United States has decided that he is no longer able to compete in the sport. He will make a formal announcement on Saturday in Beverly Hills, California, as part of the Korbel Night of Champions, a fund-raiser for the U.S. Cycling Federation.

LeMond will be one of 14 male and female racers honored at a dinner afterward. Their records and medals will be flashy but none approaches LeMond's own lines in the record book: victories in the 1986, 1989 and 1990 Tours, victories in the 1983 and 1989 professional world championship road races.

That list might have been longer but for the nearly fatal shooting in 1987 that lost him 2 of the 14 seasons he has been a professional. The glory years are long gone now and he has not finished first in a race since the 1992 Tour DuPont. He has not even ridden in one since he dropped out of last July's Tour de France.

"It's probably been expected," he said of his retirement. He has often reported—and displayed—weakness and exhaustion, especially in the mountains, but has been unable to specify the cause. Now he thinks he can.

"It's time for me to get out because of physical problems," he explained on the phone from his home in Minnesota. "It's not just age that's been responsible for my performances these last few years. It's not that I wasn't motivated or just did it for the money. I have a very big physical disability that does not allow me to compete at the world-class level. I have a physical condition that is not allowing me to race at the level I should."

The condition, he continued, is called mitochondrial myopathy. "I can't spell it," he said with a laugh, "but I can say it's basically dysfunctional mitochondria, which won't help me produce energy. My energy-delivery system has been off whack. It's a mild state that affects my performance at a high level but not my day-to-day living."

Parts of each cell, mitochondria produce energy through respiration. When they are impaired, muscles are impaired. "I hate to say it," he continued, "but it would mimic some sort of muscular disease."

According to the *Merck Manual*, a standard medical reference book, mitochondrial myopathies are among a group of progressive muscle disorders of unknown cause that are inherited through the mother. LeMond said he and his doctor believe, however, that the condition is caused by the 30 lead shotgun pellets left in him when he was accidentally shot while hunting in California on April 20, 1987. Two of the pellets rest in his heart lining.

"It's very possible it could be the lead," he said. "We're hoping to tie it to the lead because it would at least give me a clear answer for the future."

But Dr. Michelle Taube of the Minneapolis Sports Medicine Center, "who has worked the last three months researching me," is still not certain of the cause, LeMond said. "That's only the most likely theory.

"It seems to be caused by something when I'm racing really hard. We think it's an environmental problem, which means most likely I mobilize lead, which causes damage.

The more I exercise, the more I mobilize it and the more damage the lead does, especially in multiday races.

"And that's why for the last three years, after four or five stages of a race I'm at a point where I need to quit racing. It's been that way for three years now."

The major effect of his ailment, he said, has been on his ability to use oxygen during a race to restore his muscles.

Discussing the amount of oxygen he could use with each breath, he said, "I went from 6.2 liters of oxygen in February to 4.2 liters of oxygen during the Tour, even three weeks after the Tour.

"It makes sense now. When I was in the Tour, I kept saying 'I can't take oxygen in.' That's exactly what was going on. When everybody else was riding along pretty slowly and easily for them, I was riding at my max."

LeMond is not through with medical tests, which he has been having mainly in Minneapolis, near his home in Medina.

"I want to get to the bottom, I want more finalized answers," he said. "This year has been the low point of my career. I have tried my hardest, mentally pushed myself beyond what I should, mentally and physically. I went through two very bad years, '92 and '93, and I was all motivated to make a charge through what would have been the last three years of my career.

"But all of a sudden the realization came to me in the Tour de France last summer that there must be something wrong—this can't be right—and that I had to re-evaluate whether I could continue in this sport. If I could take away the problem, I thought I could still compete."

Can he? "No," he replied, a flat and forlorn "no."

"We know it's repeated itself for the last three years. I've got a medical condition. The doctor said, 'Greg, you can feel good and you might think you've recovered, but you won't have.' No, there won't be any comeback next spring. I wouldn't be myself, the Greg LeMond of '85 or '86, where I just always felt great.

"I struggled to come back after my hunting accident. I did win the Tour in '89, miraculously I think now. In the last seven years I've had four months that I felt good and in those four months I won two Tours de France and the world championship. But in the rest of those years I've been just struggling.

"I couldn't figure it out. Every year I had different reasonings: allergies, overtraining, quarrels with my dad, this and that. There's nothing more frustrating for an athlete than to be talented and then suddenly to have that talent taken away from you.

"I never needed to race and be the last guy, getting pushed up hills. And that's who I was this year. This was a do-or-die season this year for me. I did everything I possibly could, prepared myself. Either I had to have a great season or I had to call it quits. Stop.

"The last thing I want to be considered is a rider who stayed on too long. Now I'm retired. I'll try to have fun."

His ways of having fun are many and varied, including spending more time with his wife and three children, fly fishing, downhill skiing, tennis and golf, mountain-bike racing and searching for antiques.

"That's what I've done this fall," he said. "I've been going to dealers for antiques, American antiques, 18th century, early 19th century, Federal period, Queen Anne period. I've been wanting to do that for years, and I've never had the time."

Through his bicycle sales company he will retain connections with the sport. He also talked about his passion for mountain-bike racing, saying he might organize a team and might even compete in a few races. Although he may also fulfill his great dream of making it to the 1996 Olympic Games in Atlanta, LeMond knows now that it will have to be as a television commentator, not as a racer in the time trial.

As of Saturday formally, but really as of July 8, when he got off his bicycle in the middle of a Tour stage, LeMond has not been a racer.

"I want to be somewhat involved in the sport, in certain capacities but I don't know what," he said. "I'll probably make it to the Tour next year, maybe as a television commentator, maybe as a guest. Otherwise I'll be fishing in Montana."

FIRST RACE

1992

FINISHING HIS FIRST BICYCLE RACE as a professional by riding so far behind that he was alone, Lance Armstrong began thinking the unthinkable. "I thought maybe I wasn't any good," he said. "I thought, 'God, these guys are that much better than me.' It was very humbling."

Armstrong is not easily humbled. He is confident, articulate, likable and, on the eve of his 21st birthday, one of the brightest prospects in the sport. But for a few weeks this summer he was simply another rider hunched over his handlebars, pumping his legs to no great, or even good, result. In a word, humbled.

As an amateur last month, he was a favorite in the road race at the Olympic Games in Barcelona but finished far back because, as he said, "I just didn't have the best legs. I had good legs but other guys had better legs."

A few weeks later, after he signed as a professional with the Motorola team based in the United States, he was entered in his first race, the Clasica San Sebastian, a World Cup competition in Spain. The rainy weather was against him and so was the distance, 234 kilometers, many more than he was accustomed to as an amateur. "It's tough when it's 250, 260 kilometers, but 200 I have no problem with," Armstrong said.

He finished 111th, dead last, 11 minutes behind the rider in 110th place. All alone as he plowed on, Armstrong refused to quit, as 95 of the 206 starters did. "It was my first race, my first professional race, and I didn't want to quit my first race," he explained. "I didn't want to finish but I didn't want to quit either."

Bloodied in battle, he began to do well: a stage victory in the Tour of Galicia in Spain, second place in the Championship of Zurich, another World Cup one-day race, then a victory in an Italian race. It was an astonishingly successful start to his professional career and confirmed his promise as the heralded amateur who beat professionals to win the Settimana Bergamasca race in Italy two years ago.

This week Armstrong has come down to earth a bit in the Tour de l'Avenir, the Tour of the Future, a French showpiece for young and promising riders.

Although he knows that Miguel Indurain and Greg LeMond both won the Tour de l'Avenir early in their careers and thus attracted their first broad attention, Armstrong was modest beforehand about his goals in the race.

"It's sort of preparation for the rest of the season, the remaining World Cup races," he said. "I'd like to have a stage win here. Definitely. That's a goal. But the overall classification, I have to see how it goes."

By Tuesday, three days before the 10-day race ends in Brittany, Armstrong ranked 31st, about five minutes behind. He did not yet have a stage victory.

Nevertheless, said his Motorola coach, Jim Ochowicz, "Lance is riding heads up and we're very pleased. He's definitely got a winning attitude," Ochowicz added. "You don't have to motivate him."

Besides attitude, Armstrong said by phone, his form was good. "Good, but you never know, it comes and goes so quick. You get good form and there's that crest you have to hold and ride for as long as you can. It's pretty easy to go over it and start your descent."

While his form holds, however, Armstrong has a full racing schedule. He rides next in the Tour of Ireland and then in such World Cup races as Paris-Tours, the Grand Prix of Lombardy and the Grand Prix of the Americas in Montreal. "A lot of riding," he conceded, "but I'm begging for it."

He also has an inner schedule, and it calls for him to be nothing less than a great star.

Armstrong has practiced and polished the line, used it in so many interviews now that his delivery is perfect. The straight man asks the inevitable question: Are you the next Greg LeMond? "No," he answers, "I'm the first Lance," (a healthy chuckle here) "the first Armstrong."

It reads glibber than it sounds. The adjective often attached to Armstrong is "brash," but perhaps that's only his way of seeking self-protection. Speaking the Lance line, Armstrong can be understood to be asking for some breathing room, for respite against the LeMond comparison. Cut him some slack, as they say back home in Plano, Texas. Until Thursday, he's still only 20.

"I don't think it's fair to compare me to Greg LeMond," he said in an earlier interview. "He's a great athlete and I think I'm a good athlete.

"Physically, we're a lot different," continued Armstrong, who is 180 pounds to LeMond's 152. "He's a big guy but he's not as big as me. Body type, there's no comparison.

"He turned pro when he was 19 but he also got married when he was 19, so I guess he started everything a little early."

Armstrong began competing on a bicycle at 12, "just to keep busy," but focused on other sports. "Being from Texas, of course I tried football, the mainstream sports thing, then tried swimming and got into triathlon from there and then got into cycling from there."

He is honest about why he changed sports. "I wasn't any good at football. No speed, no coordination."

Swimming—1,650 meters indoors, 1,500 meters outdoors—was no different. "Again no speed," Armstrong says.

That analysis carries over to road racing. Asked to list his weaknesses, Armstrong said, "I don't have a lot of speed in cycling either. I'm not very quick in the sprint."

For his strengths, he named climbing and time trials. Somewhere in between his strengths and weaknesses he put bike-handling skills. "They've improved greatly," he thought. "A lot of triathletes don't have very good bike-handling skills because they don't ride in packs."

Riding in packs offers other advantages, he continued, including the opportunity to compare himself directly to his opponents.

"The day that you're on, you're riding and you get this feeling that's like . . ." The words trailed off as Armstrong searched for a way to define ecstasy. "You're tired and you're hurting," he resumed, "but you just look around and you can tell that the guy next to you is hurting one notch more than you and you're recovering that much faster than him, and that's an incredible feeling."

Victory is another high. "When it's going good—I should say when you're winning—it's one of the most luxurious sensations. It's an incredible feeling to win major races, to come across with your hands in the air. It's like no other feeling in the world."

Victory matters a lot to Armstrong.

"I want to be a star," he said in an even voice. "I know I want to do the Tour de France, I know I want to win the Tour de France. I think I can someday get to that level but that's a long way off, a lot of hard work. The desire is there, the ambition is there, the goal is there. It's only a matter of doing the hard work and winning the race.

"Everybody wants to win the Tour de France. Everybody from Category IV up says, 'I want to win the Tour,' yet only one guy can win it each year," he continued. "LeMond has won it three times and look at his crowds, the way he's responded to. It's amazing.

"Win the Tour de France and you're a star. I'd like to be a star.

"I'm sure I'd get sick of all the pressure and all the appearances but I'd like to try it for a while."

TEAM LEADER

1994

ONE PHOTOGRAPHER WAS UP A LADDER with a camera and another was walking around with a light meter, calling out numbers as he scanned members of the Motorola bicycle team. They were posed in front of a disused roadside chapel in Tuscany. In 1993, the team photograph had been taken in a warehouse for a high-tech look and so, yin and yang, the next year the goal was something picturesque, even touristic. "But elegant," one of the photographers explained.

Center front among the 18 riders, the four team officials, four or five bicycles and a team car stood Lance Armstrong. He deserved the position of honor: Armstrong was the team leader and he wore the rainbow-striped jersey of the world's professional road-race champion. In his first full season as a professional the year before, he won the world championship, a stage of the Tour de France, the U.S. professional championship and a $1 million prize by finishing first in a series of American races.

Winners stand center front.

Then why, in the warehouse photograph taken early the year before, when Armstrong had appeared as a professional in just half a dozen races, was he also center front?

"I was the team leader a little bit last year," the Texan said in the Italian village of Castagneto Carducci, where his team was holding a training camp. "I was certainly the team leader at the Tour DuPont and throughout the million-dollar saga. In the Tour de France I had days where I was considered the man."

That didn't wash. All those races took place months after the photograph. Who knew so early that Armstrong had such star quality? He smiled broadly and ducked his head in mock humility. If anybody knew, Armstrong knew.

"I was always worried about failing," he said. "I wanted to win, but more than that, I didn't want to fail. And," he spoke slowly now, "I don't think I have."

He was determined, he continued, not to fail while he was world champion.

"Over the last few years, people seem to think the rainbow jersey has had a curse upon it," he noted. The 1990 world champion, Rudy Dhaenens of Belgium, never won another race and had retired from the sport. The 1991 and 1992 champion, Gianni Bugno of Italy, had failed to win a major race the previous two years.

Armstrong hoped to end that spell soon, as early as the first classic of the spring, the long race from Milan to San Remo in Italy. "It's a big goal for me because it's the first big race that anybody's paying attention to, and I've heard so much talk about world champions wearing the rainbow jersey and not being able to perform in the jersey. This is going to be an event where I can showcase not only my talent but the possibilities of the rainbow jersey winning a big one.

"As a champion, you have to represent yourself well and your team and your sponsor well, but with the rainbow jersey you're also representing the sport and the jersey itself. With that comes added pressure tenfold."

How much of that added pressure tenfold was he feeling?

"None," he said flatly.

When he first began making a name for himself as a member of the U.S. national amateur team four years before, Armstrong was sometimes regarded as arrogant. Then he started fulfilling his promise by winning races and what seemed arrogant became brash. As a professional, what seemed brash became confident, ebullient, even charming and honest.

"There's no pressure because I'm prepared," he explained. "I'm ready. I've said that all along in my career—I've always said I'm ready, I'm ready, I can do this and I'm confident.

"Now I truly feel I'm secure with myself and my career. I realize I can have success. I know it's right there. It's not anything I'm worried about. It's just a matter of going out and doing it. I still have the desire to do it, like I've always had, but now I know in my heart and my mind that I can conquer this sport and that I can conquer the races."

He had felt pressure, though. "Not from the team and not from the sport, not from my friends and not from my family. But I felt a little pressure from myself because it seems I demand a little more from myself than others do."

At 22 the second youngest man to be world champion, Armstrong also appeared to be a little more worried about his reception in the rainbow jersey than he should have been. He confessed that he scented a certain resentment among riders on other teams.

"Maybe 'resentment' is too strong, maybe I'm looking at it in a pessimistic way and I shouldn't," he said. "I'm sure there are people who are jealous."

Yet, with the season just opening, he had not been in contact with many other riders. That did not dissuade him as he hinted at an unexpected insecurity.

"Surely, they're a little bit jealous," he said again of other riders. "I think most of them are thinking maybe it was a fluke, thinking it was a little bit lucky."

He did not agree. "I don't think it was lucky. I rode a great race."

Armstrong was reminded that no less a racer than Miguel Indurain, the winner of the previous three Tours de France and the second-place rider in the world championship, said afterward that Armstrong deserved the victory because he was obviously the strongest man that day.

"Not everybody has the class of Indurain," he replied.

He remembered when he knew he had won: "When I turned around, four or five kilometers to go, and just saw nobody. I turned around and didn't see anybody and the last split I heard was about 20 seconds. I couldn't believe it. I thought, 'Oh my God, I'm going to win the world championship.' Then I thought, 'Oh no, I've got another lap because this is too good to be true.' I said to myself, 'How am I going to know? I don't want to cross the line and keep going.'

"It was all starting to happen so fast. From that point on, it just all happened so quick. I said, 'I'll check the computer' and I did and it said 250 and I said, 'Oh my God, this is it.' And I thought, 'Hopefully, the computer isn't wrong.'"

It wasn't. He won the 257-kilometer race in Oslo by 19 seconds, a big lead, and ended up by blowing kisses to the crowd.

"To everybody, everybody there, the fans, the spectators. And they liked it. Before I was blowing kisses, they were sitting down and afterward they were standing up. You have to please the fans. That's part of my ideas about cycling: It's a sport, it's entertainment, sports are entertainment. You can win and not be entertaining, but I think people leave a race with a better image of the sport if it's entertaining.

"I'm here not just to do things for myself and Motorola but to promote the sport. I want people to leave and say, 'Hey, I can't wait to go to another bike race.'"

After the race, officials tried to take the new champion to meet the king of Norway but Armstrong refused to go along unless his mother, Linda, who often watched him race in Europe, could come too. "She was thrilled—she was thrilled for me." At each of many checkpoints, he had to argue security men into allowing his mother to pass through. "They kept saying only the winner can come, but I told them, 'If she's not coming, I'm not coming.'" Finally they were in a room where she watched her son shake hands with a king.

That was a long way from Texas, where Armstrong grew up as the fatherless child of a 17-year-old girl whose husband left when the boy was three. "Were we poor?" he asked, repeating a question. "No, but I certainly didn't have a silver spoon." Had it been a long time since he had contact with his father? "Forever," he answered.

Usually a man of many words, Armstrong used just one when asked if his mother had been supportive. "Very," he said. "It means more to me than just having her at a race," he continued. "It gives me the opportunity to spend time with her before the race or after the race, allowing her the opportunity to spectate the race. It's not a normal relationship anyway, being that she's young and she had me very young and she grew up at the same time I was growing up and we sort of grew up as friends and not as mother and son. So I grew up as one of her friends and when I'm not there all the time she really feels . . ." He thought about it. "Lonely," he decided.

Loneliness, any sort of unhappiness, troubled Armstrong. "I'm looking for cycling to make my life, I'm not looking for cycling to ruin my life. For some people it's certainly ruined their life or made it miserable. I've seen some cyclists that just don't appear very happy. That's the last thing I want.

"I want to be happy, I want cycling to make me happy, I want it to make my family happy and right now it's doing that. The day it doesn't is the day I'm going to stop."

A contributing factor to his happiness was the big money he began earning once he won the world championship; one report said his salary had risen tenfold to $750,000 a year.

"Everybody likes money," he said strongly. "There's nothing wrong with money. There's nothing wrong with using money as a motivation. It should be a motivation not only for athletes but for everyday people. In America, people look badly on money and don't consider it an incentive, which it is. I'm supermotivated by money. I'm not going to sit here and say money doesn't mean anything to me, because it means a lot. And I enjoy giving it back. As much as I enjoy getting money, I love to give money. Christmastime, obviously a time you give and get, I don't really care to get anything, I've got everything I ever wanted, but I like to give away stuff."

That was consistent with what he described once as his religious beliefs: "I believe in my responsibility to be a good person. I think at the end of the day, we're judged upon that. I think we're all obligated as people to be true and honest and correct."

Discussing his prospects, he was optimistic about his form and opportunities in the coming season. "I'm learning more and gaining more as far as tactics are concerned," he judged. "In the past I've been very aggressive and sometimes overly aggressive and I regret it. Certainly. But sometimes you make some mistakes when you're aggressive. I recognize those mistakes and won't make them again. So my style may appear to change but it will have the same aggression with a little more intelligence."

After more than a month of tune-up races, mainly in Italy, he would get his chance to convince doubters—real or imagined—in the first World Cup classic, Milan–San Remo. It was a special race to him because its distance, 297 kilometers, suits a rider with his strength, aggression and stamina and because he was near the front the previous year until the final climb up the Poggio Hill, where he faded.

Armstrong explained that he had not ridden his own race then but had been working for a teammate, Max Sciandri, who had since moved from Motorola. "I was left a chance to take any opportunity, if something happened to him or he was having a bad day. At the finish, I was definitely working for him because he was there and he was feeling good and he wanted help." Sciandri finished third, Armstrong 22nd.

In 1994, the team would work for Armstrong.

"I have a great relationship with this team," he said. "I count them as my friends, my best friends. And they look at me the same way. The neat thing is that the way they act toward me and the way I act toward them hasn't changed a bit. I'm still the same person with a different jersey."

As a leader, he continued, his big job was to motivate. "Head up troops," he said. "I like to think I'm a motivator. I get supermotivated myself and I feel that I can motivate. We're all on the same level here, so it's very easy for them to relate to me, to see when I'm hurting. They see when I want something, when I want to win it, even if I don't tell them.

"Sometimes I tell them, sometimes I say some things in the races and I think it gets them psyched up—how great I'm feeling or how I'm going to win. Within a race I can boldly predict to my teammates, 'Hey, I'm going to win today, guys.' Before a stage or during. I think they like that.

"Certainly, that's a little bit confident but I think if you're saying it within the team, it's a little different than if you're blurting it in headlines. But it motivates the guys.

"Another thing that motivates them is that when they have worked for me, have sacrificed for me, the majority of the time I've come through. So when it comes around the next time and I say, 'Come on guys, we've got to chase, do some work here, I need some help,' these guys are 100 percent willing to do it because they know if anybody is going to come through for them, it's going to be me.

"And the day I can't do that is the day I need to stop racing. I don't want to let anybody down. And that's part of my motivation, that when I say, 'Okay, guys, let's work,' they get up there and they're on the front hammering, chasing down somebody, leading me out.

"I see these guys hurting, I see the salt forming on their shorts, I see them sweating, I hear them breathing and that motivates me.

"I'm willing to sacrifice for them. I've shown in the past that I'm willing to work for somebody else if I'm not riding well. That's not a problem. I've displayed that and I'll continue to do that. Nobody thinks that a rainbow jersey can ride on the front for his teammates, but I don't have a problem with that. If I was in a position where I had to work for somebody else, sure."

AN ORDINARY MORNING

1996

AS MORNINGS GO, THIS ONE SEEMED ORDINARY: Fog masked the hills west of Austin, a light wind fluttered flags, and the temperature promised another shirt-sleeves day.

A commonplace morning for most people, but another wonderful, joyful morning for Lance Armstrong. He woke at 7 o'clock at his home on Lake Austin, went to the kitchen to prepare a pink grapefruit for breakfast, looked at the newspaper and then began celebrating another day of simply being alive.

"Every day I wake up, I feel great," he said later. "I say 'This is great' because six months from now, a year from now, five years from now, I may not be able to say that."

Two months ago, Armstrong was competing and finishing high in arduous, 150-mile races in Europe. He had no symptoms at all. Then, seven weeks ago, the 25-year-old bicycle-racing champion was told that he had testicular cancer and that the cancer was also in his abdomen and lungs.

Three weeks later, after the malignant testicle was removed, he learned that the cancer had spread to his brain, requiring surgery to take out two lesions.

"You can see where they did it," he said. Lifting his blue Dallas Cowboys cap, he leaned forward to show the two stitched semicircles on the top left and back of his head. Somewhat proudly, he also showed two tiny bumps on either side of his forehead, where screws held his head steady during the five-hour operation.

"I'm feeling fine," he said. "A little bit of fatigue, which means I have to take a nap every day, about two hours. This week I feel like I felt two months ago. I really do. That's no lie."

"I'm really upbeat. I'm positive. I may be a little scared, I may be very scared, but I feel very positive about how things are going."

Armstrong is scheduled to leave Monday for a week at the Indiana University Medical Center in Indianapolis, where he will receive four hours of chemotherapy daily for his third week. The treatment will be administered through a catheter that was surgically implanted and that he wears at home during the two weeks between each of four scheduled weekly sessions of chemotherapy. Taped over his heart, the outside of the device resembles, ironically, the tube that bicycle riders use to pump air into flat tires.

He had no interest in irony, though. He was concentrating on one thing only and that was survival. For him, another morning alive is a triumph.

"It used to be when I woke up every morning, I knew I was going to wake up," he said. "It was so normal I took it for granted and now I never know. We're not promised anything. We're not promised tomorrow.

"We all expect to have long and fulfilling lives, but I suggest people not take that for granted. We don't always attack life, don't do things to the fullest, and I suggest that people take advantage of life."

He was sitting in the living room of his new, white, Mediterranean-style villa, which he helped design. Circled by palm trees and clumps of flowers, the two-story house is airy and bright with high ceilings, vivid abstract paintings and stylish furniture that he chose with his decorator. This is the house he had dreamed about for years, perhaps as long ago as when he was a teenager living in Plano, outside Dallas, and growing up, as he describes it, "Okay, middle class," raised by his mother, a single parent after his father left when Armstrong was an infant.

Late that June, a couple of months before he moved in, he said, "I'm happier here than I expected to be, and I expected to be very happy." Now that he has cancer, his feelings are more mixed.

"When I started it, I must have been 22, and it showed that a 22-year-old can work hard, have success, financially do well and take on a big project like this and succeed. I've enjoyed it, I enjoy it still. But if it's gone, it's gone.

"Now it means a lot less than it did before. Houses, cars, motorcycles, toys, money, fame—it takes on a whole new meaning when you have something like this," referring to his cancer. "You realize, 'I never lived for that stuff.' No. I enjoyed it but I think something like this makes you not only look at your life, but makes you simplify your life.

"The home means more than the other things. Before, I would have been devastated if I had to sell it or move out to a little old home built in the '30s, much smaller, not on the lake, not in this price range. That's fine. I could do it. That's fine, I'm alive. That's what it's all about."

His tan from the racing season has disappeared, and he seems pale, understandably less buoyant than usual. He is holding his weight steady at 170 pounds, he said, although he admits that some of his muscle has turned to fat despite daily bicycle rides of up to an hour and a half.

"I do feel good," he said. "I'm not as fit as I used to be, but, then again, for two months I haven't done much on the bike. I'm undergoing chemotherapy and I do have cancer, pulmonary lesions that are detrimental. But the lesions on the lungs are going away pretty rapidly.

"I'm really upbeat. I'm positive. I may be a little scared, I may be very scared, but I feel very positive about how things are going."

On November 10, he even competed, with the legendary Eddy Merckx as his partner, in a local 26-mile race, the Tour of Gruene, Texas.

"I wanted to do the race to prove that I was still alive, that I was well," he said, "that therapy was ahead of schedule, as well as to prove to cancer patients that cancer doesn't always have to be a killer, therapy doesn't always have to be such a handicap."

Armstrong said that measurements of the level of proteins in his blood produced by testicular cancer have gone from a high point of above 100,000 down to 113.

"Still a way to go," he said. "That encourages me, even though the hardest part to knock out is the last part."

Those who know Armstrong best agree that he is doing well, physically and mentally. Dr. Craig Nichols and Dr. Lawrence Einhorn are treating him at Indiana University for his cancer, which was first diagnosed as advanced.

On the phone from Indianapolis, Dr. Nichols said, "He has met every benchmark of progress and there's nothing to keep us from thinking he won't be cured."

"He's doing magnificently," said Linda Walling, Armstrong's mother, on the phone from Richardson, Texas. "It's only a bump in the road. We're going to beat it. I tell him, 'Negatives don't do anything for you but bring you down,' and he knows that. 'Make this the first day of the rest of your life,' I say to him, and that's what he's doing."

Yes, Armstrong agreed, that's what he's doing.

"This is the biggest challenge of my life," he said. "From the first moment I learned this, I thought, 'Oh my God, I'm going to die.' I went from being at the top of my game, fourth in World Cup races in Leeds and Zurich, to being told I had cancer. Eventually you get over that.

"But even if you're the biggest, toughest guy out there saying 'I'm going to live,' there are cases where you do die. Because cancer does not recognize that. It does not play fair. It's aggressive, it's smart, it's tough, it's relentless, it adapts, it becomes resistant to therapies. If it wants to win, it can win."

For now, he continued, he is giving little thought to his career as a bicycle racer ranked ninth in the world.

Getting up from his chair to fetch another half grapefruit, he barely looked at a prospectus for the next Tour de France that a friend had brought him. "I think very little about that, maybe a quarter of the time," Armstrong said. "The other three-quarters are focused on my life and beating cancer. If, for some reason, I can never race again, listen, that's fine."

The 1997 Tour will be extremely mountainous and, he was told jokingly, would be a terrible Tour for him. "Cancer is a terrible tour for me," he responded.

"The Tour de France, it doesn't matter." He added: "Life is the No. 1 priority. Professional cycling is No. 2. No, to create awareness for testicular cancer is No. 2. Professional cycling is No. 3."

Does he feel it is unjust that he has cancer? "No, because cancer doesn't play like that," he answered. "It doesn't play fair—nobody wants cancer. You can say, 'Why me?' but why not me? It doesn't strike because you've done something or not done something. I was just one of the ones it happened to hit.

"No, I don't want to waste my time saying, 'Why me?' I have a problem and I want to fix it."

In the Yellow Jersey

1999

AGLOW IN THE YELLOW JERSEY of the champion, Lance Armstrong completed the final leg of his three-week journey to Paris on Sunday, mounted the last of his many victory podiums and was proclaimed the winner of the 86th Tour de France. Only the second American to win the race, the 27-year-old leader of the U.S. Postal Service team stood solemnly with his cap off as a French military band broke into the "Star-Spangled Banner" just after he was given one more yellow jersey, two more bouquets, a blue vase and a check for 2.2 million francs ($350,000).

An immense crowd watching under a blazing sun and pure sky cheered him on the avenue of the Champs-Elysées. "It's been a tough three weeks on the legs and head," he said after he crossed the last line, well back in the pack, and just before he left the victory podium to embrace his wife, Kristin, whose face was running with tears.

Two and a half years ago, the yellow jersey, vase and flowers would have seemed to be unlikely rewards for the Texan, who was diagnosed in October 1996 with testicular cancer that had spread to his lungs and brain. After surgery and three months of chemotherapy, he did not return to racing until 1998 and found it impossible to convince any team except U.S. Postal Service that he was not "damaged goods," as he put it.

Since his illness, he has dedicated himself to fighting cancer, both through an educational and fund-raising foundation that he formed in his hometown of Austin, Texas, and through his inspirational victories in what he calls "the toughest sport there is."

"I relate to cancer patients," he said at the start of the Tour. "At the same time, I can relate to the families of those who didn't make it, and that's the sad thing and probably the more emotional and motivational."

His victory was highly popular on both sides of the Atlantic. European fans who stood at the sides of the Tour's many roads this month universally said they knew about his comeback and were cheering for him to win both the race and his fight against cancer. In checkups every four months, he has tested clean of the disease for two years.

"It is a miracle," he said, agreeing with a description offered at a news conference last week. "Fifteen or 20 years ago, I wouldn't be alive, much less riding a bike or winning the Tour de France. I think it's a miracle."

The American finished the Tour 7 minutes 37 seconds ahead of Alex Zülle, a Swiss with Banesto, and 10:26 ahead of Fernando Escartin, a Spaniard with Kelme, in the overall field of 141 riders remaining of the 180 who set out July 3. Of his huge deficit, Zülle lost 6:30 on the third stage when he was trapped by a crash.

Armstrong, on the other hand, had good luck throughout: He had his first flat of the Tour on Sunday during a mainly ceremonial final stage, when it did no harm, as it could have done during a stage in the mountains.

A talented man of strong will and focus, Armstrong dominated the 3,690-kilometer Tour from start to finish. He began wearing the race's symbol of overall leadership on July 3 when he won the short prologue. Two days later he yielded the jersey as sprinters began to monopolize the daily stages on flat territory. Then he regained it on July 11, when he crushed the field in a long time trial and he never gave it up.

After the first of two days off, he solidified his position on July 13 by triumphing with a bravado attack in the first day in the Alps. "I raced in a style that people like," Armstrong said in an interview before he won the Tour's last long time trial Saturday. "I'm aggressive. People want attacks, they want to see the boys working. I've always said that I'd rather be the guy that lights the race up and finishes second than the guy that sits back, doesn't do anything and wins."

That alpine victory over six climbs astounded rivals, observers and fans not only because of Armstrong's medical history but also because he was not regarded as a strong climber. He had finished only one of his four previous Tours.

Quickly this race became cloaked in an atmosphere of suspicion and rumor that originated in the last Tour when the Festina team was expelled because of its systematic use of illegal performance-enhancing drugs. That scandal has been followed by half a dozen others in the many countries of western Europe where bicycle racing is a sport second only to soccer.

Seeking to stem what he denounced as innuendo, Armstrong said in an interview that he "emphatically and absolutely" denied using drugs. A week later, after prominent press display of charges that a banned drug had been detected during a urinalysis, he said that he had made a mistake in not acknowledging that he used a cortisone-based cream for a skin rash and that he had a medical certificate to allow its use. The International Cycling Union, which governs the sport, ruled that his use of the salve was not doping.

The U.S. Postal Service leader had other, far more believable explanations for his success in the Tour's mountains. "I'm a strong kid," he said. "I also got my weight down."

Looking lean, he carried 72 kilograms (158 pounds) on his 1.77-meter (5 foot 10 inch) frame, some seven kilograms less than he weighed a year ago. He also credited his preparation and his teammates.

In May, the team and its *directeur sportif,* Johan Bruyneel, spent a week in the Alps and the Massif Central, riding the Tour's roads and studying their pitfalls. Armstrong then went on to ride in the Pyrenees "six or seven hours there in the rain with Johan in the car.

"It paid off," he said. "I had a lot of help from my team. When we got the jersey and said we would defend it, people thought we were crazy, they said this team isn't strong enough. They proved they're the strongest team in the race."

Traditionally, the winner of the Tour gives his big victory check to his teammates and such team workers as mechanics and masseurs.

Speaking of Greg LeMond, the first American to win the Tour, in 1986 and then again in 1989 and 1990, Armstrong called him "a good friend of mine and the greatest American cyclist ever." But his victory and LeMond's were different, he continued, because

LeMond rode for French teams and Armstrong "did it with an American sponsor and an American team, seven of the nine guys being Americans.

"That is, first of all, unheard of," he said. "Two years ago, people would have thought you were crazy."

In its first two Tours, in 1997 and last year, U.S. Postal Service did not win a stage. "What we did this year is a fantastic achievement for this team and for American cycling," Armstrong said. "To think about having a mostly American team—boy, that's huge."

Armstrong's performance was praised by former champions.

"He attacks just when you should," said Bernard Hinault, who won five Tours, the last in 1985. "In the Tour, we need fighters and he's a real fighter."

Raymond Poulidor, the darling of French fans three decades ago, said, "The French admire Armstrong for the right reasons. The French always admire a man for the way he's lived his life, with courage."

Hennie Kuiper, a Dutchman who finished second in the Tour in 1977 and 1980 and later became Armstrong's *directeur sportif*, said, "After his illness, he's been thinking about his life and he's a lot more explosive and aggressive in his reactions. After that illness, he knows what life is.

"He can win everything. He will win everything. He's so strong psychologically."

Armstrong has five criteriums, basically exhibition races, scheduled this week in Europe at $25,000 an appearance. He is planning to fly to the United States on Wednesday for two days of appearances. He said he would probably ride in the next World Cup classic in Spain on August 7, but would then curtail his schedule and return to Texas, where his wife expects their first child in October.

For an encore, he said, "There is nothing. If you win the Tour de France, the only thing you can do is try to win it again. That's it.

"Next year, I'll be here."

HOW HE DOES IT

2001

CHRIS CARMICHAEL, LANCE ARMSTRONG'S coach for more than a decade, was traveling down memory lane, cruising through the years back to 1992 and a place far from home.

"I remember, I sat with this kid in front of a television set in Barcelona, Spain, for the '92 Olympics," he recalled, "and we're watching Andy Hampsten ride through this crowd on Alpe d'Huez and I remember looking at Lance and his eyes were as big as golf balls and he said, 'Man, I want to do that. He's winning Alpe d'Huez.'"

Now he has done that, becoming the second American, after Hampsten, to win what Armstrong described recently as "a beautiful stage, a legendary, mythical, cruel stage." The leader of the U.S. Postal Service team won the climb easily last week as he headed at age 29 toward his third consecutive victory in the world's most demanding bicycle race.

Year after year, his domination has raised questions. The big one is how a rider who swears he does not use illegal drugs can so excel in a sport that is believed to be riddled with doping, no matter how many officials deny it.

"There will always be speculation that athletes use drugs," Armstrong answers. "I cannot prove a negative, so it is always going to be a tricky situation. When they find a test for one thing, then somebody stands up there and says, 'Well, you must be doing the next thing.' When they find a test for that, then they say, 'Well, you must be using the next thing.' It goes on and on."

For the record, he notes that he has never failed a drug test—although neither did other riders who subsequently admitted to using banned substances—and he denies using EPO, an oxygen carrier that is the current scourge of the sport, except when he was recovering from chemotherapy in 1996 for testicular cancer that had spread to his brain and lungs.

If not drugs, what then is the answer? At a news conference this week, Armstrong attributed his power to age and experience. "And," he added, "as I continue to say, this year we worked a lot harder, even harder than we did in 1999 and 2000."

Work is certainly a major part of the answer, according to interviews with Armstrong, past and present teammates, and others in the sport.

They differ in their analyses of how a young rider of undisputed talent in one-day races became a champion in the three-week Tour de France. To explain his enormous strength in the mountains after early struggles there, they cite his loss of more than 20 pounds after the chemotherapy, improved pedaling, his racing schedule, his experience with cancer and his willingness to sacrifice so much of his life off the bicycle for his life on it.

Armstrong himself scoffs.

"I was always a good climber," he said. "I just never concentrated on it."

That is partly true: When he was riding in the Tour DuPont in the United States and climbing in the Blue Ridge Mountains and Appalachians, which are comparable to the foothills in the Alps and Pyrenees, he was a good enough climber to win that race. When he was riding in his first few Tours de France in the mid-1990s, he was a mediocre climber.

"Lance, when he was young, was a pure athlete who had no idea how to pedal a bike," said Jonathan Vaughters, a teammate on the U.S. national amateur team in 1989 and on Postal Service 10 years later. "He had incredible athletic talent, he had a lot of fat on him, but he was a big strong kid.

"His gears were always too big, he thrashed around a lot, his position was completely wrong—he was horribly inefficient. But it's a lot easier to take a really big engine that's inefficient and slowly tweak it to the point where it is efficient, rather than trying to make a small engine that's already efficient bigger.

"That's what he's accomplished, but it's taken 10 years," continued Vaughters, who now rides for Crédit Agricole. "He was a pure athlete who slowly was turned into a cyclist. Now, as a rider, he's on a totally different level from me, so I don't even consider him competition. That's a different Tour that he's riding."

The man who did much of the retooling, Carmichael, said that "weight is one part of it—he's now over eight kilos lighter after cancer," or a weight of 72 kilograms (158 pounds) now.

"Take eight kilos and add them to Lance on his finishing time at Alpe d'Huez and, if he maintained the same power output, he would have finished 3 minutes 47 seconds behind where he did finish there," Carmichael said. "And that's only Alpe d'Huez.

"The first climb was the Madeleine, the next the Glandon, so you take a rough estimate—4 minutes on the Madeleine, 4 minutes on the Glandon, 4 on Alpe d'Huez—that's 12 minutes back."

And that is roughly where Armstrong used to finish.

"Another aspect is he's older, he's more developed," Carmichael continued. "He's a different guy than he was before cancer. So he's lighter, more physically developed because of age, a better focus in his training and then just the mind-set of having gone through what he went through."

Johnny Weltz, a Dane who is a former *directeur sportif* of Armstrong's, agrees about the weight and adds his own explanation.

"The cancer was a transformation," said Weltz, now the man in the team car for CSC. "He was really pushing himself hard because nobody gave him a chance. No one hired Armstrong after he was sick until Postal Service did" and, Weltz said, "he wanted to prove that he was back.

"Before," Weltz went on, "he was a young lad with a golden contract and could do whatever he wanted, a huge contract to play around. Sometimes it's not good for a young lad to get that freedom. He was young and didn't feel he had to sacrifice for his goals."

George Hincapie, a Postal Service teammate, emphasizes the sacrifices Armstrong makes now.

"He's a true champion," Hincapie said. "I get to see close up what sacrifices he makes, what preparation he does for races like the Tour de France. I see how much he suffers in training and how much he lives to train, and it really shows when he comes to hard races like this. All the hard work he puts into his training really shines through.

"I put in the same effort, but I'm just a different type of rider. I'm not a big mountain climber—that's something you have to have inside yourself. Not everybody can win the Tour de France and Lance has that special gift."

"As long as I'm racing, the Tour will be the major objective of the year," Armstrong said. He denies that he hopes to equal or break the record of five Tour victories set by Jacques Anquetil, Eddy Merckx, Bernard Hinault and Miguel Indurain.

"To tie a record or break a record would never be my motivation," he said. "I never think of myself as a Merckx, Hinault, Anquetil or Indurain. I think of myself as a lesser rider."

Lesser or equal, he is just as meticulous as they were, which may be another part of the explanation of how Armstrong became so dominant.

Relaxing in his hotel early in the Tour, the Texan praised a rival, Gilberto Simoni, the winner of the prestigious Giro d'Italia last month, in words he might have used to describe himself: "He was looking at every detail, looking at the course, making sure his equipment was perfect, training, staying focused.

"You have to look at everything," Armstrong concluded. "And, at the end of this Tour de France, I hope that's enough."

Two Different Champions

2001

NOW THAT HE HAS WON THREE TOURS DE FRANCE, Lance Armstrong is inevitably being compared with the American who did it first, Greg LeMond—and being compared unfavorably.

The words used to describe LeMond 11 years after his final victory are the same ones when he was riding: charming, open, generous, accessible.

"And he spoke French so well," one French journalist after another points out, forgetting that LeMond was as lost as Armstrong in the past imperfect tense, not to mention the subjunctive, early in his career.

In contrast, a save-get key on most reporters' computers says that Armstrong is respected, not liked, an accusation first voiced by Jean-Marie Leblanc, the Tour's director. He also objected to the professional bodyguard who accompanies Armstrong at each daily start and finish.

Leblanc did not need to say that no rider has used a bodyguard before, especially not LeMond, who was often late to sign in at the start because he was so busy mingling with spectators and signing autographs. He could not say "no" and, in short, Armstrong can.

"Armstrong is so American," a French reporter complained a few days ago. "LeMond was so European." (The French think Thomas Jefferson was dead right when he said that Americans had two homelands, their own and France.)

The Texan has been asked many times at news conferences why some spectators booed him at the start in Dunkirk on June 7 and then occasionally again in the Alps.

At the start, he replied, his critics were fans of Cédric Vasseur, a Frenchman who was left off the U.S. Postal Service team. In the Alps, Armstrong said, he was baffled. Then, late last week, Armstrong was awarded the Lemon Prize by Tour photographers for his supposed lack of cooperation, and he decided to strike back.

"If they thought I was unaccommodating before, wait till they see me in the future," he said angrily.

He pointed out how many photographers there are—the precise number is 243, along with 754 journalists and 524 technicians and assistants—and how many times a day they called his name and wanted him to pose in some novel way.

"I won't wear a wig for them, I won't put on a dress," he said. "I will give you some action on the road and they can take pictures of that."

Turning to spectator reaction, he added, "I give everything I've got. If they like it, they can come out and cheer. If they don't, they can boo. It won't change my desire to give everything I can."

He did, however, pose laughingly on the Champs-Elysées on Sunday as he took his victory lap and the Texas state flag he was bearing dropped into his bicycle's wheel, stopping him. Despite his disdain for photographers, corporate relations are important to Armstrong, who has a handful of major sponsors, including Nike, and who gives motivational speeches for a reported $200,000 each.

When he makes a brief trip to the United States this week, a major purpose is to attend a promotional event in New York for the U.S. Postal Service, which sponsors his team. He may also visit Washington to see his former governor, George W. Bush, and Texas to see his mother. He will return to Texas for the winter and a possible tour to promote the paperback version of his autobiography, *It's Not About the Bike.*

Although the account of his fight against cancer was a best-seller in hardback, he says, "I didn't write it to sell books," and grimaces at the prospect of plugging it.

Unlike the gregarious LeMond, who seemed to have old friends at whichever race he attended, Armstrong since he was diagnosed with testicular cancer in 1996 is reserved. As he nears his 30th birthday, he is certainly less brash and frisky than he used to be.

"Friends?" he said in an interview. "Who has friends in the peloton?" the professional pack in which he works.

One answer, not offered, was that LeMond always had friends there.

The two of them, rivals a decade ago when LeMond was on the downside of his career and Armstrong on the upside, are not close and the gap will widen now that LeMond has criticized the Texan's reliance on Michele Ferrari, the Italian doctor who is accused of providing riders with illegal performance-enhancing drugs.

There are few reasons for the three-time winners to be close. One lives in Minnesota, the other in Europe and Texas; there is a 10-year age difference and their interests are different. LeMond is an avid sportsman, Armstrong not at all. LeMond grew up a bicycle nut, with posters of Tour de France and Giro d'Italia stars on his bedroom walls; Armstrong had country-and-western singers pasted there.

Where they merge is in their success in the Tour de France and in their comebacks.

LeMond was nearly killed in a hunting accident that stole two years of his career and Armstrong will shortly have the five-year cancer checkup that he describes as a milestone.

At his home in Austin in November 1996, during chemotherapy, Armstrong was discussing the get-well messages he had received.

"Every once in a while, somebody will write and say, 'I was never a fan of yours' and then they end up by saying, 'But I want to wish you well.' And I appreciate that but it's strange to me, it's a little odd, it's a little upsetting that they'd write and say, 'I've never been a fan of yours' or 'I've never liked you, never liked your image, never liked what you said.'

"I think, 'Well, I'm true to my family, I'm true to my friends, I'm true to myself, I'm true to my sport. I work hard. I call a spade a spade. If you don't like it, you don't like it.

"I figure that if I'm true to my family, my friends, myself, my sponsors, what else can I do?"

That is basically what he said after the Tour photographers gave him the Lemon Prize and when he discussed hostile fans' reactions.

"I speak from the heart," Armstrong likes to say. "What you see is what you get."

Part Two

IN THE PACK

Introduction

Candy Man

1995

UNLIKE MOST OF THE 51,000 *people in the Breton city of St. Brieuc, André Chalmel seemed uncertain whether he would turn out to watch the prologue of the Tour de France through the streets.*

"Maybe, maybe not," he said. "Probably. Maybe. It depends on what time I close the shop." The prologue started at 6:10 P.M. and ended at 9:47. For the few weeks that Chalmel has operated his candy store, the Maison du Bonbon on the Rue St. Guillaume in the pedestrian center of St. Brieuc, he has closed at 7.

Don't misunderstand, Chalmel said, he is interested in the sport. Still interested.

Now 45 years old, he follows professional bicycle racing in the papers but not closely since he is so occupied with his new business. "I do keep up. Perhaps I won't get to the prologue, but that's not to say I'm not interested in the sport."

Two posters advertising the Tour were pasted to the window of his shop. He coaches a team in St. Malo. The owner of a Category I license, he rides every Sunday morning, he said.

And, after all, although he did not point this out, he rode four Tour prologues himself.

He did not remember how he did. Chalmel was a domestique *and his job was to support leaders, to fetch their water bottles and rain capes, to block for them when they went on a breakaway, to chase down their rivals. He was nicknamed Sha-sha le Chat because, like a cat, he was quiet and sleekly efficient.*

Strong, too. He had to be to win the 586-kilometer, 18-hour Bordeaux-Paris race in 1979. Two other times, in 1976 and 1977, he finished third in that race. His only other victory, in the Grand Prix d'Isbergues, occurred in 1981. Chalmel worked for others, not himself.

He rode for Lucien van Impe, the Belgian climber, when he won the 1976 Tour. Then he became a member of the Yellow Guard, the boisterous band of riders in the yellow jerseys of the Renault-Gitane team who supported Chalmel's fellow Breton, Bernard Hinault, in his Tour victories in 1978 and 1979.

The Yellow Guard swaggered and strutted and moved like a flying wedge around Hinault, entering a room with a burst of chatter and laughter. For a few years, until age overtook all but the younger Hinault, they might have been musketeers in a Dumas novel.

But Chalmel was really not much of a swaggerer. He was Sha-sha le Chat. Passed over for the 1980 Tour, he moved to Peugeot and rode in his final year, 1982, for Phil Anderson, the Australian who spent part of July in the yellow jersey before Hinault triumphed again.

Those were the good days, Chalmel said, the Peugeot team and its young English-speaking riders, some of the pioneers. He listed the names: Anderson, Stephen Roche, Graham Jones, Sean Yates and another.

"It was a long time ago," Chalmel said, fumbling in his memory for the last name. "Robert Millar," he blurted out with pleasure. "A long time ago."

The Peugeot team is gone from the sport many years now. So are others that dominated Tours de France past. An exhibition in St. Brieuc tracing the evolution of the bicycle also portrays riders in famous jerseys that have disappeared. Who still remembers Bic, Flandria and Mercier, the teams of champions?

Chalmel had not been to see the exhibition a few blocks from his store. "Business," he explained. Nor had he visited the exhibition of racing jerseys, mostly Hinault's, near the train station. He hinted at a certain coolness with Hinault, five years his junior and the great champion that the domestique *was not.*

Chalmel sighed. He retired from racing after the 1982 season and became a leader of the riders' association, which was too weak to be called a union. Then he became a real estate salesman.

Now he operates a candy store, one of the shovel and plastic bag types where the caramels and chocolates are weighed at the counter. Business did not seem to be brisk.

Perhaps, despite the late hour, he did find time to watch the prologue. A seat down front, please, for a former member of the Yellow Guard.

Gorbals Boys Don't Cry

1985

THE GORBALS IS THE SLUM OF GLASGOW, among the worst in Europe, and it produces hard people. Gorbals boys don't cry—or, if they do, they don't admit it.

Robert Millar left the Gorbals in 1979 at the age of 20 to become a bicycle racer and rarely visits Scotland now. He is slight and soft-spoken but nevertheless hard, and he says that the witnesses were wrong and that he did not cry—not even briefly—when he was deprived of victory in the 1985 Vuelta.

"I was disgusted, I was really angry," he said a few days after the race. "I'm still angry."

He didn't seem so, sitting in his apartment in a suburb of the northern French city of Lille, waiting for a laggard sun before he began a four-hour training ride.

He did not enjoy training rides around Lille, he confessed, because the country is flat and what he most enjoys is climbing. His major amateur victories, such as the British road championships in 1978 and 1979 and the French road championship in 1979, were on the flat, but since then his successes have come in the mountains: second in the 1982 Tour de l'Avenir, second in the 1983 Dauphiné Libéré, fourth in the 1984 Tour de France. At 5 feet 7 inches and 125 pounds, he has a climber's classic build.

Millar also has a climber's classic disposition, noting that he prefers stage races to classics. "I just don't have enough concentration to do well in a classic," he said. "Maybe four times a year I can motivate myself for a one-day race. I prefer stage races—they're more relaxed."

He enjoys relaxation. For a few years Millar wore a gold star in his left ear because, he explained, "It's fashionable." He also owned a blue sapphire star. Whether cycling people liked the star or not meant little to him. "As long as you do your job properly, I don't think the boss should interfere with your life."

His apartment, with high-tech posters on the wall and pride of place given to a stereo system, seemed a long way from Glasgow, where a British magazine once reported that the young Millar had become interested in cycling after glimpsing the Tour de France on television in a shop window. "No, it wasn't in a shop window," he pointed out in correction. "It was at home." He might be from the bleak Gorbals, but his family was not that poor.

After the outcome in Spain, some people would still be throwing things and screaming but Millar was under control. "It's a matter of character, isn't it?" he asked quietly. Or, as they say, don't get mad, get even.

"Oof," he began when he was asked about the three-week Vuelta. Millar, who rode then for the Peugeot team based in France, had been leading the race for a week as it neared its end. On the next-to-last day, Millar was ahead in overall elapsed time by 10 seconds over Pancho Rodriguez, a Colombian with the Zor team based in Spain, and by 1:15 over Pello Ruiz-Cabestany, a Spaniard with his country's Orbea team. Nobody else was close, with Julian Gorospe, a Spaniard with his country's Reynolds team, fourth, 5:13 behind Millar. "I think I've won it; I think I'll be in the yellow jersey on Sunday even if it's only by one second," Millar announced happily the Friday night before the finish.

A 10-second lead can be nothing in the high mountains, where time is often lost by quarters of an hour, but it can be insurmountable in flatter country, where a leader has only to stay just behind his closest rival.

And so it was no problem for Millar, who had held off Rodriguez and Ruiz-Cabestany for days. "I was still going really well," he remembered at home in Lille. "My legs felt strong."

He needed more than legs, though. "You need luck to win a big Tour," he said. "I didn't have the luck this time." More precisely, he had the bad luck of running into a cabal of the Spanish teams in the race, which decided that after two successive victories by foreigners, it was time again for a Spanish rider to win the Tour of Spain.

Millar retold the day's event, starting, he said quietly, "from when it was important." With about 60 kilometers to go and Millar riding with the leaders, he punctured and lost some time changing wheels before two teammates relayed him up a climb and toward the front. Exhausted, his teammates dropped back and, in a scene out of a silent movie, lost contact with Millar for the day when they got to a railroad crossing and found it closed behind the leaders.

Isolated, the Scotsman was not worried. "I caught Rodriguez and Cabestany on the descent," he said. "It was snowing heavily on the top but halfway down it became dry; we were in sunlight again and taking off our rain capes when the trailing group, Sean Kelly's group, caught us and passed us."

In that group was Pedro Delgado, a Spaniard and Ruiz-Cabestany's teammate with Orbea. Delgado was sixth overall, 6:13 behind. After they passed Millar, both Delgado and José Recio, a Spaniard with his country's Kelme team, broke away from the Kelly group and began building a good lead, unknown to Millar, who trailed hundreds of yards behind.

"Delgado was already two minutes in front but I didn't know that," Millar continued. "I could still see Kelly and I wasn't worried because his group was only two minutes away." Nor, he admitted, was he worried about Delgado and, especially, Recio, who did not rank among the first 30 overall. "I didn't really know how far behind me Delgado was in overall time because I kept beating him every day and I thought he was out of the race."

Forty kilometers from the finish, the Peugeot team car alerted Millar to the breakaway by Delgado, who was by then five minutes ahead of Millar and just over a minute from the overall lead "on the road," that time when anything is possible. Millar called on the others in his group to mount a chase.

"I talked to them and asked them to ride. But they wouldn't. The Tekas wouldn't ride, Rodriguez wouldn't ride. I told Rodriguez he could protect his second place, that it was better than third. But nobody would ride. They preferred to see me lose and a Spaniard win."

The Spanish riders, from the Teka team through Zor and Reynolds, were under instructions from their managers to hold back, an agreement reportedly worked out the night before. *L'Equipe*, the French sports newspaper, said that an official of Delgado's team publicly thanked "all the other team directors for their help." The agreement surprised nobody familiar with the temporary alliances teams often make, whether for tactical advantage or for money. What did surprise observers was Peugeot's lack of foresight (was it arrogance in thinking that the race could no longer be lost or was it simply naïveté?) to enroll allies from the non-Spanish teams the night before.

"You often get collusion between teams," Millar said. "Two teams get together because one is going to win the sprint and the other is going to win the race, but you don't get the whole pack riding against one man."

He was caught in a familiar racing bind: "I didn't want to ride alone after Delgado, because Rodriguez could jump me near the finish and make up his 10 seconds. I was giving 99 percent effort but I still had to keep a bit to watch for Rodriguez jumping away. Rodriguez attacked me six times on the last climb but he couldn't drop me. About three kilometers from the finish Rodriguez said to me he wasn't going to attack but I didn't trust any of them anymore.

"I was in a group that was 15 riders and none of them was working, not even in the sprint. They all held back and sat behind me while the guys in front built as much time as possible." In truth, witnesses reported that Eric Guyot of the Skil team, a French one, did try to help Millar, but Sean Kelly and other Skil riders were three minutes ahead and out of touch.

Finally Delgado arrived at the finish, his home town of Segovia, granting the stage victory to Recio. "Kelly said he had three teammates riding with him, riding as hard as they could the last 30 kilometers, but they still lost a minute and a half on Delgado," Millar said. "I don't know if he was really flying or riding a motorbike's slipstream. That's what it's like in Spain when you're Spanish and behind a motorbike."

A large crowd in Segovia waited out the 6:13 that Delgado had trailed Millar, then burst into cheers. Thirty-six seconds later, Millar crossed the line, now second in overall elapsed time in the Vuelta.

"It seemed to me the whole race had wanted me to lose," Millar said. "I got the impression that the crowds were more hostile than usual. When you're up on the podium they boo and whistle. They throw things at you during the stage. It didn't get to me because I knew I was going to win the race then."

Afterward, when he knew he was not going to win the race, Millar ignored the crowds and the children who danced tauntingly around him. "I still had the jersey for the first foreign rider but I wouldn't go up to the podium," Millar continued. Instead he got in his team car, *l'Equipe* reported, and through the windows could be seen with his head in his heads, red around the eyes.

Sitting now in his apartment in Lille, Millar did not discuss this. All he said was, "I reckon they destroyed their own race."

The final day was a formality, with Millar ending the stage in the same time as Delgado, Rodriguez and Ruiz-Cabestany. At the finish he was 36 seconds behind Delgado.

Millar gave no thought to quitting on the final day. "It wouldn't have been right for the others on my team. They worked so hard and we had pride in what we did. All I felt was sad. The guys in the pack, they acted sympathetic but I felt they were laughing behind my back.

"What's done is done, it's history now. It's the kind of thing that happens. Well, maybe not very often—it was so blatant, so scandalous. But you have to be calm because I'll be racing with them for the next 10 years."

He was indeed calm as he answered the last few questions.

Would he ride in another Vuelta? "I'd go back to Spain, sure, with a stronger team, with more climbers."

Would he cooperate in future races with the riders who refused to cooperate with him? "If it was in my own interests, I'd do it. If it was in their interests, I wouldn't. I won't do them any favors."

Did he hold a grudge against Delgado? "There's no honor in some guy winning because everybody wanted him to win. But no, I don't blame Delgado, I blame the 15 riders who were with me."

How could he remain angry at so many people? "Easy."

A Real Fathead

1998

"TWO OR THREE MORE BRATWURST, Herr Ullrich? Seconds on the sauerbraten? Another slice of nusstorte, Herr Ullrich? Again some schlag on your coffee?"

The answer in every case appears to have been affirmative.

As the first German to win the Tour de France, Jan Ullrich, 24, was heavily in demand last winter on the rubber schnitzel circuit. "Heavily" is indeed the word. By the time Ullrich had downed his last dumpling and begun preparing for the bicycle racing season, he weighed about 10 kilograms (22 pounds) more than his usual weight of 73 kilograms. It showed, too.

"Did you see Ullrich in any of his early races in Spain?" a rival was asked recently. "See him?" the rider echoed. "You couldn't miss him."

Compounding the German rider's problems was a series of illnesses this winter, which kept interrupting his training and then his racing. By the end of April, the situation so alarmed the French sports newspaper *l'Equipe* that it devoted a full page to the unfolding calamity.

Of the first nine races on his program, the paper noted, he had quit four, been unable to start two and finished three in 78th, 97th and 134th places. In contrast to the year before, when he had already raced 36 days for a total of 5,528 kilometers, he had put in 24 days for a total of 3,484 kilometers.

Laurent Jalabert, the top-ranked rider in the world, was quoted as saying that to see

Ullrich trailing the field "provides a rather pathetic image of a Tour de France winner." Laurent Fignon, twice the winner of the Tour, accused Ullrich of a lack of professionalism and called his conduct "inadmissible." Jean-Marie Leblanc, the director of the Tour, said his attitude was "unworthy of a Tour winner."

The editorial package included a photograph of Ullrich that resembled Bibendum, the Michelin man, on a bicycle.

Enough. Sweating off the suet in Spain, where he has raced almost exclusively this spring, and in a three-week training program in the Black Forest, Ullrich is rounding into form and beginning to get some results.

When the German arrived with his Telekom team in Chambéry for the one-day Classique des Alpes, he was fresh off a second place in the time trial in the Tour of Castilla-León and a third place overall.

There is still some poundage hanging over his belt buckle, but his face is once again lean.

"Maybe now we have to deal with three kilos too much," said Rudy Pevenage, 44, a Belgian who serves Telekom as assistant *directeur sportif* and Ullrich's confidant and spokesman. Ullrich himself gives one and all the same interview about his weight, his condition and his goals—"*Nein*," which, while rich in nuance, does not survive translation.

Pevenage is unworried, he insisted. "It's still five weeks to go to the Tour, and in five weeks three kilos is no problem. He's now at a very good level—80 percent, maybe 75—and after these five weeks, he'll be at 100 percent. I'm sure."

How had Ullrich managed to put on so many pounds during the winter? Did nobody from Telekom management keep an eye on him as he traipsed from banquet to banquet?

"It's not so easy," Pevenage said. "It's easy," he corrected himself, "but I can't treat him like a kid. The problem was that Jan finished his season in September and then he likes to eat and he likes to live like everybody else for two months every winter. In those two months, he likes to get rid of his stress.

"The winter before, he gained 10 kilos but nobody saw it because he had no illness at the beginning of the season and could race the weight off. But this year, three times he had to fight a bad illness: once with his ear and two times bronchitis. So he had to interrupt his schedule and couldn't lose his kilos like the winter before."

Not to worry, Pevenage said. "He'll be ready for the Tour. His form is coming."

Confirming that, Ullrich rode a good Classique des Alpes. On the third of seven climbs, the race exploded on the Col du Granier.

As the first attack developed, who was that but Ullrich leading the pack in the chase up the long ascent? Wearing his jersey of the German national champion, he looked as comfortable as he did when he was finishing second and then first in his first two Tours de France.

By the finish of the 181-kilometer race in Aix-les-Bains, only 47 riders of the 136-man field were left. Jalabert, who rides for the ONCE team, won in a sprint, beating Francesco Casagrande, an Italian with Cofidis, and Benoît Salmon, a Frenchman with Casino.

Ullrich was in the main chasing group behind the three leaders. He finished 14th in the same time as nine others, 1:44 behind, and looked strong.

On Sunday, he left to reconnoiter some of the nearby alpine climbs that the Tour de France will pass over late in July.

As he said in a rare public comment last month: "I'm more and more optimistic about the only day that counts for me—the start of the Tour."

Not to Worry

1999

IN A RITE OF SPRING that is becoming as clockwork as the swallows' return to Capistrano, Rudy Pevenage brushed aside any worries about his protégé, Jan Ullrich.

"Same question as last year," he noticed. "Same answer as last year."

The question was: "Is Ullrich fit and ready for the Tour de France?" The answer was: "Everything is okay. I think he has a good chance in the Tour."

Ullrich, 25, was not available himself for questioning at a race last weekend in France even though he was on the preliminary list of starters for his Telekom team. Like last year, the German has not been seen often in races and, when he does make the scene, is rarely among the leaders.

Last year the problem was weight. Ullrich gained more than 10 kilograms over the winter and struggled through races all spring, looking more like another German export, the Hindenburg dirigible, than the rider who won the Tour in 1997.

"I like to eat," he explained reasonably. "That's what the winter is for."

Not to worry. By the time the Tour started in Dublin, he was near his fighting weight of 73 kilograms. But he did not win the race, exploding on the final climb on a cold and rainy stage in the Alps and finally finishing second overall when the race stumbled into Paris. That made it one victory and two second places in the three years that Ullrich has ridden the Tour.

The Telekom team, which Pevenage serves as *directeur sportif*, decided to pay more attention to Ullrich's eating habits last winter and hired a diet counselor for him.

Out went dumplings, in came carrot sticks.

Out also went weeks of lazing around his home in the Black Forest, pining, no doubt, for the gooey cake of the same name. In came a few weeks of training under the sun near San Diego.

The result was that Ullrich gained only a few pounds before he resumed racing in February.

But the German appears to be star-crossed: This year the problem is injury and illness. His spring was troubled by stomach viruses, the flu and problems with a wisdom tooth, all of which caused him to skip many of the races that he uses to heighten his condition for the only race that counts for him, the Tour de France.

At the end of May, as time began drawing short before the Tour would set off July 3 in western France, Ullrich entered the weeklong Tour of Germany. On the second stage, he crashed heavily and wound up sitting on the road dazed, in pain and needing several stitches to close a cut near his right ear. Another week of competition was lost, and then some.

"He's still suffering," Pevenage said to explain why his rider had to skip the weekend race in France. "His head hurts.

"This week he'll be training at home on the flat," Pevenage continued. "Then he'll go train very hard in the mountains for a week. And then he'll ride the Tour of Switzerland."

It was in that race that Ullrich was "discovered" by his team in 1996. Just another young rider beforehand, he did so well in the Swiss Alps that he was reluctantly added to the Tour de France team, the last of nine riders selected by Telekom.

A couple of weeks later, he demonstrated the climbing and, especially, time-trialing skills that landed him in second place behind his teammate, Bjarne Riis, a Dane.

"Switzerland has been good for Jan before," Pevenage noted. "Maybe this time, too."

Back to the Wars

2000

SOMEWHAT BIGGER THAN LIFE, but nowhere near the boy blimp that was expected, Jan Ullrich has returned to combat.

Yes, his Deutsche Telekom team is still buying his bicycle racing uniforms in the stylish stout department because Ullrich is thicker through the middle than a 26-year-old world-class athlete, a winner of the Tour de France at 23, ought to be. And, yes, he is still making excuses for the extra three or four kilograms.

"It's not my fault that I got sick," Ullrich said in an interview with a handful of German-speaking reporters this week. They relayed his insights to a few colleagues. (Ullrich speaks an unsteady English but prefers not to.)

"I trained very hard this winter, harder than ever, and then I got sick," the German was reported to have said. "My only mistake was to get sick."

His medical chart lists a heavy cold and overall, or undiagnosed, ills compounded by his bulimic nature.

This makes three years, and counting, that Ullrich has made the mistake of being sick or overweight. In 1998, he celebrated his Tour victory the previous year by showing up for the start of the season perhaps 10 kilograms—some said 15—overweight. Only in July, when he finished second in the Tour to Marco Pantani, did the scales tip at his usual 73 kilograms.

Last year, after team officials regarded more closely their star's off-season eating habits, the problem was injury and illness. His spring included a stomach virus, the flu and wisdom-tooth problems, all of which caused him to skip many of the races needed to reach peak form for the Tour.

Then, at the end of May, he crashed in the Tour of Germany, injuring his head and a knee. Aspirin cured the headache, but the knee injury grew worse, forcing Ullrich to miss the Tour.

He realized then, he said, how important that race is to him, and vowed to excel at the end of the season. That mission was accomplished when he won the three-week Vuelta a España, the sport's third-ranking race, and then the world championship in the time trial. He nearly pulled off a double by finishing with the top group in the world championship road race, too.

This year, dedication *über alles.*

"It's a great disappointment to me that all the work I did this winter has gone for nearly nothing," he said. "But, barring accident or more sickness, I'm confident about doing well in the Tour de France. I think I can be ready."

He confirmed reports that for weeks he has been riding long hours daily with teammates near his home in the Black Forest.

"I still have a month and a half before the Tour starts," he said. "Beginning now, every day is meaningful."

"Now" is the six-day Midi Libre in the south of France. It will cover about 950 kilometers and include climbs and a rigorous uphill time trial.

While he is not precisely competing in the Midi Libre—the better word might be "appearing"—the main surprise is that he showed up signing autographs, posing for fans' photographs, smiling at one and all, when the race began.

His return had been promised often since he dropped out of Tirreno-Adriatico in mid-March, trailing the leader by more than an hour.

Since then, races where Ullrich was entered had come and gone—Milan–San Remo, Catalan Week, the Critérium International, the Tour of the Basque Country—without him. Telekom officials defend his absences by saying they preferred him to recover from his illnesses and spend his time logging up to 200 kilometers daily in training rather than traveling to and from races.

"I have no illusions about how I'll do in the Midi Libre," he said. "But I'll follow that with the Tour of Germany and then the Tour of Switzerland. My condition should improve.

"The Tour starts July 1 but it doesn't really begin until we reach the Pyrenees 10 days later. Then everything decisive will be crammed into six days, from there until the end of the Alps. I really believe I'll be ready."

Barring further illness or accident, of course. Ullrich was one of many riders involved in crashes as the Midi Libre wound nervously through narrow back roads off the Mediterranean coast. Much as he hopes to do for the Tour de France, he dusted himself off after he went down, then remounted his bicycle and caught up with the race.

Thinking Man's Rider

1986

EVERYBODY LIKES ANDY HAMPSTEN. "A class person, one of the nicest people you'll meet," said Mike Neel, the *directeur sportif* of the 7-Eleven team. "A real good guy," agreed Greg LeMond when Hampsten was his teammate with La Vie Claire. "A very nice fellow," said Paul Köchli, then La Vie Claire's trainer and strategist. "He fit in well with us."

Hampsten returned the compliments. He likes and respects Neel, LeMond and Köchli. The thoughtful Köchli won his praise on another level. "He realizes that bike racers aren't just animals," Hampsten said. "He knows them well enough to know how they think and knows psychology well enough to figure out not how to motivate them but to figure out how they can motivate themselves.

"I can discuss things with him," Hampsten added in 1986 when he was still with La Vie Claire. "A lot of people in cycling are close-minded: 'There's one way of doing it and that's my way and we tell you what to do and you go do it.' That's never worked for me. It could be the best team in the world and it would never work for me."

At that time La Vie Claire was, in fact, the best team in the world—so ranked by bicycling journalists. With the Tour de France approaching and LeMond and Bernard Hinault still riding together, Hampsten knew what was expected of him. "I think it will be a good race for me," he said. "It's really mountainous and there are a lot of mountaintop finishes." The American rider is one of the better climbers around. He won a mountain stage in the Giro in 1985 and followed with a second place, to LeMond, in the Coors Classic and then a victory in the Caracol/Montañas climbers' race in Colombia.

What sort of goals had he set for himself in the Tour? "I certainly don't rule myself out of anything in it," Hampsten replied. By "anything," he meant exactly what? "Anything," he answered with a laugh. Still, he acknowledged, his thoughts were team thoughts. "The team is not structured so we all have to work for one person," he explained. "The most important thing is for the team to win. Whoever wins is secondary. In our philosophy, in our guidelines, a La Vie Claire rider has to win and we always work for each other. It used to be there's one captain on a bicycle team and everybody has to work for him. Paul Köchli prefers it to be the team has to win but he wants each rider to be out there thinking, 'Here's my moment—if I can go for it now, I'll have the whole team working for me.'"

Hampsten appeared to have settled in well with La Vie Claire, which first attempted to recruit him after his unexpected victory in the Giro stage. Hinault was particularly impressed by the manner in which Hampsten, a professional for less than a month, broke away from the pack on a climb to win that alpine stage.

"I was dumbfounded at first," Hampsten said of the offer made on the last day of the Giro. It was renewed after the Coors Classic, where he again impressed Hinault and LeMond, with whom he first rode as a member of the U.S. national team in 1979. Köchli had been watching Hampsten almost as long, recalling his climbing in the 1982 Tour de l'Avenir. "He gives the impression of being very timid, withdrawn, not sure of himself—but I think that's a superficial impression," Köchli said. "Andy knows well enough what he wants, he knows how to take care of himself, he's set very precise goals and knows how to decide what's important for him. The first impression is rather misleading. But that isn't news to me since I knew Andy pretty well before hiring him."

They sealed the deal early in the winter, allowing Hampsten to spend New Year's Day flying to Europe, far from home. He was born in Columbus, Ohio, but his family soon moved to Seattle and then to British Columbia. When he was four, the Hampstens settled in Grand Forks, North Dakota, where his parents teach English at the University of North Dakota.

Hampsten attended that university for two years although, he said, "I didn't have a strong enough interest in any subject to have a major. I was more interested in bicycle racing." He started riding with a club at 14 and, when he was 16, went for the summer to Madison, Wisconsin, "where there's a lot of racing." He moved there semi-permanently at 17, returning to North Dakota in the winter to resume classes. "There was a little bit of friction" at home, he remembered, because he would drop out in the spring term when the cycling season began in March.

Since 1981 he has been living in Boulder, Colorado, and during the European season lived in Switzerland when he rode for La Vie Claire. "I really like it in Switzerland," he said. "It's an international atmosphere and the country's so beautiful. There are a lot of small roads that go through nice forests without a lot of junk all over the place. The Jura Mountains are near my home and there's a plain, and if I go further south or west there are big, rolling hills, so I can do all sorts of training."

This work ethic appealed to Köchli. "I'm very optimistic about his career," said the Swiss trainer, whose reliance on computer-designed training regimes was more controversial before his team started winning major races. Hampsten has strong views about success, past and future—and failure. "You can't lose a bicycle race," he insisted. "One person wins it, but there aren't 150 losers.

"I've been riding so long and for the first few years, every race was fun and really rewarding. After that it got hard and I certainly wasn't doing it for the money; I wasn't receiving any. I also wasn't doing it because I'd win a race now and then. It's too hard a sport to do it for reasons like that. It got to the point where it became so difficult for me when I was competing at the world level, even though I was an amateur, I found I was motivating myself. I was pushing myself not because I wanted to win and get real excited when I win, which I do, but because I wanted to see how far I could push myself. There was no one else. It got to the point that if I had a coach who would crack the whip on me, it wouldn't do much good. It became a real personal ambition just to see how far I could push myself.

"I needed results to test myself, but I wanted to see how far I could go in the sport, which is why I jumped at the opportunity to turn professional, and to win a race after being a professional two and a half weeks was, for me, very, very rewarding. It sort of proved my whole method of keeping my high goals and trying to find a way of accomplishing them, instead of trying to win small races and then start doing the bigger races. I've tried to always do the big races and get last and then get in the top 20, the top 10 and try to get to the top.

"It was a five-year process of really hard work before I did win a big race but it paid off in a big way. My results have changed fairly dramatically, but I feel I improved only another 10 percent and it's made all the difference. I'm not the best," Hampsten said, embarrassed that he might sound as if he were implying that. "I'm not a super rider now but the 10 percent improvement has made a huge difference."

Clearly, when he talked about pushing himself, he did not mean purely physically.

"No, no," he said. "Bike racing is very physical, but it's so much beyond that. It's not like a boxing match where if you can just tolerate pain, you'll do well. In cycling, all the pain is self-inflicted. Every race comes to a point right near the end where everybody is close—all the riders are actually pretty close in physical abilities—and it comes to a point where some of the riders, who are conditioned well mentally, push themselves harder than the others.

"The decisive moment might be a hill, it might be a crosswind or it just may be after five hours of racing where the riders are really fatigued. Some people make it through that point and others who are pretty much their equals physically don't even finish the race. I try to make it through that point. I've always tried to go after the hardest races I could find, even though I wouldn't do well in them. As an amateur, it was always important for me to go to Europe and find the hardest races I could, even though I was younger than most riders, and really suffer in those races and try to learn. And I did. I learned a lot and most of it was about myself: what I needed to do to prepare myself and push myself even harder."

Why, Hampsten was asked, did he need to test himself?

"Because it's so easy to finish with everyone else, just to sit up. When the crucial moment in a race comes, I could always sit up and say, 'Oh God, my legs feel terrible' or 'I had this problem or that problem so I just finished with so and so' and I could name a half-dozen famous riders so no one would get down on me. But that wouldn't be anything for me.

"What I'd rather do is try to" . . . he paused once more, staring somewhere beyond his listener, "take more risks and try, one out of 10 times, to finish really well. To me it's more important to do well in one out of 10 races than do average in every race.

"One thing I've seen in a lot of European riders is they're in a mental rut. It's so easy to lose. It's that fire, that drive, that ambition to win that really makes a difference at the end of a race. I've seen too many riders just doing it, going through the motions. Sure they kind of hope they get in a lucky break and might win the race, but they're not attacking, they're not going for it."

He realized that his attitude of not needing to win every race was arguable.

"Some people say it's a bad attitude," Hampsten admitted. "Some people say you shouldn't try—you should decide you have to win. If you don't win, you've failed. A lot of sports psychologists would say it's a cop-out not to set your goal. Some people would say if you're just going to try, that means if you don't win, then you haven't lost anything.

"A lot of people have told me I'm not setting my goals high enough, but nobody can push me harder than myself. There's no one who can say, 'You've got to win this.' That won't do anything for me.

"A lot of people want me to win: My friends, my family, they're really proud of me when I win, and that's important to me, but it doesn't help me in a race. In a race it's me—the only one I have to rely on is myself. My teammates are important to me. I want to win for them, but bike racing is so hard that when the moment comes, there's nothing there but myself. So I can't rely on other people to motivate or push me. It has to come from within.

"I'm not saying no one is helping me. But I had to decide what I needed and had to go find it. I need a coach to talk to about training. I need to talk to the older riders about tactics and I need to learn to listen to my own body about its needs.

"I've lost a lot of races and actually been proud of myself. There are other races where I've won and it could happen that I would be unhappy with myself."

Had it ever happened?

No, Andy Hampsten confessed near the start of his professional career, it had not. "I don't win enough races to have some that I don't feel happy about."

Life Is Good

1996

BICYCLE RACING IS FUN AGAIN, Andy Hampsten said, and life is good. He became a father for the first time this winter, he feels useful to his new team after a dry spell in Europe and he has rediscovered his zest. And, he said, it's a holiday racing again in America, where he is competing in the Tour DuPont for the first time since 1990.

"It's always been fun racing in the United States," he explained. "Racing is so much more serious in Europe. The atmosphere of a race doesn't have to be so grim."

At 34 with an impressive record of victories and years of service as a team leader, Hampsten sounds ready for a mellow period. He is still looking for triumphs, especially in the serious climbing in the DuPont, but overall he has reached that point where less is more.

"I'm on a really nice team," he said. "I don't think I'd be racing anymore if I wasn't on this team," referring to U.S. Postal Service, a first-year team with ambitions but a moderate program now.

"The team is compatible," he said. "Like there are two sprinters and they totally get along, no rivalry. Not with many teams would that happen. They appreciate me. It's not that they can't function without me but I'm able to give my experience to the team. So it's enjoyable being in races with them. That's more important now to me than being on a big team and going to the best races and being right in the focus. I'd just rather not deal with big international pressures."

Hampsten looks, sounds and acts relaxed, which was not always the case the last few years when he was coping with the pressure of being a star American rider, the longtime leader of the Motorola team and then a support rider for Miguel Indurain in his quest for a fifth victory in the Tour de France.

Indurain notched that victory last year but Hampsten was not there to help. A rider who has won the Giro d'Italia, two Tours of Switzerland and twice finished fourth in the Tour de France, including a formidable first place in the Alpe d'Huez climb, Hampsten was left off the nine-man Banesto team for the Tour. He spent the summer at his home in Tuscany with his wife, Linda, awaiting the birth of their daughter, Emma.

"It was between me and a couple of other guys for the last position and the other guys were winning mountainous races," he explained. "They wanted my experience, I was riding well, I didn't have any problems but I wasn't super.

"That was a disappointment for me. The whole experience of Banesto was very good, to be with the best team, but I needed more stimulation to do better racing."

Stimulation has always been important to him. The son of college teachers in North Dakota, he is that rare rider who will wander a town after a race, looking at the architecture, tasting the local foods, visiting the museums. Hampsten always has books with him during a race. He enjoys learning languages and studied the guitar during his time with Banesto.

At 34, he is a decade removed from his debut with the powerhouse Vie Claire team based in France and headed by Bernard Hinault and Greg LeMond. While they dueled for victory in the 1986 Tour—LeMond finally first, Hinault second—Hampsten finished fourth and won the white jersey of the best young rider. He credits Hinault with having taught him how to adjust to the professional's life.

Now Hampsten is the veteran and, as he says, "If I can pass a little bit on to these guys, you can say it's a duty of mine. But not heavy-handedly."

The team will compete in June in the Tour of Switzerland, its major European race this season. It is also Hampsten's major race. His voice grew dreamy as he talked about the possibility of winning there a decade after his triumphs in 1986 and 1987. "It would be really nice to win that race," he said. "Round the circle a little bit.

"I hope it will work out that I'll have good form and I'll be leading the race and I'll tell my teammates how to work for me. But until that happens, I'll try to work for them. I want to set an example."

ROOKIE SEASON

1988

NOTHING WENT RIGHT FOR MIKE CHAVEZ in the two months after he moved from the United States to Italy to start his first season as a professional bicycle racer. Climate, food, water, culture shock, even the air he labored to breathe on training rides weakened him.

"Ever since I've been in Italy I've been fighting illness," he said after a stage of the springtime Tirreno-Adriatico race across Italy. "In the past four or five days, my stomach has been grinding and I haven't been sleeping well. My health is just not up to par." Chavez was planning to go home to New Mexico, visit his parents and see a doctor.

Greg LeMond had been through it and could express what was going on. Each year a handful of American bicycle riders come to Europe to seek glory and wealth. Almost unanimously, the Americans find European life too demanding, too different, too foreign. After a season or two they are back home. "Most American riders have different attitudes toward racing from Europeans—they're not used to suffering," LeMond says. "For my first two, three years in Europe I always felt pretty tired in races, but that's just part of cycling. The first year or two in Europe is the hardest part, just being in a different life."

He got no quarrel from 23-year-old Mike Chavez of the little-known Selca team. "I've been brought into reality," he said in his dining room in Fossacesia Marina after the day's race from Cassino Paglieta in the Abruzzi. Starting the stage in 176th place among the 177 riders, Chavez dropped out during the sole climb.

"It was a hard stage," he said. "They're all hard when you feel bad. The climb wasn't that steep but it was long, and I haven't been doing well at going uphill ever since I've been sick.

"Bike racing is a humbler. American people say bike racing in Europe is as big as football and baseball and basketball, and it's actually bigger. Much harder. You become humbled by it."

Chavez was full of respect for LeMond and the Canadian Steve Bauer, who have lasted years on the European circuit. "It's just amazing for me to be here with those guys," he said. "People don't realize how hard it is to come here and do what they've done. Until you come here and do it, you just don't realize it." He insisted, however, that he did not feel awe. "No, I don't," he said firmly, his voice rising from a monotone. "They're great racers and they do well but I don't feel there's any reason why I shouldn't do well, too."

His results have been good in other seasons, Chavez said. He began racing at 17 in Colorado, where he had moved from his native Albuquerque to become a ski racer in Vail. At 18 he was ranked 10th in the United States among downhill skiers, he explained, adding, "It turned out I was a better bike racer than ski racer."

In 1984, after racing in Vail, Colorado Springs, Denver and Boulder, he visited his brother Dennis, who was stationed with the U.S. Air Force in Kaiserslautern, West Germany, and began racing bicycles there as an amateur. In 1987, unhappy with his progress in U.S. races, he returned to Germany. "Things were very good for me. I raced very well, got good results. I'm mostly a sprinter but in the last year or two, I've been able to stay with the climbers."

An official of the Ciclolinea company, which makes bicycle accessories, spotted Chavez and recommended him to Selca, for which Ciclolinea is a secondary sponsor. A small, low-budget team that races almost exclusively in Italy—the modest Tour of Denmark was its major foreign excursion—Selca is named for its primary sponsor, a manufacturer of electronic exterminating devices.

From the day he arrived in Sicily in January, Chavez had problems. "I got really sick—seven days in bed—just before the Giro of Sicily and wasn't able to race at all. The climate, food and little bit of water I drank had something to do with it. There was a flu going around and the water made my resistance not very good. So I was the first one to get the flu among a lot of racers. It took its toll: My blood pressure dropped, just everything completely went bad. When I was in Germany I had no problems. Here the climate's been very difficult, hot and cold, hot and cold again. Also, I'm used to a real dry climate and it's very wet here."

He lives in a small town outside Imola, near Bologna, where training is difficult. "The air isn't very good because there's a lot of farmland and the farmers just burn all their fields off. And all the cars—it seems they all burn gas into the air.

"It's something you just have to get used to," he continued. "I haven't adjusted to all the different things that are happening here—climate, living constantly on the road. Every day you race from here to there and you stay in a hotel, race there, stay in a hotel." He looked around the dreary hotel on the gray Adriatic and appeared to wince.

"Professional racing is a whole different thing from amateur racing. I've learned that quick. You don't just turn pro, you don't just say 'Okay, I'm a pro now.' There are so many good riders, so many riders who can win the race."

Was he simply homesick? "I did feel that at first," he admitted. "Here you are in a whole different world. Just communicating was a very big problem at first. Sure I like home. Home's a great place, I love to go back. But this is what I want to do. I want to race.

"Everybody has good days and bad days. I've been fighting this long, I've gotten this far, I'm not going to stop now. I'm planning to go back to America for a little while, recuperate. I'll be back."

Upstairs in the same hotel, LeMond was astonished to hear that there was another American in the race. "Mike who? An American! What's his name?" He considered the news for a moment and then decided, "I never heard of him." He was not being unkind but, as he usually is, factual. Unlike most other racers, LeMond keeps track of riders and their results.

When he heard about Chavez's troubles, LeMond was solicitous. "The problem of American riders coming over is they're exposed to many different types of sickness. My father-in-law, who's an immunologist, says cold viruses, there are thousands of types. An American, when you're growing up, you're exposed to most of those. That's why having a cold is not always bad—your body builds up immunity to that virus.

"He should see a doctor about getting a viral vaccine and make sure he doesn't have something in the stomach," LeMond decided about Chavez.

Something struck a chord. "Imagine being a neo-professional on an Italian team, especially a low-budget one," LeMond mused. "My God, you're talking about a mean and hard life. If you're Italian, it's one thing, but gosh . . .

"I was lucky on Guimard's team," he continued, referring to the first professional contract he signed, in 1980, with Cyrille Guimard's Renault team. "I'd probably do it over again but now that I know everything and how hard it is, God, I'd regret doing it. I don't think my wife and I could ever go to a new country and start another job completely new that is as hard as cycling and try to adapt to a different language.

"You're not certain you can succeed. I was confident in myself but in reality I did not know what my potential was. So many things go into making a rider succeed. A guy can have the physical qualities but does he have the mental qualities to survive staying and learning? I was determined and I knew that if I was going to make it, I had to do it.

"I personally knew that I had what it took to become a good, a very good, rider, but still my first years were difficult. Some riders think, 'I'll just take a pro license out.' They think pro racing is—I don't know what they think. But it's the hardest sport in the world. The problem with jumping in too soon is you're demoralized, you don't give yourself time to adapt."

LeMond looked around his dingy room with the low-watt bulb that he had complained was too weak to read by. It wasn't much, he was reminded, but at least it was a single room; the day before he was understandably upset to find he was three in a room. He seemed to be weighing the advantages of the racer's life, especially for an American.

"It's been so educational," he decided. "You could never reproduce what I've learned. There's so much that I've learned and appreciated. I appreciate Europe now. I get to see what life is really like in Europe. I like European life—Belgium, Paris, fantastic! I've seen every major city in Europe. I'm a much more international person now. I can go to any major city in Europe and find my way around. I'm as American as you'll ever get, but I'm the kind of American who can go anywhere in the world and not have any problems."

At dinner that night, LeMond and the rest of his PDM team were in high spirits. Everybody was riding well in Tirreno-Adriatico and morale had been boosted by LeMond's victory in a bonus sprint that afternoon. The noise bounced around the hotel dining room and the uncomprehending waiters joined in laughter at the team's jokes.

In their corner, the Selca team ate silently. Conversations were mumbled in Italian and bowls of spaghetti were passed with a grunt. Chavez sat forward in his chair, a little hunched, and totally ignored. When he had finished his dinner and was heading out of the dining room, another American intercepted him and brought him over to where LeMond sat. They were introduced and LeMond promised to see him later. Chavez went out and ordered a coffee at the hotel bar.

After about five minutes, LeMond pushed back his chair and made his way to the bar too, falling into place next to Chavez. For the next 15 minutes the Tour de France winner and the untried neo-professional chatted while, almost one by one, the Selca team drifted past and looked them up and down. Although a few riders looked astonished, nobody dared interrupt.

Finally LeMond shook hands with Chavez and went back to the PDM table. After a few minutes, Chavez strolled into the dining room. His shoulders were thrown back and he walked with a bounce. Never once hesitating, he marched over to the table where the Selca officials, mechanics and masseurs were having dinner, pulled out a chair, straddled it and placed his elbows on the table. Then Chavez gave them all a radiant smile.

He continued to beam until it was time for everybody to go upstairs and prepare for the coming day's race. The next morning, the last anybody but the Selca team would see of him, he was still smiling.

A Belgian Dynasty

1999

THE PLANCKAERTS ARE A DYNASTY in bicycle racing in Belgium and, like royal families everywhere, they worry about their lines of succession. A fey son here, a weak-willed nephew there and the family will be the stuff of history books.

That is not the way the three founding brothers envisioned it. The three—Willy, born 1944, Walter, born 1948, and Eddy, born 1958—were all tough, determined riders and spoke of their pride in being Planckaerts the way other marauders might boast of being Vikings.

"In the tradition in Belgium, the name 'Planckaert' means something," Walter Planckaert, now the *directeur sportif* of the Palmans team in Belgium, said before the 54th Het Volk race began in Ghent. "The name is very hard." He did not mean hard to bear.

Willy Planckaert emerged in 1964 when he finished second in the world amateur road race championship. In a dozen-year career as a professional, he won such big Belgian races as Brussels-Charleroi-Brussels, the Circuit of Central Flanders, Across Belgium and the Grand Prix Pino Cerami. In 1966, he won the green points jersey in the Tour de France and two daily stages.

Among other successes, Walter Planckaert won the esteemed Amstel Gold Race classic in 1972, the Tour of Belgium in 1977, Across Belgium in 1977 and 1984, the Grand Prix E3 in 1976 and Kuurne-Brussels-Kuurne in 1973 and 1979. In 1976, he fulfilled the dream of every Flemish rider by triumphing in the Tour of Flanders.

Eddy Planckaert won that prize also, in 1988, and added another revered classic, Paris-Roubaix, in 1990. In 1988, he won the points jersey in the Tour de France, where he also won two stages. In major races in Belgium alone, he finished first in the Flèche Brabançonne in 1983, the Grand Prix Harelbeke in 1987 and 1989, the Tour of Belgium in 1984, Across Belgium in 1985 and 1988, and Het Volk in 1984 and 1985.

After Eddy Planckaert retired in 1991, a new generation joined the professional ranks the next year: Jo Planckaert, born 1970, the son of Willy. Because he scored 15 victories in his last year as an amateur, the throne seemed secure.

After some anxious times, perhaps it finally is. As thousands of his fellow Belgians watched, Jo Planckaert, who rides for the Lotto team, finished fifth in Het Volk and then won the Kuurne-Brussels-Kuurne race the next day. Both are demanding semi-classics over many cobblestoned climbs.

His sprint victory in Kuurne over a resurgent Johan Museeuw was unexpected. With his rather open, sweet face, Jo Planckaert does not have the intense look, the heavy brows of the other Planckaerts, nor does he have their records. "Jo is a very good rider," Walter Planckaert insisted.

"But he doesn't have my character," he admitted. "It's not the same as mine."

In his career, Jo Planckaert has fewer than 20 victories, mainly in Belgian *kermesses*, basically exhibition races. Before his big weekend, his high points were victories last year and this year in a stage of the Etoile de Besseges, a minor race that opens the season in France, and a second place two years ago in Paris-Roubaix.

"He's only 28 and this is the year for him to win a big race, like the Tour of Flanders," Uncle Walter said at Het Volk. "This is the moment."

Jo Planckaert agreed. "Being a Planckaert is special in cycling," he said in a separate interview. "It's a lot of pressure. I can live with pressure.

"I'm going good now," he continued. "I hope I can make some good races, get some good results." And then he did.

The big spring classics where the earlier Planckaerts established their name—the Tour of Flanders and Paris-Roubaix—are still more than a month away. Although Kuurne-Brussels-Kuurne is a nice victory, it will increase the pressure on Jo Planckaert.

Besides, there is another Planckaert moving up in the chain. That would be Francesco Planckaert, 16, the son of Eddy. As a junior last season, he won 30 races, most of them easily.

"Eddy is training him to be dominant," said Allan Peiper, a former fine rider from Australia who now lives in Belgium and watches the racing scene. "He makes him attack from the first kilometer. Francesco just leaves everybody behind.

"If the boy is ahead by 5 minutes, 30 seconds, Eddy tells him he's only 30 seconds up and get moving. Francesco will be in the Planckaert mold, the family will see to that."

On the Right Track

1999

THE EARLY MORNING DRIZZLE was cold, of course, and promised to continue all day, of course. That's winter in Belgium.

A lot of bicycle racers prefer to avoid the place. They spent Saturday in Spain, at the Tour of Valencia, where temperatures were in the low 20s centigrade (low 70s Fahrenheit), or in Italy, at the Trophee Pantalica, where temperatures were lower but still not the 6 degrees centigrade recorded in Ghent.

This city in eastern Flanders staged the start of the 54th Het Volk race, the traditional opening of the season in Belgium and always a gathering of tough men. Of these, the toughest—no argument is possible—is Johan Museeuw.

The king of the classics, Museeuw comes from Flanders and, as always, was the center of attention for his fellow Belgians. Before the start, young and old, male and female, surrounded the parked Mapei team car in which he sat in the passenger's seat in front. Through a slightly opened window on the driver's side, small boys passed the team's official sheets of paper for Museeuw to autograph. The mood was reverential and perhaps a bit insecure.

Museeuw crashed last April in the Paris-Roubaix race, falling in the mud and cobblestones of the Arenberg woods and fracturing his left kneecap. He was taken to a Belgian hospital and the leg was immobilized in plaster.

But his wound had not been thoroughly cleaned and under the cast his knee became septic. His kidneys and liver nearly failed as the poison spread, and even after doctors understood what was happening and corrected it, they feared that the leg might become gangrenous and have to be removed. Months of recuperation followed as Museeuw kept the leg.

At age 32 and after a decade as a professional, he had been talking about retiring. He seemed especially serious in 1996 but then won the world road race championship and decided to carry on. By 1998 he had reduced his schedule by dropping the Tour de France from his program and concentrating on the 10 prestigious one-day classics that compose the World Cup. Museeuw has won a big classic nine times, including the Tour of Flanders a week before the jinxed Paris-Roubaix in April.

Not until September could he return to competition. He tested his atrophied leg in small races and decided that as much as he would like to retire—perhaps open a bar or join the family's garage business—that was not the way he wanted to leave the sport. He signed a two-year renewal with Mapei and then spent the winter training on his bicycle, swimming long laps and working out in a gymnasium.

"I've returned to see how far I can go," he has explained. "Now that I've got my health back, I'd very much like to be at the front of races again." At the front, as in winning.

In his first couple of races in Spain last month, he did fine on the flat but struggled on climbs.

"That's natural," said his team manager and confidant, Patrick Leféváre, before the start of Het Volk. "We're not expecting too much of him now. He's got a lot of races ahead of him in the next month and a half, and after Paris-Roubaix we'll evaluate his progress.

"I think he's doing well, but this is his first real test. He's serene, motivated and very calm.

"It's amazing," he added, "amazing that he's alive and amazing that he still has his leg."

For a final amazement, Museeuw rode a strong Het Volk, 202 kilometers over 11 short but steep hills lined with treacherous cobblestones. As one rider after another wearily dropped back or out and as the pack splintered in the rain, cold and mud, Museeuw remained consistently near the front.

With about 15 kilometers to go, he even went on the offensive, speeding away from a group of nine leaders. He was quickly chased down, and an attack then by Frank Vandenbroucke, a Belgian with the Cofidis team, proved to be the winning move.

"The road was wide, the wind from the side and everybody else was exhausted from catching Museeuw," Vandenbroucke said later. "It was the right moment."

The Cofidis leader easily won the race in a sprint finish with Wilfried Peeters, another Belgian with Mapei. Thirty-four seconds behind were six riders, with Museeuw in the middle of the group, finishing a splendid sixth. Only 44 of the 199 men who started the race completed it.

Afterward Museeuw was beaming. "If you'd told me about this three months ago, I wouldn't have believed you," he said. "I'm thrilled to have been there at the finish. Was I still capable of playing a role in a race? That was my only doubt, and now it's settled.

"You can't compare me yet to the Museeuw of before, but I'm on the right track." Then, the next day, Museeuw showed just how far along the track he was by finishing second in thc Kuurne-Brussels-Kuurne race, another semi-classic. In a sprint finish, he was beaten by a fellow Belgian, Jo Planckaert of the Lotto team, after another long slog over many hills. Museeuw attacked near the finish, but Planckaert was too strong for him and won the sprint.

"It was the ideal situation for me," Planckaert said. "Johan became nervous and launched the sprint while I just could sit back and wait for the right moment."

Second Comeback

1998

BY NOW, ALMOST NO ONE BELIEVES IN Wilfried Nelissen's chances for a comeback. The second comeback, that is.

For the first one, his coach, his teammates, his many fans in Belgium, above all Nelissen himself, believed. Now, the list seems to have dwindled to just Nelissen, if even.

Listen to Walter Planckaert, the *directeur sportif* of Nelissen's bicycle team: "He's in the hospital again, another knee operation. He'll miss training for four weeks once he gets out. He had the operation Tuesday. When he gets out, we don't know yet."

In other words, the rider will not begin training until April at the earliest, far too late for the spring races. No matter what his condition thereafter, his minor Palmans team will not be eligible for any of the big races of summer and fall.

The season has just begun, but for Nelissen it seems to be over already. At 28, there are not many years left.

"It will be difficult for him," Planckaert judged. "Extremely difficult."

A teammate, Gert Vanderaerden, a Belgian like Planckaert and Nelissen, was blunt. "It doesn't look good for him," he said.

They both spoke in Sint Pieter's Plein, a huge square in Ghent, before the start of the Het Volk race. Staged over 202 kilometers, 11 short, steep climbs and stretches of cobblestones, the Het Volk opens the bicycle season in the north of Europe.

The Het Volk is a tough race, especially when the wind is blowing hard, as it was this time. As they say in Belgium, mainly when a Belgian finishes first, it takes a tough man to win such a tough race. Nelissen has won it twice. The first time was in 1993, and he became the bright hope of Belgian racing at age 22. Everything seemed possible for a sprinter as fleet as he was. But the day after his victory, as he rode in the Kuurne-Brussels-Kuurne race, he crashed, broke his collarbone and missed the classics.

Nelissen won the Het Volk again in 1994 and seemed once more to be heading for the top when he also won the Belgian national championship that June. But a week later, in the first stage of the Tour de France, as he sprinted for the finish line with his head down, he plowed into a French policeman who had moved onto the course to take a photograph of the approaching riders. Knocked unconscious by the crash at 70 kilometers an hour, Nelissen suffered a concussion and had to be hospitalized. His Tour was over. His first serious comeback began.

Was he shy now when the sprinting began?

"No, not at all," he said "It's all over now." To prove it, he won a race in Belgium that September and a few weeks later the Grand Prix d'Isbergues in France. "That felt good," he said.

In 1995, he repeated his victory in the Belgian championships and was wearing the black-, yellow- and red-striped jersey the next spring. No Het Volk victory this time but he was off to a good start until the Ghent-Wevelgem race in April.

Somehow, as the pack rode single file in a heavy wind, Nelissen hit one of the many thick wooden stakes that mark the side of back-country roads. His right knee was shattered, his thigh ripped open, his shin fractured.

Then began, and continues, his second comeback. Not until February 1997, nearly a year later, was he able to resume riding. By then, his Lotto sponsor had dropped him, and he moved from the country's only major team to Palmans, a low-budget one. When the Tour de France was starting last July, the rider who once wore its yellow jersey was finally fit for his first race.

It was one of the small ones, called *kermesses*, that nearly every village in Belgium sponsors on weekends. Among the riders from some unsung Belgian teams, Nelissen raced up main streets, out past flat farmland and then back down main streets. Even if the competition was not overly stiff and even if his team convoyed him most of the way, Nelissen still astounded the sport by winning a *kermesse* in Sint Niklaas. He seemed to be on his way back.

Late this January, he went to Spain to train with the Het Volk as his first big goal, but after a 100-kilometer ride, he returned to his hotel in tears from the pain in his knee. He rested, tried to train again and could not. Last week he had surgery to repair calcification in the knee.

Nelissen will give himself this one last year to see if he has a future as a rider, his friends say. He cannot discuss his chances himself because he does not want to be called in the hospital.

Out of Luck

1998

RUDY DHAENENS WAS RIGHT: HE NEVER HAD MUCH LUCK.

Driving to the finish of the Tour of Flanders bicycle race, where he would be a consultant for the Eurosport Belgium television channel, he somehow lost control of his car, swerved off the road and into a power pylon. He died in a hospital from head injuries, leaving a wife and two children. He would have been 37 that week.

The Tour of Flanders was one of his favorite races, not only because he was a Belgian and a native of Flanders but mainly because he finished second in the classic in 1990. Dhaenens had a special affection for races in which he had ridden well: second in Paris-Roubaix in 1986, third there in 1987 and fifth in 1985, fourth in Liège-Bastogne-Liège in 1990 and in the Het Volk in 1988, third in the Belgian national championships in 1985.

Usually he looked like a small boy who asked Santa for a set of trains for Christmas and got instead underwear and a book, but his plain face could light up when he discussed the few races he had won. The world championship in Japan in 1990 was the peak, of course.

Dhaenens and a Belgian teammate, Dirk de Wolf, managed to get out in front of the pack and, after de Wolf collided with their only close pursuer, Dag-Otto Lauritzen of Norway, and left him with a disabled bicycle, the way to the finish was clear. Dhaenens won by a second or two.

There have been unlikelier world champions. Dhaenens had also won a daily stage in the 1986 Tour de France and came close to repeating in 1989. He broke away alone and was heading for victory when he entered the final curve, 400 or so meters from the line.

"I took the corner too fast, maybe, or something happened with my wheel, maybe, and I slipped," he explained in an interview the next spring. "I still don't know," he admitted.

His bicycle skidded out from under him and he was thrown to the ground. When he got to his feet and found that his rear wheel was mangled, he could do nothing more than scream with rage as the pack shot by. Instead of being an easy winner, he was the last man to cross the finish line. "It just happened, so what can you do?" he asked those months later.

Because of an injury to Sean Kelly, Dhaenens had been promoted to lead the PDM team in the 1990 Paris-Roubaix, but he understood who he was—a dependable, unselfish rider of moderate talent, not a star.

"Laurent Fignon wins more than I do, probably because he expects more of himself," Dhaenens said, referring to the Frenchman who won the Tour de France twice.

The talk turned to Moreno Argentin, the Italian who had finished first ahead of Dhaenens a week earlier in the Tour of Flanders. "There are guys who aren't often good during the year but when they're good, they win," he said. "Like Argentin: When he's super, he wins. He's super maybe four or five days a year, but he wins four of the five times.

"I'm not like him. I'm always in the top group, usually in the front, but never win. And that's what's important in cycling races. To win, you need luck."

He had that at the world championships four months later, but by the end of the 1992 season, he had to retire because of medical problems.

Not much was seen of Dhaenens for the next few years. Then, last July, he showed up in the press room at the start of the Tour de France, looking tentative. He was working in a slight job, perhaps as a television consultant, perhaps as a representative of a bicycle shoe or saddle company. He looked pleased to be remembered.

"We must talk," he said. "I'll tell you what I've been doing. I'll be with the race only a few days," he warned.

But in the bustle of the Tour, those few days sped by, and then he was not to be found, and now he has been killed.

Full of Hope

1995

HERE HE IS, FULL OF HOPE, in Isbergues, the north of France, nowhere—a company town, 5,500 inhabitants, a couple of streets, no evident restaurant, a half-mile walk from the nearest train station. For Cyril Sabatier, Isbergues is Carthage under Hannibal, Athens in the Golden Age of Pericles. Isbergues is where it all could happen.

Maybe, maybe not.

Sabatier was lying on the massage table, wearing a gray Gan T-shirt. A towel was draped over his middle as a *soigneur* worked on his legs. Sabatier had flown up that morning from his home in Nîmes, been met at the airport in Paris by a Gan team official and then driven to a hotel in the city of Béthune. The next day he would begin his four-race internship with the team.

Every fall, the French Cycling Federation encourages the country's handful of professional teams to accept up to three amateurs for a stage, a few weeks of experience at a higher level and the opportunity to impress team officials enough so that they will sign the amateur rider to a two-year neo-professional contract.

Once in a while, that happens. Of the 109 French riders who started this season with professional teams, 30 were neo-pros. This figure was skewed, however, since 12 of them were with promotional, or second-division, teams and 6 with a team that disappeared, along with their jobs, in July.

Most of these amateurs were signed to a professional contract based on their results, not their stage, which is often a token last chance. Usually the amateur, the *stagiaire,* rides his races and then returns to his amateur team humbled. Next season, he pledges, he will ride so well that he will not need a stage to win a professional contract.

Sabatier did not think he would be saying that. He is 24 years old now, a little old to remain a hopeful amateur, dreaming about next season's results.

"If it doesn't work out this season, I think it's over for me," he said as he rolled onto his side for the massage. "It's too hard to stay an amateur—not enough teams, not enough money. Another year as an amateur? I don't think so, I don't think so. This is my last chance, I know that."

He was nervous, he admitted. "Yes, a little, yes." Tired, too. "A little of that also, yes. It's been a long season."

The champion of France among cadets, age 12, and then among juniors, age 16, Sabatier has not continued to shine these last several seasons. He did win the unheralded Tour du Nivernais-Morvan this year and did finish fourth in the amateur Liège-Bastogne-Liège, but otherwise his results have been undistinguished.

The week before he dropped out of the Tour de l'Avenir, a showcase for young talent, during an early stage.

Was that race too hard, the weather too brutal? "I was too tired," he explained now. "I wanted to save what I have left for these races with Gan."

A team official was pessimistic about Sabatier. "His chances—nothing special," the official said. "He's a good rider but tired now," said another official, Michel Laurent, the Gan manager. "He's had some good results, nothing extraordinary but he's solid. He's getting his opportunity to impress us." Still, Laurent added, "At most we'll take one neo-pro and we're looking at three. Perhaps we won't take any of them."

These are bad times for French teams. Le Groupement went out of business just before the Tour de France, La Française des Jeux announced unexpectedly that it would not sponsor a new team and both Castorama and Chazal are still seeking financial backing to continue next season. At the moment, the only French teams assured of resuming action in February are Gan, the minor-league Aubervilliers 93 and Mutuelle de Seine et Marne outfits, and Festina, which is based in Andorra. Another second-division team, La Creuse, is in the talking stage.

"There aren't many French teams, that's sure," Sabatier said. "I contacted Gan, that's why I'm here." Castorama and Chazal are also believed to be interested in him, but their future is uncertain.

"In Italy, they'll have 12 teams next season," the rider continued. "I don't know anybody there, though, so I've had no contact with Italian teams.

"This stage—it's a big opportunity. I know that. Maybe my first big opportunity and I know I have to take advantage of it."

Exactly how remained to be worked out. "I don't know what my goals are because I've never done a big race with professionals. I have no idea what's expected of me tomorrow, not yet," he said, referring to the Grand Prix d'Isbergues, his first race with Gan. "Nobody has told me anything yet. I'll find out what they want me to do later."

Finishing the 206-kilometer race over 13 short yet steep climbs was foremost on his mind. "I certainly hope to finish. That would be good for me with the team."

Actually, no, Laurent said later. "Personal results don't mean much with a young rider," he said, "because we may ask him to do so many things that he wears himself out. I don't hold it against a young rider if he doesn't finish as long as he does the team's work and that's why he dropped out.

"What I look for is whether he gets in the early breaks, does he work for the others, does he do his share of the chasing, does he ride for the leaders, giving them shelter from the wind? An individual exploit is always admirable—it certainly can't hurt your chances—but the rest counts just as much.

"What you want to know is how will a young rider fit in, how good is his attitude. Sometimes a rider's legs are terrific but his head isn't."

Laurent mentioned a French professional of great promise but lackluster results lately. "He can't focus on training and racing," the manager said. "He gets distracted. Family problems, personal problems. Girls. He's supposed to be thinking about training and racing, and what's he thinking about? Women."

Married and a father, Sabatier appeared to be distant from that problem. He had his own, although it was in the past. In July 1988, the month of his 17th birthday, he was found guilty of using steroids when he won the French junior championship a few weeks before. His title was removed.

His father fought the positive drug finding for more than two years, arguing with a thick dossier of medical reports that his son naturally produced an excessively high level of testosterone, the male hormone, and an abnormally low level of epitestosterone, a natural precursor of testosterone. A ratio between the two that is higher than 6 to 1 is considered proof of doping and the young Sabatier routinely registered a ratio of at least 8 to 1.

In 1990, the boy was finally cleared and his title restored. Had the years of testimony and doubt sapped his powers or was Sabatier simply another case of the young rider who never lived up to his potential? However delicately it could be put, that was not a question to ask a rider thinking only of his stage with Gan. In any case, he said, he had not tested positive in years and probably had outgrown whatever glandular condition he had as a teenager.

"That part's over, finished," he was saying. "What I have to think about now is the Grand Prix d'Isbergues first, then a couple of races in Italy, then Paris-Bourges, I think. That's my stage, my opportunity. Everything depends now on my legs."

How were his legs? "We'll find out tomorrow," he answered.

And if he failed in his stage, what then?

"I don't know," he said, "I haven't even thought about it. For now this is all I'm thinking about. We'll see next year what I'm doing next year."

WHEN HE SHOWED UP AT THE TEAM CAR to head for the Grand Prix d'Isbergues, Cyril Sabatier's Gan racing jersey and shorts were shinily new and spotless, obviously just out of the box. The bicycle locked atop the car, however, was his usual one. The only difference was the number, 28, bolted onto it for the race.

"There's no time to measure him for a new bicycle and build one," explained a team mechanic. "He just got here and he'll only be with us for four races, a couple of weeks."

So, for the first racing day of his stage, his apprenticeship period with a professional team, Sabatier, a 24-year-old French amateur with the VC Lyon-Vaulx en Velin team, rode his familiar yellow Peugeot bicycle.

Also on a yellow Peugeot was Anthony Langella, No. 25, a 21-year-old member of the CC Marmande-Aquitaine team and another amateur *stagiaire*. The seven other Gan riders, all professionals, rode blue Eddy Merckx models.

Sabatier and Langella were driven from their hotel in Béthune to Isbergues, about 20 kilometers away, by Michel Laurent, Gan's manager and a fine former rider. After a team meeting that morning during which Laurent outlined strategy and general duties, he took the opportunity of the drive to give the amateurs some last-minute advice.

"Tactics," he said, "pay attention to tactics, stay alert, take advice from the other riders. Stay alert. There should be lots of attacks, early attacks, so stay alert. Follow the attacks, pay attention to tactics. Listen to the others."

Laurent spoke mainly to Langella, in the front seat with him, but turned now and again to Sabatier to make sure he did not feel ignored.

Looking grim and a bit nervous, Sabatier nodded his head in agreement with everything Laurent said. Tactics. Stay alert.

The team drove in three cars to the small town of Isbergues for its 49th Grand Prix, started in 1946 to celebrate France's liberation from the Germans the year before. The countryside in the north of France is not the stuff of picture postcards, although Isbergues sits just off the main road north to Calais and Dunkirk, happily out of sight of the numerous hills of slag that show where coal once was quarried and processed. The weather is generally windy because of the nearby English Channel, and rain is common.

Once he arrived, Sabatier waited for a *soigneur* to oil his legs for warmth, then rode to the race podium to sign in. He received no introduction, for clearly the speaker had no idea who he was. Even if it is part of the Coupe de France competition, the Grand Prix d'Isbergues is a secondary race and does not waste its money (66,000 francs, or about $13,000, in prizes) on a professional introducer of riders.

Still, the race drew more than 150 riders and 19 teams, including such major ones as Lotto, Gan, Motorola, Novell and Castorama, and such minor ones as Saxon, Rotan, Palmans, Asfra and Vlaanderen 2002. There was room for anybody applying, since the Spanish teams were busy in the Vuelta a España and the Italian teams were racing on their home front.

Unsung, Sabatier started to leave the podium area when a photographer—one with a press badge, not just a fan—asked him to pose. He obliged. Then a spectator asked for an autograph. Looking pleased, Sabatier signed with his left hand.

He pedaled over to the riders' tent, where he could have some coffee or a piece of bread. Sitting on his bicycle with his sunglasses perched on his head, his right leg on the ground for balance, Sabatier gazed out at the spectators on the other side of the barriers.

He seemed happy. Perhaps he was registering the amateur riders out there, the ones in unknown team jerseys or in those of Banesto and Festina, professional teams not entered in the Grand Prix d'Isbergues. Perhaps those were the men who caught his eye, the pretenders, the dreamers, the young riders who stood there admiringly and wished, like him, that one day they would turn professional.

An official tapped Sabatier on the shoulder and nodded to the right. He rode off to the start of his first professional race.

Whatever fine feats he accomplished went unseen. Heeding tactics, covering early breaks, listening to the advice of his teammates, staying alert, especially staying alert—whatever he did after the first 30 kilometers went unseen because his team leader, Gilbert Duclos-Lassalle, attacked successfully then with two Lotto riders and began to build a huge lead.

Naturally, the team car with Laurent at the wheel went with Duclos to offer advice, inspiration, a water bottle or a new wheel if he had a flat.

Unlike a major race, where teams have two cars, one to tend a breakaway, one for the rest of the team in the pack, the Grand Prix d'Isbergues had one car for each team. If that car went up front, wheels and water bottles for the other riders were provided by a neutral support car.

Sabatier worked with his teammates to protect Duclos, going to the front of the pack and blocking by keeping the speed low or breaking the other riders' rhythm with varying tempos. The CB radio that linked the race told of these tactics back in the pack.

Certainly Sabatier would have been called on, as an amateur doing a stage, to chase down any rival who tried to overtake Duclos-Lassalle. But there was no Gan official there to see his work and judge how he would fit into the team next season.

No matter. Like so many other riders, Sabatier ran out of steam in the 13 hills. Perhaps it was all the crashes on the narrow, twisty roads that 150 riders were trying to barrel through. More likely it was what he feared, that after a long season, he was just too tired to finish the race. Langella, his fellow amateur, did finish, however.

Later, after Sabatier had showered and returned to the team car to be driven back to the hotel, to pack his bags and head for the two races in Italy, he was asked what had happened to him. Had he crashed?

"No, I didn't crash," he said. "I just ran out of strength on a hill and had to quit." He was working not to look disheartened, not to acknowledge that in the next two weeks of his stage he would not grow any stronger than he was here.

A team mechanic came up and asked him if he had pulled out because of a crash.

"No," Sabatier explained, "I didn't crash. I just ran out of strength on a hill and had to quit," he repeated, trying hard to sound matter of fact and not succeeding, not at all.

ATTACK, ATTACK, ATTACK

1998

THE BOSS, A SHOOT-FROM-THE-LIP GUY, announces that you are overpaid and underperforming. Then he talks with business rivals, trying to persuade them to take you off his hands.

When they decline, the next step in the executive handbook is humiliation. In the forum where you first became a star, you are publicly demoted to underling. The hope is that you will quit rather than accept such shame. Or sulk, possibly a firing offense requiring no buyout.

"What, me worry?" says Jacky Durand, or words to that effect. He is "you" and worse, for his purposes, French.

Durand, a famously blithe spirit, is a 33-year-old rider for the Lotto team in culturally divided Belgium. He signed a two-year contract last year. The *directeur sportif* then was so Francophone that he delegated to an assistant the job of communicating with most of his riders, who speak Flemish.

In the off-season, the tectonic plates of Belgian politics shifted and whichever Walloon faction determined the choice of *directeur sportif* for a team sponsored by the national lottery found itself among the outs. So did its man. He was replaced by his assistant, the Fleming Jos Braeckvelt.

After he injured his back in a crash while training, Durand got off to a slow start this season and struggled through races in February. No problem, he said at Paris-Nice early last month: I never met a hill I liked to climb in February. I'll be ready for the April classics and everything after that. His record supported him. In a 10-year career as a professional, Durand has won such classics as the Tour of Flanders and Paris-Tours. Twice he has been the French national champion, in 1993 and 1994.

He has won two daily stages in the Tour de France and worn the yellow jersey of its leader (even he admits it was a fluke—he won the prologue in 1995 when heavy rain began falling and slowing most of the field after he finished). Last year he briefly wore the golden jersey of the leader of the Vuelta a España.

Durand's specialty is the long-distance attack, often solo. He won the Tour of Flanders in 1992 with a 217-kilometer kamikaze ride that formed his character. Sometimes it works, much more often it doesn't, but Durand has forged an identity. He is not simply "you." Except when he is—as when the boss announces that you are overpaid and underperforming.

Late in March, Braeckvelt let it be known to the Belgian press that, judging by his results, Durand was not worth whatever unspecified salary he is paid. The *directeur sportif* added that in December he told Durand he'd better have some big results this year to help him find a new employer for 2001 and admitted that he tried to shop the rider to two French teams.

"If any team wants to take him now, he's free to go," Braeckvelt concluded. A few days later he left Durand off the roster for the Tour of Flanders. When that decision was overruled by higher officials, Durand was given the job of protecting Lotto's leader, Andrei Tchmil, over the first 150 kilometers of the 269-kilometer course.

"I asked him to protect Tchmil for 150 kilometers and he did it for 180," a somewhat amazed Braeckvelt said after Tchmil won the Tour of Flanders. Durand finished 72nd.

The next World Cup race was Paris-Roubaix, a classic that Durand says he has dreamed of winning since he was a boy. He was given a free hand.

Beforehand, in Compiègne where the race starts, Durand signed no autographs, exchanged no greetings, signed on for the race and ducked into the team's bus, away from the crowd. He looked strained.

Paris-Roubaix went well for him, up to a point. He joined the first major breakaway, at kilometer 35 of the 273-kilometer race, with 11 others. On the first few stretches of cobblestones, the 12 became seven. Then they were six, with Durand stopped by a flat. When he had a new wheel, he battled on, 55 seconds behind the leaders and alone. A second flat and a third ended his hopes of another long breakaway victory.

Long before, he visualized his triumph. "I enter the velodrome in Roubaix alone," he said. "I'm swept with shivers. I'm happy. I've finally won Paris-Roubaix." Instead, in his 11th attempt, he finished the race in 31st place.

"You never can tell," he said, "an experience like this can help you next time." True, you never know, but you suspect that by now Durand does.

Prophet Without Honor

2000

IN THE CHILL SHADOW, sweat poured from Christophe Bassons's face as he pounded away at the pedals of his stationary bicycle. Around Bassons in the warm-up area, other riders for other teams were working on their stationary bicycles, getting their legs ready for a 7.9-kilometer solitary burst through the woods in eastern Paris.

At the Crédit Agricole encampment Stuart O'Grady was also sweating and sensibly wearing a heavy jacket over his jersey. So were Lauri Aus at the AG2R trailer and Jacky Durand at the Lotto tent. Nobody else looked to be working with Bassons's single-mindedness.

Outside the Jean Delatour team truck, he wore a T-shirt. Underneath, showing its black straps, his heart rate monitor relayed data to a meter on his handlebars. Shifting gears, rising on his pedals, Bassons kept his eyes steady on the readouts.

He had a mission as he prepared for the prologue of the Paris-Nice race in the Bois de Vincennes. The nail that stands up shall be driven down, and Bassons, a Frenchman who will turn 26 in June, has been that nail for the last year. Rightly or wrongly, he has been hammered.

His problems date to the Festina Affair, the systematic use of illegal performance-enhancing drugs that was exposed in the 1998 Tour de France, implicating most of the Festina team from France. After Festina's expulsion from the Tour, some of the team's biggest riders confessed and some didn't; the case drags on in the French justice system, with a trial now scheduled late in the autumn.

Although early testimony was hazy and nuanced, it showed that Bassons was one of three members of the team to have refused to participate in the drugging. Another was Patrice Halgand, 26, a Frenchman.

They are teammates again now with Jean Delatour, a new team in the French second division with a budget of 15 million francs ($2.2 million) and the goal, of course, of riding in the Tour de France.

Bassons and Halgand took different paths to Jean Delatour: Halgand remained with Festina until this season while Bassons left and joined La Française des Jeux last year. They diverged in another way. Halgand has said almost nothing about drugs in professional bicycle racing while Bassons has never stopped talking about them.

Proclaimed as a symbol of the new rider and even the new Tour, Bassons wrote, or had written for him, a daily column for *Le Parisien* newspaper in which he talked often about drugs in the sport. Bassons especially irritated other riders when he said on television that it was not possible to win a daily stage simply on talent or class.

Finally, Lance Armstrong, the American who was winning the Tour and who is a strong believer in rehabilitating the sport by not talking constantly about doping, told him publicly to pipe down.

"Armstrong told me: 'Why don't you just go away?'" Bassons wrote in a column before the 12th of 21 stages. So he did, quitting the race and saying he felt "psychologically isolated," unsupported by his teammates.

They responded last month. In a letter signed by the eight other riders for La Française des Jeux in the Tour, Bassons learned that he had been cut out of the team prizes in the race.

They amounted to 349,300 francs, which were divided among the other riders and staff workers.

For his two weeks' work, Bassons was given the money he personally won. It amounted to 500 francs. Saying that he was entitled to 20,000 francs, he called the letter "a knife in the back" and "another example of the hypocrisy that reigns in the sport." No appeal of the split is possible.

In the Bois de Vincennes, Bassons was finished now with his warm-up and began to towel his face dry. He hurriedly signed a few autographs and turned away from a journalist trying to talk to him. "No time for that," he said. "I've got to work." Then he spent the next 10 minutes doing nothing more than adjusting his uniform before he rode to the starting ramp.

Despite his long and thorough warm-up, Bassons finished 45th in the field of 157 riders, 22 seconds behind the winner. That was Laurent Brochard, also a former member of the Festina team, who served a suspension for drug use and is now the leader of Jean Delatour. For the team, it was the first victory in its short history.

OUT OF NOWHERE

1996

VICTORIOUS IN THE TOUR DE FRANCE, Bjarne Riis rode across the last finish line in Paris with his arms upraised in a V and some big questions in his slipstream.

First, how did Riis, a 32-year-old Dane who leads the Telekom team from Germany, progress to dominating winner of the three-week Tour after he floundered in two races half that long just a month ago?

Second, what happened to Miguel Indurain, also 32, a Spaniard who rides for Banesto and who won the five previous Tours but slid to 11th this year, 14 minutes 14 seconds behind Riis?

Last in, first out: Indurain appeared to have been the victim of many factors, including age, weather, a weak team and, most startlingly, a lack of peak condition.

"Last year he looked ripped, like lean," said Frankie Andreu, an American with the

Motorola team who has ridden and finished the last five Tours. "You looked at him and 'Holy cow, man, he can rip the cranks off the bike.' This year you didn't see that kind of definition."

The first 10 days after the start in 's-Hertogenbosch, the Netherlands, were marked by incessant cold rain and even snow in the Alps. Indurain prefers heavy heat, which he found too late, and was unable to shed a bit of extra weight he brought to the Tour.

While it was no more than a kilogram and a half (about three pounds), which he expected to lose quickly in the usual Tour heat, even that little makes a major difference in the mountains to a rider of Indurain's size: 1.88 meters (6 feet 2 inches) and 80 kilograms (176 pounds).

The weight and the bad weather, combined with a team lacking the usual locomotives to help Indurain over the first climbs in the mountains, reduced his chances of a record sixth victory.

So did the odds. Four men—Jacques Anquetil, Eddy Merckx, Bernard Hinault and Indurain—have each won the Tour five times, and only Indurain has won the race five times consecutively. None of them has won the world's greatest bicycle race at the age of 32 or older.

Then how did Riis emerge at that age to beam as a French military band launched into "There Is a Lovely Country," his national anthem, to salute the winner?

Apparently, the Dane is a late bloomer. Fifth in the 1993 Tour and third last year, he did not assume the many responsibilities of a team leader until this year. Before that he was a support rider and a lieutenant in France and Italy. When he joined Telekom this season, he announced that his only goal was to win the Tour. He started slowly and was still unimpressive last month.

"In the Dauphiné and Tour of Switzerland," where he was left far behind in June, "I was sick," Riis has explained. "Not until the championship of Denmark did I find my best form."

He won that race and for the first nine days of the Tour wore the red jersey with the white cross of the Danish champion. Then he donned the luminous yellow jersey of the overall leader of the Tour, never to lose it during the rest of the 3,900-kilometer journey.

Tens of thousands of Danes, all of them exuberant and some possibly sober, traveled to Paris in buses plastered with Riis banners to help celebrate the first victory by a Dane since the Tour began in 1903. It has been interrupted only by both world wars.

Riis finished 1:41 ahead of his 22-year-old teammate, Jan Ullrich, a German. Ullrich trailed by 3:59 until he easily won a long time trial the day before the end, finishing 56 seconds ahead of Indurain in second place and 2:18 ahead of Riis in fourth.

Third overall was Richard Virenque, a Festina rider, who became the first Frenchman since 1989 to stand on the final one-two-three podium. Another Frenchman, the much and justly maligned Luc Leblanc, who rides for Polti, finished sixth, giving citizens of the host country a day to crow about. They will, they will.

For his overall victory, Riis collected 2.2 million French francs ($434,353) from a total prize pool of more than 12 million francs.

Erik Zabel, another German with Telekom, wore the green jersey of the points champion, worth 150,000 francs. Ullrich received 1.1 million francs for finishing second and 100,000 as the best rider under the age of 25.

Added to the money each received on a daily basis for wearing the various jerseys and winning five stages, it amounted to quite a haul for Telekom.

Last year the German team was admitted to the Tour at the last moment and had to share a berth with ZG Mobili from Italy. Then, over the winter, Riis was signed on as leader and the blitzkrieg began.

A Tough Interview

1998

DON'T ASK BJARNE RIIS if this is a comeback year because, as far as he's concerned, he hasn't been away. "No, really not," he says curtly. "Really not."

He knows as well as anybody that after he won the 1996 Tour de France convincingly, he finished seventh last year, more than 18 minutes behind. He knows that among his five victories last year, the only one that mattered was in the Amstel Gold Race in May, when he overpowered the field, rode alone to victory and indicated that his form for the Tour in July would be as dominant as it was the year before.

Then he encountered the Tour's mountains and found that he suddenly could not climb them with the power and ease he had shown in such abundance.

Don't ask him if he's looking for revenge because, the Danish rider insists, he's not mad at anybody or anything.

"The same," he says, "really not."

He turned 34 in April, old for a racer, but who can take revenge on time? The man who won the Tour de France last year is Jan Ullrich, a decade younger than Riis. Who can take revenge on a teammate and friend?

So, no comeback and no revenge. Perhaps he hopes to prove something this year in the Tour de France?

"Might be," he responds with his first show of animation. "But really I don't think I have to prove anything. What do I have to prove?"

He indulges in a long pause. The interview is going like a soliloquy from that other Dane, Prince Hamlet. "What do I have to prove?" he repeats. "To everybody and myself that I'm still going strong." He looks reassured by his answer.

Riis is eager, perhaps frantic, to show that he is not what some suspect: a one-off, a rider who won only one big race in a career that is now in its 12th year. A longtime support rider and lieutenant for stars, he became a star himself in his first opportunity, at 32. But the question remains, Is he star or meteor?

Like Ullrich, who gained 10 kilograms during the winter and then had to interrupt his training and racing because of illness, Riis is behind in his schedule. He crashed during a training ride in Denmark in February and broke his right wrist, which kept him out of races for nearly two months.

Although the injured wrist still bothered him in April, making it difficult for him to pull the handlebars, he said as he prepared for the one-day Classique des Alpes that he felt no discomfort now. A stickler for diet and conditioning, he looked trim.

"I don't think I'm behind in my training," he said. He finished the multiday Peace Race last month in fifth place—"Pretty good, yeah," he decided.

"And last week I won a race in Spain," he added, referring to a stage in the Bicicleta Vasca.

"No worries," he summed up, looking worried. That may be no more than the realization that the ball is over and Bjarne Riis has turned back into a pumpkin.

Telekom was a minor team when he joined it and in 1995 was allowed into the Tour only as a merged entry with the equally undistinguished ZG Mobili team from Italy. From the start, Riis instructed the team in diet (bee pollen is said to be one of his secrets), training methods and Thinking to Win.

"He's the one who took Telekom to this level," said Udo Bölts, a teammate. The emergence of Ullrich two years ago and the development of Erik Zabel as a star sprinter at the same time contributed to the resurgence.

"Riis brought us a winning spirit," said Rudy Pevenage, Telekom's assistant *directeur sportif.* "He's a real professional, always looking at the details. The other guys look to him and do what he's doing."

The Dane is famous for his careful preparation of a major race, scouting routes long beforehand and deciding where attacks are likely to succeed. In team meetings the day before a Tour de France stage, Riis will sometimes correct team officials who have mistakenly explained a bend in the road.

"They'll say it turns sharp to the right here and very politely Riis will say, 'No, it turns to the left there, they made a change over the winter,'" said somebody who knows about these team meetings.

Like Ullrich, who finished 14th, Riis rode a strong Classique des Alpes, finishing seventh, a second ahead of his teammate and rival in the Tour de France. Like Ullrich again, he left the next day to scout out sites in the Tour.

Ullrich was off to see most of the roads in the Alps, but Riis, who has already visited and ridden over these climbs this spring, was heading toward the only spot he did not yet know, the 53 kilometers between Montceau les Mines and Le Creusot where the final time trial will be held a day before the finish in Paris. Often, that time trial decides the race.

GREAT DANES

1997

CITY MOUSE AND COUNTRY MOUSE do have some things in common. They are both Danes in their early 30s, they both race bicycles for a living and they are both at the top of their sport. So what if they don't overwhelmingly like each other?

Country mouse is Bjarne Riis, a 9-to-5 kind of guy, definitely a brown bagger, who rode in the service of others for nearly a decade and rarely won a race himself. At age 32 last year, he bloomed as the leader of the Telekom team in Germany and won the Tour de France in dominating style, taking the leader's yellow jersey halfway through the race and holding it without problem.

When he retires in a few years, Riis will surely return to his hometown of Herning (population 57,000) in western Denmark, open a bicycle shop and coach youngsters, just like his father.

City mouse is Rolf Sørensen, 32, who has been a star all this decade, winning such vaunted races as Paris-Tours in 1990, Liège-Bastogne-Liège in 1993, Tirreno-Adriatico in 1987 and 1992 and Paris-Brussels in 1992 and 1994.

Back in 1991, when Riis was laboring as a *domestique*, Sørensen wore the yellow jersey in the Tour for four days until he crashed, broke a collarbone and had to withdraw. He is as articulate and outgoing as Riis is shy. Their fan clubs, Danish journalists say, are entirely different: Sørensen's tends more to the country-club set, Riis's to the blue collar. They have been rivals since they both turned professional in 1986, and each accused the other of costing him victory in the 1994 world championship road race by not sacrificing his own chances.

Sørensen comes from Copenhagen, the capital, and a city more than 20 times bigger than Herning. Since his father is an industrialist, he grew up rich and long had a reputation as a playboy, which, in this sport, meant little more than he dated women and drove a sports car. Then, in the middle of the decade, his victories turned sparse.

Now Sørensen is winning again. He was first in a stage in the last Tour de France and might have won two stages if Riis had eased off and not led the charge that overtook Sørensen in the final kilometer into Gap. He took the silver medal in the road race at the Olympic Games in Atlanta, won the Tour of Flanders and is tied for the overall lead in the World Cup.

That series of one-day classics continues with the Amstel Gold Race in the Netherlands before adjourning until August. Sørensen said that he hoped to do well in the Amstel as a stepping-stone to overall victory in the World Cup. "This is always my part of the season," he said. "Now and normally in the autumn."

That leaves only the summer as a hole in his form, but the summer is Tour de France time, a time, as Riis well knows, when victory makes a career. So Riis is not among the leaders in the springtime World Cup races; he is riding now as preparation for a peak in July.

What does Sørensen think of Riis's possibility of repeating his victory in the Tour de France? "If he rides like he did last year"—a stage victory in the Alps and another in the Pyrenees, a second place in the daylong showdown into Pamplona, second and fourth places in the two time trials, a total display of power—"he should have a chance."

City mouse looked pleased with his mild putdown of country mouse.

Reasons to Be Nervous

1994

OF COURSE HE GETS A BIT NERVOUS now in the sprint, Laurent Jalabert admitted with a defensive, lopsided grin.

Defensive because sprinters, especially first-rank ones like Jalabert, do not usually say they feel fear when a race nears its finish and dozens of riders tear for the line together in a bumping, swerving wave.

Lopsided because all his upper front teeth are missing. He lost them in a sprint.

At the end of the first daily stage of the 1994 Tour de France, Wilfried Nelissen, a Belgian who rides for the Novemail team, sped toward the finish line in Armentières. One of the French policemen on the edge of the course drifted a few feet out and tried to photograph the onrushing sprint. Nelissen had his head down, as sprinters do, and the policeman had his eye to the camera's viewfinder, which can distort distance.

Nelissen plowed into the policeman and hurtled to the ground. Right behind him, Jalabert, a Frenchman who rides for ONCE, could not avoid the bodies and bicycle and he crashed, too. Behind them, Fabiano Fontanelli, an Italian with ZG Mobili, and Alexander Gontchenkov, a Ukrainian with Lampre, also went down heavily.

Jalabert broke his cheekbones and shattered his front teeth. Bleeding from the scalp, nose and mouth, he did not lose consciousness. Nelissen did, suffering from a concussion and face and knee cuts.

"Oh I remember it very well," Jalabert, 25, said now. "I've watched the videotape but even without it I remember what happened very well." He said he tried to hide his face after the crash so that his wife would not see on television how badly he was hurt.

Both riders were hospitalized and out of the Tour, where they were among the leading sprinters. Nelissen, at age 24 the Belgian national champion, is one of the fastest men in the sport and Jalabert, not quite so fast but perhaps more savvy, won seven stages in the Vuelta a España this spring before the Tour.

The two other riders, Fontanelli and Gontchenkov, walked across the finish line, towing their bicycles. After X-rays, Gontchenkov learned that he had broken his right arm and had to quit the Tour; Fontanelli remained and competed in the next day's sprint, finishing ninth.

After a month off to recuperate, Jalabert and Nelissen have resumed racing and were among the starters in the 250-kilometer Paris-Tours classic.

"It's long, maybe too long for me," Jalabert said beforehand at his team hotel in Les Ulis, a suburb of Paris. "I still lack a little condition but I've got the morale and maybe that will make a difference."

He regained his morale, he continued, in the Tour of Catalonia, when he won a stage for his first victory since the crash. Even better, he won the stage in a sprint.

"In a sprint, yes," he repeated.

The question was delicate: Did he get nervous now in the sprint, especially if he was near the front?

"A little. When a sprint starts to go really fast, when it gets dangerous, for an instant it starts to come back to me. But even if it's difficult to forget, it's over.

"We start sprinting and I can't let it bother me," he continued. "What I think about when we start the sprint is that I have to do better than I did in the last sprint."

He shifted in his chair and tugged at his jersey. He had answered these questions before but not often.

"Something like that marks your career," he said. "But you can't let it bother you. My job is still to sprint and win races. That's what I did and I hope that's what I'll continue to do."

Unlike the Frenchman, Nelissen has refused to watch the accident on video and does not like to see photographs of it. He can sound brusque when asked if he has overcome the effects of the crash.

"Yes, yes," he answered before Paris-Tours as he fiddled with his bicycle's rear wheel. "Everything okay, no problems." He barely glanced up.

The Belgian has competed in sprints and won them too since the crash. Early in September he won a *kermesse*, basically an exhibition race, in Belgium and then finished first in the Grand Prix d'Isbergues in France.

"That felt good," Nelissen said. "But it's a small race, not like this one here."

Paris-Tours is indeed a bigger race, a World Cup classic that often is decided by a sprint at the end of the broad, long Avenue de Grammont in Tours. So it was again Sunday.

The pack was bunched as it came down the 2,400-meter-long straightaway and the sprinters were fighting and swaying for position. About 150 meters from the finish, Christophe Capelle, a Frenchman with the Gan team, was bumped, put on his brakes as he headed for the steel crowd barrier and lost control of his bicycle. Down he went and down went five riders behind him. They were all in the second wave of sprinters.

A few yards ahead, unaffected by the crash, the top sprinters continued to strain for the line. Riding in that group, Jalabert and Nelissen finished eighth and ninth, the highest-placed Frenchman and Belgian, as Erik Zabel, a German with Telekom, won by half a wheel.

"I lacked a little juice to finish the day well," Jalabert told a reporter for the newspaper *l'Equipe*, "and I've never been so well placed for the sprint in Paris-Tours as I was today.

"Only," he added, "there are always these little lights that flash in your head as if to say: Attention, danger."

No. 1 in the World

1997

SCHOOL WAS OUT IN MAURS LA JOLIE so that students could watch the start of the Paris-Nice bicycle race, talk with their favorite French riders and ask for their autographs. Richard Virenque had his clique and Luc Leblanc his, but the throng, several dozen children, that waited by the gray and yellow ONCE bus was interested only in Laurent Jalabert.

That's the way it has gone in all the towns and villages along the Paris-Nice route down the center of France.

In Dun sur Auron, spectators spent half an hour chanting his nickname: "Ja-ja, Ja-ja." In Chalvignac, after his stage victory, he was mobbed as he left the victory podium. In Châteauroux, loud applause started as Jalabert walked onto the stage with the rest of the ONCE team. When he was introduced, the applause turned into a standing ovation.

Granted, life is quiet in Châteauroux, almost in the dead center—the monument marking that spot is a few dozen kilometers east—of France. There were a few movies showing, there was a flea market scheduled and there was the railroad station, which seems to be a hangout for those who want to watch trains rush through on their way to Limoges. But the big draw was Jalabert, the only one of the 152 riders to win a standing ovation.

"There are champions that everybody admires," wrote *l'Equipe* of Jalabert. "They seem to come from another world, they have another dimension. And there are champions that everybody loves . . . because they've had their misfortunes, because they've had to earn their success, because, in addition to their talent, they resemble the rest of us."

The French understand that, and so does Jalabert, who has mixed happily with all the crowds, signing any piece of paper thrust at him, chatting with one and all. He feels special warmth toward Paris-Nice, he says, since this race was the first of his major victories last year.

This was where his career really began, he says. A year later, at 27 and in his eighth year as a professional, he is France's biggest sports hero. In one year he rose from 16th place in the computerized standings of riders to first, far ahead of the man in second place, Miguel Indurain, who has won the last five Tours de France.

Jalabert showed again Wednesday how strong he is, winning the fourth stage of Paris-Nice after a final 7.6-kilometer climb at Millau. Second in the 164-kilometer stage was Lance Armstrong, 15 seconds back, duplicating their one-two finish Tuesday. Jalabert led the race, by 35 seconds, and looked stronger every day.

"The best man won again today," Armstrong said. "It's no surprise, he's the No. 1 rider in the world."

Before last season, the public knew Jalabert mainly from the photograph showing him sitting on the road in Armentières with his face covered in blood after a policeman taking a photograph blocked the sprint finish of the first stage in the 1994 Tour. Jalabert went down, losing some teeth and breaking his cheekbone and jaw. He needed more than three hours of surgery and then about six weeks of recovery.

Something happened to him over that next winter, something that he seems unable to explain. He went from a sprinter, and not even a top one, to a winner of a season-high 22 races, including Paris-Nice, the traditional opener of serious racing after a month of tune-ups. Following that he won the Milan–San Remo and Flèche Wallonne one-day classics and the three-week Vuelta a España. He finished fourth in the Tour, winning every Frenchman's heart by sweeping to easy victory on July 14, Bastille Day.

"He did it all last year," said Armstrong. "He made a big bound. It's so alarming. He went from being basically one of the best field sprinters into being a guy who won the Tour of Spain."

Anybody who talks with Jalabert comes away unsatisfied with his answers to what vaulted him to the top. "It's the result of several years of work," he says. "Physically and psychologically, I've grown enormously."

He shies from hints that, when he was recovering from his crash, he realized that bicycle racing was more than a sport. To statements that he suddenly understood his fragility and was now overcompensating for that knowledge, he provides only a wan smile.

"I've learned to attack," he responds.

THE QUESTION

1999

"PANTANI, WHY?" SAID THE BIG HEADLINE in the Italian newspaper *Corriere dello Sport,* echoing the question that a shocked nation was asking.

There was no immediate answer from the star racer and national hero. Marco Pantani was in seclusion at home after he failed a blood test and was not allowed to start the next-to-last stage of the country's biggest race, the Giro d'Italia, which he was leading by more than five minutes.

The news that an idol had been disgraced by implications of doping sparked a wave of disillusionment among Italians. But not only Italians.

The embattled sport of professional bicycle racing this time finds itself involved in a scandal that implicates its charismatic leader—the reigning champion of the Tour de France. If bicycle racing was in trouble, now it is in crisis.

The 29-year-old Italian, the winner last year of the Tour and the Giro, showed a level of 52 percent in the count of red corpuscles in the blood sample he gave to inspectors. The permitted level is 50 percent in tests administered by the sport's governing body, the International Cycling Union. He was immediately barred from competition for at least two weeks.

On the awesome peak of the Gavia, 2,621 meters (8,599 feet) high and a major climb in the Giro, a crowd estimated at 200,000 waited vainly to cheer Pantani on. When the word spread that he had been disqualified, a great sense of anger and sadness swept the fans, according to the French sports newspaper *l'Equipe.*

"For me, it's the end of a dream," said a man identified as Francesco, 65. "He restored a sense of pride to Italy. But that's over now. He tricked us, and I can't forgive him."

Another fan, Andrea, who was wrapped in a pink flag to match the pink jersey that Pantani had worn as the race leader, was equally bitter. "This is a catastrophe for bicycle racing," he said. "Enough! It's all over. What's the point of waiting for the race to come by? Why should I applaud the riders? They're all the same."

Even Prime Minister Massimo D'Alema sounded stunned. "At this time I can imagine the bitterness felt by this great cyclist, a bitterness that I share," he said.

The newspaper *La Gazzetta dello Sport,* which organizes the Giro, devoted its first 15 pages Sunday to the case. In a front-page editorial that he described as one of the saddest articles he has written, the editor, Candido Cannavo, said: "What hurts me most is the sharp sense of betrayal, on both a human and sporting level. I don't know how far Pantani is to blame or how far he is a victim of shameless provocation, but it's betrayal all the same."

Far less prominently, the paper reported that Ivan Gotti, an Italian with the Polti team, had taken the lead in the race. When the Giro finished in Milan, Gotti donned the overall winner's pink jersey, just as he did two years ago.

Despite Gotti's victory, the team's sponsor, Franco Polti, declared that racing was in crisis. "Let's stop the sport for a year and talk about all the problems," he said. "Then begin again from zero."

Sounding equally depressed, Jean-Marie Leblanc, head of the Tour de France, said, "We thought everybody understood that times had changed. Obviously not.

"I don't know if this is the fault of Pantani alone or of somebody in his team. I only know that those who did this are irresponsible."

The blood test that Pantani failed is technically not a drug test. Introduced in 1997 ostensibly to safeguard riders' health, the tests hint at the use of an illegal performance-enhancing hormone, EPO, which bolsters red blood cells and thus the amount of oxygen that is carried to muscles. There is no blood or urine test that can identify EPO.

Pantani, who rides for the Mercatone Uno team with a shaved head, a ring in his left ear and the nickname of "Il Pirata," must pass another test of his hematocrit, or red blood cell, level after he finishes his 15-day suspension from competition.

Hours after the race set off without him, he emerged from his hotel and said that he was crushed. He noted that he had known setbacks before, including a collision with a car that kept him from riding for a year, and then added, "For now, I'd like only a little respect. I'm sorry for cycling, which, once again, comes out looking . . ." He did not finish the sentence.

But others did. A wide range of riders and officials admitted that the sport had been discredited again by an ongoing scandal related to drugs that began last July in the Tour de France.

"This is bad news for the whole family of racing," said a French rider, Cédric Vasseur of the Crédit Agricole team, at a race in France.

UP FROM THE RANKS

1992

CLAUDIO CHIAPPUCCI DOESN'T LOOK, act or sound like somebody who spent much time burning the midnight *olio* when he was a young student in Uboldo, Italy. Mostly *niente*, he says of his academic achievements, admitting that he shone only at recess, when he had a chance to play goalie in soccer. But he must have been paying attention the day his history class discussed Napoleon, another shrimp with humble origins, and his famous dictum: "Every corporal carries a field marshal's baton in his knapsack."

Corporal, at best, was Chiappucci's rank before the 1990 season. After turning professional with Carrera in 1985, he toiled as a *domestique* as team leaders came and went—Roberto Visentini, Stephen Roche, Urs Zimmermann, Flavio Giupponi. Never did Chiappucci move into their ranks. "I'm an attacker," he likes to boast. "That's my temperament. But I know what people said about me: I make a lot of noise but I don't win." Not until 1989 did he record his first victories, in the Coppa Placci and the Tour of Piedmont.

Then, in 1990, at the age of 27, he exploded: in Paris-Nice, a stage victory and the jersey of the best climber; in the Giro, 12th place and another top climber's jersey; in the Tour de France, second place behind Greg LeMond and eight days in the yellow jersey. Coming off that Tour, he finished third in the Championship of Zurich and fourth in two more World Cup races, the Wincanton Classic and the Grand Prix of the Americas. From the depths of the computerized standings, Chiappucci vaulted to second place behind the Italian star, Gianni Bugno.

Funny, but he didn't sound like a corporal now.

"My goal is to become No. 1 in the next couple of years," he said. He was talking specifically about FICP points but left no doubt that the Tour de France also figured in his ambitions. "What happened to me last year in the Tour wasn't a piece of luck," he said in 1991, referring to his second place. "LeMond was the lucky one, lucky to have a dope like me as his opponent. To tell the truth, LeMond didn't win the Tour—I lost it.

"Let me assure you it would be different now," he warned. When the 78th Tour started in Lyon, he got a chance to prove those words. Although he finished on the victory podium again, in third place this time, he still could not sway those skeptics who did not think of him as a true champion.

Among them was LeMond. "It's one thing to have a good Tour de France, it's another to win the Tour de France," he said. "There's a big difference between third and first." Or even second and first. Chiappucci, he gets no respect.

He was a grand part of the Italian Renaissance in cycling—victories by riders from the Boot in six classics and two major tours in 1990—but still people tended to write him off. Other Italian stars, mainly Bugno and Moreno Argentin, made no secret of their dislike for him and his strong ambitions. He was not always respected on his Carrera team: "When you get a puncture, he doesn't always listen when you holler at him to tow you back to the pack," a teammate complained while Chiappucci was still a *domestique.*

This animosity filtered through to the *tifosi*, the excitable Italian fans, whose hearts belonged to Bugno. Chiappucci might have finished second in the 1990 Tour and Bugno seventh, the *tifosi* said, but it was Bugno who recorded victories in the two most prestigious stages, the fabled climb at Alpe d'Huez and sprinters' showcase at Bordeaux.

Basta, Chiappucci decided, enough. "I rode for 143 days last year, more than any other rider," he said. "The same for the two years before that." He was so busy working to better himself, he added, that once again he had been unable to find time in the off-season to marry his fiancée, Rita. (Until his long-delayed marriage late in 1992, Chiappucci lived with his mother.)

In the spring of 1991, a new Chiappucci showed up after another winter spent riding cyclo-cross when he wasn't attending testimonial dinners at every school, orphanage and old folks' home in his native province of Lombardy. "Anybody who invited me, I showed up," he reported.

The corporal had grasped the baton.

He started getting star treatment from his Carrera *directeur sportif*, the savvy Davide Bofiva. Suddenly Chiappucci was a franchise rider, the right man in the right place, as Carrera, after years of glory, was no longer deep in Italian riders capable of winning races. Del Tongo had Franco Ballerini and Mario Cipollini, Ariostea had Argentin and Adriano Baffi, Gatorade had Bugno and Marco Giovannetti. Behind Chiappucci, Carrera had only an aging Guido Bontempi.

Reveling in their depth and newfound ambition, major Italian teams had ended years of isolation and begun competing seriously outside their home country. The Tour de France, not the Giro, became Bugno's prime goal as he—and Chiappucci, of course—hoped to become the first Italian to win it since Felice Gimondi in 1965. In this new international atmosphere, Carrera decided to let Chiappucci skip the traditional early races at home and go instead to Spain. While the rest of his compatriots were riding Tirreno-Adriatico to prepare for Milan–San Remo, the first World Cup classic and the showpiece of the early Italian season, he was finishing second in the Tour of Murcia and fourth in the Catalan Week, where he pulled off a rare double by winning a mass sprint in the morning and a time trial in the afternoon. That done, he returned the next night to Italy.

Chiappucci made his move halfway along the 294-kilometer Milan–San Remo, attacking at the exit of the Turchino mountain tunnel and speeding away on the descent. He cruised into San Remo a winner by 45 seconds. "Any time I can attack and make people suffer, I'm off," he said while he waited for the pack to show up.

Third in the 1991 Tour de France, second in the 1992 Giro: The FICP points were pouring in and, as Bugno languished through a dreary spring, the gap between them began to close substantially. Suddenly the No. 1 ranking did not seem such an outlandish goal for Chiappucci, the little corporal no more.

Clown Prince

2001

WITH CUSTOMARY BRAVADO, Claudio Chiappucci announced the other day that he has retired as a bicycle racer. At its most attentive, the world yawned.

First, he turned 37 last month, at least a few years beyond the usual retirement age. Second, in a team sport, Chiappucci has not had a team since 1998. He rode for the microscopic RosMary squad in Italy that year and recorded one victory, a critérium in Toulouse. Last year he was inactive although always on the lookout for an employer.

What he seemed not to understand was that his time was over: He was old, he had no results and he was stained by two drug tests he failed in 1997. Lately his name has surfaced only in official reports listing those Italian stars suspected of having used illegal performance-enhancing drugs during the 1990s.

None of this seemed to bother him, at least not publicly. From long practice, he knew how to deal with rebuke.

The rider who gave himself the nickname "El Diablo" did indeed ride devilishly—his constant attacks infuriated other riders, especially because his forays down the road were so often fruitless.

But not always. Chiappucci was unknown for the first six years of his career as a professional, which started in 1985 and which did not see him win a race until 1989. Then, in the 1990 Tour de France, he was one of four riders who broke away on the first stage and finished with a lead of 10 minutes 35 seconds. One by one, three of the four fell back as the Tour continued, with only Chiappucci resisting.

The man Greg LeMond scornfully called "Cappuccino" to emphasize his anonymity was still in the yellow jersey, five seconds ahead of LeMond, on the next-to-last day of that Tour. In a time trial, LeMond destroyed him by more than two minutes and won his second consecutive Tour. Chiappucci, though, finished second overall.

He was second again in 1992, behind Miguel Indurain, the same order in which they finished the Giro d'Italia a month earlier. That year Chiappucci pulled off his greatest exploit, a monumental attack that succeeded.

As the Tour moved through the Alps, he set off with nine companions on the second of five major climbs, shed the nine and continued alone over the third climb and for the rest of the afternoon. In all, he rode without a relay, which would have given him a chance to save some energy, for nearly four hours under a fierce sun. His solo attack covered nearly 230 kilometers and ended in easy victory in Italy, where hordes of his compatriots gave him the acclaim he so badly needed.

The feat helped him win the King of the Mountains jersey in the Tour for the second time to go with his three victories in that classification in the Giro. Otherwise, his record was spotty: a second place in the world championship road race in 1994 and victories in the Milan–San Remo classic in 1991 and the Clasica San Sebastian in 1993.

Always jokey, Chiappucci liked to play the clown, arriving sometimes on his bicycle at the start of a race with his feet propped on the handlebars or inviting his mother to come pray for him in the grotto when the Tour visited Lourdes. (She did, to no material avail.)

His final years were desolate. In 1996 he quit the Carrera team, with which he had spent his entire career, rather than share the leadership with Marco Pantani, who went on to supplant Chiappucci in the Italian fans' hearts. In 1997 Chiappucci was expelled from the Tour of Romandie for failing a blood test and then from the world championships.

The night before his ouster at the worlds, he spoke in an interview about his dreams of victory the next day in the road race. Smiling, affable, again the rascal, he was confident that he was in his best form in years. It can happen, he said, I can make it happen. And then he was forbidden to start the race.

Now he is retired, taking up the post of director of sports in his native region of Italy. He made the announcement just before the Milan–San Remo race. When they heard the news, most people looked startled that until then he had still considered himself a racer.

Grassroots Race

1999

A FELLOW WHO IS CRAZY FOR BICYCLE RACES (or was crazy for them—since the drug scandals began unfolding, he's not sure) blundered into one the other day. Nothing to it: He walked out his front door on the way to the Laundromat and there the race was.

Actually it was the warm-up to the race. Trying to look focused, small groups of riders were coming up the street, turning at the corner and heading west. Small signs announced that a dozen streets would be closed to traffic most of the afternoon to accommodate the Grand Prix of Suresnes, a town just a few kilometers from the Champs-Elysées but light years away from Paris.

Seventy riders were entered, an official announced over a loudspeaker. Twenty were from the host club, Les Bleues of Suresnes, with a dozen more from its neighboring town, Puteaux. Mysteriously, the team from nearby Reuil-Malmaison did not appear to defend the championship it won last year. The small crowd behind an optimistic number of barriers took this news calmly.

The fellow who is or was crazy about bicycle racing plopped his laundry bag at the curb, sat on a bench and, to pass the time before the start, began to read about the sport in the weekend papers.

Good news: Patrice Halgand, 25, one of only three Festina riders not accused of systematically using illegal drugs last season, won the A Travers le Morbihan race in Brittany. Not much of a race, true, but one of the rare victories this year for what was the world's top-ranked team before the scandal. More important, according to a reporter from *l'Equipe,* it was a triumph for health, virtue, pleasure and nobility.

From Germany, more cheer: The unheralded Jimmy Casper celebrated his 21st birthday by beating a top sprinter, Erik Zabel of the Telekom team, in a stage of the Tour of Germany. "Beating Zabel in a sprint, it's a dream," said Casper, who rides for La Française des Jeux. "I was just a kid when he was winning stages in the Tour de France. If I had known that one day I would beat him . . ." Two days later, Casper did it again.

Good news from Italy: The reason Ivan Quaranta dropped out of the Giro d'Italia after two stage victories was fatigue, as his team said, but fatigue brought on, as it did not say, by a night spent at a disco, celebrating. The 24-year-old Quaranta, who rides for the Italian second-division team Mobilvetta, was out dancing until 4 A.M. to mark his victories over Mario Cipollini, the Lion King. Ah youth!

Bad news, too: Sixty-seven of the 135 professional French riders showed "metabolic anomalies" in their latest round of health tests. Fifty-four of them had an excess of iron in their blood, often a byproduct of the use of the artificial hormone EPO.

And more: The Casino team in France has suspended Laurent Roux, a fine rider, for failing a drug test administered by the French police. Officials of the Italian Olympic Committee descended on a race in Spain to question Italian riders about drug allegations. The Cofidis team in France reaffirmed its suspension, with pay, of its leader, Frank Vandenbroucke, for failing a drug test. He says, nevertheless, that he will resume racing June 10 in the Tour of Luxembourg.

On the street in Suresnes, the race was ready to start. This was the sport at its most basic, with no team cars, no gangs of mechanics and masseurs, not even a *directeur sportif* in sight. An official explained that the race consisted of 55 laps in a rectangle through town, a total of 88 kilometers, with a cup and a bouquet to be awarded to the winner and top team. The course was totally protected, he continued, with wardens at each corner to prevent cars from entering. At that moment, a fire truck sounded its siren and raced toward the starting line. The riders made way, smiling.

"It's just a bunch of guys, 17 to 47, out racing," explained one of those guys after he dropped out early. He had plenty of company as heavy heat and continuous attacks wore down the pack. At about the midway point in the race, a group of 10 riders had a minute's lead and managed to keep it.

The group turned the last corner in a rainbow of color and that comforting sound of the whirl of wheels and dashed for the finish line. Far down the Rue de Verdun in

Suresnes, somebody held his arms aloft in victory. The loudspeaker announced the winner but his name and club came across in a crackle of sound.

Everybody gets to do it all over again in a few weeks when the next-door town of Puteaux presents its Grand Prix. Race time is 8 P.M. It's always a good time, even when times are bad.

THE NEW EDDY MERCKX

1987

ERIC VANDERAERDEN STILL REMEMBERS the nasty name Belgian children called him when he went on training rides. "They'd recognize me out on my bicycle and they'd scream at me, 'The new Eddy Merckx, there he is, the new Eddy Merckx!'" Not just admiring children, adults called him that, too. "As an amateur, I won two races one weekend and everybody—the fans, the writers—bombarded me with that name: the new Eddy Merckx.

"It was a typical Belgian problem," Vanderaerden explained one gray day in the spring of 1987 as he sat on a rumpled bed in his motel before the Paris-Roubaix race. "Everybody wanted to believe there was a new Merckx. I'm not the new Eddy Merckx and I knew it from the start. I never could have been. But other people didn't understand that. When they realized that I wasn't the new Eddy Merckx, they got back at me, as if I had let them down. They blamed me because their predictions didn't work out. But I never made their predictions and I never felt I let them down."

In the decade since he retired, nobody has come close to being the new Eddy Merckx, although that label has been hung on a number of young riders. Who could replace the man who won five Tours de France, five Giros d'Italia, three Paris-Roubaix, three world championships and any other race that comes to mind. Milan–San Remo? seven times; Liège-Bastogne-Liège? five times; Paris-Nice? twice; the record for the hour? of course.

The pressure of Merckx's legacy has contributed to the downfall of many a promising Belgian professional. Daniel Willems burned himself out in a series of tantrums, and Fons de Wolf took shelter in the playboy's life. A handful of others, like Guido van Calster and Eddy Schepers, proved to be simply one-day new Eddy Merckxes, winners of a race early in their careers before they subsided into journeyman roles with teams far from Merckx's Belgium.

As an added pressure, the whole of Belgian cycling went into a long decline with Merckx's retirement in 1978. Many thought the drought was over when Vanderaerden arrived as a professional in 1983 at the age of 21. As an amateur he was so dominating that the Belgian Cycling Federation was forced to waive its rule that a rider could turn professional only at 22.

"Vanderaerden made a mockery of the rule," a Belgian sportswriter explained. "He won nearly every race he wanted to win. It was bad for him and for all the others."

In his first professional race, Vanderaerden won the prologue of Paris-Nice and promptly began building his reputation as the bad boy of cycling. Mounting the podium solemnly, he refused to smile for the photographers and mumbled only a few words to the reporters. He repeated that performance four months later when he won the prologue in his first Tour de France. This was not the way a young rider ought to behave, everybody agreed, clucking about his coldness.

In the next few years, Vanderaerden added another facet to his already unhappy reputation: He seemed willing to do anything to win. In 1984 he jumped from Belgium's Aernoudt team, which promptly collapsed, to Raleigh (now Panasonic) in the Netherlands, explaining that the stronger team could help him more. That spring, in the Ghent-Wevelgem race, he was caught by the camera first getting a teammate's push near the finish and then grabbing the jersey of a rival, Guido Bontempi, to slow him in the sprint. (Both actions were unavailing as Bontempi crossed the line first by a wheel over Vanderaerden.)

That same year, the Belgian's aggressive, coming-through style was blamed for a crash in the Tour de France that sent Marc Gomez into a hospital for months to repair a shattered leg. In 1985, Vanderaerden was disqualified with Sean Kelly for mutual bumping in a sprint finish in the Tour de France. Later in that race, after Vanderaerden won a time trial, it was widely suggested that for long miles he had illegally drafted behind a Belgian press motorcycle.

Whether by hook or by crook, Vanderaerden won five stages of the 1984 and 1985 Tours de France, plus the Tour of Flanders and Ghent-Wevelgem classics in 1985. But 1986 was a disaster. Although he won the green points jersey in the Tour, he failed to win a sprint, instead finishing three times second and three times third in stages. From 24 victories in 1985 he slipped to 14 the next year, mainly in minor races. Now the talk was about another new Eddy Merckx: Edwig Van Hooydonck, then 20 years old, who celebrated his first spring as a professional by winning the semi-classic Flèche Brabançonne race.

Over the winter, Peter Post, the Panasonic *directeur sportif,* called Vanderaerden in for a talk. Post, a former racer who won the 1964 Paris-Roubaix and long reigned on the six-day track circuit, runs his cyclists on a short leash, demanding discipline, sacrifice and teamwork. He was understood to have told Vanderaerden that his results were disappointing and that he blamed the rider's lack of concentration on his business investments. There was a carrot with the stick, however. To prove Post's faith in him, Vanderaerden would become Panasonic's designated leader. "That's not an honor you earn around a table," the rider said proudly.

Early in the spring of 1987 he reverted to his anything-to-win tactics. In the Tour of the Mediterranean, an unimportant prep race, he was accused of having hitched onto a team car for a tow during a time trial. The practice is not unknown in mountain stages but is rare during a time trial, since commissaires, the official judges, usually ride in the team car accompanying each rider. In the Tour of the Mediterranean, however, commissaires were in short supply. When the furor subsided, Vanderaerden had been banned from French races for two weeks and the original Eddy Merckx, now a bicycle supplier to the Panasonic team, thundered that if the charge was true, Vanderaerden should be strongly disciplined by the team.

Sitting now in his motel room before Paris-Roubaix, Vanderaerden preferred not to discuss Merckx's anger. He dismissed the French suspension as "unjustified," adding that "it was based on only one witness, a French journalist." Looking embarrassed, Vanderaerden insisted somewhat unconvincingly that he had not hitched his illegal ride. "Who saw me?" he asked. "Who can prove it? But it is all over now," he said.

Was he hoping to take his revenge in Paris-Roubaix? "This is a different race." Then, after a pause, Vanderaerden tried to explain himself. "When I started, I had just come over from the amateurs. I wanted to keep winning. I didn't worry then about public opinion. Later I learned that it took time to move in new circles. Now I think about the reaction, what the press will think. In the first years, it all had to do with being hungry for victory. I was so hungry, I was willing to run anybody over to win."

He recalled his first Milan–San Remo race, in 1984, when he finished third and charged loudly that an Italian conspiracy had contributed to the victory of Francesco Moser. "Now I might think the same thing, but I'd put it another way." Vanderaerden smiled at the reminder that when he finished second in the 1987 Milan–San Remo, he wept openly but blamed nobody.

He spoke proudly of his sprinting skill: "It's something you're born with, you just discover you've got it," and nonchalantly about his bumping duel with Kelly in the Tour de France: "Nothing personal about it, it happens in a shoot-out between two sprinters."

Did he prefer to ride for the star-heavy Panasonic team or would he be happier on a lesser team where he did not have to share the victories? "In the short run, there's no difference." Riding for a lesser team, however, would mean that the spotlight would fall directly on Vanderaerden, a difficult position for a Belgian in the post-Merckx era. "If I'm on a lesser team, I'm No. 1 and I have to win," he said. "Kelly can handle that pressure better than I can. Here we have other possible winners. For the races I want to win, I get the necessary support. Post doesn't put the riders up against each other."

He was hopeful about Paris-Roubaix, he said, and felt strong.

Strong wasn't the word, even in the Flemish he spoke through an interpreter. The next day Vanderaerden cleared the cobblestones in fourth place and spent the final 15 kilometers chasing down three journeymen leaders, Rudy Dhaenens and Jean-Philippe Vandenbrande, both of Hitachi, and Patrick Versluys of ADR. Nearly a minute ahead, the breakaway group seemed unaware of the closing doom until Vanderaerden was suddenly among them, looking them over with what seemed to be a small smile. Five kilometers remained. "Here I am boys, and who's going to beat me now?" Vanderaerden asked them.

In the last few hundred meters, they failed to make a move as Vanderaerden bolted past and flung up his arms in victory well before the finish line. Five seconds after he crossed, the rear tire on his bicycle blew out.

The Belgian newspapers were full of his triumph the next day, calling the race an epic Paris-Roubaix in which 47 riders finished what 192 started. Many of the papers also noted that right behind the leaders, in fifth place, was the precocious Edwig Van Hooydonck. He was described more than once, of course, as the new Eddy Merckx.

TEAM WORKER

1996

RELIEF IS IN SIGHT FOR FRANKIE ANDREU, so close that he can measure it: 437.5 more kilometers, roughly 270 more miles, three more days and he will have finished his fifth Tour de France in five attempts.

"I'm pretty confident I'll make it now," he said before the start of the 18th stage Thursday. "I really had doubts that first week whether I would make it, so I'm happy." He crashed and injured his left leg and right ankle on the first stage in the Netherlands and then struggled through more than a week of rain and heavy wind.

"Every year, you say, 'Never again, it's so hard and so miserable,' and then when the Tour rolls around again, you start getting motivated and you find yourself back here. But it's not fun."

For Andreu, an American with the Motorola team, the last few days especially have not been fun. Forget about the mammoth stage Wednesday into Pamplona, where he finished 70th, 33 minutes behind. Forget about the stage Thursday, when he had to push his weary legs over 154.5 kilometers from that Spanish city to Hendaye, France, on the Atlantic.

The last few days have been draining because the native of Dearborn, Michigan, has been Motorola's point man in memorial observances for Fabio Casartelli, the young rider who died a year ago Thursday after a crash on a descent in the Pyrenees in which his skull was fractured.

On Tuesday, Andreu was the riders' representative at a small service at the monument to Casartelli at the spot where he crashed and hit a cement stanchion. Thursday morning, as the only member of the team still in the Tour who rode last year with the 24-year-old Italian, Andreu received a plaque and a bouquet from the leading rider under the age of 25, a competition that has been named for Casartelli.

"I think about him every single day I get on the bike," Andreu said afterward. "When I get on the bike, I'm doing my passion, my love for cycling, which is just what he was doing. I feel fortunate, and every day I miss him."

Then it was time to race and Andreu joined the pack for the trip over five climbs to Hendaye. Andreu is in 111th place overall, a meaningless statistic since he is the model support rider, a man who works to protect his leader, not his own interests.

The man in the overall leader's yellow jersey, Bjarne Riis, a Dane with Telekom, was untroubled, as he no doubt will be all the way to Paris, where the race ends Sunday.

For Andreu, that day will mean "a lot of personal satisfaction," he said. "If I start something, I'm committed to it, not only for myself but for the team. It's the Tour de France. A lot of people don't find any prestige in finishing it but I do.

"I agree that it's more important to race the Tour than ride it just to be able to finish. I've been trying to race it and finish, too."

Like everybody else on the Motorola team, Andreu is uncertain about his future since the sponsor will bow out at the end of this season and no replacement has yet been found.

"Whatever happens, I want to keep racing in Europe," he said. "I feel every year I'm getting stronger, although the problem is that every year the pack is getting stronger, too. I keep being a little bit behind but I'm going in the right direction. I think I can still do some damage in Europe.

"If this team can't stay together, then I have to move on. This sport is a business. So I've been talking to other teams. But I'm holding off as long as I can."

Although Andreu's first preference is to stay with his current team, he does not anticipate major difficulties in finding another employer in Europe. Andreu is known as a selfless rider and a strong one—this spring he won the Olympic trials in the United States and a place on the five-man team that will race on the streets of Atlanta. "I know what my job is there," he said. "To work for Lance Armstrong," the leader of the American and Motorola teams. "I have no problem with that. That's one of the things that's kept me on this team: being realistic about what my job is.

"I know I'm not a champion, I know I'm not going to win the classics or the World Cup overall.

"I think I make the most of my abilities. Lance is in a class of his own. So I go to Atlanta and work for him because he has the best chance of doing something. I know that.

"I know what my role is and I give 100 percent and that's the best I can ask for. Sure I would love to win more but it doesn't come so easy. At all."

Second Fiddle

1998

AMID SCATTERED CRIES OF "LA BROCHE, LA BROCHE," a nickname he despises, Laurent Brochard was making his way to the sign-in for the 18th stage of the Tour de France when the air suddenly became blaring with air horns, screams and squeals. None of the tumult was meant for Brochard but for the rider who had come up in his wake: Richard Virenque. Thus it always was.

Brochard, a 31-year-old Frenchman who rides for Festina, and Virenque, a 29-year-old Frenchman who rides for Polti, were teammates the last few years on the Festina team. Virenque was the leader, the winner four times of the Tour's King of the Mountains competition, the third-place finisher two years ago and the fans' favorite. Brochard, who wore his hair then in a long ponytail and sported a bandana over his head, was a good support rider who unexpectedly won the world road race championship in 1997 but was dogged by bad crashes that limited further feats.

They were both part of the nine-man team that was expelled from the last Tour after Festina officials admitted that the riders used illegal performance-enhancing drugs. Although Virenque has not made such a confession, Brochard has, and he served a six-month suspension before he was reinstated by Festina with a 50 percent pay cut.

In this Tour, Virenque has won the polka-dot jersey of the best climber again, ranks fifth overall—the highest-placed Frenchman by eight places—and is again the darling of the French public, which continues to post signs of support along every route.

Brochard resides in 81st place, drew little encouragement from the fans even when the race passed through his native region of the Sarthe and has accomplished nothing. Even Friday, the last real chance for a Frenchman to win the country's first stage before the grand finale in Paris on Sunday, la Broche (the spit, as in a rotisserie) was not part of any attacks, not even the late one by 13 riders that produced a winner. Although the flat stage was watched by crowds so enormous that a visitor hesitated to recycle a peach pit or apple core out of the window of his car in fear of skulling a spectator, the start was delayed for the second successive day by a worker protest, this time farmers angry about something. Only Virenque's many fans seem to have no grudge against the Tour, and it tried to ban him.

THE PELOTON IS TOGETHER AS IT PASSES THROUGH A TOWN IN A WHIR OF WHEELS AND THE FLASH OF TEAM JERSEYS.

The young Chris Boardman, right, king of the time trials; a triumphant Greg LeMond, below left, as he won the 1989 Tour de France; and a despondent Laurent Fignon, below right, as he lost that race in a time trial.

Over the dreaded cobblestones of the Arenberg forest comes the pack in Paris-Roubaix.

The pack in Milan–San Remo heads down to springtime on the Italian Riviera.

FESTINA RIDERS LYING AS THEY DENIED DRUG USE. GRAEME OBREE ON HIS HOMEMADE BICYCLE.

Tens of thousands turn out in Villava, Spain, to honor Miguel Indurain, the local hero.

Johan Museeuw, Belgium's king of the classics.

In Italy, the *tifosi* hang a banner to encourage Marco Pantani.

Bernard Hinault, top, with his familiar glare, whips through a time trial.
Amid snow and fog, the pack heads for the sun in Paris-Nice.

Bumping along the cobblestones on one of the dozen short hills in the Tour of Flanders.

Robert Millar, top, in the jersey of the Vuelta's leader; Eros Poli, bottom left, dreaming the possible dream on Mont Ventoux; and Laurent Jalabert, bottom right, after the 1994 Tour de France crash that cost him his front teeth.

gan
gan
CREDIT LYONNAIS
PINARELLO
MAPEI
QUICK-STEP
MERCKX
QUICK-STEP
MAPEI
MAPEI
COLNAGO
QUICK-STEP

In bicycle-made Brittany, the crowds are always huge for a race.

Gilbert Duclos-Lassalle, top left, wearing a victory smile. Jan Ullrich, top right, leading the Tour de France with Bobby Julich in his wake on a climb. Axel Merckx, bottom, bearer of a fateful name in the sport and determined to make his own mark.

Up a hill in a Belgian village goes the pack in Liege-Bastogne-Liege.

Claudio Chiappucci happily on the attack, as usual.

Lance Armstrong, wearing the Tour de France's yellow jersey and looking resolute, leads Marco Pantani on a climb.

Like Virenque, Brochard is not granting interviews during the Tour. But he does not wear the enigmatic smile that his former leader does. Brochard is stony-faced in his silence. The only sign of individuality is the way he wears his long hair now, in small, tight, beaded braids.

"Forget that part," said Neil Stephens, another former Festina rider, who retired after the expulsion and is one of three members of that nine-man team not to have confessed to doping. "Underneath, he's very timid and a gentleman."

Brochard has had his moments other than the world championship. In the 1996 Tour, he became one of the dozen Frenchmen ever to have won the stage on July 14, the national holiday, and in 1993 he was second in the French championship. The world championship, however, was his apex.

When he came home to Le Mans, the mayor presented him with a medal. The city's soccer and basketball teams both asked him to throw out the first ball at their games. His fan club numbered 300. A month after his victory, 2,000 supporters flocked to a rally at a race track near his home to honor him.

Brochard talked about a recurrent dream after he won the championship: "I see myself passing the line, my arms raised, I hear the speaker screaming my name, I'm up on the podium, and they're giving me the rainbow-striped jersey. It fits me like a glove."

He was not allowed to ride for France and defend that jersey after the Tour expulsion. On Friday, he was in Festina blue when he crossed the line in 50th place, simply another face in the crowd, and just ahead of Virenque.

In Defense of Virenque

1998

MOCKED NOW AND ENTIRELY ABANDONED, Richard Virenque responds with the spirit of the adolescent he remains: In a temper tantrum, he said that he is through with professional bicycle racing. If the sport doesn't need him, he raged, he doesn't need it. (Offstage sounds of feet being stamped and doors being slammed.) Nobody loves him.

"He would love to continue and make dreams come true," his older brother explained, "but he is not being given that chance."

In other, less-shimmering words, because of his involvement in the doping scandal that became known in the last Tour de France as the Festina Affair, none of the 20 or so top teams is willing to hire the star climber and team leader at his salary of about $1.6 million a year.

Alas for him, many of those teams are not willing to hire him at any salary. His years of cockiness, his frequent and public criticism of rivals, his many small snubs are not forgotten. And even those teams, like Rabobank in the Netherlands or Vitalicio in Spain, that bear no grudge, have no money left in their budget after they filled their rosters months ago.

At age 29 and in the peak years of his career, Virenque has become—made himself—extremely damaged goods. By continuing to insist, as is his right, that he is not guilty in the Festina Affair, he has lost his credibility. In less than half a year he has plunged from the darling of the French media and fans to an object of ridicule on a nightly television program, where his moronic puppet is portrayed wearing a helmet of hypodermic needles.

Defending himself, he never addresses the issue of whether he took the illegal and artificial hormone EPO or the equally illegal human growth hormone. Seven of his eight teammates have admitted this and been rehabilitated: All have jobs for the next season, which starts in February. The eighth teammate retired, leaving only the team leader still battling the tides.

Virenque's unvarying defense is that he has never failed a drug test. By now, everybody else understands the difference between not proving positive in a doping test and not taking drugs.

That was the point of the Festina Affair, in which the team's *directeur sportif*, its doctor and its chief *soigneur* admitted they had engaged in a systematic program of supplying and administering illegal performance-enhancing drugs while keeping the riders within medical bounds where they would pass cursory tests. Only when the French police showed up with sophisticated tests was the lying exposed. Then the *soigneur*, Willy Voet, long Virenque's confidant and surrogate father, named him as one of those most active in the program.

So, mercifully, 12-year-old girls have stopped squealing his name. All those spectators who stood at the sides of the Tour's roads bearing signs of support after the expulsion of his team—"With You, Richard," "No Tour Without Festina"—have decided that they can do "Without You, Richard."

His sponsor offered him a chance to return if he would admit all and, incidentally, take a 50 percent pay cut. Virenque rejected both conditions.

Even for those who think him a twit and do not for a moment believe his threat to quit, there has been something unseemly about the way Virenque is being pummeled. Everybody is piling on. He says the evidence shows his red-cell level was below the limit of prima facie guilt of doping and the press quotes unnamed doctors to dispute his reasoning. Sealed court dossiers are published in the tabloid press. The newspaper *Le Monde* suddenly analyzes his character under a headline "The Man Who Wanted So Much to Be Loved," as who doesn't?

Suddenly also, newspapers are noting that Virenque never wore the Tour's yellow jersey for more than a day, and that back in 1992; that he may have finished second (1997) and third (1996) in the Tour but never first; that he may have been King of the Mountains in the Tour from 1994 through 1997 but that his record in other races is nearly nil.

Television commentators now talk about how eager Virenque was to be interviewed, how much he craved attention. The same commentators fail to remember the Tour stage of July 18, 1995, when the Italian rider Fabio Casartelli was killed in a crash in the Pyrenees and the French cameras stayed with Virenque as he rode to victory over a demoralized field. The commentators' celebration was so splashy and went on for so long that Italian journalists with the race circulated a petition of protest—which, predictably, was ignored.

Virenque deserved his day of glory, the French argument ran. The country didn't have much else to cheer about in that Tour. Now the script has changed and Virenque is yesterday's hero. The frenzy has turned against him, sulking and out of work.

Too bad for him. If you can't kick a man when he's down, the crowd asks, when can you kick him?

Back in the Saddle

1999

ANYBODY OUT THERE remember the Alka Seltzer commercial that warned against trading a headache for an upset stomach? You do remember it? Franco Polti doesn't.

Polti, the head of an Italian company that makes electrical appliances, sponsors the professional bicycle team that bears his name and that ranks fifth in the world. He announced at a news conference in Paris that the team had hired Richard Virenque, the bad boy of

French cycling, while firing Luc Leblanc, the somewhat reformed and definitely faded bad boy of French cycling. Make that Alka Seltzer a double.

Neither announcement was a surprise, the rumors having flown about Leblanc for months and about Virenque for a week. "He's a great rider," Polti said of Virenque. "He's got character. That's why I said let's sign Virenque. I like riders like Virenque."

He was also forthright enough to say that his company is hoping to double its business—vacuum cleaners, irons, coffee machines—in France and thought a French star would attract publicity.

Virenque returned the compliments. "I'm happy and proud that Mr. Polti has shown confidence in me," he said as photographers cried "Richard!" in a perfect imitation of the way French teenage girls do—or did before he was implicated in a drug scandal and expelled from last year's Tour de France.

"It's a chance to restart my career," the rider said. "I thank the boss for giving me this opportunity." Both he and Polti used the word "rehabilitate" often.

The contract is for two years and no salary figure was made public although, with performance bonuses, it is believed to equal the $1.6 million he made last year with Festina, a French team.

Yes, that's the same Richard Virenque who announced in a hissy fit a month ago that he was retiring at the age of 29 because nobody believed in him. Translated, that meant nobody would hire him.

Virenque insisted that his announcement of his retirement last month was sincere, while noting that he had been negotiating with Polti since October. After his announcement, two teams in Spain and two in Italy, including Polti, intensified negotiations.

The sticking point with all of them was money: Virenque makes a lot of it for a rider with few victories. Virenque said he was unsure of his program with Polti, which has a strong climber in Ivan Gotti, who won the Giro d'Italia in 1997.

"I hope, I wish to participate in the Tour this year," Virenque said. "The Tour is my reason for living." He said his priorities were the Tour, the Vuelta a España and the world championships, which will be held in Italy this year.

Much less attention was paid to the fate of Leblanc, who did not attend the news conference. Brash and self-centered, Leblanc might have been a role model for Virenque, with whom he has feuded for years. Now 32, Leblanc has not had much success the last few seasons and was let go, although his contract still has a year to run, for unspecified reasons.

One of them may have been the way he unilaterally withdrew from the Tour last summer to protest doping investigations.

In a discreet way, Polti said, "We've given Leblanc a lot of chances."

Another team official offered a bit more: "It's up to the lawyers now. As far as we're concerned, he's no longer with the team. But if we have to take him back, we'll take him back."

Progress Report

1999

SO, RICHARD VIRENQUE, how's the Tour de France going for you?

"Very well, thank you," he said in one of the few in-depth interviews he has granted. "Good-bye. Have a nice day."

Adhering to his oath of silence toward the unfriendly press during the race, Virenque is letting his performance speak for him—that and his fans. As far as performance goes, the controversial Frenchman is wearing the polka-dot jersey of the Tour's top climber and hopes to win it for a fifth time, nearing the record of six set by the exalted Féderico Bahamontes and Lucien van Impe.

Virenque also ranks seventh overall, 10 minutes and 3 seconds behind the leader, Lance Armstrong of the U.S. Postal Service team, and aimed to improve that position once the race got through its second rest day and launched into the first of two days in the Pyrenees.

"Anything can still happen," he said in another slip of the tongue a few days ago. "We've got to wait for the Pyrenees. Everything depends on whether Armstrong cracks there. If he doesn't, the best I can hope for is the podium," the one-two-three set of steps at the Tour's finish in Paris.

Until then he is content to be just another face in the crowd in the gunslinger all-black costume he wears on social occasions, such as dinner, while his Polti teammates sport the yellow and red jersey of their sponsor. During the race, he wears the top climber's jersey, which he gained mainly by finishing sixth on each of two stages in the Alps. True to his habits in his glory years, Virenque does not deign to accumulate points by contesting each hill along the way, preferring to make his mark in a big way.

He has 174 points, followed by Mariano Piccoli, an Italian with Lampre who does rush to the attack on the small hills, with 142.

If he remains generally unpopular with other riders, the 29-year-old Frenchman has kept his strong grip on his fans. He is cheered loudly at daily sign-ins.

Conversations along the sides of the Tour's many roads show that most of his older fans regard him as a sort of populist hero, a rebel whom the system has tried and failed to break.

He was first banned from this Tour, then reinstated by the International Cycling Union, the overlords of the sport. Although he is still under formal investigation and has been accused of doping by former team officials, including his longtime masseur, Virenque has not admitted it.

From the start of the race, the roads have been dotted with pro-Virenque posters and banners. "Go, Richard," "Courage, Richard," "Thank you, Richard," they read.

"I Believe in You, Richard," said a sign on a recent morning. The couple holding the sign were asked why, exactly, they believed in Virenque.

"Because they're all drugged," the man said, pointing to the pack gathering at the starting line. "Why should Richard be singled out?"

Out the Front Door

1995

AT THE AGE OF 41, GILBERT DUCLOS-LASSALLE understood that it was time for him to retire from bicycle racing. No question about when—he decided during the winter that this would be his last season—the question was how.

"I want to go out by the front door, *la grande porte*," he explained. "It's a choice I made, to retire, go out by the front door, leave when I'm still riding well.

"Too many riders stick around one season too many, then have to leave by the back door. I'm taking the front door."

The Frenchman, who rides for the Gan team, spoke while standing in the parking lot of a hotel in Béthune in the north of France. For the last time in his 19 seasons as a professional racer, he was watching a team mechanic assemble his bicycle for a road race the next day. The height of the seat was checked, the gears adjusted, the tires spun. Duclos-Lassalle looked satisfied.

"Yes, it's my last race on the road," he said of the Grand Prix d'Isbergues. "I've got several races on the track afterward—Grenoble, maybe Bordeaux—and a few critériums, but this is it on the road."

A native and resident of the southwest, he likes racing in the north. The wind, the rain and fog suit his image as one tough rider.

He has to be tough, of course, to have made it to 41 when most riders retire at 33 or 34. He had to be tough to overcome an accidental shooting—Duclos-Lassalle is quite the hunter—that shattered his left hand a decade ago. He was back riding in months.

And he had to be tough to last 19 seasons in a career that saw him acclaimed in 1979, when he won Paris-Nice and become a great French hope, and then was nearly forgotten for a decade while he registered just one big victory. That was Bordeaux-Paris in 1983.

Late in the 1980s, he stopped being a team leader and dropped down to road captain, the veteran who decides tactics during a race, looks out for the leader and instructs the young. A road captain gives and obeys orders.

In 1990, he yielded his best chance for a stage victory in the Tour de France when, far ahead of the pack in his own region of the Pyrenees, he was ordered to stop and wait for his leader, Greg LeMond, whose tire had punctured just as his opponents attacked. Duclos-Lassalle waited, helped LeMond catch his opponents and finally rode with the triumphant American into Paris.

The thrill of the team's victory lap on the Champs-Elysées more than made up for the lost chance at a stage victory, Duclos-Lassalle said. Road captains are expected to talk like that.

After the 1990 Tour, he thought he might last another season or two. In 1992, he changed his plans. That was the first time he won Paris-Roubaix, a race designed for tough guys, riders who can take the pounding over the cobblestones, the choking dust when the weather is dry, the slippery mud when it rains.

The next year, he won Paris-Roubaix again. Once might be a fluke, two consecutive victories were a career. Just short of his 39th birthday then, Duclos-Lassalle became a national hero in a France short of people to admire.

"I've had many fine moments—Paris-Nice, Bordeaux-Paris and the two victories in Paris-Roubaix," he said in the parking lot as the work on his bicycle was finished. Neither officials of his Gan team nor his fans minded that he had not won a big race since 1993.

If he did not win, he did continue to ride hard, trying to win. He remained a rider of the old school, a reminder of the Peugeot team that dominated French racing in the 1970s when he joined it.

"Nineteen seasons, always with the same team," he said. "Different jerseys—Peugeot, Z, Gan—but always the same team." He will remain with Gan next season as a public relations official.

Knowing that this season would be his last, he cut his schedule, picking his spots. No Tour de France last July, not at his age. The Grand Prix d'Isbergues, a secondary race in the Coupe de France competition, seemed a good place to finish his days on the road. Fans in the north adore him.

The night before the race, he was told that the Gan riders were expected to sign in a bit early for the 11:30 A.M. start.

"A ceremony," explained Michel Laurent, the team manager. "They want to make a speech about you." Duclos-Lassalle beamed.

Sunday morning, he rode away from the ceremony with a bouquet, words of praise for his endurance singing in his ears.

The race started with two circuits of the town of Isbergues and Duclos-Lassalle quickly attacked, showing them all how tough he can still be. He led the pack out into the countryside, was caught, attacked again, was caught again.

At kilometer 30 of the 206-kilometer race, with a strong head wind blowing, he attacked again and was joined by two Lotto riders. That was the last the pack saw of them. When their lead exceeded 11 minutes with more than half the race done and the pack indolent in its chasing, it became clear that one of the three would win. As he said later, Duclos-Lassalle knew he would not be that man.

His companions, the Lotto riders, were prepared to play him between them. The tactic is simple and almost always efficient: Teammate A attacks, forcing the rival to use his strength to catch him while Teammate B follows along in the slipstream. When A is caught, B attacks. Eventually the rival is exhausted and either A or B jumps off alone to the finish line.

The race never quite came to this cat-and-mouse game. Teammate A, Sammie Moreels, set the pace over every one of the 13 hills, with Duclos-Lassalle always second and Teammate B, Frank Corvers, behind them both, saving energy in their draft. With six kilometers to go, Corvers attacked and opened a lead of 50, then 100, then 150 meters. Duclos-Lassalle could not respond. Corvers finished first by 50 seconds. His arms raised, as if in victory, blowing kisses to the huge crowd, Duclos-Lassalle was an easy second over Moreels.

Afterward they made a few more speeches about Duclos-Lassalle—a monument to bicycle racing, he was called—and gave him four trophies. One was for having been the most combative rider in the Grand Prix d'Isbergues.

He received it with a special look, a special smile, understanding that he had gone out of the sport exactly as he wished, by the front door.

Exit Motorola

1996

THE RACE OF THE FALLING LEAVES they call the Tour of Lombardy, the Italian classic that just about closes this dismal bicycle racing season. What began in February as a time of hope and surprise ends later this month in failure and shock.

The Motorola team was in Milan for Lombardy and will race next at the World Cup finale, the Japan Cup outside Tokyo. After that, oblivion.

"The end of an era or something like that," said George Noyes, the team's chief mechanic, trying to sound chipper. "Life goes on," added Geoff Brown, one of his assistants. "One door closes, another opens, hopefully," said Paul Sherwen, the team's publicity director.

Noyes and Brown have been selling bicycles off the back of the Motorola truck at the last few races. They would willingly sell the truck, too, but it has already been bought by the new Cofidis team in France.

Everything must go since the team must. For $500, about $1,000 less than it is worth, a friend of the team—and who isn't these days?—can have Sean Yates's titanium training bike. It's pretty used but so, in truth, is Yates, 36, who was planning to retire to Britain even if the team had found a new sponsor.

Jesus Montoya, 33, is also retiring, to Spain. The ailing Lance Armstrong, Frankie Andreu, Bruno Thibout and Kevin Livingston have signed with Cofidis; Laurent Madouas with Lotto in Belgium; Max Sciandri, Andrea Peron and Flavio Vanzella with La Française des Jeux, another new French team.

Bobby Julich is leaning to a team in Italy and Axel Merckx has said yes to Polti in that country. George Hincapie is going with U.S. Postal Service. Somebody thinks Max Van Heeswijk will join Rabobank in the Netherlands. Kaspars Ozers and Gord Fraser seem to be unaccounted for.

The riders, a generally young and talented bunch, should make out fine. What of all the others—the team officials, masseurs, mechanics, the doctor? So many uncelebrated people, the ones who made it work. In its six years of Motorola sponsorship, the team was highly regarded for its precise organization, its ability to get different groups of riders to their scattered races in comfort, without the helter-skelter atmosphere many other teams endure.

What happens now to the ones who massaged the riders, picked them up at the airport, adjusted the saddle height of their bicycles, inspected their tires, packed and held out lunch bags in the feed zone of so many famous and obscure races, got their luggage to their hotel rooms, found them a glass of milk at 3 A.M., did their laundry and monitored their training?

Noyes: "I'm taking next year off, recovering, hoping Mr. Ochowicz finds another sponsor for 1998." Late in August, Jim Ochowicz, the team's general manager, gave up his search for a sponsor for 1997 and immediately began looking for one for the year after that. "If he finds a sponsor, we'll start again next August or September, I hope. That's hopefully, that's ideally. It remains to be seen if I can handle standing still for a whole year."

Brown: "I've signed with U.S. Postal Service, so I'll be on the circuit again next year. They're based near Geneva but on the French side of the border, so I'll be moving down there from Belgium. The reality is that everybody needs a job."

Sherwen: "I've had a foot in both camps for the last few years and now I'll be dedicating a lot more time to my television career: Channel Four in the U.K., ESPN and ABC in America, SABC in South Africa, SBS in Australia. I do a monthly magazine worldwide called *Velo Magazine*, which is a half-hour program. So I've got a lot of work on my plate. I'm also thinking about something I've been dabbling at for a long time, which is a safari company." Sherwen, a former strong professional racer and once the British champion, grew up in Kenya and Uganda.

Noël Dejonckheere, European operations manager: "First we have to clean everything up. And then after that I'm going to spend some time with my family, take a holiday, do a bike trip for a week and then do a walking trip with friends around Mont Blanc, four or five days, going from hut to hut. If Jim finds something for '98, we have to start working again."

Eddy DeGroote, part-time *soigneur* and jack of all trades, full-time English and Dutch teacher in Belgium: "I have a few contacts, maybe it will be a French team. I've worked with Belgian teams, Dutch teams, an American team and maybe now it will be a French team."

John Hendershot, head *soigneur*: "Yes indeed, I am retiring and very happily. My wife and I are going to start a boarding kennel for dogs, probably in Colorado but maybe Texas. My wife is an animal trainer by profession and worked in several zoos, including the Bronx Zoo. I'm counting on her to handle the mind work and I'm going to do the shoveling. I resigned in the middle of the year. I'm burned out. This is my 13th year doing it full time and my seventh year in Europe with the team. I'd rather leave with people wishing I would stay than stay with people wishing I would go."

Ochowicz: "We're still capable of doing this business and I'm hoping we find a sponsor. I'll be going back home to Wisconsin to work from there. We have to downsize the corporation to squeeze out six or seven months without income while we try to find that sponsor for 1998."

Massimo Testa, the team doctor: "The last 11 years I took a lot of time from my practice, a family doctor and sports doctor, so maybe it's time to stay a little longer at home in Como. I have no motivation to work for another team full time. My wife is American, so I would like to start something in the United States as a coach to individual athletes. But I'm always available to work with anybody from this team."

Max Testa was a youngster working at the University of Pavia in 1985 when the 7-Eleven team, newly turned professional, arrived in his native Italy from the United States to race in the Giro d'Italia. The team's Italian sponsor, Hoonved, a maker of vacuum cleaners, thought a doctor ought to look after the riders in that three-week race.

"They called a doctor who was 50 years old and had worked 20 Giros but he didn't want to work for the team. He said it was not good for his reputation, he was always working for big teams, not little ones from America that nobody had heard of, and he sent me there instead. It was the first American team in Europe. We won two stages in that Giro and I've been with them ever since, 11 years.

"It's sad, you know, like a school vacation, everybody going in a different direction. We were a good team, a little different. It was a big challenge to work with people from so many different countries. So I'm happy. I was lucky to have this job. But you know the good times are not coming back."

Testa shook his head, tried a feeble smile. Yes, you knew that about the good times.

ER-OS, ER-OS

1994

THE HEADY DAYS ARE OVER FOR EROS POLI. No more daily bouquets of summer flowers, no more crowds of young fans chanting his name. Er-os, Er-os. Ah well, Poli says.

When he mounted the podium to sign in for the Paris-Tours bicycle race, several hundred French spectators applauded politely, quietly, just as they applauded politely, quietly, all the other foreign riders. The loud cheering was reserved for French riders.

The race announcer welcomed Poli, proclaimed his victory in the Mont Ventoux stage of the last Tour de France. "A solo attack, climbed alone up the gigantic mountain, the pack chasing him but unable to catch him. Ladies and gentlemen, the winner of the glorious Mont Ventoux stage, Eros Poli." Polite applause.

That same introduction during the Tour started a daily commotion, which became a clamor when Poli took the flowers given him as the race's most aggressive rider and, with a soft smile, passed them out. That was nearly three months ago. Does anybody remember?

"Yeah," Poli said with enthusiasm during an interview. "One guy, before Paris-Brussels, stopped me and asked me, 'Are you Eros Poli?' Just the day before the race, I was doing some shopping in Compiègne, and I said, 'Yes,' and he said, 'Great, fantastic,' and asked me to sign an autograph."

The fans dwindle down to a precious few but Poli does not mind. He knows who he is: a 31-year-old Italian rider for the Mercatone Uno team, a professional for four years and no star. He is a support rider, a spear carrier, and content to be who he is.

Once he might have thought he could become a star. That was in 1984, when he was one of four riders who won the gold medal for Italy in the team time trial at the Olympic Games in Los Angeles. But even as an amateur, he was usually no more than a support rider.

On the national team he worked for Mario Cipollini, the great (just ask him) sprinter, the same man Poli has worked for in his professional career. "On the national team they asked me to prepare the sprint for Cipollini," Poli remembered. "For me it was perfect."

Blocking the wind and setting up a slipstream with his full 6 feet 4 inches, clearing rivals out with his 190 pounds, Poli is a splendid lead-out man. Cipollini rides behind him for the last few kilometers, husbanding his strength, and then zips past and dashes for the line in the final few hundred meters. He wins a dozen sprints that way every season.

"I'm in this team just to work for him," Poli said. "My program is to work for him. It's very difficult to work for myself. I'm strong enough in the sprint to finish fourth, second, third but not first. And it's very important to finish first. Second is nothing. So my specialty is to help Cipollini."

During the Vuelta a España in May, Cipollini crashed when he was elbowed into the crowd barriers by a teammate as they both sprinted for victory. His head injuries and subsequent loss of balance were so serious that he had to skip the Giro in June and the Tour de France. The teammate who put him down, Adriano Baffi, rode the Tour but withdrew after a few stages. That left Poli out of a job, as he put it, and free to seek a victory.

He chose a flat stage, 259.5 kilometers from Rennes to the technology theme park of Futuroscope in western France. "That was a special stage for me—no mountain, all flat, I'm not dangerous for the general classification because I'm way behind the yellow jersey and I feel very, very strong."

He bolted away alone at kilometer 60 and opened a huge gap. Over the silted Loire River, past vineyards and fields of wheat, through alleys of birch trees he went, building a lead that reached a maximum of 18 minutes 30 seconds at kilometer 115. Then the pack came to life. With 30 kilometers left, he was caught. His breakaway had lasted 166 kilometers and 4 hours. Exhausted, he finished 15 minutes behind the winner.

A few days later, he again attacked alone. This time he faced the 1,909-meter-high (6,263 feet) Mont Ventoux—21 kilometers long on a grade of more than 8 percent for 16 kilometers and nearly 10 percent for the rest. "There it was hard. Hard. But I had 40 kilometers of descent, so that was easy."

He did not think he could last, or even get away.

"Not exactly, but I tried. I said that in the first 20 kilometers of my attack, if I could have 5 or 7 minutes' lead, I could try. Then with 100 kilometers to go, I said I could have 40 kilometers to go downhill but I have 20 kilometers to go up. So I need 20, 25 minutes." He had nearly 24, lost almost 20 of them uphill, kept most of the rest downhill and won easily after his 171-kilometer breakaway.

As a souvenir, he said, he has a photograph of the way he crossed the finish line, somehow making a sweeping bow while he pedaled.

He also has his memories. "Maybe now I know I won a big stage because now my form is not good and I remember when it was. A long year—Giro, Tour de France, 100 races. Just three months ago it was so easy. Not so easy but . . ."

Despite the Ventoux victory, he insisted that he has no personal ambition other than to serve.

"No problem. I'm more popular now in Italy but that doesn't change my life. I don't feel more important, nothing special like Cipollini. He wins 10, 11 races a year, I won a stage. In the four years I'm a professional, this is my second victory."

Nothing has changed in his head?

"No," he said quickly. Then he thought about it, his long face moving. "No, nothing." He smiled. Eros Poli was that rare being, satisfied.

Iron Man

1986

FATIGUE DOESN'T START IN THE BODY but in the head, Sean Kelly likes to say. That maxim has been used against his chances to win the Tour de France: In his head, the argument runs, Kelly is convinced that he cannot win the race. His record for futility in the Tour supports this view since, after winning five stages by 1982, he has not crossed a finish line first again, coming in second 11 times.

The trouble is never his condition, because he always seems to be in shape. "A rider says to me, 'I go out training two hours every morning,'" he says. "But I ask him, 'What about the afternoon?'

"I'm not the type to stretch out on the sofa and read the newspaper to relax after a training ride. My life is riding, eating, sleeping."

And so Kelly raised no eyebrows one recent spring when he attended the funeral of Michel Goffin, a Belgian rider who succumbed to injuries suffered in a fall in the Tour du Haut-Var, left church with his wife, took his bicycle out of the trunk of his car, changed clothes in the car and bicycled the two hours back home in Belgium.

"He left here at the end of January and he hasn't seen a suit of clothes since—he wears only cycling equipment and has no social life whatsoever," complained (or boasted) his father-in-law, Daniel Grant, to the *Irish Times* one season.

Grant said his daughter Linda "has seen him for only six weeks since January."

Two other stories about Mr. and Mrs. Kelly come from the British book *Kelly* by the Irish journalist David Walsh:

After a race in the Netherlands in 1984, Linda Kelly was sitting on the family car, waiting for her husband. When she got down, she left a mark where her hand had rested. Kelly wiped away the mark without a word. Mildly annoyed, Linda complained that her husband's priorities were first his car, then his bike and finally his wife, Walsh wrote. "Kelly heard the accusation, turned and with a look of deadly seriousness told his wife that she had gotten the order wrong: 'The bike comes first.'"

During a sports seminar in Dublin, Kelly was asked about sex and bicycling: "Taking the question with total ease," Walsh reported, "he replied: 'I think it is an understandable question, whether a top rider should abstain before a big race or not. My policy is to abstain for a week before a one-day classic and about six weeks before a major Tour. Usually I am away from home a long time before a major Tour, so there is no problem there.'"

Such seriousness has impressed Europeans since Kelly came to the Continent in 1976 just before he turned 20. By then, he had twice been Ireland's junior champion and, after he won a stage of the Milk Race in Britain in 1975, he was named to his country's team for the Olympic Games in Montreal. First he rode under an assumed name—Alan Owen—in the Rapport Tour of South Africa, which was forbidden to international competitors because of the country's racial policies of apartheid. Found out, Kelly was banned from Olympic competition for life and suspended from amateur racing for six months.

Once the suspension ended, he signed with an amateur team in Metz, France. He was a sensation, winning 17 races in four months. This attracted the attention of Jean de Gribaldy, a French aristocrat and former racer who ran a furniture store in Besançon to help finance the professional teams he operated on low-overhead budgets. The Frenchman piloted his private plane to Dublin, hired a taxi to drive 110 miles to Tipperary and interviewed Kelly aboard a tractor at the family farm in Carrick-on-Suir. Kelly signed on to become a *domestique* for de Gribaldy's Flandria team in 1977.

Those were the glory days for the Belgium-based team, whose two stars, Freddy Maertens and Michel Pollentier, terrorized the pack in classics and the flatter stages of major Tours. Kelly learned his trade slowly as a pilot fish, setting up Maertens for his strong final sprint.

"Experience gives me my strength," the Irishman says. "For my first five years as a professional, I took the time to learn my trade." By 1980 he had developed into a fearless and swift sprinter for the Splendor team, winning five stages and the points championship in the Vuelta and two stages in the Tour de France, but he did not really blossom until he rejoined de Gribaldy as the leader of the Sem team in France.

The leader's role fits Kelly well. "The Irishman is the best leader you can have," said a former teammate, Jörg Müller, a Swiss. "He's a real boss in every sense of the word—steady, willing to give a break to his riders." Jean-Luc Vandenbroucke, a Belgian, put it another way after Kelly went down in a mass fall in a race in Spain. "He had a scarred back, ripped shoulders and torn skin on both hands," Vandenbroucke said. "That night, five minutes after he got in bed, he was sound asleep. The next day and rest of the race, I never once heard him complain. In fact, he was in good spirits all the time.

"Somebody like me, who was suffering only because it was a tough race, I was ashamed to admit that my legs ached."

This toughness extends to his conduct on the road. Kelly has been disqualified three times for roughness in Tour sprints and is regarded as one of the premier "arrangers" in the pack, somebody who will rig alliances and victories.

As the leader of a traditionally underpaid and weak team, Kelly often needs the alliances with presumed rivals to further his own ends. For the rigging of victories, there is no defense, and Kelly—a close-mouthed man who has been known to answer a radio interviewer with a nod—has never offered one. In a recent Tour of Lombardy, the prestigious classic that closes the season in Italy, he refused to sprint after the lumbering Giambattista Baronchelli at the finish. Kelly was content with a cynical second place and whatever rewards it brought. Strongly criticized, he answered words with actions, as always, by winning a critérium in Paris the very next day.

King Kelly

1993

OCTOBER, NOVEMBER, DECEMBER: Much of the year is left for those who mark it by the calendar. For those whose measure is the bicycle racing season, the year is near its end.

All that's left are two World Cup races, in Italy and France, and the Montjuich climb in Spain. In less than two weeks, there's nothing except six-day races on European tracks and such Asian oddities as the Japan Cup and assorted spins around Australia.

The transfer period for riders who are moving to new teams officially opened October 1, but anybody who waited until then to plan for next year is in grievous trouble. Although the occasional *domestique,* a low-paid nobody, may still find a job, rosters began to calcify as early as July.

For a star like Sean Kelly, a rider who commands—or at least asks for—a big salary, these could be worrisome days.

"He wants to go on if he finds a good team and gets good money," said Kelly's agent, Frank Quinn, on the phone from Dublin. "I'm telling teams, 'Kelly's available.' They're interested but in the next breath, the teams say their budget is gone." He rated Kelly's chances of riding next year at 50-50.

Kelly puts it a bit higher: 60-40. Salary is not the only negative factor; age and recent performance weigh against him, too.

A critérium is not much of a race to win—just an exhibition, really—but so far this season it's all Kelly has won. Once. He did it in the Netherlands in July, when most other stars were competing in the Tour de France.

While there are riders who base their careers on critériums in Belgium and the Netherlands, Kelly, even at 37, is surely not among such small fry. Not King Kelly, the winner of 33 races in 1984 and the dominant classics rider of the mid-1980s. His record in the one-day events includes two victories in Milan–San Remo, two victories in Paris-Roubaix, two in Liège-Bastogne-Liège and three in the Tour of Lombardy.

King Kelly? He was an emperor. A victory in the Vuelta a España, two victories in the Tour of Switzerland and seven consecutive victories in Paris-Nice. Consider his record in 1986, when he won his third consecutive Super Prestige Pernod award as the season's top rider: first in the Grand Prix des Nations, Tour of Catalonia, Paris-Nice, Milan–San Remo and Paris-Roubaix; second in the Tour of Flanders, Paris-Brussels and Tour of Lombardy; third in the Vuelta; and fifth in the world championship road race.

Now there is the sole critérium victory.

"This year wasn't a very good one for me," he agreed. "I had a crash that knocked me out of the classics for a while, out of Liège-Bastogne-Liège and the Amstel Gold." Coming out of a left-hand bend, he crashed in the Flèche Wallonne in mid-April and strained his groin. "If you get knocked out for two weeks, that sets you back an awful lot."

Some big names are retiring from the sport this year. Laurent Fignon called it quits in August and Stephen Roche a little later, and both are four years younger than Kelly. Nevertheless, Kelly said he was in no rush to leave. Despite repeated rumors that he will not be back when the new season starts in February, Kelly strongly denied that he had made any decision.

"I never said this was my last season—that I never said," he said by phone from his home in Belgium this week as his 3-year-old twins, Nigel and Stacy, played in the background. "I'm stopping sometime but I haven't said just yet."

The decision, he continued, will be made soon after the Tour of Lombardy in Italy. Kelly last won Lombardy in 1991, and another strong performance could sway any doubters.

Can he still win a big race? "I think I'm capable of winning classics, yes," he replied. His hard gaze, those cold eyes, could be felt over the phone. "I've been going well the last three weeks and that gives me confidence for another season. It's really only in the last few weeks that I've been getting the sort of form that I should have during the season."

His fourth place in the Paris-Tours race a week ago is proof that his physical strength is back, but is it too late?

"The motivation is there now," said Quinn, his agent. "And his poor season this year will only spur him on more. We're willing to take a fair reduction in salary from this year."

Kelly is believed to have earned about $600,000 this year from the Festina team based in Andorra. That's a lot more money—about 100 times more—than Kelly earned when he began his professional career in 1977.

"I've seen a lot of change," he said. "The bicycles have changed, the style of racing, the standards have improved, as they have in all fields of sports.

"There are many more riders now at a higher level than there were in the 1980s," he added. "Then you had 15 or 20 riders at the top and there was a step down to the next. Now you have 60 or 80 riders up there."

Are the riders better now or better trained? "When you train better, you become a better rider," he replied. "You have to push yourself to the limit—that's what makes the top riders. Some people can't do it but that's what makes the good ones and the great ones."

As he nears the end of his career, Kelly voices no regrets. "Regrets," he says, repeating the word. "No, I wouldn't call it regrets. But if I could go back and start my career again, there would be things I would change, of course. Everybody would.

"The number of races—I rode too many," he said. "I was going from one race to another, at the beginning of the season especially." He estimated that for years he rode "160, 170 maximum," days a season, or 40 to 50 days more than are customary now. "Then by the time the Tour de France came around, I paid for that," he said.

Although he finished as high as fourth in the Tour in 1985 and fifth in 1984 and won the green points jersey four times, he was never a contender for final victory.

Kelly did not rule out the possibility of signing for another year with Festina, which is undergoing a cutback after a disorganized and unsuccessful season. But if it has no room for him and nobody else does either, he said: "I'll return to Ireland. I don't know what I will do, I haven't really decided as yet."

Quinn summed it up this way: "He has no plans for next year—no driving sports cars, no farming, no doing television commentary. He wants to go on racing."

Kelly seemed uninterested in discussing retirement plans since, in his mind, he is not yet old. Measured by the calendar, perhaps not; measured by this racing season, certainly.

Late Bloomer

1998

THERE WAS A CHILL IN THE AIR and the dark clouds of early morning promised rain. The fields of nearby farms were bare and stalked by hunters. At the start of the Paris-Tours race in suburban St.-Arnoult-en-Yvelines, the gutters were flecked with leaves.

The professional bicycling season is nearly finished. Paris-Tours, a World Cup classic, will be followed on successive Sundays by the world road race championship in the Netherlands and the Tour of Lombardy in Italy, another World Cup classic, before anybody who is still left on the road goes home for the winter.

Hold back the night: The races are ending and Ludo Dierckxsens is just getting started. Let this season continue till February, when a new one begins. He has waited so long for the opportunity and now he bursts with desire.

Dierckxsens calls it ambition. "I'm feeling very strong, healthy and ambitious," he said in his skillful English during an interview. "Ambitious," he repeated.

The Belgian rider for the Lotto team was fresh off a victory in the testing Paris-Bourges race after an impressive three weeks in the Vuelta a España, where he finished

34th overall and second and fifth in two stages. Late in August he was second in the Grand Prix Ouest–France and two weeks before that he was third in the Hew Classic in Hamburg, a World Cup race.

"I've made 600 points this year and I think I'm in the top 50 now," he said. That's top 50 among the world's 900 or so professional riders. He started the season with no points at all because in his previous four seasons as a professional he competed only in the smallest of races, mainly *kermesses,* or afternoon spins around, around and around villages in Belgium. The prizes are minor, as are the teams and contestants.

This year Dierckxsens broke out, moving from the second division in Belgium to Lotto, the only first-division team in his homeland—the big leagues after serving time on the uncelebrated Saxon, Collstrop and Tonissteiner rosters.

"For me," he said, "this is the first year that I have an international program. It's my fifth season with the pros and now I'm in a big team and now I get a chance to ride internationally. And I took that chance."

He did, and he was 33 years old—turning 34 in a few days. When the season ends in a few weeks, he will be two years older than most riders are when they retire.

"I think I can do four, five more seasons," he said jauntily. "I hope so anyway."

Where was Dierckxsens, with his shy smile and vanishing hairline, all those other years before he turned professional at 29, seven or eight years later than most professionals?

"I was working in a DAF truck factory," he said. "Painting trucks for eight years. I had a wife and son and it was steady work. At that time, cycling was a hobby for me. I trained after work but it was pure hobby" while he rode in amateur races.

Then DAF laid off 50 percent of the workforce, not including Dierckxsens.

"When that happened, I had the opportunity to go with the pros and I thought, 'Even though I still have my job, from day to day you can lose it.' So I joined a pro team and I'm very happy I did. After three years, I could have got my job back at DAF. I had to make a decision. And I'm still riding.

"At the beginning my wife wasn't too happy," he admitted. "She didn't like bicycle racing. But if you can earn more money, it's always better. That's why I'm riding, not only for the pleasure but for the money. That's what a professional does."

He has no regrets, he added, that he did not change careers earlier. "You can't turn back time. It's a pity, but no regrets. You can't make up lost time. It's past. You can only live in the present time."

Dierckxsens has been living well in the present. "I was 12th in Paris-Roubaix, fourth in the E-3 Harelbeke, I rode a very fine Tour de Flanders, 13th in the Tour of Galicia."

Three days after Paris-Roubaix in mid-April, he crashed in a Dutch race and broke his right wrist, forcing him out of races for two months. Since then he has risen from his role as a *domestique,* or worker bee, with Lotto to a place on the Belgian national team in the world road race championship.

"I'm a joker or wild card," he said. That means he will not be protected like the team's two leaders, Andrei Tchmil and Peter van Petegem, but will not have as his primary task protecting them. He will be free to ride his own race.

"I think I have a chance there," he said. "My condition is the best it's been this season."

Lance Armstrong, who rode with Dierckxsens in the Vuelta, said: "He can win the worlds. He's a strong guy, a savage. Very aggressive, that's his style. That's the way he can win the worlds if team tactics go his way."

First, of course, was Paris-Tours and the Belgian was not daunted by the fact that the flat race is usually won by a sprinter, which he is not.

"Mostly sprinters win but not always," Dierckxsens said. "I have a chance and I think I have to believe in that chance. Now there are many people who believe in me."

Meeting His Fans

1996

WHEN HE GREETED HIS FAN CLUB, Laurent Roux would have preferred to be alone—off, say, on a huge breakaway in the Tour de France or, even better, a huge and victorious breakaway. Then, like some champions of old, he could have gotten off his bicycle, eaten an ice cream and signed some autographs before resuming his triumphant ride.

Instead Roux was simply another face in the Tour de France pack when it whizzed past an open-air celebration by his supporters that recalled the days when the bicycle race was somewhat closer to the people than modern corporate practices allow.

Roux did his best to make the rendezvous. Sometime earlier, he joined a five-man counterattack to a breakaway, which might have gone somewhere and thrilled his fans, but it was quickly swallowed by the pack.

After that, he could do no more than wave at kilometer 117 of the 15th stage in this 83rd Tour, which covered 176 kilometers of engagingly rolling country from Brive-la-Gaillarde to Villeneuve-sur-Lot in the southwest.

He missed a swell time, complete with free foie gras and the wine of Cahors, two products of the region—as is Roux—in what obviously served the rest of the year as a cow pasture. A seven-person band, including three on accordion, played such tunes as "Go Laurent, He Can Win" and "To the Champs-Elysées, Perhaps He Can Win."

What's with the "perhaps?" That's no way for a fan club to think. All together now every last one of the 262 members of the Association of the Supporters of Laurent Roux: When the Tour ends Sunday in Paris after covering 3,900 kilometers in three weeks, he's a cinch to win.

But not today. Massimo Podenzana, whose fan club, if any, is based in his native Italy, glided across the finish line the winner by 37 seconds after he shed his companions in another long breakaway by low-ranked riders.

Second to the Carrera rider was Giuseppe Guerini, an Italian with Polti, and third was Peter Van Petegem, a Belgian with TVM, 50 seconds behind.

Podenzana, twice the champion of Italy, completed the stage in 3 hours 54 minutes 52 seconds, a stunning average of 44.9 kilometers an hour considering the heavy heat, which reached 33 degrees centigrade (92 Fahrenheit). Where are the snows of yesterweek? A week ago, the Tour had to shorten a stage in the Alps because of a blizzard.

The man who took the leader's yellow jersey that day, Bjarne Riis, a Dane with Telekom, continued to wear it as all the contenders finished 5:38 behind. They were content for a third day to watch each other and await the Pyrenees, where the battle will be joined at the highest level.

That is not yet Roux's. Just 23 years old and in his third year as a professional, he ranks a creditable 40th among the 135 riders remaining. Showing strong spirit, Roux has often gone on the attack in the Tour for his TVM team, which is based in the Netherlands. He joined TVM after his first employer, Castorama in France, folded at the end of last season.

The picture postcard that his fan club was selling for 5 francs (about $1) noted that he has twice been selected to represent France in the world championships, that he won a race in Picardy and finished second in the Classique des Alpes in 1994 and won a stage and finished third overall in the esteemed Tour de l'Avenir in 1995.

This year he has won a stage in the Route du Sud and finished second in the French championship road race.

He has a nice smile, looks good in his team jersey and wears a discreet ring in his left ear. What more could a fan club ask for?

So the tables in the press room after the stage into Tulle were covered with invitations for the hundreds of reporters who travel with the race to attend the shindig in his honor. "Thanks in advance for coming by," the paper read. "Friendship and thanks for your encouragement," Roux wrote underneath.

The food, the wine, the conversations with the people who line the sides of the Tour's many roads were all a throwback to the time, about a decade ago, when such encounters were common.

Let the race go through the village of Renazé, for example, and the members of the Madiot Boy's Club—the punctuation is theirs—always set up trestle tables bearing food and drink in honor of Marc and Yvon Madiot, two fine French riders. Let the race pass through a town in the Dordogne or the Auvergne where a former champion lived and the festivities were repeated.

Everybody, from reporters to team mechanics to the drivers of the race's hundreds of cars, was welcome to enjoy a quick plate of cold cuts, a slice of bread, a bit of gossip. Then, with the race approaching, back into the cars and on down the road.

Nowadays the practice is discouraged by the Tour's organizers. Probably there are insurance risks and possibly there is a feeling that these meals are not quite as chic an image as the race wants to present. Like the homely broom that used to serve as a mast on the bus, known as the broom wagon, that sweeps up riders who have quit the race, the fans' lunches have disappeared.

The signs at the cow pasture said, "Vive Laurent Roux." Second the motion and, add to it, "Vive the Laurent Roux Fan Club."

Little Brother

1993

LIKE ALL RIDERS IN THE TOUR DE FRANCE, Prudencio Indurain had a day off and, like many others, he spent it with his family.

One of his three sisters came with his father from Spain, as did several cousins, although his mother was reported to have stayed home because somebody had to watch the family farm near Pamplona. As for Prudencio Indurain's brother, he was already here. Wearing the yellow jersey of the race's overall leader, Miguel Indurain is seeking his third successive victory in the Tour.

That makes life somewhat difficult for Prudencio Indurain, who ranks 133rd among the 139 riders left. This Tour de France, his first in two years as a professional, has not gone well for the little brother.

If he were the loose, jokey kind, Prudencio Indurain might object that he is in fact the bigger brother, bigger in height and weight. But he is dignified and a bit weary of all the media attention he has been getting. So he simply stares off to the side during an interview and recites the facts: "My height is 1 meter 88 (a tick above 6 feet 2 inches) and Miguel is 1 meter 86. My weight is 78 kilograms (172 pounds) and Miguel is 76 kilograms." Prudencio is 25 years old and his brother 29.

He treats the inevitable next question with the same factual monotone: "I'm a normal rider and he's a great champion. He's got a different metabolism than mine and everybody else's."

That is, according to Spanish journalists, his stock reply to the question why, even factoring in their ages, one brother has won the last two Giros d'Italia and Tours de France, the two biggest races in the sport, and the other has yet to win his first professional race.

Prudencio Indurain would be amazed to know that, as the Tour travels around France and now into the tax haven and duty-free mall of Andorra, his stock reply in hundreds of interviews has taken on the glow of poetry. "He's an eagle, I'm simply a sparrow," *Le Parisien* translated the answer this week.

People seem to want a bigger story in Prudencio Indurain than he is willing to offer. He refuses to provide pathos.

There was, for example, the time trial on July 13 in which Miguel Indurain finished first and Prudencio Indurain last, 17 minutes 48 seconds back. Afterward, little brother acknowledged the joke that the pack had been caught in an Indurain sandwich, but he noted that it was a joke among their Banesto teammates, not his joke.

And he made no excuses. He did not dwell on the problem of competing in the world's most difficult bicycle race with a left thumb badly injured, and at first feared broken, in a crash a few days before the time trial.

The thumb bothers him still, making it difficult to grasp the handlebars or squeeze the brakes, he admitted a few days ago. "I've got a bad hand but I've never thought of dropping out," he said. "I've got to hold on and wait for better days."

The best day of all, he continued, would be Sunday if his brother wore the yellow jersey at the Tour's finish in Paris.

His thick, dark eyebrows tightening with his seriousness, Prudencio Indurain makes clear his role: "My big goal is to help the leader, be up there with him and do everything possible to help everybody else keep helping him." That is the classic definition of the duties of the *domestique,* the teammate who has no identity except with his leader.

Prudencio Indurain explains that, in the Tour, he is a brother in few ways. He dismisses the talk that he made the nine-man Banesto team only because of his relationship.

"People think I'm here because of him," he told the French newspaper *l'Equipe.* "That no longer bothers me too much. I know I made it by my own efforts. I'm here, that's all. I finished the last two Giros with Miguel and I'm still with him in the Tour."

Asked the other day if his brother, a veteran of nine Tours now, had warned him how hard they are, Prudencio Indurain laughed and said, "I've realized how hard it is by myself."

He has had some bad days, including the time trial and the Alps, and Monday struggled in 104th in the first of three days in the Pyrenees. Of the 28 remaining young riders, those 25 or under this year, he stands one from the bottom in overall elapsed time.

But he has also had some good days. In the team time trial, when Banesto surprised everybody by finishing seventh and limiting Miguel Indurain's loss to his main rivals to little more than a minute, Prudencio Indurain was praised for staying right behind his brother during his powerful pulls at the front.

"I rode behind him when he set the pace because I knew better than anybody else how fast he can go," he explained. "I could say, easier than anybody else, 'Slow down.'

"But I didn't," he added proudly.

The Indurain brothers share a room in the many hotels of the three-week Tour. At the team's dinner table, Prudencio Indurain says, "I'm more open than he is. I speak, he listens."

Upstairs, in their room, they talk about family or common interests. "We like the same things: nature, the land, hunting. Only in the bedroom are we brothers. The rest of the time we're teammates.

"It's important to have a champion on your team—it boosts everybody's morale. When he's your brother, it doubles the feeling."

Gérard Rué, a Frenchman who rides for Banesto, compares the brothers this way: "They're both decent, quiet, sympathetic people, alike in every way.

"Except, of course," Rué adds with a smile, "on the bicycle."

The Expatriate Life

1993

GÉRARD RUÉ IS SPENDING ANOTHER bicycle season far from France. He frowned at the reminder. First Switzerland, now Spain. "It seems like a nice country," he said, "but of course I don't know much about Spain yet. It's only been a month or so."

He was more decisive about Switzerland, where he spent a year as a rider for the Helvetia team.

"It wasn't easy to get along with the Germans," he said, declining to elaborate. When he left Helvetia after the 1991 season, he complained that a French rider—this French rider, in any case—found it difficult in a country where the food, language and customs were not French.

Everything was French with the Castorama team, which Rué rejoined. Castorama, sponsored then by Système U, was his team from his professional debut in 1987 until he went to Switzerland in 1991. Now ranked 51st among the world's 900 professionals, Rué had productive years with the French team but none as good as that season with Helvetia: sixth place in Milan–San Remo, second place in the Critérium International, third place in the French championship, 21st place in the world championship and a splendid 10th place in the Tour de France.

Still, it was Switzerland.

Rué is very French, he conceded. He was born in Brittany 28 years ago this July and likes everything about France and being French.

Not quite everything. He frowned again, his eyebrows arching, his long chin jutting.

He had just been asked about the race that forced him once more into exile. That was the national championship in June, a race in which Rué saw a chance to become as French as a racer can be: a champion, the wearer of a jersey slashed with the blue, white and red of the French flag.

"The French jersey is a beautiful one to wear," he said. "Quite a distinction." His voice grew deep and lively. "I think that for any professional racer, the jersey of a national champion is most important."

The thought made him sit straighter. Then he rubbed his thumb against his first two fingers. "That, too," he said.

Money, glory, the tricolor jersey, a career in France—Rué came within 8 kilometers of them all in the French championship. Half a lap from the finish line, he was off alone, 35 seconds ahead of the pack and feeling strong, when a teammate, Luc Leblanc, led a charge to overtake him.

Setting the pace for a handful of rivals, Leblanc soared by the astonished Rué. So did those who traveled in Leblanc's slipstream. Rué finally finished seventh, 40 seconds behind Leblanc, the winner.

A rule of the sport is that teammates do not attack each other; if a rider is alone at the front of the field, a teammate blocks for him, trying to slow rivals, not speed them along.

"If Leblanc hadn't attacked, Rué would have won," said Laurent Fignon of the rival Gatorade team. "You don't do that when you have a man ahead. It's a little disgusting."

Leblanc was unapologetic. "I'm sure Gérard understands," he said after climbing down from the victory podium and embracing his mother. "We were both strong but that's the way races go. Too bad there's just one jersey."

Stomping away from the finish, Rué was furious. "With a lead of 35 seconds and half a lap to go, I would have won. I deserved better. I don't know what anybody else thinks of his victory but for me, it's Luc's victory, not the team's."

Later, Leblanc was asked if he thought he and Rué could continue to work together on the Castorama team. Oh sure, he answered, not to worry.

"I know what he'll be going through in the next few hours. You think I've never been disappointed in a race myself? I'm disappointed for him. But only the jersey counts and

I've wanted this jersey so much for so long. I would have gone to the ends of the earth to win it."

Raymond Poulidor, the French bicycling favorite a quarter of a century ago, has long known the 26-year-old Leblanc and is fond of him. Nevertheless, Poulidor sums him up this way: "Luc's a kid. A nice kid, but a kid."

He spoke after the French championship but before the world championships in Spain, where Leblanc defied team strategy by attacking alone near the finish, pulling rivals with him, while the French were attempting to keep the leaders together and set up a sprint finish for another rider. Rué was on that team, too. By then he had announced that he could not stay with Castorama another season.

Still bitter? Rué was asked the other day in Fontenay-sous-Bois, a Paris suburb, where he was awaiting the start of the Paris-Nice race.

"Yes, oh yes," he replied. "It's a bad memory, the worst I have."

But there is a bright side, he continued. Now in Spain he rides for the Banesto team, the top-ranked one in the sport, which is led by Miguel Indurain, winner of the last two Tours de France and the last Giro d'Italia.

"Banesto, we're a little like a family. With Castorama it was good times, too. I had four years with Castorama and they were good years. And then the last year wasn't so good. After the championship, I had to get out."

He would not say more about Leblanc or the race, preferring to talk about the present and future.

With Banesto, Rué's obligations are clear. "In the Giro and Tour de France, I'll ride for Indurain, but in the classics I'll be on my own. I hope to do something there. And then, of course, there is the French championship again." A final frown.

No Third Chance

1999

THIS TIME THEY DIDN'T GIVE JAY SWEET A REPRIEVE.

He finished the first Tour de France stage in the Pyrenees the same way he finished the first stage in the Alps—so far behind everybody else that he had to be eliminated, according to the rules, because of the difference in his time and that of the winner.

Rules are rules, the judges said, even though they had the grace not to say that in the Alps. In fairness to them, though, how many second chances does anybody get? Sweet got one, but not a third chance.

"Wish me luck," he said before the stage Tuesday. The rest day on Monday had helped, he added, but his left heel still bothered him. "Maybe it's just bruised, but the team thinks it may be chipped," he said.

In general, Sweet felt less tired even though he knew that at the end of the day he would be exhausted. He knew that because he had been exhausted every day for more than a week.

Why was he hanging on, going through all this suffering and sometimes even humiliation? "The only time I get to see the other riders is at the start," he said with a laugh.

As the Tour's *lanterne rouge*, the red lantern that used to hang from trains to signify their tail end, Sweet was weary of jokes about whether he intended to defend his jersey. There isn't a jersey for the lowest-ranked rider in the Tour although there used to be a black one for the last man in the Giro d'Italia.

"Why am I hanging on?" he said. "Why not? I've gone through so much already, I might as well keep going. I don't want to give up, I want to finish in Paris.

"I want to finish," he repeated, his voice growing softer.

Sweet is a 23-year-old Australian who is riding in his second year as a professional for the second-division Big Mat-Auber team from France. For his first Tour de France, he was the last man selected for the team that was given the last nine numbers—and handed out alphabetically. Sweet wore No. 199, the final number in the race. (He was also tired of jokes about the last number belonging to the last rider, as if it were an omen.)

Most days he rode so far behind that he was alone, with only the handlebars to talk to, as the riders say.

"A lot of times when you're out there on your own, you start asking yourself why and what for," Sweet said. "I guess it's a personal goal. I mean, this is the Tour de France. The Tour de France is the biggest sporting event in the world and I'm part of it. I've started it, I want to finish, I'm determined to finish."

That determination carried him through the first time he finished outside the time limit. Sweet was dropped, or left behind, on the third of six climbs that day in the Alps on the way to Sestriere, Italy. He caught up with a group of stragglers and stayed with them on the descent, then was left behind even by the stragglers on the next climb.

"It was a terrible day," he said recalling the miserable conditions. "It was raining, it was cold, it was hailing, there was a head wind and I did most of it on my own."

That was for 68 kilometers over three major climbs in one of the heaviest rainstorms people in Sestriere could remember.

"On the last climb to Sestriere, there were no spectators," he said. "Everyone had gone home.

"The work crews were waiting for me to finish so they could pack everything up," he continued. "I sprinted the last kilometer, trying to make the time cut. So it wasn't like I was just riding along, enjoying the scenery."

Sweet said: "I was going flat out the whole way to make it. A lot of guys might have given up, but I kept going all the way to the finish. At first, I did feel quite sorry for myself and then I said, 'Wake up. Let's get the job done.'

"Then when it started raining and hailing on me, I actually thought, actually thought there was someone up there making everything as worse as possible. And all I was thinking was 'You're not going to break me, you're not going to break me, I'm going to break this, I'm going to break this.'

"I was three minutes over the time cut," Sweet said. "The judges said it would be unfair to put me out over three minutes." So he was reinstated.

Perhaps the judges realized that Sweet had accomplished one of the epics of the Tour, like the rider who repaired his broken bicycle at a forge in the early days of the race before World War I or the rider in the 1930s who gave his wheel to his leader, who had a flat, and then sat on a wall at the side of the road and wept at his lost chance for victory.

Sweet did not see himself in a Tour epic. "This race, it's not going to break me," he repeated. No one wants to be last, and to keep going when you're last, you gain some respect." Then he went to ride the first stage in the Pyrenees. He finished 13 minutes outside the time limit, once again sprinting the last kilometer.

Jay Sweet, sweet Jay. Whatever befell him, and it seemed better not to ask, he left the race with respect gained.

A Man of the Tours

1992

THE SANCHEZ FURNITURE STORE in the Plaza de Zaragoza in San Sebastian, Spain, has a front window packed with bicycle jerseys, caps and posters, including a giant one of Miguel Indurain on the victory podium in Paris last year after he won the Tour de France.

The Kasvi barber shop on the Alameda del Boulevard has in its window one of the leader's yellow jerseys that Indurain wore on his way to Paris.

On the Calle de Reina Regente, a bakery has a huge photograph of the Basque rider Marino Lejaretta in a yellow jersey, which he wore briefly a few years back. Also in the window are two signs with the battle cry "Aupa" flanked by somersaulting exclamation points in the Spanish manner.

A delicatessen in the Avenida Felipe IV displays the work of an artist in the neglected medium of cold cuts. He has mapped, in chorizo, the route of this 79th Tour de France.

In short, San Sebastian has taken El Tour to its bosom. That is not surprising, since the Basques of northeastern Spain love bicycling and boast a dozen riders in the Tour and 23 amateur bicycle clubs in the three Basque provinces.

That love is the reason San Sebastian was willing to pay $1 million to be host to the Tour on its first visit here since a one-day stage in 1949.

This charming seaside city of 180,000 residents is part of the heart of the Basque country, perhaps the aorta. On Sunday the Tour traveled 194.5 kilometers through the auricles and ventricles.

At the finish of the race into and past the cities and pueblos of Gœipuzcoa Province, the winner was Dominique Arnould, 25, a Frenchman with the Castorama team from France. Second, half a bicycle length behind, was Johan Museeuw of the Lotto team from Belgium and third was Max Sciandri of the Motorola team.

In his excitement at having held off the pack after a lengthy breakaway, Arnould raised his right arm in victory less than 10 meters from the finish. He then glanced back, saw a horde of riders bearing down on him and resumed racing, not coasting. Museeuw was not quite able to catch the Frenchman.

Although all the favorites finished in the same time, the overall leader's yellow jersey changed hands.

Indurain, the defending champion, dropped to third place behind Arnould in second place and Alex Zülle, who took over the lead by winning a bonus intermediate sprint and gaining six seconds that were deducted from his overall elapsed time.

Zülle, a Swiss who rides for the ONCE team, was second by two seconds to Indurain in Saturday's prologue.

That foreigners finished first, second and third in the first stage was fitting. This is Blanche Dubois country: Kindness to strangers is as native to the Basque as to the bedouin. Yet many hearts must have yearned for another victor—Marino Lejaretta, for example, the man in the yellow jersey in the bakery's photograph.

As he says, he was still dreaming of victory as recently as this spring. A victory before his fellow Basques in the province next to his own Vizcaya would have capped his last season as the undisputed strongman, the iron horse, of racing.

But in mid-April, not long before his 35th birthday, Lejaretta crashed in a race outside nearby Bilboa. When he awoke in a hospital, he had broken ribs, a punctured lung and fractured vertebrae in his back. His career was over.

Now a guest of honor of the Tour de France, he cut the ceremonial ribbon for Sunday's stage. This is the first Tour de France that Lejaretta has not ridden in since 1985. It is, in fact, one of the few of the three grand tours he has missed since then. Almost unbelievably, for the last three years he has ridden in the Giro d'Italia, the Vuelta a España and the Tour de France—a total of about 11,375 kilometers from each mid-May through each July.

All told, he rode 11 Vueltas, 7 Giros and 8 Tours. He rode them well, too, finishing fifth in the 1989 and 1990 Tours de France, fifth in the 1991 Giro and third in the Vuelta the same year.

The only other rider who has ridden in all three Tours for three consecutive years is Bernando Ruiz of Spain, who did it in 1955, 1956 and 1957. Nowadays, a rider who tackles two of the Tours in the same year is considered to be a workaholic.

Lejaretta did not ride simply the Tours once he turned professional in 1979. He competed in nearly every race possible in the eight-month calendar and rode them well. Among his 56 victories are the Vuelta in 1982, two Tours of Catalonia and three Grand Prix of San Sebastian.

Like Zülle, the new wearer of the yellow jersey, Lejaretta rode for the team sponsored by ONCE, the Organizacion Nacional de Ciegos Espanoles, or national federation for the blind. Among other jobs, they staff lottery booths throughout Spain, selling tickets and making change by feeling the size and texture of peseta banknotes.

A huge ONCE poster at several strategic spots in Basque country shows a sightless man wearing a racing jersey and sitting alongside a bicycle. Above his head, the poster says, "The Other Marino." It is both mawkish and touching.

Traveling the stage in an organization car as an honored guest, not a racer, the original Marino surely understood that feeling.

A Happy Story

1991

EVERY TOUR DE FRANCE should have at least one happy story, and here it is:

The next time somebody attempts to justify a dirty deed by announcing that life isn't fair, Ronan Pensec intends to set him straight. "Life, she's fair," he says, practicing his English. "She's more than fair."

Pensec knows. A day short of his 28th birthday, the Frenchman can look back on a childhood marked by the death of his mother when he was 7 and of his father 10 years later.

"I learned young to live life," he says.

To pay his bills, he became a bicycle racer in his native Brittany and was successful enough to turn professional at age 21. His results have been respectable, including a sixth place in the 1986 Tour de France and an eighth place in 1988. He missed the 1987 race after injuring a heel and spent that July bemoaning his bad luck.

"For a bicycle rider to miss the Tour de France is bad," he said. "But for a French bicycle rider to miss the Tour, it's a calamity. A tragedy. Worse."

Pensec spoke those words early in May, during the Tour DuPont in the United States, and his tragic tone was portentous. At that point he faced the very real possibility that he would miss this 78th Tour de France.

The problem was eligibility. His new Spanish team, Seur, did not rank high enough to gain an automatic invitation and was hoping to qualify as one of six wild cards. Seur's chances were slim, unlike those of Pensec's former team, Z, based in France. It is led by Greg LeMond but, before the American was hired, Pensec was Z's main rider.

In the Tour last year, Pensec was one of the four riders who broke away on the first stage and established a 10-minute lead. Fourth overall, he attacked on the first day in the mountains more than a week later. On his 27th birthday no less, Pensec took over the yellow jersey. That lasted only two days, as the pressure and the travail of climbing got to him. He eventually finished the Tour in 20th place but first won a special place in the hearts of his fellow Frenchmen.

What endeared him to them was Pensec's sweetness. Although he dresses in the punk mode and formerly wore his black hair spiked and sometimes tinted, he is really a sheep in wolf's clothing. Face to face, his manner is reasonable and polite.

"Listen," he said after donning the yellow jersey, "you're not going to hear me announce to the world tonight that Ronan Pensec is going to win the Tour de France. All I know is that I'm going to climb Alpe d'Huez in yellow."

Then, after he faltered in a hilly time trial and lost the jersey, he accepted the defeat with grace.

At the end of the season, Pensec announced that although he was happy riding for LeMond, he planned to join Seur. He would more than double his salary, to $400,000 a year, and become a team leader again. But those were not the only reasons he was leaving.

He wanted to see more of the world, he explained during the Tour DuPont. He knew France well and the United States a bit from races and vacations there, working on his English and shopping for motorcycles.

There's a whole world out there, Pensec said, and he wanted to become a citizen of it. Who knows? he said, maybe he would ride for an Italian team next.

These hopes began turning sour when it grew increasingly doubtful that Seur would be invited to the Tour de France. It did not help that Pensec had a bad spring, missing 18 days with assorted ailments.

The bad news came in mid-June: Seur had not made the list but was the first alternate.

"It broke my heart," Pensec said. "To hear that I would not be in the Tour was really hard on me, dramatic." Adding to the heartbreak was that on July 15 the Tour would finish a daily stage in Quimper, his hometown in Brittany, and resume there the next day.

He wanted terribly to be part of the race in front of his neighbors. "It would mean so much to me and my wife, Armelle," he said.

Late in June Pensec raced well in Spain and two Sundays ago he finished a good 14th in the French national championships. Then he began making plans to spend Tour de France time in some of the minor races that dot the calendar in other countries.

Last Monday, however, he was asked to be in Madrid. Representatives of the Amaya team, which had already accepted an invitation to the Tour de France, wanted to meet with him and officials of the Seur team. Amaya's goal was to buy his contract.

"Oh, I was very, very happy when I heard about this," Pensec said. "The Tour de France is my life, and the stage is in my town."

Signing a rider from another team in mid-season is rare but not unknown, and the deal was done quickly. Everybody was happy: Amaya got a rider it wanted, Seur was relieved of a big salary during a time of small races and Pensec made it to the Tour.

"A lot of people were happy, me most," he said. "I get to ride in the Tour de France after all and go to Quimper."

Quimper, a city of 50,000, is known for its shellfish and painted pottery. On holidays, the women delight in wearing traditional costumes, including the tall Breton bonnets decorated with lace.

Quimper has many charms. Mainly, for Ronan Pensec, citizen of the world, it's home.

COMPUTER MAN

1993

TONY ROMINGER IS MAN, not computer, right? Definitely. He laughs, he sings, he pays his taxes and goes on vacation, he feels pleasure and pain—especially when somebody with the wrong access code tries to interface his microchip.

"No, no, no," Rominger protests, "oh, that's not right. Look at me," he commands with a laugh, "I'm a human. Just like you."

The rest of this report from Mainframe XV672 follows:

Rominger, a 32-year-old Swiss who ranks second among the world's riders, has a reputation for being programmed for victory by his sports doctor. Just pop in the floppy disk, people say, and Rominger will do the rest.

Despite his insistence that he is flesh and blood, he sometimes makes it sound otherwise. After triumphing in the Tour of the Basque Country this winter, for example, he retreated to the training hills near his home in Monaco and announced that he would not race again until the Liège-Bastogne-Liège classic, some weeks off.

"By then I will be perfectly programmed to win," he said in French, one of several languages he speaks. He was close as a prophet, finishing second in a sprint at the end of the long, demanding one-day race.

Somewhat stolid and deadpan, Rominger is a rarity in the sport in predicting victory. He also forecast his second successive victory last month in the Vuelta. He is less optimistic about his chances in the Tour de France, saying only that he hopes to make it onto the three-step victory podium when the race finishes.

Far back in the field after a disastrous team time trial, Rominger will know more about his chances after the individual time trial, the Tour's first major shakeout. Then come the Alps, another testing ground.

Rominger does not seem to be worried. After all, he is under the care of an Italian sports doctor who lays out a program that the rider follows like a, well, machine. The essence of the program is to spend less time racing and more time preparing to race, reversing the conventional wisdom that races are the best training.

"You look at my program, I don't do so many races like other riders," Rominger said in an interview. "I go home and prepare for races. I don't go to races for training, I go to races to win. That's the difference between me and the others."

Following his victory in the Vuelta, Rominger got with the program by spending a month at high altitude, training and building up his red corpuscles, which carry oxygen to the muscles. Not many riders would throw away a month of their racing season but off Rominger went to Vail, Colorado, accompanied by his family and the doctor, Michele Ferrari.

"I enjoyed Colorado very much," the Swiss said. "The weather wasn't so good, much snow still, but the people were nice. Good training, too. I know me very well, I'm riding such a long time, I know what kind of training I have to do."

When he returned, he rode a leisurely Tour of Switzerland, skipping any further work, including the Swiss championship because his Spanish team's sponsor, Clas—a dairy cooperative in Asturias—did not enjoy the prospect of having its name subordinated on the red jersey with a white cross of the Swiss champion. The possibility of a Rominger loss was not written into the software.

This general confidence in Rominger's strength is one reason he is rated among Miguel Indurain's main rivals in the Tour de France. Only Indurain, who is seeking his third successive victory in the Tour and who is the overwhelming favorite in the time trial, surpasses Rominger in the computerized standings of professional bicycle racers.

Another reason Rominger's chances seem to be high is that, if he is not quite the powerful time trialist Indurain is, the Swiss is considered to be a stronger climber. The 80th Tour's two days in the Alps and three days in the Pyrenees will offer many opportunities to gain time on the Spaniard.

Finally, not having ridden the Tour since 1990, when Greg LeMond won, and the Giro d'Italia since 1989, Rominger has not been humiliated by Indurain, who has won both races twice in the last two years. Therefore, unlike Gianni Bugno and Claudio Chiappucci, Italian rivals and the two primary carriers of the disease, the Swiss does not have an Indurain Complex.

Andy Hampsten, the fine American climber with Motorola, defines the complex: "People would rather be beaten by the same guy as be beaten by different people. I think the Italians do accept that Indurain is going to win and they're used to that, so they'd rather Indurain win again than their rival does."

Rominger appears to be respectful but not awed by the record of Indurain, who will be 29 next week.

"Between us we have won all the major tours for the last two years," Rominger likes to point out, a little like the corner grocer boasting that he and John D. Rockefeller have $12 billion in the bank between them.

Nevertheless, Rominger has proven that he can win races, including Paris-Nice in 1991 and Tirreno-Adriatico in 1990 and 1989 plus such prestigious classics as the Tour of Lombardy in 1992 and 1989 and the time-trial finale of the World Cup in 1991. The first two are run in the winter, the second two in the fall, which points up Rominger's lack of results thus far in the Tour de France.

It is always run in July and he suffers from hay fever in the summer, although the problem is said to be under control. Before it was, he finished 63rd in the 1988 Tour and 57th in 1990, skipping all other participation since he turned professional in 1986. He has ridden for teams in Italy, France and now Spain, adding language skills in those countries to his native German, his careful English and the Danish he learned from his mother.

Another summertime problem is that, unlike most racers, Rominger much prefers the cold and even the rainy cold to heat. So far the Tour has been moving clockwise around France under blue skies and a sweltering sun.

"The heat will be a problem the first week only," he said, "but it shouldn't be a hard week, so I think I'll get used to it." He should know better when the Tour reaches Madine Lake in northeastern France for the race against the clock.

BACK FOR MORE

1995

THE LAST TIME THE ENIGMATIC Tony Rominger appeared in the Tour de France he was not so much appearing as disappearing, explaining in the six languages he speaks how he had collapsed physically but certainly not psychologically.

In second place overall and trailing Miguel Indurain by an insurmountable five minutes, Rominger had coasted to the side of the road and quit with nearly a third of the Tour ahead. Stomach problems, the Swiss rider insisted, definitely not a loss of morale. In French, German, Italian, Danish, Spanish and English—definitely not a loss of morale.

The news conference was held in the red-brick city of Albi in a hotel meeting room and, on the wall behind Rominger, a Rotary Club plaque proclaimed, "Service Before Self."

He posed for one more photograph dozens of times and then he was gone. Back in his tax-haven home in Monaco, he rested for a few weeks, enjoying a vacation with his wife and their two young children, and then rehabilitated his psyche by winning bicycle races. First was the Grand Prix des Nations, then two successful attacks on the world record for the hour's ride.

This year he began slowly before winning the Tour of Romandie and then the Giro d'Italia. At age 34, he remains No. 1 in the computerized standings, comfortably ahead of Indurain, No. 2. It was Indurain's record for the hour ride that he broke last fall.

Indurain, Indurain—there's that name again. "I admire him," Rominger says. "If I don't win this Tour, I hope he does."

Now Rominger has reappeared in the Tour de France, explaining in his six languages how his defeat last July had enriched him. "I learned to lose," he said. "I learned that I have nothing to lose. That is also important. I learned to accept."

If he did not win this Tour, which starts in a few days, he would accept? "The world would not end," he said. "That is what I learned."

Surrounded once again by cameramen, he spoke after taking the Tour's cursory medical inspection. Despite traces of the flu in the recent Tour of Switzerland, which he did not finish, and minor stomach problems in the Giro, which he won easily, he appears to be in splendid condition.

"In Switzerland, he looked ready," Lance Armstrong said. "I've never seen Rominger look like that. He was lean. Straight away, I thought, 'Whoa!'"

So Rominger is ready physically. Is he psychologically? Perhaps his bland, almost casual, attitude toward this 82nd Tour de France is part of his new code of acceptance. Or perhaps it's a mind game.

"I was more motivated for the Giro than I am for here," he said. "Now I am here and we will see what I can do.

"Besides, my goal is not to win the Tour de France but to win one big Tour a year, the Giro, the Vuelta, the Tour de France," Rominger said. "That is enough for a cyclist. I have already done it in the Giro. So I have fulfilled my goal."

He won the Vuelta in 1992, 1993 and 1994. In that period, his best finish in the Tour was second in 1993, and he was a co-favorite with Indurain last year until the Spaniard dominated him and everybody else in the first time trial.

A few days later, Indurain sped away in the first mountains and the Tour neared its finish for Rominger. Sapped by dysentery, he quit after the Pyrenees.

What about his comment this week that the Tour is really a race for second place behind Indurain? He smiled, not embarrassed by his apparent concession.

"But he has to be the only favorite," he said of the Spaniard, who is seeking his fifth consecutive Tour victory. "For now, there are a lot of guys who want to have a great race and make life difficult for him. I am here, I will do the best I can. More you cannot ask."

Armstrong, among others, asks for more.

"Don't fall for it," warned the American rider. "He's playing a game: If he gets second, he said all along he'd get second. If he wins, oh God, he's really great. If he says he's going to win and gets second, he's disappointed everybody. It's an old trick."

Yes, but is it this time? Only Rominger knows.

La Longo

1999

THE SECOND HALF OF THE bicycle world championships—on the track this time, not the road—begins Wednesday in Berlin with a familiar face missing. Despite her lust for one more gold medal, and maybe another one after that, Jeannie Longo seems to realize that it will not be won on the track.

La Longo has more world championship gold medals than most people have toes, but she wants another. At the end of the month she will turn 41 and her weatherworn face is startling among the smooth brows and cheeks of her so-much-younger rivals, but still she wants another gold medal.

And after that one, how many more? The Frenchwoman doesn't say and will not discuss retirement, as she has refused to do since she ended a brief withdrawal to hearth and home by winning the most recent of her 12 gold medals in the 1997 championships in Spain. That one was in the time trial, her third triumph against the clock.

She has also won on the track in pursuit and the points race. But the last of her five victories in the women's road race occurred in 1995 in Colombia.

What passes in bicycle racing for a whole generation has emerged since then. Such champions as Diana Ziliute and Edita Pucinskaite, both of Lithuania, are 23; and Zulfia Zabirova of Russia, Fabiana Luperini of Italy and Hanka Kupfernagel of Germany are 25.

They demonstrated their vigor this month in the elite women's road race around pastel Verona, Italy. The easy winner was Pucinskaite, whose gold medal accompanied the bronze one she won in the time trial. Second was Anna Wilson, 27, an Australian who was also second in the time trial. Third was Ziliute. Longo finished ninth, her same rank in the time trial.

Before the road race, she was somewhat chatty as, national team by national team, the 120 riders were called to the starting line. The French team was the eighth of 31 to be summoned and the women rolled out in a group—but not quite.

Five of the six were in formation. The last, Longo, was, as always, off to the side, not really part of a team.

Not until the next team, the one from Australia, was called did Longo answer her inner clock and begin pedaling to the line. She stayed bunched with the Australians until the race started, and then again she was on her own, off on an individual quest.

Bicycle racing is what she does: She and her husband, Patrice Ciprelli, a Frenchman who is her coach, spend vacations at velodromes in such places as Mexico City as she attempts to better her world record for the hour's ride against the clock.

In low-echelon competition, Longo still delivers. Last spring she won the French pursuit championship for the umpteenth time. But she dreams bigger: Longo does not rule out an appearance at the Olympic Games in Australia next year to defend the gold medal she won in the road race in Atlanta in 1996.

Despite her age and evident decline in power, her rivals take her seriously.

"She's a great athlete," Wilson said as she awaited the start.

"Know her?" she repeated. "I can't say I know her at all."

Kimberly Smith of the U.S. team was also respectful. "She's a rider to be feared," she said. "She could easily spring a surprise today. Know her? Just a little bit. I'm not close to her, if that's what you mean."

Another rider, who pulled a face of disdain on condition of anonymity, was more critical. "Nobody really knows her, I think," she said. "She does have that reputation.

"But," she admitted, "she's certainly been a great racer."

Lanterne Rouge

1992

THE LAST SHALL BE FIRST, THEY SAY, and for a brief moment in this Tour de France, Henri Manders was. First, that is. He had been last, or very near it, most of the rest of the time.

As the Tour neared its end the next day in Paris, Manders ranked 129th among the 130 men remaining of the 198 who set out in Spain. He was nearly 15 minutes ahead of—or behind, depending on outlook—Fernando Quevedo in the battle to become the 79th

Tour's *lanterne rouge,* the red lantern that used to hang on the back of every French train to signify the end.

Their personal race was relatively tight until stage 18, when Manders finished a splendid 10th into Tours while Quevedo was 130th and last, 7 minutes 21 seconds behind Manders. That doubled the Spaniard's deficit—or lead—in the fight to be *lanterne rouge.*

First things first: Manders, a 32-year-old Dutchman who rode for the Helvetia team from Switzerland, won a bonus sprint on July 20. Let the record show that his victory occurred in le Péage de Vizille, at kilometer 23 of the 15th stage, 198 kilometers from Bourg d'Oisans to St. Etienne.

Manders collected six bonus points and 5,000 French francs (a bit less than $1,000). The money was the whole point of his bravado.

"I was in a group of 15 riders out ahead and I thought, 'Let's try to pick up some money to pay my fines that I got in the mountains,'" Manders said. "When I won the sprint, I thought, 'Ah, my fines are paid.'"

Then, zip! zip! zip! the rest of the breakaway passed Manders. That was it for him as Numero Uno and he didn't care. Laurels are not accepted at the bank where fines are paid.

He declined to reveal how much he had been fined—"Not a lot"—presumably for accepting or soliciting uphill pushes from spectators.

There was not much else to talk about in the way of triumphs, and Manders wore the look of a man who knew what was coming. He was in his seventh Tour de France and had finished the last three in 144th place, 113th place and 104th place. It was not significantly better before then, either.

How did it feel to be almost the *lanterne rouge*?

"Almost," he repeated emphatically. "It feels not so nice, no. It's not an honor anymore."

There was a time, no more than a decade ago, when the *lanterne rouge* was a highly publicized distinction. Riders actually slowed down to lose time and become the last man in the standings, knowing they would be constantly interviewed and, because of the press coverage, would be invited to many of the critériums in the Netherlands, Belgium and France that followed the Tour.

Those days were over, as much a part of the past as the entertainment the Tour used to provide after a daily stage. A decade ago, the shows offered such attractions as Yvette Horner, the queen of the accordion, or a faded French chanteuse like Dalida. Now the entertainment was by a British band dressed like the Blues Brothers, Jake and Elwood, and singing, quite terribly, Rolling Stones numbers.

Nor did a Tour employee still set up a movie projector to show flickering highlight films of past Tours on a wall in the village square. The highlights, without the shadows of moths in the projector beam, were shown on nightly television now and the villages had mainly become ski resorts and big cities. Now, also, the Tour organizers frowned on coverage about lack of success, like the *lanterne rouge,* feeling that it detracted from the leaders. And the critériums were much reduced in number, too.

Allan Peiper, a 32-year-old Australian who rode for Tulip and remembered the old days, had an added explanation. "Nobody would try to become *lanterne rouge* now," he said. "It's too risky that you'd be outside the time limit" on a stage, while seeking to drop down, and would be eliminated.

Peiper had never been the *lanterne rouge.* "But I've been pretty close every time, like I am now," he admitted. He ranked 124th. "It doesn't matter. It used to be a bit of a novelty because the *lanterne rouge* was invited to all the critériums, and now it's nothing. If you're last . . . you're last. But last is better than fourth last, I suppose. The other end of the scale, you see."

Peiper was asked if there was any embarrassment in being last.

"No," he said. "These days, if you finish the Tour de France, if you're a bloody 20th or last, it's all the same. It's pretty hard, you know."

Manders agreed with that assessment but thought there was another reason that so few of the starters in Spain would finish. "It used to be an honor to finish the Tour, and I don't think today that riders race to finish. They want to win a stage and show themselves off."

He won a stage himself, in 1985. "Seven years ago, yes," Manders said. "And I finished that Tour, too. When I've finished this one, I've finished seven. And I've been in seven. It's not a record, of course, but I'm proud of it. Like everybody else, I've been quite sick sometimes, but I've always stayed in and finished the Tour de France." As he would the next day, and as Quevedo would, too.

Last things last: Quevedo was a 27-year-old Spaniard with the Amaya team and was thrilled with his showing, he said.

"Last year, in my first Tour, I had to drop out with four stages to go. This year, I'll finish. Much better. Who cares if I'm last, I'm still in the Tour."

When he went to sign in for the stage, the Tour's announcer, the warm-hearted Daniel Mangeas, introduced him to the huge crowd of fans.

"Quevedo may be last," Mangeas declared, "but he'll be there on the Champs-Elysées tomorrow and he'll go back to Spain Monday on the same plane with Miguel Indurain. Think about that when you think of the *lanterne rouge*."

Quevedo, who understood French passably, thought about it himself and broke into a big grin.

A Man of Modest Goals

1991

GINO DE BACKER HAD MODEST GOALS as a bicycle racer, perhaps because, at age 29 and in his fourth year as a professional, he had just one victory to his credit. That occurred in 1990 in a *kermesse*, or one of the many minor races held in and around villages in the Low Countries. The place was Desselgem, Belgium, not far from his home in Destelbergen.

Before that, De Backer's main achievement was a fifth place in the 1988 Paris-Tours race, a World Cup classic. His dark face breaks into a sunny smile when he remembers the sprint finish in Paris-Tours and the cheers of tens of thousands of spectators lining the long straightaway to the finish line.

By now the Belgian had learned that most riders are measured by more than the cheers of the crowd. If they ride, as De Backer did, for the B squad of a second-echelon team like Tonton Tapis in a race as distant from home base in Belgium as the 1991 Tour DuPont, honors are what count.

But De Backer had no hope, absolutely none, of winning the Tour DuPont and carrying off the $50,000 that went to the victor. Nor could he realistically dream of winning a daily stage ($800) or the championships for sprinters ($1,000), climbers ($2,000) or even best young riders ($1,000).

At mile 49 of the stage from Richmond to Wintergreen, Virginia, De Backer saw his chance of an attainable goal, however modest.

"I hoped to win the jersey of the most aggressive rider," he explained hours later. So

De Backer attacked. Of the 102 other riders, all remained indifferent except for Dave Spears of Team Canada, an amateur. Not bothering to chase, the pack watched placidly as Spears sprinted after and joined De Backer. Helped by a crash that blocked the pack briefly, the two quickly disappeared on the rolling and twisty road.

Twenty miles later, their lead was up to 7 minutes 30 seconds, its peak. The pack had passed through a feed zone by then and been slowed by the usual confusion as riders snatched their lunches on the fly and transferred sandwiches, pastries and fruit from small sacks to the pockets of their jerseys.

That accomplished, a desultory chase began. Neither De Backer nor Spears was dangerous—the Belgian ranked 59th, the Canadian 70th at the start of the day—but various teams' tactics dictated that the road ahead be clear by the final climb to the resort of Wintergreen.

The focus should have been on De Backer but, for his hour of glory, he chose an empty stage. The back roads from Richmond were bordered by nothing but untended and overgrown fields, many of them unfenced. Houses were rare and spectators even rarer. At the few crossroads, state policemen were posted to hold back traffic that had not arrived. Only at a bonus sprint in the town of Scottsville did a small crowd gather, and there Spears was first across the line.

"Nobody," De Backer remembered later. Nobody to witness his feat.

He and Spears relayed each other through eerily empty Virginia, passing stands of loblolly pine, ash and maple. Side winds stirred tulip trees and fields of black-eyed Susans: still life with bicycle racers.

And their lead was coming down. By mile 78, it was 3 minutes 40 seconds and, despite their steady pace, by mile 80 it was 3:15. By mile 88, when the two began climbing a long hill, the lead was barely 2 minutes. Spears was stroking easily on the climb while De Backer began to struggle. He was soon left behind.

"I felt good," De Backer recalled. "The other guy, he didn't want to wait. He wanted to go alone, he said good-bye. An amateur," De Backer said contemptuously.

He was quickly swallowed up by the pack, which continued after Spears. A few minutes after De Backer was caught, Spears reached the town of Faber, an outpost of civilization. Alone, he raced past a post office, the Mount Shiloh Baptist Church, the Faber Volunteer Fire Company, a line of train tracks leading to some big city somewhere.

People were out and cheering.

As he turned onto Highway 29 South, traffic was backed up for a few hundred yards and drivers had left their cars to watch. Applause and shouts of encouragement greeted the Canadian as he passed the Meander Inn and the Stoney Creek Golf Course.

And then, of course, it was Spears's turn to be caught. At the finish, he was 10:39 behind the winner. De Backer labored in 17:31 behind at the mountaintop.

"My legs were good on the climb," De Backer said, "but my coach said to me, 'Easy, easy, there's another race tomorrow.' I've got a chance there if I make it over the hills, then maybe on the flat or in the sprint."

He was pleased with himself and his performance, but curious. Had he won the prize as the most aggressive rider? he wondered. "I think not," since he had not been notified.

It seemed kinder not to tell him that the honor had been voted instead to Spears.

Champion for a While

1997

THE CHAMPION'S BOUQUET OF SPRING FLOWERS sat in the front of the team car. George Hincapie, the champion for not even an hour and a half, sat in the back, trying not to cry.

"They can't do this," he said. "They can't do this," he repeated, again and again.

Hincapie, 23 years old and a leader of the U.S. Postal Service team, had just been stripped of the title of American professional champion, which he won earlier Sunday in the CoreStates USPRO Championship bicycle race in Philadelphia. Officials ruled that, after the rear wheel of his bicycle went flat and was repaired with less than 10 miles to go in the 156-mile race, Hincapie was illegally paced back to the front group of riders by his team car. The penalty was to void the national championship he won by being the first American to finish the race.

"After his flat, he rode behind his team vehicle an excessive amount of time, more than two minutes," said Shawn Farrell, the head international official for the race. "I've never heard of a case where somebody motorpaced that long, that far, in front of so many people."

Mark Gorski, general manager of the U.S. Postal Service team, disagreed on several counts. "We paced him into the caravan, which we have the right to do," said Gorski, who rode in his team car. "We were in front of him for 15 or 20 seconds. On the second warning, we pulled over."

Gorski, a gold-medal bicycle sprinter at the 1984 Olympic Games, argued that the officials should have penalized the driver of the car, not Hincapie, for any infraction. The team will protest the decision to the sport's rulers, the International Cycling Union in Switzerland, Gorski said, not sounding optimistic.Veteran observers of the sport could not recall a precedent for the disqualification.

"Riders have been put out of a race for holding onto a team car and getting a tow," said Paul Sherwen, a former Tour de France rider who was an official for the championship's organizers. "But I've never heard of a rider who was disqualified for being motorpaced."

Gorski also questioned the 80 minutes it took the three commissaires to make their decision. During that time, Hincapie mounted the victory podium, received his flowers and his jersey, acknowledged proudly that his parents had come from New York City to watch him and then attended a news conference.

"Tremendous, tremendous," he said immediately after he finished. "I've worked for this in this race for the last four years." His highest previous placing in the U.S. championship was 10th in 1995.

A native New Yorker who raced in Central Park as a boy and now lives in Charlotte, North Carolina, Hincapie would have succeeded his teammate, Eddy Gragus, in the red, white and blue jersey. Instead it went to Bart Bowen, a rider for the Saturn team who was also U.S. champion in 1992.

Hincapie said he had two flats during the long race in ideal weather, just enough of a breeze to offset heat in the low 80s. The first flat occurred about halfway through and the second with two laps left.

"A really bad moment," he said. "But I got repaired quickly and my teammates helped and I rode hard to get back with the front group.

"I've looked at so many riders in Europe wearing national champions' jerseys and thought, 'I want to be that,'" said Hincapie.

Later, when he was sitting in his team car after he was told about his disqualification, Hincapie said he would not return the jersey he was wearing. He did not speak defiantly. He was shattered.

Trying to console him, a friend pointed out that he would not turn 24 until late this month. He has many more championships ahead of him, many more chances to win, the friend said.

Hincapie brushed the words away. "This was the year," he said. "They can't do this." He ducked his head then and covered his eyes with his hands.

A Change of Luck

1994

THE HOTEL ROOM MUST GO for $125 or $150 a night and the bicycle leaning against a wall would fetch $3,000, maybe $4,000. Bobby Julich was sitting up in bed, watching something on a big color television set, waiting for his turn on the masseur's table downstairs and eating a banana. Good-bye to hard times. That was last year.

Julich is bright, articulate and glaringly polite. He is patriotic, in love and devoted to his parents. Mainly, at age 22, he is one of the great hopes of American bicycle racing, a tall, lean rider who climbs strongly, time trials well and holds his own in a sprint.

Most teams would have been happy to have a young rider with his attitude and talent under contract, people thought. But they were wrong. Because an opportunity was missed, because his luck turned wrong and his timing went bad, Julich spent last year riding in the United States as an independent professional without a team, a sponsor or a support staff. He was alone in a team sport.

Food and water during a race? "I had nobody waiting in the feed zone," he remembers, "so I just carried everything. It looked as if I had a little backpack on.

"Many times I ran out of food, many times I ran out of water," he added. "Coming through a feed zone, once in a while I would try to snag a bottle from somebody but, more times than not, they would pull it back."

Massage, which riders receive daily during a race to refresh their leg muscles? "No such thing," he said. "I didn't have a rub for the whole year. I threw my legs up on a wall, if I had time and energy, and just rubbed them down a bit. Throw them up on a wall, keep the circulation going, maybe use some baby oil."

Travel money and other expenses? Julich went through $25,000 in savings as he paid his way to and from races. "You start to throw away an empty water bottle during a race and then you think: 'They cost $5 each. This is going to cost me $5.'"

Race results? "I didn't have many major results," he continued in a flat voice. "I was close but no cigar in quite a few instances. I forgot how to win, I forgot the winning attitude, I forgot the whole approach to winning."

That was last year. This year, Julich is riding as a member of the Chevrolet/L.A. Sheriff team and has just finished the Tour DuPont in a splendid seventh place among the 112 riders who started. He enjoyed the DuPont, Julich said at the end, in High Point, North Carolina, a bleak, furniture-making center where wing chairs far outnumber people. He was pleased with his performance and with that of his team. He enjoyed the racing and the attention. The attention, ah the attention—press conferences, interviews throughout the 12-day race, fans asking for autographs, the loudspeaker blare of his name and team at the start of each stage. Last year he was anonymous.

"There are so many good riders out there and you never hear of them because they're not on teams," he said of his year as an independent. "I'd come to the start line in a race and I'd have on a jersey that was blank and they'd say my number but not my name, and two or three guys behind me they'd say, 'Oh, there's X with Coors Light or Y with Motorola' or whatever.

"You couldn't get on a team because no one knew you were in the race," he continued. That wasn't it, of course. That was later. There was another reason earlier.

As a rider who finished fifth in the DuPont in 1991, when he was a 19-year-old member of the U.S. national amateur team, and then 10th the next year, Julich received offers to join professional teams. In retrospect, the best offer came from the Gatorade team in Italy at the end of the 1992 DuPont. "The offer was there but I was kind of talked out of it," Julich explained. "I was 20 years old and a bit intimidated by going all the way over to Europe and not knowing Italian, not knowing anyone on the team.

"And I was a little bit scared by the whole European regimen. I thought that people who just aren't ready and go over to Europe and get thrown into the meat grinder just get spit out. And that's not what I wanted."

He liked better an offer from Mike Neel, formerly coach of the 7-Eleven and Spago teams, to join a new American team funded by the Rossin company in Italy. "He has a reputation for bringing around young riders, for bringing them to success," Julich said of Neel. "He offered a team with half its races in America, half its races in Europe. I thought that would be the best deal for me, to get my feet wet in my first year as a pro:

half over in Europe, but if things went bad, I'd be able to come back to America."

The sponsorship for the new team fell through, as it sometimes does in the sport, and Julich found himself without an employer as the 1992 season was opening. The precise date, he noted, was January 26, "when I was waiting for my first paycheck, for the go-ahead to have our training camp in Santa Rosa, California, the next week. Instead, on January 26, I was left high and dry.

"I frantically called every team in America—Saturn, Coors Light, Motorola, L.A. Sheriff, IME, everyone, just looking," he said. "I told them I understand you guys have made your budgets already. Just get me to the races, you don't even have to pay me.

"That wasn't good enough because, as I found out on my own last year, just getting to the races is a major, major expense. Even if they didn't pay me, it was still going to cost them between $20,000 and $30,000 in lodging, transportation, equipment, all that sort of thing." No team had that much money left in its budget.

He did not call the Gatorade team in Italy. "I figured I had my opportunity there and I didn't take it and . . ." A long pause. "I was kind of embarrassed to call and say 'I wasn't going to go on your team but my contract fell through and can I get back on?' I had enough sense not even to ask.

"So I raced as an independent all year," Julich continued. "What drove me was to convince a team, regardless that it was late in the season, that Bobby Julich was a worthwhile rider to have on a team. Time and time again, when I would get results, I would go around to see if anybody was interested. Still it was no takers."

At last he received an offer to join a Portuguese team for the few weeks that constitute the heart of the American racing season. "It was a Portuguese 'professional' team that was more of a club team—just a bunch of guys over here for a free vacation," he said. "They promised to pay me but they didn't. I was supposed to go over and do the Tour of Portugal with them and maybe stay in Europe the rest of the year, but that fell through. The ticket never came in the mail. But at least I got into races without paying an entry fee.

"What was a kind of bummer was that I'm from America and I'm very proud of that and I had to wear a jersey that said Portugal on it," Julich recalled. "So everyone thought I was from Portugal. People would say, 'Gosh, you look like a guy that was on the U.S. national team last year,' and I'd say, 'That's me.'"

His voice was subdued now. "And I finally cracked mentally and financially," he said. "In early August."

WAITING IN THE MORNING SUN for the airport shuttle that would start him home to California from the Tour DuPont, Bobby Julich was relaxed. There was nothing to worry about, he knew. What the organizers of the DuPont had not taken care of, his Chevrolet/L.A. Sheriff team had.

His bicycle was bundled into its traveling bag, his luggage was at the curb, the shuttle to the Greensboro Airport ran dependably every half hour, his plane ticket was confirmed. People had seen to things.

Life is easy for Julich, 22, in his comeback from a year as an independent professional, a solitary rider in a team sport. Last year, Julich had nobody but himself to see to things.

"I would go to the races, get there on my own, be really tired when I was starting a race because of all the logistical stuff—calling the organizer, making the plane reservation, making the car reservation," he recalled. "But that was the easy part.

"The hard part was getting on the plane, paying for your bike, once you get to your destination, get your bike, get your stuff, rent a car. By this time it's probably 9, 10 o'clock at night. Then you try to find something to eat, drive around when you have no idea where you are, look for some buffet thing, all you can eat, some low-priced thing, try to get a decent meal and stay away from the food poisoning that sometimes goes hand in hand with those all-you-can-eat places and then after that try to get close to the race site and find a hotel.

"And by that time it's usually 12 or 1 o'clock in the morning and you have to get up and drive an hour to a race and it starts at 9 o'clock. You're up at 5 trying to eat. It was just a couple of hours' sleep a night.

"So it was difficult before I even started a race. And then, getting into the race, I had to cover every breakaway. If there was a Coors, a Saturn, an L.A. Sheriff and a Subaru, I had to be on it, no matter who it was, when it was, because that's the combination that's going to go up the road.

"And if it wouldn't work, I had to come back and another would go and I had to go again. I had to go with every single breakaway that looked dangerous to me, just to make the money to keep going."

At last, he said frankly, he cracked.

"It was a series of cracks, really," he explained. "More of a three strikes sort of thing.

"The first major crack came when I was unable to do the DuPont" in 1993, he said, after he learned that his sponsor had withdrawn too late in the season for him to join another team. The DuPont was closed to him because major multiday races do not admit independent riders.

"That was when I realized I'm in big trouble," he said. "I always had a positive attitude and figured a team would pick me up by DuPont time. And when I was sitting on my couch in California and watching the prologue on TV, I really had a little problem there. I was depressed beyond all belief. I was pretty much ready to bag it right there. My girlfriend, Angela, helped get me through."

Then he was recruited by the Portuguese team that, although it failed to pay him, gave him entry to such major races as the CoreStates U.S. Championship in Philadelphia.

By the CoreStates, Julich continued, "I started to come on, I started to feel strong. I was in the final breakaway. After 155 miles, with 5 more to go, we got caught. That was the second blow. There I was in a seven-up breakaway and even if I got seventh, it was going to be about $5,000, which would have done amazing things for my financial status and my morale.

"I believe if I had had that result, even seventh, some team would have picked me up. After that I got depressed again for a couple of weeks and again my girlfriend pulled me out."

Several weeks later, at two races in California, he took the third strike.

"I went to a race in San Rafael and it was so hot, about 110 degrees, honestly. I started the race with what I thought were two water bottles, but I guess when I turned my bike upside down to get it in the car, one of my bottles fully drained out." With no support staff, Julich had nobody to pass him more water.

"I got dehydrated, cramped up, wound up making no money. The third strike was that I had never missed a race in my life, but the next day I missed the race in San Jose because I thought it was at 4 and it really was at 2:30.

"And that was a sign right there. I had never missed a race, I had never made that mistake. And that was it for me. I just went into major depression from there, which taught me a lot about myself. I never thought I'd fall into major depression. You hear a lot about it happening to people but I never thought it would happen to me."

How bad was his depression?

"I didn't want to do anything, I didn't want to leave the house, all I did was sit there. The only time I went out was to get food. All I did was watch TV. I was a total slug.

"I spent so much of my time watching TV and thinking, 'When am I going to pull out of this?' And that day wasn't coming. That signal never came.

"I felt as if I hadn't raced in years. I'd read about the guys racing or watch them on TV and think, 'Gosh, I used to do that.' My girlfriend tried to pull me out of it but I think I was pushing her away. All I wanted was to be left alone.

"Finally . . ." A tortured pause. "I remember sitting there and I felt so fat and I'm usually pretty skinny and I looked at myself in a mirror and I was so embarrassed."

From a weight of 160 pounds on his 6-foot frame, he had ballooned. "I had been a successful athlete and in a month, a month and a half, my whole life had gone to pot. I felt like a total failure for the first time in my life."

Writing off 1993, Julich decided to try one more time to find a team for the next season.

"I think many people could have bowed out and said, 'That's it,' but I've always had a competitive instinct and I couldn't say it," he said. "I felt like I've never been a quitter. If I'd given up, I would have learned that when things get hard, just give up."

Julich resumed training in California and began phoning and faxing teams to ask about a job for 1994. In November, the Chevrolet/L.A. Sheriff team made an offer.

"I said 'I'll take it.' There was no counteroffer by me, no bargaining."

Dave Lettieri, the *directeur sportif* for the team, is pleased with his new rider. "He's a young guy, very talented," he said during the DuPont. "He fits in well and we're very happy with him."

Up to the DuPont, Julich had recorded seven victories this season. "Once I found a team, I began to feel like an athlete again," he said.

Julich refuses to describe 1993 as a wasted year. "In retrospect, last year was the best thing that could ever happen to me as a person and an athlete," he said. "I matured light-years. I know now when things go bad it's just for a brief time. You have to trim off the peaks and fill in the valleys because life and sports are an everlasting roller coaster.

"The lesson I learned last year was an overdue lesson. I always had it handy for me. I may have deserved a lot of things I received but I wasn't appreciative and now I've seen the other side of the fence, I know what it's like, how hard it is, and I don't believe anyone can become successful without all the help you get."

After the Crash

1999

THE 1999 TOUR DE FRANCE TOOK THE DAY OFF MONDAY, its first of two this year, and, unhappily, Bobby Julich was not here in the Alps with his Cofidis team preparing to attack the mountains and fulfill his long dream. It began in 1986, when he was 14 years old and watched on television as Greg LeMond became the first American to win the Tour de France.

That changed his life, Julich says. He dropped the other sports he played at school in Colorado and concentrated on racing his bicycle.

Julich won his share of races, joined the U.S. national team and then turned professional in 1993. He experienced some terrible times, too, including the collapse of his first team and the year he had to spend as an independent rider in the United States, eating up his savings as he paid his way to races, hoping for another chance. Eventually he got it and wound up riding in his first Tour de France two years ago. He finished 17th, then vaulted to third last year.

"I learned so much last year," he said this spring. "There were a few times when I was nervous and caught up in the situation. I was second for a couple of weeks and I began thinking, 'I don't have much higher to go but I can really lose a lot.' I was kind of playing it safe.

"People can maybe say I wasn't aggressive, but the situation I was in, I couldn't deal with it like a seasoned veteran. The next Tour I want to lay it all on the line and give myself a 100 percent chance of winning."

He was laying it all on the line in the time trial in Metz when he came down a hill too fast and crashed, ending his race in a hospital where an examination revealed that he had broken ribs and a broken left elbow. He was flown home to Nice during the day.

Beforehand, he was confident, saying that he expected "a great time trial."

"I'm feeling good, my legs are good, my morale is super. I'm arriving at the first time trial unscathed and very motivated."

Even the pollen allergies that troubled him in races in June had lessened, he said. But, as he said months before, sitting in the sunshine in Nice, where he lives during the season with his wife, Angela, "Destiny has been a big part of my career.

"Success doesn't necessarily mean you'll be happy and failure doesn't necessarily mean you'll be miserable. It's seeing the bright side of the situation you're in and not thinking too much about the bad things.

"The hardest place to be is at the top because you're going to get knocked off. And the people who get back there are the people who've learned to deal with failure as much as success."

Julich talked about a number of topics in bicycle racing, including drugs.

"I just hope the riders take more responsibility," he said. "Winning at all costs is not worth it. There's honor in second, third, fifth, 20th place or even finishing 100th. You don't measure human beings by the number of bicycle races they won."

Why did winning the Tour de France mean so much to him?

Because it's the biggest race, he said. "But I'm not in this sport to say that I'm the best at anything. I'm in this sport because I love it, first of all, and second to see what my limits are.

"I know that a lot of people pass their heyday and think, 'What if I would have taken it a little more seriously?' or 'What if I had taken advantage of that opportunity?' or 'What if, what if?'

"This is such an easy sport," he joked before he went home. "Do a lot of training, don't get sick, don't get injured. What was it Eddy Merckx said when somebody asked him how to become a top rider? Ride lots."

Little Mig

1995

BIG MIG HAS GOALS, such as winning his fifth successive Tour de France, to match his nickname. So does Little Mig, such as completing the race and maybe, just maybe one of these days, crossing a finish line in the mountains with the main group.

Not winning the stage, understand. Little Mig knows his limits. He simply wants to share the thrill of being one of the first 10 or 15 riders across. Even the first 20 or 25, as long as they are in the first group. Whatever the number, that first group is called the leaders.

Guess which Mig—Miguel Indurain, the Spaniard who rides for the Banesto team and wears the overall leader's yellow jersey, or Miguel Arroyo, the Mexican who rides for the Chazal team and wears the Chazal jersey—was closer to fulfilling his goals Monday, the race's day off?

Sigh. Indurain has spent the last week propelling his 6-foot-2-inch, 174-pound frame across the finish line in first, second and third places. He leads the Tour by 2 minutes 46 seconds.

In 59th place among the 129 remaining racers, 1 hour 40 minutes 35 seconds behind, stands the 5-5, 130-pound Arroyo.

"The pace is so fast, too fast for me," he said a few days ago, when the Tour was still on the flat. It was indeed fast then, more than 40 kilometers an hour. Sunday it was about 5 kph slower but there were some big mountains to get over: two climbs rated fourth category, the lowest, in length, steepness and general difficulty; two rated third, one rated second and one rated first.

In a horde of riders 28:05 behind the winner, Arroyo arrived in 59th place.

If only he could do better, he said in an interview. He is doing his best: A veteran of the ADR, Z and Subaru teams and now in his second season with Chazal, the 28-year-old Mexican has always ridden to his maximum potential when the climbing begins.

"It's so important to the team for me to do something in the mountains," Arroyo said.

For the second year, his Chazal team was allowed into the 21-team Tour on sufferance: It is a low-budget French team and the publicity it engenders in the Tour for its sponsor, a wholesale vendor of cold cuts, is all that stands between it and extinction. No Tour, no spurt in the sale of salami, no team.

The race organizers understand this and feel a special responsibility to a French team. By the same logic, Arroyo, Chazal's best climber, is not the team leader.

"No, it's Jean-François Bernard," he said. "It's a French team, you know." He referred to a French rider who not only has seen better decades but also has announced that he is leaving Chazal next year for a new French team.

Under Bernard's leadership, Chazal has scored exactly one victory this season. It happened in a minor race not long before the Tour and just after the team was warned by the race's organizers that their invitation might be withdrawn unless Chazal riders started showing results worthy of a Tour entry.

"Maybe in the mountains I'm the leader," said Arroyo. "It's a big responsibility. My form is good. I finished seventh in the Dauphiné, and in the mountains there I finished with Indurain and Richard Virenque."

Not here, though. In the first alpine stage last Tuesday, the Mexican was 45th, 19:01 behind Indurain and nearly 15 minutes behind Virenque, who is wearing the polka-dot jersey of the Tour's top-ranked climber. The next day, Arroyo finished 52nd into Alpe d'Huez,

15:25 behind Indurain and 13:31 behind Virenque. Sunday, he was nearly 25 minutes behind Indurain and 23 behind Virenque.

In the big picture, the Chazal team has been equally undistinguished, ranking 16th among the 21 Tour entries in total elapsed time. In prizes so far, Chazal has won 31,500 francs (about $6,200) as compared with the 579,550 francs for the ONCE team.

Ordered by their *directeur sportif*, Vincent Lavenu, to display the team jersey and move some garlic sausage, the riders were semi-visible during the first week on the flat in Brittany, northern France and Belgium. Especially were they to be seen after 3:15 P.M., when French television usually begins its daily Tour coverage.

Since then, however, in the Alps, the long and difficult stages in the Massif Central and now in the Pyrenees, Chazal has entered a Bermuda Triangle. The team has not cut the mustard, let alone caused it to be spread on the sponsor's mortadella.

Arroyo is on a mission. After the Tour's day off Monday, which included a long training ride, he has two stages left in the Pyrenees to finish with the leaders and blaze his team's name into the nation's delicatessens.

Can he do it? It's doubtful. This job calls not for somebody as modest and soft-spoken as Arroyo but for a real hot dog.

Reluctant Tiger

1995

THE BIG BOYS, THE CAPOS, were up in Belgium, fighting out the Tour of Flanders over such monuments of bicycle racing as the Kwaremont, Bosberg and Mur de Grammont hills.

There was a time when Jean-François Bernard would have been there, too. Instead, he was in the capital of Brittany for the Grand Prix de Rennes, in which the greatest difficulty was the unremarkable Tabor uphill past the municipal swimming pool. Instead of the World Cup in Flanders, Bernard was riding in the lesser Coupe de France. Instead of the big boys, the competition was Frank Hoj, a 22-year-old Dane who turned professional this year with the Collstrop team in Belgium.

"This is actually an important race for me because all the big riders are in the Tour of Flanders today," Hoj said. "So I definitely have an opportunity to show what I can do, if the conditions are right."

They weren't and he didn't, but Hoj was speaking in that golden time when anything is possible, before the start of a race. Leaning on his bicycle in the Esplanade Charles de Gaulle as 14 teams assembled, he was chatting with a fellow Danish neo-pro, Soren Petersen, 28, of the Rotan Spiessens team, Hot Dog Louis co-sponsor, also based in Belgium.

Unlike Hoj, Petersen was not the competition for Bernard. "This race doesn't mean so much to me," Petersen confessed. "A good training race because I've been sick the last two weeks. Maybe be in the front group and do something, but mainly training."

Those words echoed Bernard's. This was only his second race of the season, which began for nearly everybody else early in February following months of roadwork. After a winter spent looking for a job, Bernard did not get on his bicycle until January 20. "Until then, nothing," he admitted.

He, too, was in the Grand Prix de Rennes for training, he said, and he, too, thought maybe he would do something but mainly it was training. At age 33 in May, Bernard has been around long enough to know the rest of the cliché: "But if I can help any of my teammates, if I can help the team, of course that comes first."

When he said that, Bernard was sincere. The team always comes first for him. He is a rarity, a rider who has been and still could be a team leader but who prefers to work for others. The role of team rider, the *équipier* who shelters his leader from the wind and chases down his rivals, who sacrifices his personal chances and often his wheel for a leader, suits Bernard.

It suits many other riders, too, of course. None of them has finished third in the Tour de France, however, or been acclaimed as the next great French star.

Bernard has—eight years, a terrible crash and a knee operation ago. Since then he has renounced the responsibilities of a leader and the pressure the position generates. A leader is expected to win, after all. When a team labors to set him up for a victory and he cannot bag it, the leader is liable to lose respect, his own and his teammates'.

That was the problem: Bernard did not win many races. A time trial here and there, even a major time trial like the one up Mont Ventoux in the 1987 Tour, but otherwise little.

The next three years, while he was leader of the Toshiba team, were empty. In 1988 he crashed in a badly lit tunnel during the Giro d'Italia and injured his back. The next year he developed fibrosis in his left knee and needed an operation and months of recuperation. In 1990, a saddle sore and another operation forced him out of the Tour de France.

In 1991 he moved to Spain to ride for Banesto, which already had two leaders, Pedro Delgado and Miguel Indurain. There was no need for a third leader, especially a Frenchman, so Bernard went as a proclaimed lieutenant. That is to say, a worker.

For the last four seasons he led Indurain up mountains, pacing him relentlessly until rivals—and Bernard himself—cracked. Then Indurain swooped away to victory, as leaders are supposed to do. Bernard followed, not that far behind, just enough to keep the pressure off.

"I'll never be a leader," he admitted in 1993 in an interview with *l'Equipe.* "I can't be someone that you can count on 100 percent and if you ask that of me, I lose half my power."

Some suspected him of vast insecurity, others of dilettantism. A butcher's apprentice as a youth, he later developed a taste for expensive cars and became a collector of fine wines. He often neglected to train, preferring to spend his time hunting with friends or simply at home with his wife and two children.

Along the way with the Banesto team, he won a few races, most notably in 1992 when he was first in Paris-Nice and the Critérium International. Last fall Bernard quit Banesto. "I wanted a change of air," he explained in Rennes. "I was there four years and it was time to change, time to come back to France, do something else, ride with a young team, take another road."

Eight teams were interested in hiring him, he continued. The problem was that Bernard insisted any new employer should also have to hire his buddy, Philippe Louviot, 31, another team worker, who was left without a team when Novemail folded.

Perhaps one of the many faxes Bernard said he received from prospective employers carried the message that only team leaders can dictate the hiring of a friend. Team workers do not enjoy that power.

Budgets were made, rosters were filled, the season began and Bernard would not waver. He and Louviot were a package.

"We know each other a long time, since we were amateurs," he said in Rennes. "We rode together for Toshiba and we've been close for years. And we absolutely want to stay together."

Only Chazal, a low-budget French team with a lust to appear in the Tour de France and a need for a rider with Bernard's name value, was willing to buy the package. An associate sponsor was found to pay his and Louviot's salaries.

Despite the late start, Bernard seems unworried. "No problems at all," he said before the Grand Prix de Rennes. "My only goal is to be ready for the Tour de France, to get there in good form. Anything before then, it's not important."

He rode strongly for most of the race's 193 kilometers, dropping out with a few circuits of the city still to go. He was here just for the training, maybe to do something, maybe to help the team.

"I feel good with this team," said Bernard, the reluctant tiger. "There's no leader at Chazal. I think there are three or four riders, myself included, who are free to ride our own race. But leader? That's not what I'm looking for."

DUBLINERS

1998

PLUMP, STATELY STEPHEN ROCHE is one of the major spokesmen for the start of the Tour de France in Ireland, as befits the native of Dublin who won the race in 1987 and whose photograph, in full racing gear, still hangs everywhere in that city years after his retirement.

Sean Kelly, who rode 14 Tours and won the green points jersey four times, is also honored in Dublin, but not nearly as much as he will be when the race passes into County Tipperary and his hometown of Carrick-on-Suir.

The late Shay Elliott, a pioneer Irishman in professional bicycle racing and the holder of the Tour's yellow jersey for three days in 1963, has been similarly celebrated, as has Martin Earley, a clever, hardworking team rider and the winner of a Tour stage a decade ago.

In the publicity buildup for the Tour, no Irishman seems to have been forgotten except for Paul Kimmage. His name appears nowhere except in the *Sunday Independent,* the Irish newspaper for which he writes, and on the book he wrote, which has just been reissued eight years after it scandalized many in the world of professional bicycle racing. It also sold 15,000 copies, which he calls "pretty good for a sports book," and won an award in Britain as the best sports book of 1990.

Titled *Rough Ride,* it tells how Kimmage and some other riders used drugs—mainly amphetamine stimulants and steroids—to be competitive.

"I was never a cheat," he wrote. "I WAS A VICTIM," he insisted in capital letters.

"My perception at the time was that we were victims of a corrupt system," he said in an interview before news broke of the drug scandal involving the Festina team. Kimmage did not feel that the system had improved since he retired in 1989 during the Tour de France, the third he rode in his four-year pro career.

"The drugs problem has changed," he said. "It's moved on from amphetamines and steroids to EPO."

EPO multiplies the red blood corpuscles that carry oxygen to the muscles. Because it thickens the blood, it is suspected in a handful of rider deaths attributed to heart attacks.

"That's a bad change, a very bad change," he added. "It's a change that happened due to earlier neglect by the authorities." He was referring notably to the International Cycling Union, which governs the sport.

"This attitude of sweeping it under the carpet, the law of silence, has done a lot of damage to the sport," Kimmage said. "I think they're paying for it now."

So is Kimmage, in his way.

"I haven't been treated very kindly in the run-up to this race," he said. "If I wasn't working as a journalist, I wouldn't be here now. I'd be on the other side of the barriers. I believe that very strongly.

"I'd by lying if I said it didn't sadden me, it didn't disappoint me hugely. To be fair, when they list Stephen and Sean and Shay and Martin, they've won stages in the Tour and written their names in the legends.

"But I do believe there's an underlying current of, 'This guy's written a book that we didn't like and now we're going to make him pay for it, we're not going to let him forget it when the Tour comes to Ireland.'

"I love the sport," he continued. "It was from love of the sport that I took the decision to write the book. Because it would have been easy to take a new job on the paper, say nothing and be buddy-buddy and pally-wally with everyone.

"But what sort of service would I have done to the kids who were coming into the game? The attitude is 'You cannot be anti-drug and pro-sport.' I'm totally pro-sport. They perceive that if you talk about drugs, you do damage to the sport, which is absolute, complete nonsense."

Roche disagrees. He and Kimmage were more than friends before the book, which is full of flattering—Kimmage now calls them "fawning"—references to the rider who in 1987 won the Tour, the Giro d'Italia and the world championship road race. They were the tribute paid to a star by a *domestique*, a rider whose finest result was a sixth place in the amateur world championship.

"I don't know what's up with Paul," Roche said in an interview. "Paul wrote his book and I was stung by it. We talked a couple of times and I told him I didn't like it. No, we haven't been reconciled.

"He has to wake up sometime and realize what he's doing to sport in general. Yes, it's okay to wake everybody up to the danger of drugs, I do agree, but at the same time there's a limit as to what you can say. He's said it once, okay, but he keeps saying it again.

"I say kids today need sport to keep them out of trouble, to keep them away from drugs, to keep them out of delinquence," Roche added. "So encourage them to ride a bike. Don't tell them that if you want to ride a bike well, you have to take drugs. Say it a little, but don't go on and on, please."

To which Kimmage would reply: "The book was written to highlight the ambivalence of the authorities to the problem. They were the target. It wasn't the bike riders. The book wasn't written to portray those who do drugs as baddies and those who don't as goodies.

"Once the system addresses the problem and the guys keep taking stuff, they're no longer victims," he added. "That's when they become cheats.

"But the authorities haven't answered to the problem," Kimmage said, his face darkening even before he knew of the Festina scandal. "They have to, they can't keep ignoring it."

THE GREAT CIPO

1998

MARIO CIPOLLINI, the biggest hot dog outside the dreams of Oscar Mayer, has come to Ireland for the start of the Tour de France with a bicycle as green as a shamrock.

The star Italian sprinter and showman arrived with his Saeco teammates and the 20 other teams of nine men each who will set off in the three-week race. The riders began showing up for cursory medical examinations at Dublin Castle in the afternoon and few are likely to attract more attention than Cipollini.

Ireland is fair bicycle racing territory and his exploits, including four daily stage victories in the recent Giro, appear to be well known here.

Cipollini has no Gaelic and less English, so will be spared explaining to the natives that his bicycle was not painted in honor of the Emerald Isle. Like his yellow bicycle, it was painted in honor of Cipollini. He rode the yellow bicycle last year during the two days he wore the yellow jersey of Tour leader. This year his eye is on the green jersey of the points leader, hence the green bicycle.

A notoriously feeble climber, Cipollini does not have a bicycle with the red polka dots that denote the King of the Mountains. But, as befits a clothes horse who boasts that he has a pair of shoes for every day of the year, he does have in his Tour suitcase the red, white and blue, star-spangled outfit that he wore last year to honor the American makers of his Cannondale bicycles and the black and blue soccer jersey of Inter Milan with the No. 10 of Ronaldo that he wore on a victory podium in the Giro.

He and his team are fined every time he appears in anything but his regulation team jersey and black shorts but, hey, life's meant to be fun, Cipo says.

For all his sartorial bluster, his pet cheetah and Via Veneto scruffy good looks, the 31-year-old Cipollini is surprisingly soft-spoken. He does not predict victories and never humiliates his rivals verbally. While he may refer to himself as The Lion King, Il Magnifico and even, a few years back, unblushingly as the Italian Stallion, he does not say he is the best sprinter in the sport. He agrees, however, with anybody who does say so.

"It's not easy being among the best for 10 years," he said during the Giro, where he tied Eddy Merckx's career record of 25 stage victories. "It's more difficult every year for me to train, to suffer. My biggest boost is that I win, which makes it worthwhile. I still feel an indescribable joy when I do. There's nothing like winning."

And he keeps winning. After his triumphs in the Giro early in June, he won four stages in the Tour of Catalonia, his tune-up for the Tour de France.

His overall strategy will be the same as last year: finish high in the short prologue on Saturday and then try to win the first road race around Dublin on Sunday or the second stage to Cork on Monday, gaining enough bonus seconds for victory to don the yellow jersey and wear it to France on Tuesday. For more than a week, the Tour's terrain will be flat—ideal for sprinters.

As always, Cipollini will rely on his Saeco teammates to overtake any breakaways and power him to the front near the mass finish. Saving energy, he will tuck in behind his lead-out man, Gian Mateo Fagnini, and then burst past him and presumably everybody else with 100 or 150 meters left.

Any sprint finish in the top 25 of the 189-man field will give him the points, on a sliding scale of 35 down to one, that count toward the green jersey. That is Cipollini's main goal in this Tour, he says, but to win the jersey, not just keep it for a few days, he will have to get over the Pyrenees and Alps and make it to Paris.

It will not be simple. In his four previous Tours, citing the heat and general weariness, he has been unable to finish. "They say I can't do it," he says, "but I think I can. When I get something in my head, I go for it."

FLIGHT OF THE EAGLE

1990

THE EAGLE OF VIZILLE FLEW OVER HOME SOIL. All along the way, past the dappled meadows and scarlet stands of poppies of the Vercors region, he was treated with respect, as eagles usually are.

There was a time not so many years ago, however, when Thierry Claveyrolat carried the nickname in affectionate mockery. "Eagle" is usually reserved for such great climbers as Féderico Bahamontes, the Eagle of Toledo, who, legend says, once made it to the top of a mountain in the Pyrenees and was able to halt and eat an ice cream before the other riders joined him. Bahamontes won the King of the Mountains jersey in six Tours de France. In 1959 he won the Tour itself and his yellow jersey still hangs in the rafters of the cathedral in Toledo.

Claveyrolat excelled in smaller races and smaller mountains for most of his career. Then, in 1989, he spread his wings. "For a while I thought I would become the world champion," he remembered. "I thought of it, I really thought it would happen."

His face puckered as he recalled the world championship course in Chambéry, France, and how he and eight others attacked on the eighth of 21 laps and built a lead of nearly five minutes. By the bell lap, Claveyrolat was one of three riders still ahead, by 11 seconds. At that point, his teammate Laurent Fignon led the pursuit, pulling with him Greg LeMond and Sean Kelly.

"It would have been better to believe in Claveyrolat," said another French rider, Charly Mottet.

Paced by Fignon, the threesome caught the leaders and LeMond went on to win the final sprint, with Claveyrolat fifth and Fignon sixth.

"If somebody had told me before the start, 'You'll be in front for 180 kilometers and finally finish fifth,' I would have been awfully happy," Claveyrolat admitted months later. "But because of the circumstances, I feel terrible. It would have been understandable if the Spaniards or the Italians had ridden after me, but not my own team.

"Winning would have been everything. For me it would have been more than a dream. But there's no point still thinking about it. I'll never forget the world championship at Chambéry, but it's time now to think of other things."

Those other things included, of course, the Tour. Suddenly, at age 31, Claveyrolat bore the nickname of Eagle with pride. For the second successive year he was wearing the polka-dot jersey of the King of the Mountains in the Tour. In 1989 he lost the jersey when he had to quit in the Pyrenees because of a broken wrist, but now he was in sound health and even better form, winning the first alpine stage and finishing fourth at Alpe d'Huez.

He explained that he had been inspired by his many fans in this part of the Alps near Grenoble. Claveyrolat comes from the town of Vizille, just outside the city limits.

His supporters were back for the time trial from Fontaine, another suburb of Grenoble, to Villard de Lans. After his efforts the two previous days, the soft-spoken Claveyrolat did not expect to do well and seemed unsurprised when he finished 28th in the field of 170 remaining riders.

"I did my best," he said, "but I just didn't have anything left after the mountains." The fans who chanted his name along the route understood. "He's not a winner of the Tour de France, no," said Georges Delombre, who wore the cap of Claveyrolat's RMO team. "But he's a very good climber, he's won a stage of the Tour and he's one of us."

In the Vercors, Claveyrolat was "the regional," the local favorite, and in the countryside, where the Tour remains the favorite sport of summer, the tradition of cheering on the regional is strong.

In the village of Engins, for example, Maurice Francol had just led a herd of goats down from pasture and into a barn when the first rider in the time trial whirred past his farm. Francol barely turned to watch Antonio Espejo of the Kelme team taking the curve. "I'm not much of a cycling fan," Francol confessed. "Farmers are too busy to spend the day watching even the Tour de France."

Would he be back by the road when Claveyrolat went by in the afternoon?

"Of course," he said. "He's one of us." Francol gestured at the craggy foothills of the Alps across from his barn. "He comes from the other side but he's still one of us."

Up the road a few hundred meters, near the banner that marked the summit of the Engins hill, Brigitte Durand was working at a snack stand. She is usually a secretary at the village hall but was helping sell sandwiches and such drinks as sodas, mineral water and beer.

"We're just here for the day, to make a little money and to cheer the riders," she explained. "Claveyrolat especially, of course. He's the regional." At her side behind the wooden counter, Monique Dalbion nodded. "Claveyrolat especially, of course," she echoed.

Hours later, his back knotted and his jersey soaked with sweat as he climbed, the Eagle of Vizille came through Engins. The two women left their stand, which had sold out, and stood at the side of the road to join the chorus shouting, "Thier-ry, Thier-ry."

The rider swept left at the World War I monument. On the steps of the Restaurant du Barrage, a café really, a few farmers came out to join the cheering. Francol stood near his barn, where chickens scratched in the dirt, and applauded.

In a few seconds, Claveyrolat had left Engins behind as he rolled past the limestone hills overshadowing the road. He was on the descent now, with another long and tiring climb still to come. "Vas-y, Thierry," "Go, Thierry," the signs said as he approached the finish. He was weary by then and lost 2 minutes 49 seconds to the winner, Erik Breukink, falling from 15th to 16th place overall.

"That's done," Claveyrolat said. "I get my next chance in the Pyrenees." The Eagle of Vizille awaited another day to rise, to glide, to soar again.

What Else Can He Do?

1998

THE PRESSURE ISN'T OFF, CHRIS BOARDMAN SAID, but it is diminished. The 29-year-old Englishman had just won the prologue in the Prutour, the first major bicycle race in Britain in four years.

Thousands of fans on the scene in Scotland went wild, as they probably did in the rest of the United Kingdom, where the race was shown live on television.

One of us. Our Chris. "Well done, son," the Scots shouted in a language remarkably akin to English.

The adulation was almost enough to make him forget his problems. It's only three months into a racing season that lasts through October, but already for Boardman, who rides for the Gan team based in France, this has been a long year and one full of pressure.

He knows how to deal with it, he insisted. "Being a pro, you've got to accept the pressure as something that comes with the job," he said a couple of hours later, relaxing in his hotel. "Nobody likes pressure, but you've got to deal with it."

How else could Boardman have set a record in winning the gold medal in pursuit at the 1992 Olympic Games, and twice, in 1993 and three years later, have broken the world record in the most acclaimed performance on the track—the one-hour race against the clock? How else could he have won three world championships? How else could he have won the prologue twice in the Tour de France, the last time as recently as a year ago?

Between then and now, something has gone wrong. Boardman says it himself, as if his record of no victories until the Prutour prologue on Saturday and then a repeat Sunday on a 128-mile stage to Newcastle, England, did not say it for him.

"Things haven't gone great this year," he says, despite the two victories. He knows that the Prutour field of 18 teams of six riders each is made up mainly of amateurs and second-level professionals. In his major races on the Continent, he has been riding without power—"I'm just missing that explosivity," he admitted—fading in climbs and not coming close to dominating races against the clock as he has since he turned professional late in 1993.

"I did it more on experience, motivation," he explained, referring to his victory over the 2.6-mile prologue course in Stirling, Scotland, with a steep ascent from the town center to the 13th-century Stirling Castle. Hard by the statue of King Robert the Bruce, who vanquished the English at the nearby battle of Bannockburn—"sent them homeward to think again," as "Flower of Scotland," the unofficial national anthem, puts it—Boardman crossed the line in 6:08. That was two seconds faster than George Hincapie, an American with the U.S. Postal Service team.

"I think technically I rode it quite well," Boardman continued, analyzing his performance. "I didn't make any mistakes."

The race ends Sunday in London after 825 miles of zigs and zags through England and

Wales. The Prutour, sponsored by Prudential, is an attempt to resuscitate the sport of bicycle racing in Britain, which has not had a major stage race since the Kellogg's Tour of Britain ended in 1994.

As the top British rider and the only one with an international reputation, Boardman is the fans' focus.

"A Brit in Britain," he describes himself, noting that he did not ask to be given No. 1 in this race. His thoughts, however, are more on the Tour de France and the rest of his season.

"You realize you may very well be on a plateau or even on the descent," he said, "but that's one of those things you don't want to talk about. You don't know where the top is until you're looking back at it. There is no peak until you start down the other side.

"For myself, it becomes a whole lot less interesting when you hit that plateau. This is one of those jobs that the amount of yourself that you put into it, the sheer time it absorbs of your life, when you stop getting rewards, you ask, 'What am I doing this for?'"

Boardman leaned back in his seat and summed up this bleak season. "I've had illnesses, but looking back on it, I couldn't say, 'That was it, That was it.'

"It gives me a certain peace of mind as a rider when I can say, 'What else, what possibly else, can I do more and I can answer 'nothing,'" he concluded. "That's a certain comfort. You can sit back and get on with the job, which is pretty much where I am now."

LAST SEASON

2000

"WHO'S LEADING THIS RACE?" Chris Boardman asked idly half an hour after he finished a tough uphill time trial in the Grand Prix Midi Libre. Told that he was the leader, Boardman looked surprised. "I'll be at least two minutes back when it's done," he said with finality.

He was right. When all the riders had finished, the king of the time trials was 2 minutes 28 seconds behind the winner.

Forty-third place is not usually the spot to find Boardman, a 31-year-old Englishman who won the pursuit race—basically a time trial—at the 1992 Olympic Games, set the world record for the hour's ride against the clock in 1993 and again in 1996, and was world champion in pursuit in 1994 and 1996. The list goes on: world champion in the time trial in 1994 and three times winner of the prologue of the Tour de France and three dozen other races against the clock since he turned professional in 1993.

So what went wrong in the race in the village of Laguiole, the knife capital of France? The short answer is that nothing did.

"My form is, believe it or not, very good at the moment," Boardman said. He would have won the time trial in the Four Days of Dunkirk race this month except that a dog wandered into his path and he had to swerve and slow, costing him an estimated eight seconds in a race in which he finished second by 23 hundredths of a second.

Another part of the short answer is that in the Midi Libre the uphill terrain did not suit his metronomic style, all power, position and ability to bear anaerobic pain. His forte is smoothness, not the constant breaks in rhythm when he had to keep getting up out of the saddle on the 15-kilometer climb.

The long answer—one preferred by the articulate, even philosophic Boardman—is that, as he prepares to retire at the end of the season, his role in the Crédit Agricole team and his performance level have changed. Not necessarily diminished, he said, but changed.

"I think I'm capable of still doing some big things, just not the volume I used to do," he said. "There's still a lot of pressure and a lot of it comes from myself. Like today: Even when the odds are all against me, I just hate to fail."

Stacking those odds was the enormous amount of work he did the day before at the head of his team's pursuit of a breakaway rider. Crédit Agricole had the leader's jersey in the race and protected it successfully by first catching the breakaway after a long chase and then setting up its sprinter for a stage victory.

Boardman did much of the labor at the front during the stage, acting as a *domestique,* or ordinary worker, rather than the star he has been throughout his career.

"I'm probably the best-paid *domestique* in the bunch," he joked over a cup of coffee as riders in the time trial continued to finish singly in the street outside. Low in the overall standings, he was one of the first to start the individual race against the clock.

"I like to think that if it's not my turn, I'd hold up my hand and say, 'Okay, somebody else is better suited to do the job.' At the moment, the logical thing for me is to be a *domestique.* I'm giving for the boys, that's not a problem. You've got to do it and I like doing it.

"It's a different kind of responsibility and you've got to give everything you've got until you're empty.

"Still, I would have liked to have done a ride here. I've done some of the best training I've done in two years. When it's your last year, you get a bit irritated when you're looking good all the time and getting no payback at the moment. I want that payback."

Whether he gets it or not in the Tour de France and the Olympic Games in Australia, he is definite about not seeking it during another season on the road.

"I said from the outset that I would retire at 32," an age he reaches in August. "It gets to the point where what you're putting in doesn't equal what you're getting out. You're getting more disappointment than you are elation. It just gets to the point where it's no fun anymore.

"You're constantly trying to train not to fail. It happens to everybody, it's quite logical and natural. This is where I'm at.

"I'd really like to do well for my self-respect. I don't want to do what some other guys do, take the money and ride out your last year. I don't want to be like that. I want to give everything I've got till the end of the year and get some results. That's my motivation.

"It's like doing the last one in a set of 10 intervals in training—you know you can give it your all, even though you're knackered, because it is the last one."

Come, Join the Party

1999

"WHAT ABOUT THE FESTINA SCANDAL?" demanded the man standing under the banner that read "Salins, Jura, with Cédric Vasseur." "Who cares about the TVM scandal?"

"Listen, my friend," he continued to a man he first met two minutes before, "drugs and doping are not what the Tour de France is all about. The Tour de France is about Cédric Vasseur, you and me. The Tour de France is about sports and a good time.

"Forget doping, my good friend. Go eat some chicken."

The chicken—"not as bad as you might think," judged a man with a plate of it and fried potatoes—and three kinds of sausages, each with fried potatoes, plus wine and beer were all for sale at a picnic lunch organized in the town of Salins-les-Bains to celebrate the flypast of the Tour de France, including Vasseur, a 28-year-old Frenchman who rides for the Gan team.

Vasseur is not from the town, a porcelain center in the Jura, but from the north, at least

600 kilometers away. How he happens to have a 100-member fan club here and why the club decided to organize the day's festivities, which attracted hundreds of people who do not belong to the club, testify to the enduring strength of the world's greatest bicycle race and the sport itself despite the doping scandal that has enveloped them.

"The cycling public in Europe is an educated public," said Graham Jones, a Briton who rode in five Tours between 1979 and 1987 and finished three of them, "and they do, rightly or wrongly, know what goes on, and to a certain extent they've accepted that."

Members of the Cédric Vasseur Fan Club, many of them eating lunch in a big tent with four long tables and an accordionist singing on the stage, expressed more than acceptance. Men and women, young and old, they were uninterested in discussing the expulsion of the Festina team from the Tour, the arrest of half a dozen riders, team coaches, doctors and masseurs and the confessions of five riders who started the Tour that they had used such illegal performance-enhancing drugs as the artificial hormone EPO.

"It happens, it happens," was a typical comment. "That's not why we're here."

"That side of cycling doesn't concern us," said Claude Meyer, an organizer of the club and the lunch. "We prefer to concentrate on the good side, people like Cédric."

Meyer, 47, met Vasseur, then 23, when he was an amateur in the Tour du Franche–Comté, and Meyer, as he put it, was "no more than a cyclo-tourist and a big fan." Vasseur, he continued, is a *chic type*, or swell guy, and they quickly became friends. Vasseur's father, a former professional rider, is also a *chic type* and a friend of Meyer's. Both Vasseurs began coming to Salins-les-Bains for occasional races, and the fan club was formed.

When Vasseur wore the overall leader's yellow jersey for five days in the last Tour, Salins went crazy, Meyer said.

Vasseur was pretty happy himself. "It was fantastic," he said in an interview earlier in the Tour. "My father won a stage in the Tour de France but didn't get the jersey, so I was first in the family.

"It changed my life. People looked at me differently, they waited for me to ride past. This year I'm not expecting to win it again but I'll try to do my best and do a good Tour de France."

Vasseur has ridden well, ranking 24th overall and fourth in the King of the Mountains competition as the race ended.

"Cédric is giving it his best," Meyer said. "That's what the Tour is about, giving it your best, not drugs.

"All of this is in honor of Cédric and the Tour. Go look at the collection of old bicycles we have here, the old racing jerseys."

Salins is just another small town in France. For a few hours, though, Salins and the Place Aubarede, where the celebration was held, were the center of the small world of bicycle racing.

"The Cédric Vasseur Fan Club Welcomes You," said a banner across the road, and the welcome was sincere as long as nobody tried to talk about illegal drugs. "How about a sausage, my good friend?" the man said when the topic came up.

Vasseur addressed the issue Thursday, after he finished 11th at the end of a long breakaway that ended in a mass sprint.

"This is the third long breakaway I've ridden in that was caught near the line," he said. "Luck smiled on me last year but not this one. The Tour is the most beautiful race in the world and I owe it my glory and the most beautiful moments of my career. I owe it a debt.

"Many people go to a lot of work to organize this race, many people travel to our roads to applaud us, the riders accept many sacrifices to get ready for the Tour. It's a pity that the party might be spoiled. We all have to work so that the Tour remains a jewel of France's heritage. Sports must make that happen."

A Different Ending

1993

A LITTLE MORE THAN A YEAR AGO, Graeme Obree decided that he was "totally fed up with cycling" because he "had nothing from it whatsoever."

He did not mean honors, since Obree had won a fair number of amateur races in a dozen years of competition in his native Scotland. He meant money. At the age of 27, Obree, a dropout from studies in engineering and economics at Glasgow University, the bankrupt owner of a bicycle shop, was unemployed and broke.

"On the money side I was on the dole and that was it," he continues. "I had no money and a mortgage and a wife and a son. Last October I said, 'I'm through with the bike, I'm never going to ride again.' But there's not a lot of jobs floating around in Scotland, so soon I was thinking about making a comeback and what I was going to do was write a book about my experiences.

"Then a friend said, 'You don't have an ending.' What I needed was just one goal for one season for the ending of this book."

Obree pauses and his face breaks into a smile, possibly at his own bravado. The goal he chose was the most revered distance record in the sport: the hour's ride against the clock. The racer, alone on a track, goes just as far as he can in 60 minutes.

Since Henri Desgrange, the founder of the Tour de France, set the record of 35.325 kilometers an hour in 1893, it had been pushed up by a line of champions. Fausto Coppi covered 45.848 kilometers in an hour in 1942, Jacques Anquetil reached 47.493 kilometers in 1956, Eddy Merckx reached 49.431 kilometers in 1972 and Francesco Moser broke the 50-kilometer barrier—as big a psychological wall as the four-minute mile for runners—in 1984 when he covered 51.151 kilometers. Nobody had exceeded Moser since, although a few had tried and many had dreamed of trying.

"The hour record is everything," Obree says. "There's only so many people who have held it." They number less than two dozen, including Coppi, the winner of five Giros d'Italia and two Tours de France; Anquetil and Merckx, each the winner of five Tours de France; Moser, the winner of the Giro and innumerable classics, including Paris-Roubaix three times—and Obree, the most feared time trial rider in Ayr, Scotland.

Last July 16, on the bicycle track in Hamar, Norway, he covered 50.689 kilometers in an hour, fell 462 meters short of Moser's record, said "I'm going again tomorrow" and spent a sleepless night, fearing leg cramps.

Riders usually space record attempts three or four days apart, but Obree did not have that option since the officials who had to time his ride to make it official were leaving late the next morning. "What drove me on," he says, "was desperation. Desperation, necessity. It was the last chance."

Had the money for the record attempt run out? "Hardly," Obree says. "I didn't have any in the first place. Basically I didn't have any money and I saw my chance of getting any money slipping away. If I could humanly do this thing, I was going to do it."

For the second attempt, he changed bicycles, riding on one he designed and built himself partly with material from the family washing machine. Lacking the horizontal bar that usually runs from the saddle to the handlebar post, the bicycle has a distinctive curve to the handlebars, which the 5-foot-11-inch, 160-pound Obree grips in a tight and nearly flat aerodynamic tuck, far over the bars.

The position is usually described as "an egg" and he is alone in using it.

He set off early for the track. It was 8:50 when he got there and he was nearly in a frenzy. "Where's my bike? Right. Where's my helmet? Right. Let's go.

"I got on the track and did a few laps" to warm up, Obree continues. "Normally the starter fusses about, but I was wanting none of that. I said 'Okay, you ready?' and I just went away. And once you start, you're doing it, that's right, you're doing it."

And he did it.

Riding a revolutionary bicycle valued at about $100 and jutting far over the handlebars as he pushed a monstrously big gear, Obree became the new holder of the hour's record. An hour after he started, he had covered 51.596 kilometers, or 445 meters more than Moser. The gunshot that signaled his breaking of Moser's record came with more than a minute of the ride left.

Obree was in Paris recently to ride in the Open des Nations track meet. He was not there as the hour record-holder since Chris Boardman, an Englishman, recorded 52.270 kilometers an hour to break Obree's record a week after he set it. The Scotsman was invited instead as the world champion in the pursuit race, in which two opponents set out at opposite sides of the track and race for four kilometers. Obree won the title in August on the same track in Norway where he set his hour record.

"So many people still think of me as the hour record-man, not the world champion," he mused. "Although I held the record only seven days, I'm one of the names on the list now. It was my one chance of doing anything, of winning anything, of being one of the big names."

He is anything but bitter, he insists, that his hold on the record was so short. "I was expecting it," he says of Boardman's success on the track in Bordeaux. "Because it wasn't my best possible performance because I'd ridden the day before. But it may be the best thing that's happened. Now I have another go at setting the record next year. Thanks to Mr. Boardman."

Obree was shown a photograph of him crossing the finish line at the end of his hour's ride with his right hand cocked into a fist in the air and a grimace mixing exhaustion and triumph on his face. What was he thinking then?

He looked silently at the photograph for what seemed to be a long time. Then he spoke: "I thought, at last, after all these years, at that moment . . .

"The best was when the gun went before I actually finished the whole hour. When that gun went, ah! Nothing could go wrong—I couldn't finish or a puncture or the fork snapped before I got to the end. If I dropped down dead then, if I dropped down dead, my epitaph would be written already. I had broken the record.

"After all those years of struggling and saving pennies to buy a loaf of bread, it had all been justified. Everything had been justified, all those years. Everything had been justified as soon as the gun went.

"As soon as the gun goes, that's me covered the distance he covered already. Everything else was extra. The gun goes after you've got the distance, it's a distance record. I was sailing and if I'd wound up dead, I'd still have the record."

Since then, and especially since he set a speed record while winning the pursuit race at the world championships, Obree has had no financial worries. Turning professional and sponsored now by the Bic pen and razor manufacturers, he has ridden without much success in a handful of road races and with great success on the track at the six-day races that fill the European fall and winter. Each appearance brings him a fee of several thousand dollars in addition to his Bic contract. Hard times are definitely over.

The schedule is full through January, when the road season begins to replace the one on the track, said Martin Coll, 29, Obree's brother-in-law and manager. "We go to Grenoble tomorrow, two days later it's Dortmund, two days later it's Geneva, four days later it's Munich, three days later it's Bordeaux. We have to go from Bordeaux to Ghent to race there and then straight back to Bordeaux and we race two days there and then to Vienna, a week's invitation to Vienna.

"This is a money-making thing for Graeme," Coll continued. "Next winter they'll want to see him again at these tracks. Whether he gets some medal of any color at the world championships next year, they'll be wanting him indoors at the six-day races. For the demand, you know. People will be wanting to see him again."

Coll and Obree were having a late breakfast at their hotel in Paris, Coll drinking coffee, Obree eating a basket of croissants while he compared his new life to a merry-go-round. "You don't know who's the person who's going to pick you up at the airport, you don't know what hotel you're going to, you have no facts and figures."

Life has changed. "Totally," Obree says. "In terms of security. You can't have a good outlook on life if you can't afford anything, so my outlook on life has improved. Otherwise I'm the same guy except I don't see my wife as often."

"And you don't drink as much," Coll throws in.

"I don't drink at all now," Obree admits. Known before as no stranger to a daily pint or two of beer, he stopped drinking in September because of liver problems complicated by a lingering lung infection. "Also drink isn't good for performance."

He seemed a bit surprised to be asked why he was riding the merry-go-round.

"Why?" he echoed. "Because it's my job. It's what I'm good at. At the moment this is what I'm good at and you know what they say: Do what you can when you can.

"I'm also doing it for the money. I've got to get as much money as I can. But it's got to be performance-driven. I'll do the performance, Martin will try to get as much money for me as he can. Obviously we go to races where the best money is if there's not too much traveling involved.

"What money means to me is not all those zeroes in the bank, a fancy car or whatever else. It's no more sitting there and thinking what I can't afford to buy.

"You won't live any longer by having money; life will be just as short as it would be without money," Obree decides. "You've got to make the most of life."

That includes the book he planned to write a year ago. "I'm still going to write it," he says, "but obviously it will be a bit different. Especially the ending. The ending will be nine-tenths of the book now."

Part Three

RACES AND PLACES

Introduction
THE TOUR CAME HERE

1995

MONSIEUR PATRICK, OWNER AND MANAGER *of a hotel on the Place du 11 Novembre in Saugues, was tending bar the other evening and cheerfully explaining the difficulties of his chosen career.*

"Down here at 7 in the morning to serve the guests' breakfasts, closing at 1 in the morning," he said as he wiped glasses, steamed milk for coffee, poured wine and drew a few beers. "Sometimes a guest wants to leave at 6. Where do you buy croissants at that hour? You have to buy them the night before and store them in the refrigerator.

"Vacations? We've taken eight days off in the two years since we bought the hotel. When can we go? In the spring and summer, it's the tourist season. In the fall, it's the banquet season."

By "banquet," he possibly exaggerated. The awning on the restaurant attached to his hotel advertises crêpes and pizzas. Saugues is in the Auvergne, a region in central France not notorious for its cuisine, but even such local delicacies as stuffed cabbage, duck breast with blueberries and almost anything with chestnuts qualify better as banquet fare than a pizza.

"In the banquet season," he persisted, "we serve up to 250 people a day. Otherwise 150.

"Days off? You can't close a hotel one day a week. Bills to be paid: The hotel had 25 rooms when we came here, we knocked down walls, made it into 18 rooms, fixed the plumbing, put in an elevator." He rubbed his thumb over his first two fingers in the familiar gesture.

"No vacations, no days off, down here at 7, up to bed at 1," he said in good-natured summary. "And the worst? The worst is that I don't even get to watch the Tour de France on television. Too busy. Too busy even for the Tour de France."

For the first time in his monologue, his face lost its smile. The rare bartender telling his troubles to a customer, he seemed distraught. If there had been a drink in front of him, somebody would have offered to fill it up again.

"The Tour de France could come right past the hotel," he continued, "and I couldn't even watch it on television."

The Tour indeed remains a benchmark in the heartland, la France profonde. *The race is in distant Brittany or the Alps and people in other regions watch on television. More than 40 million Frenchmen see the race on television, the organizers of the three-week Tour say. The bicycle race rolls through or near town and people turn out. Fifteen million people flock to the sides of the Tour's roads, according to the organizers.*

What else is there to do in a pleasant town like Saugues? Four concerts were scheduled this summer, not including the accordion festival on August 13. There will be two conferences to discuss a local legend, the Bête du Gevaudan, a sort of werewolf, it seems, to whom or which a museum is being built.

The lamb fair lies ahead on Friday and the mushroom festival comes two days later. The rest, as a Dane said, is darkness.

The next morning some of the people of Saugues were up early. Four old men in the sort of caps that old men wear were gathered in the Place du 11 Novembre outside the hotel, talking about the Tour de France. A Frenchman, Laurent Jalabert, had won the previous day's stage in a grand exploit on Bastille Day, the national holiday, and the four old men were feeling particularly proud to be French.

"The Tour de France came here a few years ago," one of them told a visitor. "This town, Saugues. The Tour."

The daily stage ended or started here?

"No, it came here. Passed through. This town, Saugues. The Tour."

Who won that stage? He didn't know. Who won that Tour? He couldn't recall. All he could remember was that the Tour had come through town. This town.

"Unforgettable," he said.

A Taste of Spring

1995

FOR MONTHS, ONE GRAY DAY has trudged bleakly after another. No sun, no sign of spring. Winter, still winter outside the window and inside the heart.

But not all hearts. Mario Cipollini and Gianni Bugno have tasted spring.

In the south of France, as television proved last weekend, the bicycle racing season has begun: There was the pack, gliding along the back roads of Provence, past hills that had to be dotted with early lavender and shiny with the new leaves of olive trees. There was the sun and, when it baked the hills, there would be the scent of thyme.

The riders wore shorts and short-sleeved jerseys, the uniform of spring. Spring—Cipollini, Il Magnifico, has been waiting nearly a year for spring.

Late last April, in a sprint finish in the first stage of the Vuelta a España, he was shouldered into a crowd barrier and crashed heavily at high speed. Because the Italian was not wearing a helmet when he thudded onto the road, he suffered a severe concussion.

Cipollini is fearless, just ask him. Was fearless.

After the crash he suffered from fierce headaches and found he had lost his zest for the sprint. If he retained his speed over the final 200 meters, he no longer felt able to abandon himself to the fury of that charge. He did not get back on his bicycle until September.

The Tour of the Mediterranean was his first competitive race since the Vuelta. On the third stage, from Maugio to Berré among the green hills outside Marseille, Cipollini let it out, attacking with half a kilometer left.

He coasted over the line, sitting up while the other sprinters were still pumping. Cipollini's long hair was blowing behind him from under his helmet, and his arms were outstretched, palms down, in his familiar gesture of victory, like a holy man blessing his flock. "Thank you, boys," he told his Mercatone Uno teammates.

Before the race finished he recorded two more sprint victories, but the first was the best. "It was as good as winning the world championship," he said.

Bugno returned from another sort of disaster. Last August, during the world championships in Sicily, the rumor went out that he had failed a drug test. Not drugs exactly but caffeine, which is prohibited in extraordinary amounts as a stimulant.

Found guilty, Bugno was banned from the sport for two years under rules of the Italian Cycling Federation. On his appeal that the international laws of racing took precedence over national laws, the sentence was reduced to the standard three months.

That was not a whitewash for Bugno, who has long been a man of fragile morale and complex problems. Six years ago, when he was still a minor rider, he began seeing a psychologist to help resolve his timidity. He also had to overcome severe vertigo, or dizziness and fear of falling when he descended a mountain at high speed. The trouble was laid to a bad crash in the 1988 Giro d'Italia and to a congenital obstruction in the canals of his inner ear.

As a cure, Bugno underwent ultrasound treatments laced with music, mainly Mozart. "I listened to Mozart at different speeds and degrees of loudness for a month," he reported. "After that, the vertigo was gone."

Soon an allergist found that Bugno could not tolerate wheat, milk and milk products, and changed his diet. Retooled, Bugno became a champion, rising to the top of the professionals' computerized rankings.

In the 1990 Giro, he won the prologue and kept the leader's pink jersey for the rest of the race. In the Tour de France that year, he won both the climbers' big stage at Alpe d'Huez and the sprinters' at Bordeaux. In 1991 and 1992 he won the professional road race championship.

The last two years have been lean, however, with only an unexpected victory in the 1994 Tour of Flanders to slow his decline. Everything soured: He lost confidence in his *directeur sportif* with the Polti team, he was divorced, he moved from Italy to Monaco. The positive drug finding and the two-year ban confronted Bugno, at age 31, with the probability that his career was through.

Like Cipollini, the Tour of the Mediterranean was the first race of the season for Bugno. On Saturday, he worked hard to spring a young MG teammate, Davide Rebellin, off and away on the 9-kilometer Mont Faron climb near Toulon. When Rebellin could not shake a rival,

Bugno overtook them both and swept to victory himself. Wiping the sweat from his face, he stood in the sun and said he hoped this victory would simply be the first.

On Sunday, the sun moved from Provence to Paris and the street market was suddenly full of flowers: crocus, pygmy iris, narcissus, primula in all the colors of the rainbow jersey. Down south it was dark and overcast.

The Tour of the Mediterranean ended in the streets of Marseille with a climb up the Notre Dame de la Garde hill, 550 meters long and a grade of 20 percent. Like the Mont Faron ascent, this was asking a lot of the riders early in the season and few were up to it. Bugno zipped to another easy victory, both the stage and the overall.

Because he wore only the slightest smile, he might have seemed remote, even indifferent, when the television cameras moved in afterward and the questions began. His answers were banal.

As Bugno knows, for weeks to come, a bright sun will be exceptional. Prudence and caution are called for. Down in Provence it felt like spring, but was still winter.

A Helping Hand

1997

THE FILIPINOS SAY IT NEVER HAPPENED. No, no, no, they insist, it's a misunderstanding.

"An exaggeration," said Julius Enagan, the team trainer. "I don't know why people think this. Nothing like this occurred. Come, we speak to the rider."

He summoned one of the riders on his six-man team in Le Tour de Langkawi race in Malaysia: No. 186, Carlo Jazul, who was checking his bicycle.

"Did Bugno push you across the finish?" the coach asked.

"No, no, no," Jazul replied.

"You see." Enagan placed his arm around Jazul's shoulders. "Bugno comes up to him in the race and puts his arm on him like so and he says, 'You're a good boy, a good boy.' But push him across the finish? It never happened. No, no, no. It is not allowed. The penalty could be severe," Enagan said.

A check of the records for the stage showed that indeed Jazul had finished nearly two minutes ahead of Gianni Bugno, the star Italian rider. Obviously Jazul had not been the one who was pushed, so could deny it truthfully.

But the records showed that two other riders on the Philippines' team—Arnel Querimit and Enrique Domingo—finished seconds behind the Italian.

Sitting on the tailgate of his Mapei team car, Bugno was rubbing sun block onto his face and nose.

Ciao, Gianni. Did you help a Filipino rider make it to the finish line after the climb in the Genting Highlands?

"No, nothing," Bugno said. His eyes darted left to right and back again. "Not allowed to push another team."

A racer may help a teammate by pushing him uphill or even across the finish but assistance to a rival could too easily be mistaken for interference. The Filipino *directeur sportif* and Bugno knew the rule book: Pushing an opponent costs each rider a fine of 200 Swiss francs ($135) and a time penalty of two minutes. That's a lot of time in a sport that measures daily stages in seconds.

So, no, no, no, it never happened. Yet a handful of people saw it happen about 750 meters from the finish after a steep 18-kilometer climb.

Bugno noticed that a Filipino rider was struggling and near collapse. Bugno turned back down the road, rode a figure eight, came up behind the rider, put a hand in the small of his back and pushed him uphill until they were close enough to the line for the other rider to get across under his own power. That elegant gesture kept his rival in the race.

Ciao, Gianni. This time the questioner brought along an Italian journalist to translate. It helped also that the Italian journalist was an old friend of Bugno's.

"Sure, I helped him," the rider admitted. "I did it because he's one of us. I don't know his name or who he was, not even his number. All I know is that he was in bad trouble. We have to look out for each other, no?"

It would be nice to think that Domingo was the beneficiary of Bugno's generosity.

Flash back 10 days to the airport in Kuala Lumpur, where the 150 riders were waiting to be flown to the start of the race in Sabah. Hanging out for six hours while tickets were distributed, security was cleared and the plane loaded, everybody was bored and growing irritable.

Bugno went for a stroll and passed the Filipino team members sitting on the floor. They recognized him and jumped to their feet. The amateurs rushed him, crying "Bugno, Bugno," and asked him to pose for photographs. First was a team picture with Bugno in the middle, then individual shots of each of the six riders and their handful of officials with Bugno. He kept smiling throughout.

Afterward, somebody asked a rider if he really knew who Bugno was or just that he was a foreign professional rider.

"Bugno, of course," the rider responded. "A great champion. Two times in the world championships. The Giro. The Tour de France. I know Bugno. He is in all our racing magazines. One of my heroes."

That rider was Enrique Domingo.

The Hell of the North

1985

THE DAY BEFORE THE PARIS-ROUBAIX RACE, the organizers came across a road crew busily repairing potholes in a village street that was to be part of the course. The potholes, the workers said, had to be filled immediately, the battered cobblestones quickly covered with tar. The organizers argued for a delay, but the workers were adamant. The road was unsafe, they insisted, a menace to traffic. "Exactly!" the organizers replied.

That argument won a postponement of repairs until after the 172 riders in the 1985 Paris-Roubaix had bounced through the potholes and over the cobblestones. "It's not a bicycle race," Bernard Hinault often complained, "it's a cyclo-cross." The winner of Paris-Roubaix in 1981, he thereafter refused to take part in the race.

In deference to its age (first run in 1896) and standing (winners in addition to Hinault include Fausto Coppi, Eddy Merckx, Francesco Moser and Sean Kelly, a roll call of champions), Paris-Roubaix is politely called "the queen of classics." But its other subtitle better describes the race: "The Hell of the North."

Truly it is a form of hell, more than 250 kilometers of back roads paved for 50 kilometers with cobblestones, usually made slick by April rains and mud.

And if the rain is an enemy, the cold is another and the wind a third: In the flat country of the north of France, there is no protection as the wind whips across farms and coalfields to fight the riders from the front along much of the route. But the main peril is the cobblestones, called *pavé* in French and "Belgian blocks" in parts of the United States. Generations ago they were carried as ship's ballast to America and wound up lining the streets of cities in the East. They were long lasting but crude, and finally they gave way to paved roads that were kinder to automobiles.

Even in the French countryside, cobblestones are now rare in all the areas frequented by tourists, but in the north, with its desolate landscape of slag heaps and steel mills, there has been no pressing need to replace the stones to lure automobile traffic onto back roads. Every year another section may be tarred over, but the Paris-Roubaix organizers seem to be able to find the country lane here or the forest trail there with its cobblestones still gleaming wickedly in the rain.

Yet even in dry weather the cobblestones are a torture, battering the racers in the hands and arms as the shock vibrates up the bicycle, puncturing tires, destroying wheels and wills. In the rain they also cause skids and mass crashes, and the earth into which the stones are set becomes a sucking mud through which the riders sometimes have no way to proceed except by running, their bicycles on their shoulders.

Despite the song, April in Paris is usually not a time of chestnuts in blossom but a dreary month of rain, and so it was this time. It rained heavily the week before the race and the sky was dark as the riders gathered in the Place Charles de Gaulle in Compiègne, a town 82 kilometers north of Paris and the traditional start of the race, despite its name. The riders showed up in ponchos and knitted caps, and spectators began to put their umbrellas up as the race moved off on the blacktop road leading away from the town where the World War I armistice was signed.

Even before the rain there were a few punctures and a mass crash, both inevitable in a pack so large: 23 teams, seven from Italy, six from France, six from Belgium, four from the Netherlands.

Quickly 13 riders broke away and by kilometer 22 their lead was up to 2 minutes and 44 seconds. By kilometer 36 it was 5 minutes and they dropped a rider who punctured, the unlucky Marc Gomez. Three years before, Gomez was a 27-year-old neo-professional who became the toast of French cycling by winning one of his first races, the Milan–San Remo classic. The next year he became the French professional road champion but then was badly injured in a fall in the Tour de France. The year after that, in 1984, he was hurt again in a fall on a training run as he attempted to rebuild his form, and his season was shot until after the Tour. He rode a strong Tour de l'Avenir, the Tour of the Future, a fall stage race that was dedicated to putting the spotlight on young riders and giving older professionals a final showcase before teams signed up their riders for the next season. Nobody was saying that at 30 Gomez needed this sort of exposure or that his job was threatened, but he obviously needed a bit of glory to stop the rumors that he had failed too many times ever to be a winner again.

So, 23 seconds behind the breakaway group, he slogged on, with the rain streaking the dark goggles he wore to protect his contact lenses. Gomez was riding perhaps a bit closer to his La Vie Claire team car than he should have been, but who could blame him for seeking that extra help in drafting?

As he fought a strong side wind alone, his chances of catching the leaders just a few hundred meters ahead of him were gone. By kilometer 42 he was 55 seconds behind the breakaway and by kilometer 58 he was 2:15 down and the team car had left, dropping back to the pack in case La Vie Claire's leader for this race, Greg LeMond, might need a wheel. Five kilometers farther, Gomez was resigned, a leisurely pedaler as he waited for the pack, 2:42 behind, to reach him.

The pack was in no hurry, which allowed the breakaway to set a rapid pace: After two hours the lead riders were 20 minutes ahead of a schedule based on the maximum expected speed of 40 kilometers an hour. For anybody who punctured, this fast speed meant a hard ride to get back, as Francesco Moser learned at kilometer 72, where he waited for a new wheel, surrounded by seven of his teammates.

Moser had won Paris-Roubaix three times and now was making one of his last attempts to tie Roger de Vlaeminck's record of four victories. Paris-Roubaix, which he first rode in 1974, is an ideal race for men like Moser, strong men, strong enough to survive the bouncing and spills along a course where power and will are all, tactics nothing. "My team is weak and that troubles me," Moser said nevertheless. "Everybody says that Paris-Roubaix is a special race, one in which you don't need teammates around you. That may be true on the cobblestones, but you need them before."

He need not have feared: His Gis team towed him back well before the cobblestones started at kilometer 113, and then it was up to him. At age 33, Moser seemed too old to equal his victories in 1978, 1979 and 1980, but he also seemed too old the year before to break Eddy Merckx's record for the hour's ride against the clock, which he did easily, and too old to win the Giro d'Italia for the first time in 11 attempts, which he did a little less easily.

"I won't say that I'm too old—no, it's not that," the Italian rider said before the race. "But I know you can't hope for anything in Paris-Roubaix if you're not willing and able to give 100 percent of yourself. I'm a fatalist. I've known for a long time that you have to accept the cobblestones, consider them as just one part of the race, if you hope to ever get over them. You've got to accept them, forget them and adapt yourself to the violence. Mostly you've got to have luck and try to stay near the front so that your team car can get to you quickly if you puncture. We'll see. It's probably my last Paris-Roubaix, and that doesn't bother me at all."

At kilometer 99, a curtain of rain awaited the riders, the sky black to the horizon, great sheets of water being whipped along by a wind from the right. Quickly, by kilometer 106, the sun was out and glinting on the water running through furrows in fields showing the first green stubble of spring.

Until now the race might have been any of the lesser spring classics, Milan-Turin, say, or Paris-Vimoutiers—a cold and rainy jaunt through the countryside on well-surfaced roads. But now came the first cobblestones, slick from the rain, muddy on both sides of the 10-foot-wide road; in extremis a rider might negotiate his way down this dirt track, banging in and out of the water-filled dips, and later some did. The *pavé* came in short stretches—1.5 kilometers from Salesches to Escarmain, 0.6 of a kilometer (barely a city block) on a gentle hill outside Bertain, no early section longer than 2.1 kilometers—but they came so frequently that the clear roads between sections were forgotten.

The pack began to break up, shattered by mass falls, slowed by the stones and mud and the armada of press cars and the photographers' motorcycles that slewed and fell across the road. The rain pelted down again at kilometer 125, soaking the leaders as they filed along a road so little used that grass grew on the slight rise down its middle. At kilometer 132, near a huddle of new homes with an arrow pointing the way to the Sansome British War Cemetery, the pack was split into five major groups and already some riders were through.

Covered with mud, Pascal Poisson of the Renault team and Marc Sergeant of Lotto took a shortcut, veering away from the race route and down a quiet road with signs pointing the way to the city of Valenciennes, the first of two feeding zones and therefore a rendezvous with team cars. Ahead of Poisson and Sergeant were other small groups of riders going home with their heads down after only eight kilometers of cobblestones.

Until Valenciennes, the race had been heading north and now it turned northwest, with the western crosswind becoming frontal and bringing rain again. Ahead at kilometer 154 lay the oaks, birches and cypresses of the forest of Arenberg, the single-most feared stretch, 2.4 kilometers lined with brutish stones of uneven height and irregular placement, a dark place made mad by the beating of television helicopters hanging over the trail. Nearly 25 years ago, the race organizers feared that Paris-Roubaix had gone soft and ordered their scouts to find new challenges, and somebody remembered this forest, now under government control, where the roadbed dated to the early 18th century. "I've never seen cobblestones like this," an official said. "They're not paving stones but huge rocks, a foot long, a foot and a half high. We've found the perfect place for Paris-Roubaix, dangerous but magical."

Through this unmagical place the riders stormed with faces haunted under their coating of mud. It covered their arms and legs and even their backs, thrown there by rear wheels. Led by Theo de Rooy of the Panasonic team, the breakaways were dispersed now, only 3:58 ahead of the pack paced by Eric Vanderaerden, also of Panasonic and winner a few days before of the esteemed Tour of Flanders. Close behind him were the other favorites—Moser, LeMond and Sean Kelly.

At kilometer 190, far too early as he later admitted, Moser made his move. Why did he attack so far from the finish with 5 Panasonics near the front to lead a counterattack? "I wanted to be sure to reach Roubaix in time to catch the first plane home to Milan," he replied testily. Then he confessed that he hadn't been sure where he was but he knew he wanted to be out of there. "I just attacked because I was afraid of falling, of losing my balance among all the motorcycles blocking the road, and I thought it was better to ride at the front."

With his own teammates close behind to aid him, de Rooy refused to participate in Moser's attack, so the Italian was forced to fight the wind alone. He managed to build a lead of 1:15 at one point, 67 kilometers from the finish.

As he passed through Bersée, at kilometer 204, swinging right at the statue to the town's war dead, Moser looked wan and strained. Soon he was caught, with Vanderaerden attacking just after an ugly stretch of potholed road turned sharply right and the crosswind became a tail wind. By the cobblestones at kilometer 218, Vanderaerden had joined Moser, with Kelly and Hennie Kuiper leading the chase. By kilometer 231, on the cobblestones of Templeuve, Moser's race ended: He fell, and Vanderaerden was gone by himself.

He held off his pursuers for a while, then fell back and was caught. At kilometer 245 of 266, it was anybody's race with only a handful of anybodies left: Kelly, LeMond, Marc Madiot and Bruno Wojtinek of Renault, Eddy Planckaert of Panasonic, Rudy Dhaenens of Hitachi and Jef Lieckens of Lotto. Moser and Kuiper were a minute behind and fading fast.

Finally, at kilometer 251, the rider who decided to go off was Madiot, two days short of his 26th birthday and still a perpetual *espoir*, a great white hope with the Renault team, never a winner of a classic as a professional but the 1978 winner of Paris-Roubaix for amateurs. Madiot had long had a reputation for being either—at his best—self-effacing or—at his worst—timid. However, this time he broke away confidently and there was nobody able to chase him down over the final 14 kilometers, three of them laced with cobblestones.

Madiot's pursuers all had good excuses. "I had the bonk, the *fringale*, at the end and I couldn't do it," LeMond said. "The wind was too much, the worst I've ever felt it here."

Kelly put it differently: "Madiot was just too strong. After chasing Vanderaerden, I had nothing left."

Madiot opened his lead to more than a minute and, as he passed under the red flag that marks the final kilometer, the Frenchman was able to reach down and shake hands with Cyrille Guimard, the Renault team manager, whose car escorted the rider in.

"Those last few kilometers, it was fantastic," Madiot said. "You don't feel tired then. All you hear is people cheering. All those people and there you are, alone."

Just short of two minutes later, Wojtinek, a native of the north, finished second, punching the air in triumph before his fans. Kelly beat LeMond in a sprint for third place and Moser and Vanderaerden came in together, in 12th and 13th places, 5:41 behind. Of the 172 riders who started, 35 finished, among them Marc Gomez, in 28th place. He was nearly 27 minutes behind, long enough for some of the other riders to have ended their showers, washing the mud of Paris-Roubaix off their bodies, and to have left for home or the next race.

Going to Court

1992

LATE IN THE AFTERNOON OF AUGUST 28, 1988, after seven hours and 274 kilometers of bicycle racing around the Belgian town of Ronse, the world championship road race dwindled to a duel between two men in the starting field of 178. With less than 100 meters to go, nobody ahead of them and their closest opponent two bicycle lengths behind, Steve Bauer and Claude Criquielion sprinted toward the finish line and glory.

It was a breathless moment for each: Criquielion, a Belgian who in 1984 first won the championship and the adoration of his French-speaking countrymen, and Bauer, a Canadian who finished third in the same world championships just a month after he was a close second in the road race at the Olympic Games in Los Angeles in 1984. Both tore ahead at speeds above 46 kilometers an hour.

Seconds later, Maurizio Fondriest of Italy hurled his arms upward in victory, an astonished smile on his face as he glided across the finish line. Behind him came Bauer, who appeared to be near tears.

Far behind them came Criquielion, walking and dragging his mangled bicycle with his right hand. His left hand was raised in the official sign of protest. He placed 11th after he walked across the line, which the rules permit if a rider brings his bicycle across, too. He looked angry, exceedingly angry.

On Monday, three and a half years later, a Belgian judge is to announce in criminal court with whom Criquielion should have been angry: Bauer or himself. In what is believed to be an unprecedented lawsuit in professional cycling, Criquielion sued Bauer for assault. If he wins, he intends to seek more than $1.5 million in damages for the loss of the world champion's rainbow-striped jersey.

"I haven't heard of any riders who believe in Criquielion's case," Bauer said this past week before he started the Paris-Nice race. It finishes Sunday and he expected to be home in Belgium when the court decision was announced.

"What riders say about the case," Bauer continued, "is 'It's still on?' They can't fathom it."

Criquielion refuses to comment these days and did not show up in court on February 3 in Oudenaarde when final testimony was heard. Now 35, he retired from the sport after last season and lives on his family farm near Ronse.

Last year, when he was willing to discuss the case, Criquielion insisted that he sought not vengeance but justice. "Never, never," he said when asked if he had dropped his lawsuit. "Without him, I would have been the world champion. I want justice."

Thousands jammed the streets of Ronse to see the finish and millions in Europe watched it on television. What they witnessed was an opening sprint by Bauer, who veered right, about a meter from waist-high spectator barricades, on the final small hill. Criquielion responded by chasing Bauer down and then trying to pass him on the inside, between the rider and the barricades. The Canadian, who had been standing on his pedals, sat down, shifting into a lower gear and losing a bit of speed. His right elbow then flew up.

Suddenly the Belgian crashed, grazing a policeman who was standing in the road, then hitting a stanchion of the steel barricades. His bicycle fell to the right, the rider to the left. Bauer wobbled but stayed upright.

Race judges saw all this, too. "Rider No. 36, Bauer, Steve, who finished second, is disqualified for actions deliberately unsportsmanlike and dangerous," the judges announced, referring to the elbowing that was presumed to have unseated Criquielion. It is the only disqualification, other than for positive drug testing, in the 64-year history of the race.

What nobody saw, according to Bauer, is that Criquielion bumped him while trying to pass. What nobody understood, Bauer adds, is that his elbow flew up reflexively as he tried to keep his balance.

One of his witnesses, Bauer continued in an interview, was a professor of biomechanics who had studied film of the race supplied by the Belgian BRT network. "He analyzed the sprint from a biomechanical point of view, not a tactical point of view: reaction forces, balance forces from the point of collision on. Basically he was very good for my defense, proving that Criquielion hit me first, that he made contact first.

"The experts appointed by the court also said Criquielion made contact with Bauer first," he added. "From that point on, there's no sprint. We're two riders out of balance."

He called Criquielion's charges "laughable, utterly ridiculous." But, Bauer added, "It's really been a serious matter." For weeks after the race, Belgian police stood guard at Bauer's home in Gullegem because of threatening mail from Criquielion supporters. There have been no further incidents.

Despite the crash and lawsuit, the Canadian has continued to do well professionally, finishing second in the prestigious Paris-Roubaix race in 1990 and wearing the leader's yellow jersey for nine days in the Tour de France that year. Last season, as he passed his 32nd birthday, his career slowed. Riding for the Motorola team, he recorded only three victories, two of them in the Tour DuPont, in which he finished sixth.

To this day, Bauer said, he does not know who would have won the sprint if there had been no collision.

"I was feeling good and that's why I led the sprint out and forced him to go to the left side and into the wind," he said. "He was going good, too, I can't deny that, but if he was going so good, why'd he pass on the right? If he had tried to pass me on the left, into the wind, it would have been a good sprint."

He paused and thought about the race, about the lawsuit and about Criquielion. "What a dummy," he decided.

A Long Wait

1997

"FORTY-ONE YEARS," sputtered Albert Bouvet, even more red in the face than usual. "Forty-one years that I've been waiting."

Bouvet has been waiting that long to have his burden lifted, to get out from under the heavy sorrow of having been the last Frenchman to win the esteemed Paris-Tours race. He does not say it but he thinks it is a disgrace that no Frenchman has won Paris-Tours, an arrow through the heart of the country, since he did it in 1956.

He sighed. "For 41 years, it has been a very sad story," he said at the start, wearing a badge that bore his name and his identification as the last French winner. "Very sad."

The race is 101 years old and was dominated by French riders from the first year through the mid-1950s. Twenty-eight times a Frenchman has won it, second only to the Belgians' 37. But not since 1956. Since then the winners have included Italians, Dutchmen, Germans, Belgians, of course, an Irishman and—can this be true?—a Dane and an Australian.

A Dane? Not a Frenchman but an Australian? Bouvet's eyes rolled. What next, an Eskimo? A Bosnian?

"Impossible," Bouvet said, "not possible." He laughed bitterly. "Very sad."

He was entirely sincere. Another man might glory in his reputation as the last French champion; not Bouvet. He was always a team player. He is more proud of having served Jacques Anquetil in his first Tour de France victory in 1957 than he is of his own triumph in Paris-Tours.

The years ease from Bouvet: His thick white hair turns dark, his jowls and gut recede, he is again the trim, 26-year-old Bouledogue (pronounce it "bulldog") de Fougères, his hometown in Brittany. He wears the glorious Mercier team jersey and he is riding Paris-Tours in a strong wind, as always, and is far back in the race.

He is not happy, he did not want to be here and he has lost a lot of money, he thinks. A short time before, he had finished second in the Grand Prix des Nations, a long time trial, and was offered 60,000 francs (then less than $1,000) to race on the track in Rennes the day that Paris-Tours was held on the road.

"Sixty thousand francs, even old francs, you don't refuse that," he remembers. But his team insisted he ride Paris-Tours, in which he finished 25th the year before, winning all of 5,000 francs. He was not angry, he insists; he was, after all, a team rider. The track is where he performed best—French champion in pursuit in 1958 through 1960 and again in 1962, silver medal in pursuit in the world championships in 1957 and 1959—but if Mercier wanted him on the road, onto the road he went.

Midway to Tours, 250 kilometers from Paris, he is far behind when his coach pulls alongside in his car and asks with some asperity, "You riding or not?" The rider is stung.

"Ten kilometers later, I was at the front," Bouvet says.

About 40 kilometers from the finish of that Paris-Tours, on a short descent from a hill, Bouvet attacks with an Italian rider. They build a small lead, not even two minutes, before Bouvet leaves behind his accomplice. Alone, the Frenchman holds off the pack for 25 kilometers: "Near the finish, I was this close to dropping the adventure, to sitting up and letting them catch me. I didn't believe I could do it."

At the line, he was perhaps two meters ahead, but ahead. Two meters, two centimeters—he won. His prize came to 700,000 francs. He never again came close to winning Paris-Tours, but what Frenchman has? In the last decade, none has been closer than fifth place. When his racing days were over, Bouvet became a journalist, writing mainly about bicycle racing, and then an official of the Tour de France.

Before he retired in 1995, he had risen to director of competition, which meant that his was the voice everybody heard on the radio linking the Tour, screaming at cars ahead of the race to move out of the riders' way, bellowing at photographers' motorcycles that he had taken their number for interference, yowling at one and all to clear the road. Albert Bouvet was quite excitable, to tell the truth, but in his retirement he is calm. Somebody else is in charge of keeping press cars and motorcycles out of sight of the race, and he is happy to be merely an honored guest.

Not this day, however, not the Sunday of Paris-Tours. He paced the street where the race started in the suburb of St. Arnoult en Yvelines. (The "Paris" part is as flexible as the "Tours.") French chances of victory were slight. Paris-Tours is almost always won in a sprint, and the best native sprinter, Frédéric Moncassin—although he had not won a race this year—had called it a season and was home near Toulouse. The second-rank French sprinters were just that. "Maybe Nazon," Bouvet said of Damien Nazon, a French sprinter who blew everybody away in the minor Tour of China two years ago. "Maybe Jalabert," he said of Laurent Jalabert, the top-ranked rider in the world and, more important, a Frenchman. Maybe anybody, as long as he was French. Please not another Italian, Belgian, German, Dutchman, Irishman, Dane or Australian. Not a Swiss. Not a Samoan.

Six hours later, it was a Ukrainian. In a two-man sprint, Andrei Tchmil, a Ukrainian who was born in Russia and is seeking Belgian citizenship, beat Max Sciandri, an Italian who rides as an Englishman. In that stew of nationalities, there was not a French gene. The highest ranked Frenchman was in 22nd place.

The only one who had seemed capable of victory was Jalabert, who was in front alone with 35 kilometers to go and a lead of about 30 seconds. He held out for 20 kilometers before he was caught.

Albert Bouvet slowly got out of an official car to watch the finish. His head was low and his face strained. He seemed to have been weeping. "I hoped," he said. "When Jalabert attacked, I thought it was possible. I allowed myself to hope."

An old man pushed up to him in the crowd and gave him a photograph. Bouvet looked at it closely.

"Look," he said, "this was 40 years ago." The cream of French racing was in the photograph. "This one here, that's Louison Bobet," Bouvet pointed out, "that's François Mahé. Here, that's Anquetil. And here," his finger stabbing a rider with a big smile and a look of ease, "that's me."

He peered up at the sky and spread his arms wide. "Maybe next year," he said.

THE PRIDE OF LIONS

2000

IN THE DIN OF THE OUDE KWAREMONT, the dozen young men standing on a muddy shoulder of the cobblestoned road were not looking down the hill for their first sight of the breakaway in the Tour of Flanders. Unlike the thousands of others there, they were looking up, up at the two television helicopters, as they waved large flags of a black lion rampant on a yellow field.

In this part of divided Belgium, the flag of Flanders takes precedence over the black, yellow and red national flag. All down the Oude Kwaremont and on the 15 other hills of the race, spectators flapped smaller versions of the flag of Flanders that had been distributed minutes beforehand. On some hills the larger flags formed a canopy under which the riders struggled toward the crest.

Spanish Basques do this, too, at bicycle races, but they are always joyous. Not here, where faces were earnest. Joy does not seem to be a Flemish virtue. Hardiness is.

Johan Museeuw is certainly hardy. Two years after he almost lost his left leg to gangrene because of a crash in Paris-Roubaix in 1998, he is winning major races again. ("They call me the rider of the 1990s," he said after finishing first in the classic Het Volk in February, "so explain to me, please, how I won the first big race of 2000.")

In a pretty tribute to Museeuw, who has won their race three times, the organizers of the Tour of Flanders decided last year to pass through Gistel, his hometown. That went so well—big crowds, good feelings—that the visit was repeated this year.

Again the town turned out in hordes to cheer its native son. In truth, the 34-year-old Museeuw is more than that. He is such a hardworking, down-home person, and his career has been marked by so many successes, that he is a natural hero throughout Flanders.

In Gistel, just inland from Ostend on the North Sea coast, there are two public shrines to Museeuw. One is his father's garage and car dealership, where the son's many trophies are kept. The other is the Gasthof Tourmalet, an inn where many of Museeuw's jerseys—the yellow one he has worn in the Tour de France, the rainbow-striped one he won in the world championship road race, the Belgian champion's one—are displayed.

On show, too, are the jerseys won by a former proprietor of the Gasthof Tourmalet. That would be Sylvère Maes, who named his inn for the mountain in the Pyrenees that the

Tour de France has been climbing since 1910. Maes won the Tour in 1936 and 1939, winning four stages the first time, including the one from Luchon to Pau, presumably over the Tourmalet. In 1939 he won two stages and the polka-dot jersey of the King of the Mountains, shining that year in the Alps.

Two big fish, then, from one small town, separated by generations. Contemporary photographs of Maes show an open face with a prominent nose and chin, which caricaturists loved. The record books say he was born in 1909 and do not give a date of death.

Outside his inn, where the race took a left turn on its way across the flatland to the first of the hills, the crowd waiting to cheer Museeuw and the other riders was loud but not rowdy. The Flemings do enjoy honoring their big men. They are especially proud that so few Walloons from the French-speaking other half of Belgium have managed to win the Tour of Flanders. It's too tough a race, Flemings say with a significant look; it takes tough men.

Another one of these is Eric Leman, who is tied with Museeuw for the most victories in the Tour of Flanders. Now 53 years old and a soap manufacturer, Leman won the race at the start of the 1970s, when he was also winning five stages in the Tour de France. After Museeuw's hometown was visited last year, Leman or a friend asked the race organizers to pay him the same honor.

So, at Ingelmunster, 40 kilometers after Gistel and still before the first hill, the riders turned off the main road and passed through a series of suburban streets. Surrounded by friends, Leman was waiting at the curb. He looked fit and proud—another lion of Flanders.

The tributes were touching and the show of pride understandable. Insulated by language and culture, the Flemish perhaps need to show their flag. But it went wrong at the school in Meerebeke that traditionally serves as press headquarters after the finish.

One classroom was marked "*Preszaal (NL)*," meaning it was exclusively for Flemish speakers. Another, across a courtyard, was marked "*Salle de presse*," meaning it was for French speakers and everybody else not fit for entry into the first room. Us and them, the signs said and, other than the Flemings, nobody reading them was remotely reminded of lions.

The Northern Front

1995

THE BICYCLE RACING SEASON OPENED on the northern front last weekend, moving from the temperate breezes of the Riviera and Andalusia to the stinging cold and daylong drizzle of Belgium.

"The rain is no problem, not for Belgian riders," said Eddy Planckaert, formerly one of those riders and a distinguished one. Sitting in the comfort of the Bloso Sports Center in Ghent, Planckaert was discussing the Het Volk race, which he won in 1984 and 1985.

"It's the most beautiful race of the beginning of the year," he continued. "If you win, you have a lot of publicity, as much as if you win a classic."

The Het Volk, which was first organized in 1945 by the Flemish newspaper of that name, is a classic—an important one-day race—but not a classic classic, not a great one-day race, not one of the 11 classics that compose the World Cup and not a classic that means much outside Belgium.

"For a Belgian rider, a victory here means he's got a job for next season," said Claude Criquielion, another formerly distinguished Belgian rider. "No matter how well he does the rest of the year, a victory here wins him a new contract. That's how important this race is to the Belgian people.

"For everybody else," Criquielion admitted, "it's not a very big race."

But if the Het Volk's meaning is narrow, it is profound.

"For a Belgian sponsor especially," explained Jean-Luc Vandenbroucke, the *directeur sportif* of the Lotto team based in Belgium and yet another formerly distinguished Belgian rider, second in the Het Volk in 1984 and third in 1981. He was surrounded by dozens of fans who were standing content in the cold rain and gazing at bicycles and riders as teams began arriving for the race.

"It's very important to win the Het Volk because it's the start," Vandenbroucke continued. "The Belgian people have waited impatiently for the season to start and here it is."

Belgian fans, among the most intense in Europe, have been waiting for more than their season to start three weeks after the campaign began in Spain, Italy and southern France. Since the great Eddy Merckx retired nearly 20 years ago, those fans have been waiting for another great Belgian champion, some rider swift and voracious enough to show the world how rock-hard Belgians can be and how triumphant.

Instead the fans have had to settle for Planckaert, Criquielion and Vandenbroucke, among others: Respected riders, winners all, but not one a great champion. Those three are retired now. The new Eddy Merckx is still slouching toward Brussels.

In Ghent, inside the sports center, riders were entering rooms to change into racing uniforms while hundreds of fans wandered the corridors. Bicycle racing is an immediate sport—fans are not held back from the athletes by long lines of policemen but are allowed to mingle, to seek autographs, to exchange a few words with the riders before and after the race.

For many Belgian riders, this was as close as they would come to big-time adulation. The Het Volk attracted 24 teams of 8 riders each, and some of those teams were the minor, small-budget ones that usually appear only in Belgian and Dutch *kermesses*, insignificant criterium races through villages to break the torpor of a weekend.

Asfra, Palmans, Zetelhallen, Cedico, Tönissteiner Saxon, Vlaanderen 2002, Espace Card: Who outside Belgium has heard of these teams? Here they were, competing against such giants as Mapei, Motorola, Festina, Gan, Castorama, Polti, Novell, TVM, Lotto and Le Groupement. Those are the teams that will go on to all the races, the classic classics, that are closed to the Asfras and Espace Cards.

Over the hall's public address system came an announcement for the fans to please stop blocking the corridors. A few young children looked tentatively at their fathers, who shrugged and continued to point out the gearing of this bicycle and the handlebar rake of that one. Not until the riders began leaving the sports center did the fans follow.

The rain was pelting his Brescialat team car as Eric Vanderaerden spilled six or eight small sandwiches and pastries, each wrapped in tin foil, from a bag and began packing them into the back pockets of his jersey.

A decade ago he was another new Eddy Merckx, a feared sprinter, an excellent rider of short time trials. Then he lost just enough power and ambition and gained just enough age to become no more than another respected Belgian rider. He is in his mid-30s and his face has lost its sleek look in a web of deep lines.

Third in the Het Volk in 1992 and 1993, Vanderaerden had little pressure on him. "I'm with an Italian team now, so this race is not so important to me," he said. "I hope to do my best, no more."

His goals for the season were equally limited: "To win something. Last year I didn't win a race so I hope to do it this year."

Perhaps he will, but not in the Het Volk. Somewhere during the 205-kilometer race past Flanders' waterlogged fields, through sodden villages and over 11 steep, slickly cobblestoned hills, Vanderaerden dropped out. So did many others in the 192-man field. Eighty-five riders made it to the end back in Ghent, with 39 more finishing but being disqualified because they were outside the acceptable time delay.

Despite its tiring hills and winter weather, the Het Volk is often decided in a mass sprint finish. This day, however, three riders broke away at kilometer 55, on the climb up the Oude Kwaremont, and managed to stay away, aided by a passing train that kept the chasing pack blocked at a railway crossing for two minutes.

For a Belgian fan, the three riders represented a problem in loyalties.

One was indeed Belgian—Edwig Van Hooydonck, second in the Het Volk in 1990 and third the next year—but he rides for the Novell team based in the Netherlands. Another in the breakaway—Andrei Tchmil—rides for the Belgian Lotto team but is Russian. The third was no problem at all: Franco Ballerini, an Italian who rides for the Mapei team in his homeland.

Ballerini proved to be the strongest. In the final few kilometers, with the pack half a minute behind, the Italian attacked three times and twice was caught by Van Hooydonck and Tchmil. They could not respond the third time.

By six seconds and about 200 meters, Ballerini was so clearly the winner that he had time to applaud his performance and straighten his jersey before he coasted across the line with his arms upraised.

He became only the fifth foreigner in half a century to win this most beautiful of Belgium's early season races. Belgian fans would have to wait at least another year to cheer in the rain for one of their own.

Paying a Debt of Honor

1996

THE TRAVELER ON THE FRENCH ROAD D105, one lane each way in the Cantal region of the southwest, would almost certainly be heading toward some destination other than Chalvignac. Pleaux, perhaps, or Mauriac, which are at least towns, or Aurillac, which is, stretching it a bit, a small city.

Chalvignac is a village. Population 600. A post office, a couple of cafés, a few dozen houses surrounded by pastures and planted fields that are just now turning green. D105 climbs a hill to Chalvignac, offers a pleasant view of the Dordogne River, bends broadly through town and then heads off to the horizon, to Pleaux, perhaps, or Mauriac.

Not many people stop in Chalvignac. Last year the Paris-Nice bicycle race was supposed to finish a daily stage here and, to hear residents talk a few days ago, it was going to be one of the bigger events in the village's history.

The weather turned to snow that day a year ago, however, and the wind was sharp and strong, blowing the snow across D105 and blocking it. After fighting the wind and snow for a while and falling far behind the race schedule, the riders refused to go farther. Rarely is a bicycle race canceled because of a storm, but this one was.

Paris-Nice moved off in cars and buses to wherever the teams were staying that night. The next day the race resumed far from Chalvignac.

The village was installed early in this year's itinerary. "A debt of honor," said Josette Leulliot, who has directed Paris-Nice since 1982, succeeding her father, Jean Leulliot, who started the race in 1933. "Yes, exactly," she continued. "A debt of honor that we owe to Chalvignac."

This year the weather was fine and the race proceeded here without incident. On the long climb up the hill, Laurent Jalabert, the French star, attacked early and gained a 16-second victory, taking the overall leader's white jersey. Afterward he stood on a shoulder of D105, signing autographs and chatting with people from the village, a millionaire wearing short pants on his visit to Chalvignac.

The village turned the day into a holiday, complete with fatted calf. It was turning on a spit over a fire in the main square. "All the animals that we serve come from our farm," a sign announced. For 65 francs ($13), lunch comprised cold cuts, a slice of roast beef, the local whipped potatoes called *aligot* and finally an assortment of cheese. For 50 francs, no cold cuts.

Other stands sold sandwiches—pâté, cheese or sausage—and waffles and crêpes. For drinks, this being France, wine was cheaper at 7 francs than water (8 francs).

The villagers had set up a big tent in the square and, after the race, they gathered there to listen to a few speeches of welcome to the race, to drink a glass or three of pastis and to nibble at pieces of the local cheese, cantal and Roquefort.

A band was going to play and each table in the tent held copies of songs for a sing-along. The top sheet was titled "To the Country Market," a regional waltz with words by Rene Labourel and music by Altero Betti. Roughly translated, the verse runs: "In this country is born / The most beautiful market / On the bank of the Dordogne / Where every Saturday night / Chalvignac receives / All the kings of folklore."

In part, the refrain: "Chalvignac, I love you / With your great market / Each week-end / I come to enjoy / The good products of the Auvergne." In all, there were three verses, each one followed by the refrain.

The singing had not yet started when it was time for the Paris-Nice troupe to head for that night's hotels, far from Chalvignac, but no doubt the celebration went on into the night.

As they say in this sport, it is not enough for people to come to the race. The race must also go to the people.

Bananas

1997

"IT'S A NICE VILLAGE, NICE ENOUGH," the man said. "Calm. Unchanged for a long time." He looked up and down Laheycourt's main street, the rue Général Porson. "Poor," he decided. "Poor."

The houses in sight, most of them two-story stone row houses, some of them modern tract homes, looked nice enough. But the man said he was a lifelong resident of this village in Lorraine, so he should know.

A couple of other men waiting for the Tour de France to pass through said most people worked in the few steel factories still active in the area, or on farms. The Tour's roads through Lorraine, in eastern France, pass one vast farm—wheat, corn, potatoes—dotted with villages dozens of kilometers apart.

"It's pretty enough here," said the gendarme blocking traffic on an approach road to the main street. He was from another village, 50 kilometers away. "Champagne is prettier country than Lorraine in places," he said, "and Lorraine is prettier country than Champagne in places." That seemed to sum it up for him and, looking down the road to make sure the Tour wasn't approaching, he waved some cars through.

The civic pulse beats slower in *la France profonde,* deep France, than it does in the cities. At the town hall, the most prominent notices announced a trout fishing contest in the river Ché and a lecture, with slides, about developing the memory. (There were other notices but who can remember them?) Yes, all streets would be closed to traffic hours before and minutes after the Tour de France whizzed into and out of the village.

Which was why the visitors had stopped in Laheycourt. They were with the Tour and had gone ahead of the race to find food.

The village had one café and the two men seated at the bar were eating French sandwiches: a meter of bread surrounding a slice of ham thin enough to watch the Tour through. The sandwiches looked enticing to people who had not eaten since breakfast, eight hours earlier.

Two ham sandwiches. No ham sandwiches left. Two cheese sandwiches. No cheese sandwiches left. In that case, two ham and cheese sandwiches. The man behind the bar smiled.

What sandwiches were available? No sandwiches were available: There was no more bread. The day was Wednesday and the village bakery was closed. Even if it had been open, there was no more ham or cheese or sausage or lettuce or tomato or jam.

Outside, the posted menus offered, among other starters, warm goat cheese salad or the gourmet salad of greens with foie gras and smoked salmon. Each cost 40 francs (about $8). For a main course, choose among the fish, *lotte* or *sandre,* or try the dozen snails Alsatian style (68 francs). The slab of beef in port sauce was 75 francs.

Price was really no object. If it had been, the café offered pizzas, too, and onion tarts.

Everything on the menu, the man behind the bar explained, was as available as a sandwich. Which is to say, not at all. The kitchen had closed early because the Tour de France was passing through. In a few moments, the café would close entirely so that everybody could see the race. The kitchen would reopen in three hours if the visitors cared to wait. Alas, they couldn't.

They found instead a small grocery store whose stock of food other than canned goods was bananas. Rich in potassium, which reduces leg cramps, a banana is otherwise not as satisfying a lunch as, say, a gourmet salad with foie gras and smoked salmon, but it is infinitely more satisfying than the memory of breakfast.

Eating his bananas, one visitor was reminded of a story: More than a decade ago, an imperious Frenchman, Jean de Gribaldy, was the *directeur sportif* of a professional bicycle team that he recruited, trained and clucked over with more than moderate success. The team, then sponsored by Sem, a manufacturer of grass seed and other agricultural wonders, was run on a small budget and won its share of small races and parts of bigger ones. But it was habitually crushed in the Tour de France by the Panasonic team, a powerhouse that operated on a much bigger budget.

Now de Gribaldy, the man said, fancied himself an expert on, among other items, riders' diets. He preferred fish to meat, for example, and insisted on small portions. He was particularly opposed to bananas as a food, feeling that they did not digest easily and sat instead on a rider's stomach for hours, slowing him in decisive sprints.

In one Tour de France, de Gribaldy's team was being overwhelmed as usual by Panasonic for all the major prizes and stages, managing only to reap crumbs. One morning, leaving the hotel they shared, members of the Sem team saw the Panasonic riders receive part of their rations for the day—the sandwiches, pastries and sweets they would carry in the back pockets of their jersey until they reached the halfway feed zone and received more of the same, on the flypast, in a muslin bag. What the riders were being given in abundance as sandwiches were long pieces of French bread with the soft white removed and replaced by bananas.

"Look, look," a Sem rider said to de Gribaldy. "We can't eat bananas but Panasonic eats bananas."

De Gribaldy, the man said, did not skip a beat.

"Thank God," he replied. "If they didn't eat those bananas, they'd win everything in sight and there would be nothing left for us. Thank God they eat bananas."

Over the Border

1995

IN THE END, ALMOST EVERYBODY AGREED, it was the Kazakhs' fault. Definitely. Not the Italians' and not the Belgians' either.

The only dissenters might have been the Kazakhs themselves, the seven-man team in the first Tour of China bicycle race and their handful of mechanics and officials. But who was listening to them? Who spoke Kazakh other than the Kazakhs?

Certainly not the Chinese border guards—the friendly men and women in the green uniforms of the army and the scowling men in the white uniforms of the police, bearing enough gold braid on their caps and shoulder boards to humble the chairman of the U.S. Joint Chiefs of Staff.

Somebody in that group, or perhaps it was the nervous man in the sharkskin suit on the bus who looked like a police undercover agent and, the rumor mill said, turned out to be a police undercover agent, decided that the Kazakhs' visa was irregular.

Not exactly irregular, the rumors had it, but sort of Russian. Since the breakup of the evil empire, Kazakhstan has been an independent country, but before that—well . . .

And everybody knows how the Chinese feel about the Russians or are supposed to feel about them or used to feel about them. (In fact, the language barrier was not that great since fair-skinned Kazakhs, the bulk of the team, speak Russian but that would surely have confirmed suspicions.) Perhaps it really was true, as the first rumor had it, that two riders, no, make that four riders, did not have Chinese entry visas. No, make that the entire Mapei team from Italy and the entire Collstrop team from Belgium did not have individual visas but each one sheet of a collective visa that was not acceptable to somebody in a green or a white uniform or even a sharkskin suit.

Or something.

In any case, the entry of the Kent Tour of China into China was delayed for nearly two hours at the border with Hong Kong after the departure of the race from Hong Kong was delayed more than an hour on the other side of the border. Exit and entry forms were the problem, the rumors said.

The time passed in a jovial way at both rest stops, with people being told to pile off their four yellow double-decker buses and then immediately being told to please, please, get back on the buses. At one point in China the dozen accompanying journalists were told to leave the buses with their baggage, which did wonders to uplift the mood of the many representatives of the race's sponsors and advertisers aboard.

Once down, the journalists were told to get right back up. A mischief maker re-entered his bus and announced that the authorities had decided instead to round up all petty bourgeois elements, namely businessmen, for re-education clinics. Just joking, folks.

The crossing point was at Shenzhen, a Special Economic Zone, which is often written with the "S" in "Special" barred vertically into a dollar sign.

The business of Shenzhen, a charmless collection of skyscrapers, building sites and corrugated tin sheds, is—what else?—business. As the buses carrying the Tour of China entourage sat first on one side of the frontier and then the other, members could notice a reversal of stereotypes: on the Hong Kong side, meadows and fish ponds; on the China side, a horizon full of high-rises and the national bird of China, the crane, as in building crane.

Of course, the Tour of China did make it across, speeding through the city with a police escort. The buses pulled into the Shenzhen Sports Complex, a huge soccer stadium, more or less on schedule, a good two hours before the riders began the first stage. Somebody seems to have anticipated a bit of delay at the border.

And the first stage of the first professional bicycle race in China began on time, too, 2 P.M. Shenzhen Sports Complex time. Fifty-five kilometers and 1 hour 18 minutes 22 seconds later the stage ended in a victory by Damien Nazon, a French sprinter with the Castorama team, which, unlike Shenzhen, will go out of business at the end of the year.

A lot Nazon cares. He will sign after the Tour of China with the Banesto team in Spain led by Miguel Indurain and heretofore lacking a fine sprinter. The 21-year-old Frenchman, who was an amateur until a few weeks ago, is their boy. He proved that by beating one of the better sprinters around, Djamolidin Abdujaparov, an Uzbek with the Novell team, whose name was as unpronounceable to the Chinese announcer as it was to the American one.

Third was Robbie Ventura, an American with the USPro team. The pack of 104 riders, divided into 15 teams of 7 men each, crossed the line mainly in the same time as Nazon.

The race finished at the Mission Hills Golf Club, a decidedly palatial sprawl. Several hundred people, some in elegant golfers' clothes and some wearing the conical straw hat of the peasant, gathered there to watch the racers in mild weather under overcast skies.

Parts of the route, a sleek new expressway that was closed to all traffic but the Tour of China's, were also lined with crowds. Bicycle racing at the amateur level is a somewhat popular sport in China, where the bicycle is more commonly used as a means of transportation for people and goods.

At least in Shenzhen, cars do not seem to be rare but they are not plentiful either. Each of the 15 teams had a car for its own use in the race and some were requisitioned taxis with their meters hooded.

The oldest appeared to be the vehicle given to the Saturn team from the United States, which showed more than 725,000 kilometers on its odometer. That will have to be turned back to a respectable 600,000 kilometers before the car is sold in the next decade or two.

To the Great Wall

1995

BEFORE THE TOUR OF CHINA BEGAN IN HONG KONG, Slava Ekimov said that although he was the only one of 105 riders to be accompanied by a wife, he had not come along to have a vacation. For her it was a vacation. For him it was work.

Ekimov, a 29-year-old Russian racer for the Novell team based in the Netherlands, proved that when he won the last of six stages by 10 seconds and the overall race by a mere two seconds.

"This is a good victory for me," he said as he rubbed a towel over his face to wipe away sweat and traces of Beijing's industrial pollution. Airborne grime never sleeps in China's cities, not even on Sundays, when workers continue to build apartment houses, office blocks and roads. "This victory is worth a lot to me," Ekimov added.

Specifically, it was worth $50,000 in the total pot of $200,000, which made the first Kent Tour of China the world's fifth-richest race after the Tours of France, Italy and Spain and the Tour DuPont in the United States.

The DuPont and the China are organized by many of the same people—Medalist Sports, Inc., in America and Medalist Offshore Ltd., in Hong Kong—and they know what attracts bicycle teams to foreign climes, especially after the European racing season ends in mid-October.

Ekimov's six teammates flocked around him at the finish to thump his back and shake his hand. Traditionally, the winner's share of a race is divided more or less evenly with his teammates and support staff. Irina Ekimov made the scene, too, pecking her husband on the lips.

Second by two seconds in the final stage, a 22-kilometer time trial at the Olympic Complex in north-central Beijing, far from any crowds, was Steve Hegg, an American with the USPro team, who led the race for its first four stages.

He lost the leader's yellow jersey Saturday to Daniele Nardello, an Italian with the Mapei team whose future appears unlimited, given that he is just 23 years old. Nardello, first in Paris-Bourges and second in the Tour of Lombardy this season, finished fourth Sunday, 10 seconds behind Ekimov. He entered the time trial, an individual race against the clock, with an eight-second lead over the second-placed Russian.

The Italian gained that by finishing second Saturday in a stage to the Great Wall while Ekimov was third. Both were in a sprint finish with the winner, Alessandro Calzolari, another Italian with Mapei.

Things might have been otherwise. Once the race finished its total of 500 kilometers, 10 seconds were deducted from Calzolari's overall time for his victory. For second place, Nardello received a six-second bonus and, for third, Ekimov got four seconds.

If the low-ranked Calzolari had let his teammate win, the reasoning ran, the extra four seconds would have given Nardello the overall victory by two seconds over Ekimov, instead of vice versa.

"Bah," said Patrick Lefévère, the *directeur sportif* of the Mapei team here. "Many things could have happened. That's bicycle racing."

Ekimov was clocked in 25 minutes 28 seconds for the flat and undemanding spin at the Olympic Complex and out onto a closed, six-lane highway in the midst of urban fields, gleaming new apartment houses and dilapidated small houses.

The final stage through urban decay contrasted with the one Saturday, 132 kilometers from the outpost of Huairou to the Great Wall. As any schoolgirl knows, especially one with an *Encyclopaedia Britannica* at her elbow, the Great Train Robbery, no, Great Trek, no, Great Victoria Desert, no, Great Wall of China, here it is, ran for 6,400 kilometers east to west, and parts of the fortification date to the fourth century B.C.

In 214 B.C., Shih Huang-tri, the first emperor of a united China, ordered work to begin in earnest, connecting a number of defensive walls into a single system with watch-towers. Substantially rebuilt in the 15th and 16th centuries, the wall is about nine meters high, with its towers a meter higher.

The stage's route offered a blend of the 21st century in the riders on their advanced bicycles and perhaps the 18th century in the many peasants out working their fields with no more than hoe, shovel and rake. The only piece of farm machinery seen in more than three hours in the hills 90 kilometers north of Beijing was a mule hitched to, and walking nonstop around, a small mill to grind ears of corn into flour.

Other ears were stacked in cribs or drying on roofs in the many villages the race passed. The sole spots of green in the fields were cabbages coming to harvest just in time to be trucked into Beijing, mounded on sidewalks and sold for pickling as a winter vegetable.

As it remained for the time trial, the weather was splendid: sunny and mild instead of snow, which covered the ground about this time a year ago. Above the haze of pollution, visible even in the hills, the sky was pure. At each brick and stone village, people turned out to see the race go by. Peasants, laying down their wooden, sledlike backpacks and their $50 Phoenix steel bicycles, seemed dumbfounded by the racers' $5,000 titanium bicycles and the accompanying fleet of about 25 cars and trucks.

The road kept climbing, steadily but rarely sharply, over three hills before plunging over each peak into a valley. In the distance, the hills receded fainter and fainter, just as they do in scroll paintings. Now and then a faraway Great Wall observation tower could be glimpsed through leafless poplar and birch trees.

Suddenly the road came out of the hills, turned from one and a half lanes into four, began mounting again and, there before the riders it was—the Great Wall, snaking overhead.

Mutianyu, the finish line, was out of the way to limit disturbance to the major tourist thoroughfares. There were no souvenir stands, with their cries of "Look, look, cheap, cheap." There were no jade Buddhas or Mao caps with a red star, no picture postcards and no sweatshirts imprinted "I Climbed the Great Wall."

Mainly there were the hills and the awesome wall. The Tour of China, in a grand part of its splendor, indeed.

A MAN ALONE

1997

GEORG TOTSCHNIG'S BIG ADVENTURE started shortly after 10 A.M., a bit less than five kilometers into the Liège-Bastogne-Liège bicycle classic, in the town of Beaufays, just outside the city limits of Liège, as the riders were moving gently uphill, trying to work up a little warmth for themselves on a cold morning.

Probably people were still chatting in the pack, as the riders do when they are moving out, still going nowhere.

The 188 riders did have a destination, of course. First was Bastogne, deep in the Ardennes and the focus of the Battle of the Bulge in World War II. After Bastogne, the destination was the same Liège the pack had just left.

Liège-Bastogne-Liège is the oldest of the sport's classics, started in 1892 and run nearly every year since except for a few years at the turn of the century and during World Wars I and II. It is a demanding race, including a dozen of the short hills that keep Belgium from being flat as a table. Nobody in memory has won Liège-Bastogne-Liège with a breakaway from start to finish because the route is 262 kilometers long, the winds usually strong and those hills murderous on tired legs.

But the lack of success on long breakaways has not curtailed them. Nearly every year, somebody goes off on an early attack, builds a big lead and then is caught 80, 90 or 100 kilometers from the finish, where the real race begins. This time it was Totschnig's turn.

He is a 25-year-old Austrian who rides for the Telekom team in Germany. At the start of the season, he ranked 79th in the computerized standings of the world's top 900 riders. In 1997 he recorded one victory, in the championship of Austria. The year before he finished a splendid ninth in the three-week Giro d'Italia and demonstrated climbing ability. He was hired during the winter by Telekom to offer support in the mountains to its leader, Bjarne Riis, the winner of the 1996 Tour de France.

A worker bee, then, and no reason to get excited if he attacked early, especially if he went alone and had nobody to take a turn setting the pace and sheltering him from the wind on the long trip south to Bastogne and the return over most of the dozen hills.

By kilometer 26, he had a lead of 4 minutes 10 seconds. By kilometer 35, as he rode parallel to a stream dotted with fishermen, his lead was 6:15.

Past apple and wild cherry trees in flower, past small herds of cattle in pastures, past dark hillsides posted against hunters and foamy brooks posted against fishermen, Totschnig flew, fighting a head wind.

The slightest sprinkle of rain turned to snow and, far behind him, the race radio reported team cars being called to the pack for riders who wanted another jacket. By kilometer 50, when his lead was at 11:20, the sky lightened in the southwest. By kilometer 69, Totschnig was being pushed by a tail wind, and his lead, as he crested a hill and had a view of the shadowed valley below, rose to 14:10. In a field, a trough of water for cattle was covered with a film of ice. At the first major hill, the Côte de St. Roch, 900 meters long with a 12 percent grade, a big crowd of fans waited at the summit, kilometer 81. It was snowing lightly again.

Into Bastogne Totschnig came, turning right at the Patton tank that commemorates the battle there and heading back north. He had already grabbed his musette of sandwiches, fruit and cakes at the feed zone, kilometer 98, when another rider surged out of the pack, in pursuit.

The chaser was Ermanno Brignoli, 27, an Italian with the Batik team, unranked by the computer in his fourth year as a professional, another worker bee. The pack let him go, too.

Brignoli caught Totschnig eventually, although it took a while. The Austrian was far and away first over the next three hills but looking weary as he struggled against the strong wind that shook the dark boughs of the Ardennes trees. By the third of those hills, the Côte des Hézalles, 1.1 kilometers long at a grade of 11 percent, his lead over Brignoli was down to 2:30, with the pack four and a half minutes farther back.

The sun was out now, and the dark clouds of morning had turned to white puffballs. In the pack, riders were calling to their team cars to return jackets.

Looking weary, Totschnig responded to fans' applause by rising from the saddle and putting some extra effort into the next climb, the Côte d'Aisomont, kilometer 171, nearly 5 kilometers long with a grade of 5 percent.

He was first there by 50 seconds over his chaser and then, on a steep and sinuous descent, he was overtaken.

Totschnig had been out alone five hours. Nobody ever wins Liège-Bastogne-Liège with a start-to-finish breakaway but somebody usually tries.

At the next climb, the Côte de Stockeu, kilometer 178, slightly more than a kilometer long at a grade of 12 percent, Brignoli was the first rider over, followed by Totschnig and then the pack, 3 minutes back.

Not long after that, first Totschnig and then Brignoli were caught and the real race began. The exact spot was kilometer 193 of the 262, the start of the climb up the Côte de Rosier, 4 kilometers with a grade of 6 percent.

There were still six hills ahead.

Brignoli never did finish the race. Totschnig did. He was 108th of the 112 riders who made it, 15:55 behind the winner, Michele Bartoli.

For his victory, Bartoli, an Italian with MG, received 100 World Cup points, or enough to put him into a tie for the lead in the 10-race competition, 200 points in the computer rankings, or enough to move him from fifth in the world to third, and 500,000 Belgian francs ($14,300).

Totschnig gained no World Cup or computer points with his 108th place. By finishing, however, he won the King of the Mountains prize, 100,000 Belgian francs plus 10,000 more for each of the five hills he conquered. As the custom is, he shared the money with his teammates, keeping for himself the exploit.

A Family Business

1999

FINALLY, THE GRAY OF WINTER BEGINS yielding. In the park, crocuses stand in white rows; down the street, forsythia bushes have flared yellow; on the balcony, the withered jade plant puts out green leaves.

Another hint of impending spring was on the road, moving at 40 kilometers an hour along the western flank of Burgundy in a stream of rain-soaked jerseys. That was the Paris-Nice race, which since its origin in 1933 has subtitled itself "The Race to the Sun."

There is always sun in Nice, the organizers of the race say, even when there isn't. Sometimes at the finish of the weeklong race, after so many promises of sun and gaiety on the Côte d'Azur, almost everybody groans at the sight of more pewter skies. Everybody but the organizers. They are less interested in the weather than in the fact that another Paris-Nice race has ended and now it's time to begin working on the next one.

The organizers are mainly members of the Leulliot family, headed by Josette

Leulliot, who took over the sponsoring organization, Monde Six, in 1982 after the death of her father, Jean Leulliot, who began the race.

There are at least three other Leulliots in the organization plus people who have married into the family, and all of them hold day jobs, too—Paris-Nice and the three minor one-day races that Monde Six operates are a passion but not a living for them.

Jacqueline Leulliot, for example, works in a travel agency and has a clause in her contract that gives her this week off every year to head the press office for Paris-Nice. "I do this because I helped my father when he ran the race," she said, "because my family still runs the race and because I love this race."

Since Paris-Nice cannot entice daily television coverage because it cannot afford to share the costs, she comes around at the finish line to show her notes to waiting reporters.

"So and so, number such and such, has attacked and is being chased by so and so, numbers such and such," she says, reading the information that her sister Josette has phoned from the front lines of the 1,354-kilometer-long race. Josette Leulliot is one of the few race directors who, before a daily stage, stroll along the crowd barriers with lists of the starters to distribute to spectators.

But in an increasingly multinational Europe, where even the currency—the unseen euro—will issue someday from one big vague place, there may not be room for an artisanal race such as Paris-Nice. Last year, the Société du Tour de France let it be known that it was interested in acquiring Paris-Nice and giving the creaky old thing a coat of shellac and modern business techniques, just as it has done for two Belgian races, the Flèche Wallonne and Liège-Bastogne-Liège.

Negotiations are continuing, and the advantages are clear: The Société du Tour de France has the money and the clout to attract the big teams and the star riders who are skipping this 66th Paris-Nice. Among the teams not here are Telekom, Banesto, Mercatone Uno and ONCE; among the absent riders are nearly everybody in the top 15, including Laurent Jalabert, the French national champion and a participant in the last 10 editions of Paris-Nice and the winner of the race from 1995 through 1997.

His ONCE team is boycotting the race in its continuing protest over police searches for illegal drugs in the last Tour de France, which the team quit.

"Laurent says that between him and Paris-Nice, it's a love affair," Josette Leulliot has said. "We share that feeling. It's a shame for him. It's a shame that we've gotten to this state."

The Festina Affair, as the drug scandal is known, has cost Paris-Nice some of the sponsorship the race needs to meet its 6 million franc ($1 million) budget, she admitted: "We've had to tighten our belts." The overall prize list amounts to just under 800,000 francs, leaving the race far behind its competitors. "Other races are sponsored by newspapers with lots of money," Jacqueline Leulliot said, "or companies with lots of money. We're still just a family business."

For how much longer? "Big fish swallow small fish," she said. "That's the way life is and that's the way bicycle racing is. Or is becoming."

In a New Role

1999

BUSY, BUSY, BUSY. "Everything's calm today because we've done all we can beforehand," Laurent Fignon said as he bustled around the city hall in Vincennes, on the eastern fringe of Paris, looking into different rooms, checking this, double-checking that.

For somebody who was organizing his first Paris-Nice race, Fignon did seem calm. "I've got a very efficient team," he said, letting his eyes roam first into a room marked "press," then one marked "officials," then one marked "secretariat," then—whoops—into one unmarked, where a woman wearing a blue, white and red official sash was joining an apprehensive couple in holy matrimony.

Three out of four was acceptable. His attitude said, Better to check than to assume. He himself said, speaking generally, "There's a lot to learn."

A two-time winner of the Tour de France early in the 1980s, Fignon has organized one-day races for the past few years but says that the weeklong Paris-Nice race dwarfs anything before.

"It's not like you're putting together eight one-day races back to back," the 40-year-old Frenchman said. "This is a whole, an entity." He is especially happy with what he described as his mix—"stages for sprinters, stages for climbers and then the time trial on the Col d'Eze to sort things out."

Although the Col d'Eze climb in Nice was long a standard part of the race, it was dropped in 1996 for reasons never made entirely clear. Perhaps it had something to do with television coverage, without which a race passes into the shadows.

Paris-Nice has been living in those shadows for the past few years. First the television coverage dwindled, then many top teams decided to ride instead in the rival Tirreno-Adriatico race in Italy. Sponsors and welcoming cities became harder to find for "The Race to the Sun."

Last year, the Leulliot family, which had organized Paris-Nice for decades, decided it was time to sell the property. The organizers of the Tour de France were interested, but it was Fignon, heretofore the man behind such minor races as Paris-Bourges and the Polymultipliée de l'Hautil, who unexpectedly won the bidding.

"I've always said that if one day I could organize a major stage race, I wanted it to be Paris-Nice," he said then. "It's a race everybody knows."

But there have been problems, he admits. The drug scandal that nearly scuttled the 1998 Tour de France is still unresolved and in the public consciousness. "Potential sponsors continue to reject cycling," he said. "Then we've had some difficulties getting all the necessary official permits and authorizations. There are so many different authorities."

Another problem is the quality of the field of competitors. Lance Armstrong and Alex Zülle, first and second in the last Tour de France, both withdrew because of illness and lack of form. A day before the start, the race's favorite, Frank Vandenbroucke, fell in his home in Belgium and may have broken his left wrist; he, too, had to withdraw.

Such other stars as Laurent Jalabert, Jan Ullrich, Abraham Olano and even Michael Boogerd, the winner of Paris-Nice last year, are riding instead in Tirreno-Adriatico.

Nevertheless, a good-sized crowd watched his buffed-up version of Paris-Nice as it began in the Bois de Vincennes with a short time trial for 160 riders divided among 20 teams.

Some improvements were obvious: a closed-circuit, large-screen television set at the finish to allow spectators to see the action, a club car for sponsors and other guests, a daily presence on television. Since his retirement as a racer in 1993, Fignon has worked as a consultant for the Eurosport television network. He has persuaded it and a French network to show his race.

In return, he said, he made the stages more telegenic by putting small and large climbs near the finish, hoping to ensure action. The return of the Col d'Eze uphill time trial was vital to add to the suspense, explained the man whose blackest memory must be the time trial on the last day of the 1989 Tour de France, when Greg LeMond made up a 50-second deficit and beat him.

"These changes are just the start," Fignon said. "Give me a few more years to really put my mark on the race."

PARIS-ROUBAIX

1992

FRAMED ON THE WALL, a *Miroir-Sprint* magazine cover showed a tight-faced Eddy Merckx pedaling through the rain, alone except for his motorcycle escort. An *Equipe* special edition portrayed Roger de Vlaeminck pulling away in heavy gloom from his closest chaser. From the cover of *Sport Club*, Fausto Coppi stared defiantly, only his forehead white where his cap had kept the dust off. Another *Equipe* showed Greg LeMond trying to smile, minstrel-like, through a mask of mud.

Pausing now and again to sign an autograph, Rolf Sørensen was admiring the Paris-Roubaix art show a day before the bicycle race itself. Sørensen, a Danish rider for the Ariostea team in Italy and a wearer of the yellow jersey in the last Tour de France, had stepped back into his youth. "I was 5, 6, 7 years old when I became a fan," he said. "That's the way I started: looking at pictures. Eddy Merckx, everybody. My favorite riders were Merckx, of course, de Vlaeminck, all the big riders."

Two decades later, his favorites have barely changed. "I still have Merckx as an idol, de Vlaeminck, Francesco Moser. Also Hinault. He's the last, I feel the last, really big, big rider who won everything."

Sørensen had stopped at a booth with a display of Bernard Hinault photos, mostly from the Tour de France. Hinault did not like the Paris-Roubaix race, the Hell of the North, and stopped riding it soon after he won it in 1981.

"It's a special race," Sørensen said of the 96-year-old Paris-Roubaix, where cobblestones cover 57.6 of the 267.5 kilometers. When the weather's wet, the cobbles are treacherously slippery; when it's dry, dust from the road chokes the riders. In any weather, the cobblestones leave the riders' bodies, especially their arms and hands, beaten and weary.

Sørensen, 26, is a rising star of professional bicycling, a favorite in the World Cup series of classic races, which he surely would have won last year if he had not broken his left collarbone in a crash in the Tour de France. Like Hinault, he does not consider the Paris-Roubaix classic his race. Unlike Hinault, however, Sørensen has never finished higher than 51st in five entries. (Sunday was no better: He fell, badly injuring some ribs, and could not finish.)

Some other riders consistently do well in Paris-Roubaix, which really begins in

Compiègne, well northeast of Paris. Merckx won the race three times, as did Moser and Rik Van Looy. De Vlaeminck won it a record four times.

Hennie Kuiper won it just once, in 1983, but as he proudly noted: "I rode Paris-Roubaix 14 times and was in the top 10 seven times. I have all the places, including the most important—I won it.

"In my living room," Kuiper said, "there are no photographs from my career but there is a big cobblestone. It's the trophy they give to the winner. And every morning when I wake up, that big cobblestone looks at me."

The Dutchman, now 43, is the *directeur sportif* of the Motorola team and so shares his secrets about the race.

"You must wait until the last two sections of cobblestones," he said. "You must not attack too early, you must keep feeding and drinking—it's 270 ks on the cobblestones and you burn a lot of energy. Sometimes when you're too concentrated and nervous, you forget that.

"But the real secret is good legs."

Kuiper had them in 1983 when he fell twice and recovered each time to get back quickly with the lead attacking group. Sixteen kilometers from the finish, he went off alone, building a lead of a minute 30 seconds. Then he rolled into one of the many potholes that lace the many cobbles.

"I broke my rim," he remembered, "so I had to wait for the team car. Seconds are like hours then. When you wait and can do nothing, you go crazy." The mild-tempered Kuiper screamed with rage as he waited for a new bicycle. "By the time the car came, Madiot, Moser and Duclos-Lassalle were right behind me and I got another bike with only a few seconds' lead." It was enough. When the race finished on the track at Roubaix, Kuiper was 1:15 ahead of Gilbert Duclos-Lassalle, in second place.

"Second again," Duclos-Lassalle wailed. In 1980, when he was in just his third year as a professional, he finished second to Moser in Paris-Roubaix. That was the last of the Italian's three successive victories; he was 29 and at the crest of a glorious career on the road.

For Duclos, just 25, it was only a beginning. Earlier that season, after he won the Tour of Corsica, Paris-Nice and the Tour of the Tarn, he was widely proclaimed as the next great French rider. That was a judgment the two second places in Paris-Roubaix seemed to confirm and a major victory looked to be not far off.

Early last Sunday, Duclos was still waiting. In the nine intervening years, he has had an honorable career, winning his share of small races, but never a really big one. Among his 60 victories were sprinkled such names as the Midi Libre, the Tour of Sweden, the Grand Prix of Plouay and Bordeaux-Paris. Since his lamented second place, the closest he had come to victory in Paris-Roubaix was fourth in 1989.

Duclos-Lassalle will be 38 in August and has become one of the oldest professionals in the sport. Time saps ambition and corrodes skill. Yes, Duclos has lost much of his youthful swagger. He has surmounted a hunting accident in which he nearly destroyed his left hand and has borne the change in status from team leader to road captain—the honorary rank accorded to veterans because they have been there before. Winners are never road captains.

But road captains, as Duclos showed, are sometimes winners.

Coming out of the Arenberg forest, a 2.4-kilometer trench of ancient cobblestones and rutted shoulders, he had worked himself toward the front of the pack. He remembered, he said later, that Moser attacked at this very spot in 1980. Moser believed in shattering the pack with sudden accelerations that left his rivals heavy in the legs and without conviction they could catch him.

Off went Duclos-Lassalle. If, by Kuiper's standards, he attacked far too early, Paris-Roubaix has no rules except that nobody wins by remaining passive. A couple of others joined Duclos and they began to overtake the early leaders, shedding some, keeping others. Within 40 kilometers, Duclos and three companions had a clear road ahead to Roubaix, 70 kilometers away. A flat reduced the group to three and then, with 46 kilometers to go, Duclos sped away alone, nearly two minutes ahead of the pack.

His lead gradually came down but he never was caught. Too many chasers watched each other and waited for somebody else to make the first move. Occasionally somebody did and members of Duclos's Z team, especially LeMond, caught and neutralized them.

For the first time this year LeMond was in wonderful form, peaking for the one classic that motivates him. Yet he played the team game, working for the Z rider in front, refusing to attack, chasing down rivals, blocking.

Over the seasons, Duclos-Lassalle had not won big races but he had influenced a few. Two years ago, when LeMond might have lost the Tour de France because of a flat tire in the Pyrenees, Duclos was far ahead and hoping to win the stage. Instead, he obeyed orders, stopped, waited for his team leader and helped him storm back to the front. Now LeMond was thanking him again.

With 17 kilometers to go, Olaf Ludwig of the Panasonic team broke free and tried to overhaul Duclos-Lassalle. With 14 kilometers to go, Ludwig narrowed the lead to 50 seconds. With eight kilometers to go, it was 38 seconds, with five kilometers to go, 32 seconds, with four kilometers to go, 28 seconds. Ludwig had waited too long.

Far enough ahead to remain out of sight, Duclos rolled on. Long before he reached the dangling red triangle that marks the last kilometer, he knew he had the race won. "When I got there," he reported later, "I said, 'Too bad for him, but it's over.'"

Ludwig was a lap behind as Duclos-Lassalle sailed around the track and crossed the finish line. Both his arms were upright in a victory salute, both his fists were clenched, and through the dust of Paris-Roubaix on his face, he was wearing a smile that, for a man nearly 38 years old, could be called boyish.

A Letter from Korea

2000

OPEN LETTER TO THE PRESS DEPARTMENT of the Société du Tour de France:

Thanks loads, *mes amis,* for the invitations to the Paris-Tours race and to the presentation of the next Tour de France, two events I have not missed in decades. This year, though, I must decline with regrets less strong than expected.

One lives now in Seoul, a fine place but not a model for bicycle racing. True, just outside the city there are hills—the South Koreans call them mountains—but they would rate as no more than Category III climbs in the Tour, next to the lowest in height and difficulty, that would break up a race nicely. The problem, though, is that there is no way to clear the heavy and constant car traffic off the roads, where a bicycle rider has a good chance of ending as a fatality statistic.

Nevertheless, one enjoys Seoul and its friendly people. The city is not half as pretty as Paris, possibly because it was captured and recaptured four times in a war half a century ago while France somehow managed to preserve its capital. *Zut,* history is bunk, as an American philosopher said.

As for the food, it is different. You French may eat such exotica as cock's comb—a friend and bon vivant says it is best pan-fried and is mainly cartilage with a taste he describes as "crunchy"—but the Koreans far surpass this by eating antler. *Mais oui,* the growth on the deer. No, it is not impossible; I have myself found it lurking in a stew.

The weather? Much like France's, without the steady rain and low skies and gray gloom. What one always appreciates about Paris-Tours is the chance to see autumnal fields and falling leaves, that sense of closure to a racing season that began amid the green buds of spring.

Same here. On a drive north in the countryside, one remarked the pumpkins in fields dotted with stalks of withered corn and the year's final bales of hay. Soon, they say, it will snow.

You would point out now that Paris-Tours was held two weekends ago and I would say that the mail arrived late.

One saw the result briefly somewhere: Andrea Tafi, an old favorite, constantly cheerful and hardworking, won in a three-man breakaway in the rain. In memory I saw the long, straight finish between the plane trees along the Avenue de Grammont and pictured Tafi thrusting his arms aloft as he crossed the line near the Hôtel de Ville. Swell race, Andrea, congratulations. You win a big one every year.

If Paris-Tours is over, the presentation of the next Tour de France is still ahead, as always the last Thursday in October, this year October 26, in Paris. The time is 11 A.M., which means, as always, noon.

One will miss the usual crowd, everybody decked out in jackets and ties instead of the customary shorts, everybody looking thoughtful as they examine the map that has just been projected onto the big screen.

Too many mountains? one asks team officials afterward. Not at all, say those people with strong climbers. Far too many, an unbalanced course, say those without. Then they all agree that it is the riders and not the roads that determine the race.

I'll miss all that, but in my mind I can see it already. On the big day, just for a moment as the route is unveiled, all of you think of me and, in Seoul, where one doesn't race on bicycles, I'll think of you.

In the Big Time

1996

VINCENT LAVENU SMILED AT ONE AND ALL, shook any hand in reach, turned appropriately solemn to discuss his team's prospects in the Paris-Roubaix race.

Paris-Roubaix! Definitely the big time. The Hell of the North. The centennial edition of Paris-Roubaix, 263.5 kilometers long, 50 of those kilometers over cobblestones, was run Sunday with four hours of coverage on European television.

This was more like it for Lavenu, the *directeur sportif* of Petit Casino-C'est Votre Equipe. Nodding happily, he turned realistic. "What chance do we have against some of these teams?" he asked. "Big cylinders, some of them. We're small cylinders."

He knew what he was talking about: The only member of his six-man team who would finish was Jaan Kirsipuu, an Estonian, in 16th place. Lavenu is no fool but, even in realistic moments, he is enthusiastic.

"It's beginning to happen for us," he said. "Two second places, you noticed that? Two second places. For us, the season really begins now."

The two second places, scored last week, were in the distinctly minor Circuit de la Sarthe race. Lavenu's team is usually found in minor races, not in such crown jewels as Paris-Roubaix.

When the World Cup of one-day classics began in March with Milan–San Remo in Italy for the 22 first-division teams, his second-division team was riding in Cholet-Pays de Loire deep in France. When the big boys were riding the Tour of Flanders in Belgium, his team was at the Grand Prix de Rennes in deeper France. Next weekend, when the 22 first-division teams ride Liège-Bastogne-Liège in Belgium, the second division will be in such small-time races as A Travers le Morbihan and the Tour de la Côte Picardé in deepest France.

Morbihan! Picardy! Backwaters. Lavenu winces. His heart yearns for Liège-Bastogne-Liège, the big time.

The problem, of course, is money. With an annual budget of 6.5 million francs ($1.5 million), he cannot compete for star riders with the first-division teams: Banesto spends more than $6 million a year, Mapei and Gewiss ditto, ONCE don't ask.

Gan, the sole first-division team in France, has a budget of nearly $5 million. In contrast, the five French second-division teams range from a bit above $1 million (Mutuelle de Seine et Marne) to not quite $2 million (Agrigel–La Creuse).

As a small team with a small budget, Petit Casino-C'est Votre Equipe is eligible only for the World Cup races in its own country. Of the 11 World Cup classics, that means just Paris-Roubaix in the spring and Paris-Tours in the fall. In between, it is the small time: Cholet, Rennes, the Tour of Armorique, places virtually unknown to first-division teams. Picardy!

The 40-year-old Lavenu is daunted neither by the races nor by his team's lackluster performance this season. He will not react the way Willy Teirlinck, the *directeur sportif* of Collstrop, a minor Belgian team, did this month when his riders showed no spark in a multiday race: Teirlinck recalled his staff from the feed zone where the riders grab bags of sandwiches, fruit and cake and made them finish two daily stages in the cold rain without lunch, without fuel.

Collstrop and Petit Casino have the same number of victories this season—none—but it is not Lavenu's way to be harsh. He remembers how it felt to be a minor rider trying to stay with those with stronger legs and more talent. Instead of anger, he offers understanding.

"It's a young team with a lot of spirit," Lavenu said hopefully earlier in the season. The only Petit Casino rider with a name is its leader, Armand De las Cuevas, whose talent is often obscured by his attitude. Last year the Castorama team that he led suspended him without public explanation from mid-July through the end of the season in November.

"He's a rider of high quality, a little different, but a leader," Lavenu said. "His signing will give us a little more cachet."

Cachet is what Lavenu desperately needs. In his fifth year as a *directeur sportif,* his goal is, as always, an invitation to the Tour de France. He usually makes it and his overmatched team always rides dismally. But it's the big time and Lavenu bubbles the entire three weeks.

"The Tour de France is the main goal of all French teams," he said. "I think De las Cuevas is an extra trump."

The Tour's organizers have already issued invitations, all of which were accepted, to the top 18 teams in the computer rankings. Petit Casino ranks 23rd. Four wild cards will be awarded in June and Lavenu is optimistic.

"We'll go to the Tour de France," he began confidently, "if we deserve to." His voice dropped away on the last few words.

Petit Casino is not alone in its despair. These are hard times for French teams, which cannot find sponsors to provide the millions needed to compete for the best riders. Blame it on the economy, which remains torpid with 3 million people unemployed. Growth projections for the year were revised sharply downward three weeks ago, from 2.8 percent to 1.3 percent, barely a pulse.

So Lavenu has to make do with small sponsors. Starting in 1992, it was Chazal, a regional merchandiser of cold cuts. This year it is Petit Casino, a chain of coffee shops in supermarkets, that is contributing more than half of his team's budget.

"Listen," he says, "the name is not just Petit Casino. The 'C'est Votre Equipe' is very important." It means "It's Your Team" and literally it is; anybody out there wanting to be a sponsor, send a contribution.

"'C'est Votre Equipe' is a concept to let the public become part of the team, to have a say for a minimum of 150 francs," he explained. "Already we have 1,200 supporters, even people in Belgium, Luxembourg.

"In France, our supporters range from people on welfare to the heads of companies. They send us their checks, we send them information, a team book, and we'll do that all year long. A drawing will be held to see who follows a race with us, rides in the team car. And all year long, information about the team."

Personal checks accepted, no credit cards. The address: France Cyclisme Promotion, 9 Rue du Genevois, 73000 Chambéry-le-Haut, France. From his heart, Vincent Lavenu says thanks and looks forward to seeing you at the team's next race, A Travers le Morbihan. Morbihan! Picardy!

ACROSS AN EMPTY LAND

2000

BECAUSE THE AVEYRON *DEPARTEMENT* in south-central France is one of the least-populated in the country, mainly long stretches of pasture or fields of grass waiting to be cut into hay, there were few witnesses to the finish of René Joergensen's doomed dream.

He deserved better than just an old woman in a black beret standing at the gate to a farm and watching with an uncomprehending gaze. Farther down the road, two men held the bridle of a horse and peered over a hedge.

About 120 riders in the Midi Libre race also saw Joergensen accept what had become inevitable, sitting up on his bicycle and letting the front of the chasing pack envelop him. They do not count as witnesses, however, since they have seen it so many times that their testimony would be sparse. The newspaper did not even mention his feat because it did not count as a feat—that status is gained only in the rare instances when a long, solo attack succeeds.

The bland facts: Joergensen, a 24-year-old Danish rider for the Memory Card–Jack & Jones team from his homeland, sped away from the pack at kilometer 54 of a 206-kilometer hilly stage, built a mammoth lead, was allowed to remain ahead for three hours and then was slowly overtaken and finally left behind. It happens all the time in bicycle races.

"I know that," Joergensen said after the stage finished in the grim town of Décazeville. "But sometimes it works. If you never try, you never win. You have to take that chance."

Once he accelerated in his attack, Joergensen hesitated a few hundred meters ahead of the pack, waiting for companions to share the work ahead, to take their turns pulling into a slight head wind while the others rode in the slipstream and saved energy. But nobody joined him.

Off he went. Joergensen worked hard to build his lead, standing out of the saddle on every small rise and using his thick thighs to power his legs. From the outskirts of Castres, where he started, he rode straight north, around Albi, past long fields of grain and vegetables, through played-out coal-mining towns at the top of the Tarn *departement.* His lead reached its maximum: 14 minutes 40 seconds.

Spectators were plentiful in the Tarn, especially in the feed zone, where Joergensen snatched a white lunch bag from a team worker at the side of the road. The rider transferred a few foil-covered sandwiches and pieces of cake to the back pockets of his jersey, and began to eat and drink. He needed the fuel: He was 79 kilometers from the finish and more than 13 minutes ahead.

Into the Aveyron he went, crossing the town of Nauçelles, where lines of schoolchildren screamed encouragement. Far behind him, the pack awakened and began riding hard in pursuit. The Crédit Agricole team had a leader's yellow-and-red jersey to protect, and other teams had their sprinters to think of when the finish line neared. With 64 kilometers to go, Joergensen's lead was down to 9:31.

It continued to drop, of course, since one man is no match for 120. With 46 kilometers left, on a narrow road with a barnyard stench hanging over it, the Dane was only 2:30 ahead. The press cars behind him were ordered to move out and leave a clear field for the pursuers.

Joergensen held out a while longer, making it first over the day's third climb with a 14-second advantage. He might have yielded then, in front of a good-sized crowd at the peak, but he pressed on to a bonus sprint two kilometers farther down the road. Another crowd waited there.

Just out of its sight, just after he had gained his last prize of the day, he was caught. The old woman in the black beret saw the pack flow by Joergensen, who returned to anonymity. He finished about half an hour later in 94th place, 2:53 behind the winner.

"A hard day," he said. "The wind was from the front all the time—a long day. One hundred twenty-five kilometers alone, that's long. Today I wasn't lucky. But maybe next time I'll make it to the finish alone.

"Alone," he repeated. "Out there today it was like I was all alone in the whole world."

Recipe for a Race

1999

THERE WAS A LULL IN THE BICYCLE RACING drug scandal and, far from the police stations and courthouses in Paris and Lille where so many riders and officials are spending their days now, the organizers of the Midi Libre race tried to keep the sport where they feel it belongs—on the road.

The Midi Libre is a small, low-pressure race held for six days every mid-May in the southwestern part of France where its organizer, a newspaper of the same name, circulates. Because its dates, May 18 to 23, conflict with the start of the prestigious, three-week Giro d'Italia, the organizers sometimes have trouble attracting big names.

But the race always go on, passing over the high hills of the region and through its picturesque places—Montpellier, Castelnaudary, Carcassone—the capital of that French dining specialty, the meat and bean dish called cassoulet. Although its ingredients vary from town to town, it is consistently satisfying and authentic—as bicycle racing itself was before the doping scandal began to give it all the credibility of professional wrestling.

The scandal, which emerged in the Tour de France last summer, has affected even the bucolic Midi Libre race. Philippe Gaumont, one of three French riders who are under investigation by the Paris drug squad, failed a doping test there last year after he won a daily stage. He was subsequently cleared on a technicality.

This year the race has another problem: Foreign teams are shunning France because of its widespread police investigation of doping. In addition to customs scrutiny of team buses and cars coming into the country, the investigations are being carried out on at least three fronts by different police organizations and judicial authorities.

The first of these is in the northern city of Lille, where a broad inquiry began last July when a worker for the Festina team was found behind the wheel of an official Tour de France car full of illegal performance-enhancing drugs. More than a dozen persons have since been placed under investigation, a step short of being formally charged, in that case.

In another case, the Paris police's drug squad rounded up 15 persons late last week on suspicion of using and providing illegal substances. Most of the suspects were released—drug use is not usually a crime in France, although possession and supply are—but two among the five who are still under investigation continue to be held.

The third major investigation is centered in the Champagne city of Reims, where a van belonging to the TVM team from the Netherlands was seized more than a year ago and found to contain illegal drugs. While three persons have been placed under formal investigation there, the case has languished.

The TVM team announced this week that it will not participate, as scheduled, in the Midi Libre race. At least three other big teams that usually show up—Banesto and ONCE from Spain and Rabobank from the Netherlands—will also skip the race this year, the organizers said.

Banesto and ONCE have also voiced doubts about riding in the Tour de France in July, citing their discontent with the police crackdown. Both dropped out of the last Tour in protest and participated in few French races this winter and spring.

The teams are not shunning Italy, where drug investigations are also widespread at the judicial, if not the police, level. In Spain and the Netherlands, two other centers of the sport, there have been no known investigations.

The Midi Libre's organizers took the news of the TVM pullout well. "I'm sad but not surprised," said the head of the committee, Roger Béné, in a phone interview. "Not surprised because some foreign teams have been avoiding France this season. You know why."

He said that 17 teams would appear. There will be big teams like Telekom, Saeco, Lotto and the major French squads, and then there will be those from the French, Italian and Belgian second divisions.

So the race, subtracting teams here, adding teams there, will be a little like the different regional ways of making a cassoulet, he agreed: Instead of preserved goose, there may be duck; instead of lamb, pork; there may be no sausages at all. But, he promised, whatever the mix, it will work.

Directeur Sportif

1996

"*AL LAVORO*," JOHN EUSTICE SAID IN ITALIAN—time to work. Professional bicycle racers hear that all the time. The seven riders of the Amore & Vita team got to their feet, straddled their bicycles and began rolling toward the starting line.

"Have fun," Eustice called after them in English. Perhaps some other *directeur sportif* has said that once in the century that people have been racing bicycles. Eustice looked as if he said it often. "One of my jobs is to keep them loose," he explained. "Europeans can come over here and feel displaced. I try to keep them happy."

He knows from long experience what keeps a racer happy. In 1975, at 19, he became one of the first Americans to ride in Europe, starting with an amateur team in Italy. Before he retired in 1986, he had ridden for teams in Belgium, Germany and France as well as Italy. In 1982, when he was a member of the Sem team in France, he won the U.S. professional championship. He repeated that feat in 1983.

"I went back to Europe with the star-spangled jersey on and tried to look impressive," he continued. "I didn't. Like a lot of guys, I had to work too hard for others instead of myself."

For the last decade, Eustice has been what he terms "an asterisk" in the sport: He organizes races, including the former Kmart Classic in West Virginia and the forthcoming Olympic trials there; he runs training camps in Arkansas, New Jersey and West Virginia; he has been a technical consultant for U.S. television at the last four Tours de France.

Rider, organizer, agent, talent scout, analyst—until now, Eustice had done it all except serve as a *directeur sportif,* the coach of a team. In the current Tour DuPont, he is head of Amore & Vita, a 16-man, second-division team in Italy that sent seven of its young riders. Amore & Vita, which is also competing in Europe with its A team and officials, was looking for an American coach who knows racing and speaks Italian. Eustice was looking for an opportunity.

"I was so nervous the first few days because I never did this before," he admitted. "Now it's better. It's rewarding doing this. I really like this job.

"I stayed away from it and I now I find I love it. It's like going back into a cult."

As whistles blew and horns sounded, he slipped into the driver's seat of his team van before he began following the pack. The van was ninth in line among the 16 teams' vehicles, a ranking based on the teams' overall standings.

Ahead were such major outfits as Motorola, Mapei, Festina and Rabobank, and Amore & Vita's place was unexpectedly high. Unexpected, that is, to anybody other than Eustice. With five first-year professionals and two second-year professionals, the team would not have been considered likely to place a man second in the stage into Richmond, third into Raleigh, North Carolina, and fifth into Greensboro, North Carolina. All those places had been taken by the team's sprinter, Glenn Magnusson, a Swede. The day before, 700 meters from the finish in Greensboro, Magnusson was fighting it out for victory when his front wheel hit a pothole and cracked in two.

"Andriotto led him out," Eustice said, referring to Dario Andriotto. "He was fighting half the Mapei team to get position. Andriotto wouldn't have believed a week ago that he could ride equal against Mapei, but he does now."

To Eustice, his riders' results were easily explained: "A little team with a big spirit can give everybody else a hard time. We've got the spirit and we've got some talent, too." He did not add that Amore & Vita had an enthusiastic *directeur sportif*—himself—who was eager to see how far he could push his riders in 12 days and whether their accomplishments would shine some light on his own managerial skills.

"I'm a good coach," he decided. "I did everything wrong as a rider, that's why I'm a good coach. I can see things coming and say, 'Uh, uh, I lost three years that way.' I would give up everything else to run a team. I am good at building a team. Morale, excitement, that I'm good at.

"Like De Pasquale," he continued, referring to Maurizio De Pasquale, a strong climber.

"I gave him the responsibility of team leadership. He was a little nervous at the beginning but now he's accepting it.

"The first day, he came back and got water bottles and I said, 'Stop that. That's the last time you do that.'" The team captain, Eustice was saying, does not do the work of a support rider. "He's there. Now he's getting used to his role, he likes it, he's starting to command the other guys.

"And they're happy listening. He's smart. He sees everything that's going on. Everything. And a good person. The guys listen to him. So he's the soul of the team right now."

How had Eustice decided to make De Pasquale his leader on such short acquaintance? "Observation," he explained. "Talent spotting. What I know."

The geographic profile of the day's stage in the Tour DuPont lay on the dashboard of the team van Eustice was driving. Marked in pencil were three points where riders could win bonus money. First came the sprint at Stuart, Virginia: $5,000 for the first man, $3,000 for the second and $2,000 for the third.

The DuPont is one of the richest races in the world, offering prizes of $200,000, including $64,500 in bonuses, or *primes* as they are called.

In addition to the Stuart primes, the climb at Cahas would pay $1,000 to the winner and the climb at Lynville another $1,000.

The overall winner when the stage finished in Roanoke, Virginia, would gain $2,500. That one was not marked on Eustice's map. As *directeur sportif* of the young Amore & Vita team, he was being realistic.

In Magnusson, he had a sprinter who had already finished second, third and fifth in DuPont stages, so there was hope for the Stuart prime. In De Pasquale and Andrea Patuelli, he had two climbers whom he thought capable of staying with the leaders in the Blue Ridge Mountains. But he knew he had no rider who could both climb and sprint and contest the finish in Roanoke. In only his first week as a *directeur sportif,* the 40-year-old Eustice knew how to balance buoyancy with common sense.

So the Stuart sprint meant less to him than other concerns. First was his worry that Magnusson might not make it through the first of four days in the mountains to contest the last few sprints before the DuPont ends.

Mile 17 of 110: Magnusson drops back and raises an arm for assistance. The Amore & Vita van moves up on Magnusson's left. He looks weary. The metal plates on his shoe soles, which lock into his pedals, need some oil.

While the mechanic leans out and tends to that, Eustice asks, "How you feeling?" The rider smiles, nods. "Good job, baby," the coach says.

Mile 24: Leon van Bon, a Dutchman with Rabobank, wins the Stuart sprint. Magnusson decided not to contest it. "A lot of guys are tired," says Eustice.

Mile 30: Filippo Meloni, an Italian, falls to the rear, signals for the van, passes in three empty water bottles and takes five full ones. He stuffs them into the pockets of his jersey and even into its neck. He will distribute the water to his teammates on this hot and muggy day.

"Hold on, do what you can do," Eustice instructs him in Italian. "He's exhausted and sick," the coach explains. "He's been raced too much this year and came here sick. All he can hope to do is hang on."

Mile 38: Luca Maggioni, another Italian, signals for water, takes two bottles and rides off. "My problem child," Eustice says. "He's doing nothing in the race, and I tell him to at least get water for the others but he just gets it for himself."

Mile 50: Malcolm Elliott, an Englishman with Chevrolet/L.A. Sheriff and a fine sprinter, stops. Since there has been just one small climb and he has not been left far behind, he must be quitting for other reasons, probably stomach troubles. "That's what we want," Eustice says, "get rid of the competition." He thinks about that. "You feel sorry for him, but that's racing."

Mile 56: The field shatters on the Sugarloaf Mountain. Four Amore & Vita riders are left behind, three stay with the leaders. Eustice guns the van past his stragglers after giving each water and a supportive word. He is heading for the first group and his three riders there. "Be tough, hang tough," he tells Maggioni.

Mile 58: Magnusson is in a small group behind the leaders. His eyes are glazed with the uphill effort. "Good boy, hang on," Eustice says, passing him two water bottles. "He's seen his limits," he says. "Now he knows how far he has to go."

A thunderstorm erupts and hail begins pelting the road. Eustice and his mechanic worry how many of their riders can make it to the finish without crashing or finishing so far behind that they would be disqualified.

In the end, everybody on the team except Maggioni, the problem child, made it. He stopped in the storm, was picked up by a support car and will spend the rest of the tour riding in the second van with mechanics, masseurs and spare wheels. De Pasquale, the team captain, was the highest finisher, 23rd, or 16 seconds behind Lance Armstrong, the stage winner. Magnusson was 81st, or 13:22 behind. "He lives to fight another day," Eustice announced exultantly.

"It's so rewarding doing this," he added, his face alight. "I really like doing this. I get so crazy during a race. I really love this job."

Learning on the Job

1992

CHASING HIS BIG DREAM, Eddie B. is in France today. He was in Switzerland yesterday, in Italy the day before and he will head for Germany tomorrow. "Everybody is dreaming about something, I'm dreaming, too," he explains. "I'm dreaming big dream."

Vast dream, really. Eddie Borysewicz, who is universally known as Eddie B. because Americans could not pronounce his name when he arrived 15 years ago from his native Poland, built the U.S. amateur bicycling program that won handfuls of medals at the 1984 Olympic Games in Los Angeles.

"When I started, was nothing," he remembers. "No office, nothing. I was the first guy, who don't speak English. I have only a telephone and have even to buy a desk. That was '78, okay? We make big steps. I have so many riders who win the Olympics, world championship medals."

Now, at age 53, after his highly successful career teaching amateurs, Eddie B. is in his first year as a professional *directeur sportif.* The two versions of the sport are about as similar and as different as college and professional basketball.

"So far, so good, extremely good, even more than I expected," he says of his Subaru-Montgomery Securities team. "Nice bunch of guys, enthusiastic. These guys not complain.

"Our results are good and everybody is surprised how well we go. That does not mean we have no problems—we have a lot of problems." (One of them is that just when his English grew rapid and picturesque in its shortcuts, everybody else began speaking Spanish or Italian or French, which he has not used in 15 years.)

Undaunted, Eddie B. dreams his dream: He will build the best team in the sport, and he will do it soon. "We're going to be the top team in the world," he says flatly. Top team? "Top team. We need for this a couple of years and we need luck."

Also money, victories, more staff, more experience, more than his current 10 road riders, more time in the day—the list of "mores" is long, headed by more money. In a sport dominated by teams that spend at least $5 million a year, Eddie B. has a budget of $1.4 million.

"It sounds like a lot of money if you don't know much about professional cycling," says one of his riders, Rob Holden. "If you do understand the sport, you know what a small budget it is." Holden was speaking at the team's hotel in Nantes where, like his coach, he arrived after driving two days with two teammates from a race in Italy.

"Drive, that's us, that's what we can do," Eddie B. said. "That's not Buckler, okay, that's not Panasonic," referring to two Dutch teams with the money for plane fare and luxurious private buses.

Star riders for those teams were in Italy last weekend, racing the Milan–San Remo classic, which began in 1907. The smaller fry were in western France, preparing to ride Cholet-Pays de Loire, which began in 1978. It bills itself as the first French classic of the season, defining a classic not as a venerable and prestigious race but merely as a one-day event. People more disinterested than the race's promoters would rank Cholet-Pays de Loire as a semi-classic.

Whatever its standing, Cholet-Pays de Loire offered—in reduced amounts—just what the hallowed Milan–San Remo did: money, publicity and points in the riders' computerized standings. For the many teams that did not have the money or points to enter Milan–San Remo, Cholet-Pays de Loire was an opportunity to race, to get a foot on a low rung of the ladder and begin ascending.

So such barely known professional teams as Collstrop, Assur Carpets and La William came from Belgium. Cermia represented Spain, Pro Road Project Japan, Chazal and Eurotel France and Subaru-Montgomery the United States.

"We're an American team based in America with American sponsors and some American riders," Eddie B. said. "Also some European riders. I think we well represent Subaru, Montgomery Securities and America, okay? To have another American team present in Europe and doing well, that will help American cycling grow."

Despite its American roots, his team will compete almost exclusively in Europe this season. A major reason is that the points a team needs for big races are more readily available in Europe than in the United States. They are known as FICP points, from the initials in French, the language of bicycling, of the International Federation of Professional Cycling.

"Without FICP points, nothing," Eddie B. points out. "We're collecting FICP points and we're learning." Already this season, which began in February and runs into October, his team has won enough points in races in France and Italy to advance from 40th in the world to 27th. The top 20 teams automatically qualify for World Cup races and the top 16 for the Tour de France, Subaru's major goal.

But not this year. "This is a testing year: What can we do? What can the riders do? What kind of experience do we need?" Eddie B. asks.

"This is a learning experience for me," he added. "I'm learning about professional cycling. It's new for me. I can make several mistakes this year that I will eliminate next year.

"Next year is going to be our real season in Europe. We did not come from nowhere, we are not nobodies. We are already a very competitive team. Next year we'd like to be in the Tour de France and I believe we will be in the Tour de France.

"Only we need a little bit more money. We need a doubled budget. We're not looking for $5 million or $8 million like the big teams. For $3 million we can produce results like big teams. Because we're hard workers."

Lacking money, Eddie B. turns to friends and contacts he has made in his many years in the sport. An official of the French Cycling Federation helped him hire Denis Roux, one of the team's more experienced riders but one left without a job when his Toshiba team folded last season. A doctor for the Italian Cycling Federation monitors the health of Subaru riders. A friend in Germany supplies offices, storage space and a phone number for race promoters to call.

Outside the hotel, in the chill evening, his team mechanic was struggling to fit a bicycle rack atop a car. Eddie B. noticed this and went to help, tugging the rack into place and trying to tighten its bolts. Not many *directeurs sportifs* have to bother with such chores, he was told.

"I worked like this when I started in American cycling," he replied, hammering the rack with his hand. "I made some history in amateur cycling and right now I try to do my best in professional cycling. My disadvantage is I don't know races. I am learning about these races.

"But that's nice," he added. "Next year I'm going to have different experience."

FOR ALL HIS DREAMS OF BUILDING the best team in professional bicycling, of competing with the big boys over the Alps and Pyrenees in the Tour de France, Eddie B. was gloomy about prospects in the undemanding Cholet-Pays de Loire race. The course might be flat but so were his riders.

"Please don't expect very good results from us," he cautioned. "Guys too tired. Only riders who have a chance to be top 10 have to finish. Others can stop when they want. We're taking this race as a warm-up."

That went for Eddie B. himself. When he finished driving the 205 kilometers of the course behind his Subaru-Montgomery riders, he planned to stay at the wheel and leave immediately for his distant headquarters in Germany. "Problem. I need to be in Dortmund and in Belgium at the same time to talk to agent and sign the contract for next races."

Races can mean money since some promoters pay start fees for a team or a star to show up. While the Tour of the Mediterranean in France paid Subaru-Montgomery nothing, the team will get nearly $7,000 to ride in the Tour of the Basque Country in Spain. "So we get rolling, okay?" Eddie B. says enthusiastically.

For a small race, Cholet-Pays de Loire paid what it could. "Little money, 5,500 francs." Eddie B. considered dropping out of the race because two of his better riders, Denis Roux and Mike Carter, were sidelined with knee tendinitis and the others were fatigued after traveling two days from their last race in Italy. But the no-show penalty was 10,000 francs ($1,785), which he decided was too steep.

Subaru would race, but with limited goals and as one of the smaller teams in the 18-team race—only five of its riders mounted the podium in the Place General de Gaulle in Cholet and signed in as several hundred spectators clapped intermittently.

"The American team, Subaru," intoned the race announcer, Daniel Mengeas, usually a warehouse of minutiae about riders. This time he was stumped. Eddie B. had entered Nate Reiss, who has ridden almost exclusively in the United States; Rob Holden and Chris Walker, who have ridden almost exclusively in England; Martin Aun, an Estonian who rides almost exclusively nowhere but is so eager that he competes for expenses only, and Janus Kuum, a Norwegian who was born in Estonia.

First to report, Subaru-Montgomery set a bad precedent for the announcer. The major teams in the race—Lotto, Castorama, Z, RMO, PDM, Lotus, Buckler, Tulip, Helvetia and GB-MG—all sent B squads packed with young, unknown riders, while reserving their stars for the previous day's Milan–San Remo classic in Italy.

The minor teams—Chazal, Eurotel, Cermia, Pro Road Project, La William, Collstrop and Assur Carpets—sent their A squads but these riders had few glories to be sung; if they had more, the riders would have been invited to join major teams. As one nonperson after another trooped on stage, Mengeas wilted.

Then, to the blare of horns as team cars tried to form a line, the riders mounted their bicycles and freewheeled out of town. The real starting point was 7 kilometers away, where a herd of black-and-white cows gazed forlornly at the 143 riders. They set off uneventfully and only the changing color of pastured cows—now brown and white, now mostly black, back to black and white—proved that time was passing.

Chatting with his mechanic, Alain Dénegre, in the back seat and a guest in the front seat, Eddie B. worked to maintain his position in the long line of team cars. He had drawn No. 4 out of the hat and pronounced it lucky for obscure reasons. Its real advantage was that he was close enough behind the pack to see quickly if any of his riders needed help.

For that reason, different *directeurs sportifs*, those with numbers in the teens, kept trying to jump the line. The biggest offender was the canny Cyrille Guimard of Castorama, whose number was so high that he violated the rules and failed to post it in his car's rear window. That way, perhaps, nobody would realize he was cutting in.

At kilometer 12, the radio linking team cars reports a crash ahead. Eddie B. quickly stops and Dénegre leaps out, carrying two replacement wheels, but just as quickly returns and reports no Subarus involved. At kilometer 15, a rider jumps away from the pack and builds a lead of more than a minute. Eddie B. does not worry. "One rider not dangerous," he decrees. "Five serious, 10 dangerous but one, no problem. Too much head wind today."

Kilometer 17: Reiss drifts to the rear of the pack and raises his right hand, asking for help. He wants to pass to the car three jackets that Subaru riders have taken off as they begin to work up a sweat.

"Nate, PDM and Lotto are talking," Eddie B. warns. "The cars pull alongside and they talk. Maybe friendly talk, 'How are you?' maybe making a deal. If they move to front, watch out. Tell the boys."

Reiss nods and the car drops back. "Warning never hurts," Eddie B. says. Guimard again tries to cut in front.

Kilometer 33: "There's my boy," Eddie B. shouts, gunning the motor, as a rider far ahead pulls over to the right side of the road with a flat. When he draws nearer, Eddie B. realizes that the rider is from Eurotel, which wears the same Day-Glo yellow hat as Subaru.

Kilometer 80: Holden calls for help. "I can't turn the pedals," he says. A 14-man breakaway has developed and left the other riders split into small groups, fighting strong crosswinds. "You can't go, drop out at feed zone," Eddie B. says. Then he races off to see if any Subaru riders are in the breakaway. He doubts it since the radio has not mentioned his riders' numbers but race radios are not always accurate. Besides, Subaru has drawn numbers in the 90s and the French for Walker's 97—four twentys, ten, seven—is too complicated for Eddie B.'s rusty language skills.

Among the decipherable numbers are two riders from the Castorama team—11 through 20—directed by Guimard. His car has long deserted the line, as it is allowed to do if a team has riders in a breakaway.

Kilometer 98: Eddie B. pulls up to another large group of riders and counts two more Subarus. If there is only one group ahead, he has two men up among the leaders, fighting for prize money and points, which go to the first 10 finishers. "We have to go!" Eddie B. announces, jumping the curb and speeding on the sidewalk to get past riders spread across the road as they battle the wind. Just before he hits a road sign, Eddie B. whips the car back into the road, ahead of the riders. "Sometimes like that," he says, "but it's my boys."

Kilometer 128: Finally the car reaches the next bunch of riders, including Reiss and Aun. "A bunch went and I tried to bridge over with two Castoramas and a Zed but the Castoramas wouldn't work," Reiss reports. "We could have made it if they worked."

"Better two in the top 14 than four in the top 40," Eddie B. says, meaning that if the Castorama riders had cooperated in trying to overtake the leaders, they might have towed along the whole chasing pack.

"That's racing—miss the break, you miss it. Like life." He consoles Reiss. "It's over," he says. "You did good." The chasing group slows, knowing it cannot overhaul the leaders. By the time Laurent Desbiens of Collstrop reaches Cholet and easily wins the race, the chasers are far behind. Aun is the only finisher for Subaru, 44th, 25 minutes back.

Somewhere on the slow trip to town, his guest tells Eddie B. that it wasn't surprising Castorama led the attack and refused to chase: The sponsor, a chain of hardware stores, is especially popular in this part of France and Guimard, who has guided riders to seven victories in the Tour de France, comes from nearby Nantes.

Eddie B. thinks about this. "I didn't know," he says. "Too bad you didn't tell me before so I tell them to watch Castorama."

And he adds: "That's education. I'll remember that next year."

The Wrong Climate

1998

THAT FELLOW WITH THE BOOGIE-WOOGIE TIE and the long face at the Tour de France presentation was Yvon Sanquer, who has spent the last four years trying to make chicken salad out of chicken feathers. Just as he seemed to be perfecting the formula, his laboratory was closed.

"Finished," he said. "It's over." He tried a smile, which, with the loud tie, was meant to show that he was still in there battling. The long face said otherwise.

"The team is through," the *directeur sportif* of La Mutuelle de Seine et Marne continued. "A pity. Maybe we'll return after a season away, but I doubt it.

"The sponsor was more than correct," he said. "They signed for three years and then gave us a fourth. But in this climate, it's impossible to find a new sponsor."

"This climate" is the doping scandal that enveloped and ruined the Tour de France this summer and that dominated the race's presentation in Paris.

Known as the Festina Affair for the team that was expelled from the Tour for systematic use of illegal performance-enhancing drugs, the scandal is far from over. Team officials and riders continue to be questioned in the French cities of Lille and Reims and some, like Cees Priem, the *directeur sportif* of the TVM team from the Netherlands, have not been allowed by the courts to leave France and go home since July.

At the highest level of the sport, the reaction is still mainly talk, appeals to morality and plans for frequent and independent medical examinations of the racers, but no outpouring of funds to develop tests that can trace the synthetic hormone EPO, the more-sophisticated PFC and human growth hormone in blood or urine.

Sponsors, however, are beginning to move. Three French teams—Cofidis, Big Mat–Auber and La Française des Jeux—have pledged 1 percent of their budgets to drug control and have established a code of conduct that dictates the suspension and eventual firing of any rider found positive in a doping test.

Another sponsor, Casino, has announced its withdrawal after next season, a year earlier than previewed. The photograph of one of its riders being led away and charged by the police with drug trafficking presumably did not move groceries for the supermarket chain.

Festina, the Spanish watchmaker that gave its name to the scandal, has taken a convoluted path: Its president, Miguel Rodriguez, said early in the Tour that if an intention to use drugs systematically was proven, he would immediately terminate his contract, which runs until 2001. But when team officials and five riders confessed to just such practices, the sponsor stuck by the racers.

Festina even boasted that the notoriety had been good for business. Then, late last month, the sponsor announced that while it would keep the budget steady at 35 million francs ($6.3 million) a year, it would spend 4 percent of this in the fight on drugs, would concentrate on developing youth teams and would cut each professional rider's salary by 60 percent.

Take it or leave it, the riders were told. Some took, some left.

Out went such stars—and admitted illegal drug takers—as Alex Zülle, who joined Banesto in Spain, and Laurent Dufaux and Armin Meier, who moved to Saeco in Italy. Richard Virenque, the team leader, who consistently denies doping despite others' testimony to the contrary, refused the cut in his 12 million-franc annual salary and is negotiating a new contract in Italy.

If his face wasn't so long, Yvon Sanquer would probably laugh at these developments. His team, La Mutuelle de Seine et Marne, was never accused of doping—it could barely afford aspirin, let alone EPO at $100 a pop. La Mutuelle de Seine et Marne was sponsored by a French health insurance company, which put up most of the annual budget of 6.5 million francs. That's small change in the sport.

Having so much less to spend, Sanquer worked with riders having so much less to offer. He initially built his second-division team around unproven youngsters and discarded veterans. Told long beforehand that his sponsor would drop out at the end of 1998, Sanquer curtailed the youth program this season and relied on veterans, hoping they would win just enough times to attract a new bankroll.

By the end of the summer, his plan began to work. In La Mutuelle's colors, Gilles Maignan, 30, won the French time trial championship, Françisque Teyssier, 29, won the esteemed Grand Prix des Nations. At last, La Mutuelle was rolling.

"Too late, too late," Sanquer said. "Maybe it would have been enough in another year, but now, where do you find a sponsor in this climate?"

A Furtive Fellow

1997

HE HAD A FURTIVE LOOK, which set him apart from the other people in the pressroom at the Tour de France. The others looked bored, happy, busy or any combination of these but not furtive—they belonged. The green card with an individual photograph that hung on their chest said so. The fellow with the furtive look had no green card.

Then how did he get past the two guards at the door and into the pressroom? No problem there: Lots of people do it. They like to take photographs of reporters at work, popping bright lights into their eyes. Then they look uncomprehending when a reporter asks if he can visit their grocery or shoe store some afternoon and stare at them, maybe even take photographs while they try to make a sale.

There are also people in the pressroom who do have the proper accreditation, that green card, but have never been known to write an article. Didier, the super fan, is one of them. He shows up at every Tour, and many other big bicycle races, struts a bit and never misses a buffet table. He represents a press agency named for himself and no doubt based in his living room, good enough for whoever issues press credentials.

Unlike Didier, the furtive fellow did not strut. He was too old for that—at least early 50s—and too heavyset. He looked hunted. His eyes were never still, as if he was searching for the person, among the hundreds in the pressroom, who would betray him to the authorities and cause him to be evicted.

Until then, he showed up in the pressroom day after day wherever the race traveled. He seemed to be carrying more, too, all of it clutched tightly to his body: In Rouen, at the start, a black briefcase; by Pau, midway through, a couple of filled Tour plastic bags joined the briefcase. He gave the impression of a man fleeing a fire with all his possessions.

Everybody else needed a pass, but he circulated in the by-invitation-only area before each day's stage and waited at the fenced-off finish line afterward. At the long time trial in St. Etienne, where the riders set off individually to race the clock, he collected autographs from dozens of them, crossing the barriers with impunity to chat with riders as they warmed up on rollers. He took photographs, using the kind of camera that gets turned in at the developer's.

It got to be too much, a few reporters felt. Generally they don't like super fans, believing that even if they do no real harm and never get in the way, they burlesque the seriousness of the job. (If that sounds pompous, it is.)

Near the end of the three-week race, some of these reporters discussed the furtive man and whether he should be turned in and barred from the pressroom, the finish line, the warm-up area and all the other places where only people with the right papers could go. No decision was made.

The furtive man was around for the last stage, of course, the one on the Champs-Elysées in Paris. Once the riders sprinted across the final line, they all headed for a nearby hotel, and so did he. This time he was clutching not only the briefcase and the plastic bags and his camera and a notepad for autographs but also the hand of a boy in his early teenage years. The boy had thick glasses, a vacant stare and a heavy way of walking, as if he was dragging his thick legs, not striding.

His father was pointing out riders to his son, walking hand in hand to where they were getting off their bicycles, calling them by their first names and introducing the boy.

He had spent his Tour making friends and now he wanted them to meet his son. No reason to be furtive about that, is there?

MESSENGERS OF SPRING

1986

THE CYNICAL MONSIEUR DUPONT locked his country post office, slipped into his government-issue blue overcoat with the gold buttons and drove to the highest hill overlooking the village of Vaudebarrier.

"It's a fraud and a cheat—no question about that," he announced to somebody already atop the hill, peering down the valley to catch sight of the pack in Paris-Nice. "I know, we all know, that races are being bought and sold," Monsieur Dupont continued. "You see it now even in the Tour de France. Money talks and everybody listens." He rubbed his thumb over his first two fingers in the universal gesture. "It's all fixed, all the races."

Then why was he standing on the edge of a stubbled cornfield on a cold day in March, waiting for Paris-Nice to stream by?

"It's a cheat and fraud," Monsieur Dupont explained, "but it's spring." Yes it was. After a winter of cyclo-cross and six-day track races, of gossip from training camps and official team presentations, of minor races in the south of France and Spain, the professional season was off to its real start with Paris-Nice.

What if the calendar said early March? What if the air was so frigid at the prologue in Paris that many of the riders preferred to sit in their team cars while awaiting their turn to set off? What if some riders wore warm-up suits during the time trial and Eric Heiden of 7-Eleven sported an Andean shepherd's cap with earflaps instead of an aerodynamic helmet? ("We're like automobiles," said Alain Bondue of the Système U team. "When they're cold, they don't go very well either." Even so, he finished third in the prologue, seven seconds behind the winner, Sean Kelly.)

This day, the third of the race, started 60 kilometers north of Vaudebarrier, in Burgundy. The town was Chagny, lying in the heart of some of the best-known vineyards in France; Rully was a few kilometers up the road, Chambertin a few kilometers down it. Gnarled and leafless, the vines looked dead. A thick layer of frost had built up overnight on automobile windshields and the fields were crusted with snow. On this morning, the world started black and white.

"How cold is it out there?" Greg LeMond asked.

"About 60 degrees," a friend joked.

"I'll bet it is—in your car, with the heater turned way up."

He was leaving the dining room of his hotel, an ugly gray blockhouse designed for tour buses. Nearly all 11 teams in Paris-Nice had spent the night there before going by car to the village of Buxy and the start of a 225-kilometer stage to the city of St. Etienne.

LeMond was right: It was 60 degrees Fahrenheit in the car with the windows rolled up and the heater turned on, but about 25 degrees outside in Buxy. A few hundred children stood bravely at the riders' sign-in, stamping their feet, while the town's band tried to provide some bracing martial music. Nothing helped.

The pack set off slowly, the riders watching their breath puff out before them as they moved toward the start of the first long stage of the French season. Only Bondue had his mind on anything but the weather. Rolling slowly, he found himself next to Eddy Planckaert, a Belgian sprinter for Panasonic.

"What if somebody just took off?" Bondue asked dreamily.

That is not the kind of question Bondue should have been asking. As he said later, "The only training I had for Paris-Nice was to shovel the snow at my parents' house."

Besides, the Frenchman is not celebrated as a climber and the topographical profile of the stage showed a series of hills building to two climbs rated second category in steepness and length. Bondue is a track specialist, the winner of the silver medal in pursuit at the 1980 Olympic Games and the professional world champion in pursuit in 1981 and 1982. On the road, his best showing was a second place in Milan–San Remo in 1982.

Planckaert knew all this—knew at least that Bondue had no chance over the hills ahead. The sprint specialist looked over at the track specialist and gave his answer to the question "What if somebody just took off?" Devilishly, Plackaert said, "Go for it."

And Bondue did. Since Kelly was leading the race and Bondue was third, a few of Kelly's teammates went after Bondue before thinking better of it on the first hill. "I looked back and saw they wouldn't catch me," the Frenchman said later. "I felt good. I decided to keep going."

Somewhere, as he headed south, the day began to catch color. What had been black fields turned muddy brown and then the slightest bit green. The leaden sky changed into a washed blue and the sun burned just bright enough to clear the fog off the hills and light up the road ahead. The snow was melting quickly at Vaudebarrier, where the cynical Monsieur Dupont was now cheering his first bicycle race of the year.

Bondue remained far ahead of the pack, reaching a peak of 19 minutes 44 seconds at the village of La Clayette, 80 kilometers into the stage. A stiff 20-kilometer climb here and Bondue moved strongly up to the Col de la Buche, but was laboring 35 kilometers later at the Col des Sauvages, the first of the second-category climbs. The pack had also woken up. Was it the change in the weather that stirred the other riders or simply the realization that a breakaway had to be reeled back in?

With Kelly's Kas team setting the pace, Bondue's lead began to drop. By the last climb, at Duerne, 45 kilometers farther along, the messenger of spring was only three minutes ahead. He struggled up the hill first, taking the points that gave him the mountain jersey, before the other riders whooshed by. Submerged in the pack over the last 45 kilometers, Bondue reached St. Etienne in 78th place for the day, losing 16 minutes 32 seconds to the leaders. "It might have worked," he said. "I tried. I lost."

The next day the sun was out gloriously. Over a course even more mountainous than the day before, the sprinter Eddy Planckaert ("Go for it") broke away for 120 kilometers and led the pack by as much as nine minutes before he was caught. What was a sprinter doing in these climbs?

High on a hill watching Planckaert zip through the sunshine stood a couple of Frenchmen. One of them gestured out over the hills where the pack was riding hard on this almost balmy afternoon. "There are the fellows who've brought the good weather," he said. "There are the boys we have to thank for spring."

Blockbuster Classic

1988

FOR DECADES, BIG WAS BEAUTIFUL in the Milan–San Remo race. As Lenin observed, "Quantity has a quality all its own," and here was quantity galore: a race nearly 300 kilometers long, enlisting at least 300 riders. Nothing else in the sport approached that combination. Gerrie Knetemann, the Dutch racer for the PDM team who has ridden Milan–San Remo more than a dozen times, remembers even vaster fields. "I've ridden with 450 riders," he said.

And now, no more. Alarmed by injuries and even deaths on the road, the International Federation of Professional Cycling has limited races to 200 riders. Milan–San Remo, whose packed, narrow roads made it notorious for crashes, was widely regarded as a major target. "You spend all day trying not to crash," Knetemann said. "Picking a winner is like playing bingo."

Martin Ducrot of SuperConfex confirmed the danger. "It's very nervous," he said. "Even when you start with just 200 riders, when half of them are left, that's 100—a dangerous number." He was seconded by Fred de Bruyne, who won the race in 1956 and who now works for the Panasonic team as a liaison man. "It's always nervous at the start. Italians are nervous riders. The trick is to stay in front at the start and try to avoid the falls."

Dangerous or not, riders covet victory in Milan–San Remo, the first classic of the season. "There's always a good winner," Knetemann said. "I've never seen a mug win it," added Allan Peiper of Panasonic. "It's the greatest race there is. You've got to ride hard, you've got to stay at the front. The last 90 kilometers are unbelievably hard. I think it's the best race of the year. Only a champion wins it, only a champion." Not quite since the race began in 1907, but almost.

If the playboy Fons de Wolf won in 1981 and the journeyman Marc Gomez the next year, Eddy Merckx finished first seven times. Most of the legendary names of cycling are found among the victors: Petit Breton, Christophe, Bartali, Coppi, Bobet, de Vlaeminck and Gimondi. Francesco Moser won in 1984 ("You've got to take a chance on losing it to win it," he said after his victory following 10 failures) and Sean Kelly in 1986.

Fresh off his seventh consecutive victory in Paris-Nice, Kelly was unaccountably chatty as he stood before the 1988 start in Milan's Piazza de Duomo. The new rules complicated his strategy, he said, because they limited the 31 teams to six or seven riders instead of the usual 10. "You can't control the race now, you can't put anything together with seven men," Kelly complained.

Around him riders sat with their backs on the cathedral as masseurs rubbed wintergreen into their legs. The piazza was packed with team cars, policemen, riders, journalists and even a scattering of worshipers on their way to 9 A.M. mass. The *tifosi*, the celebrated Italian fans, were out in force, applauding the Del Tongo and Bianchi teams as they followed a motorcycle escort provided by the *polizia stradale*. "Vai Baffi," go Baffi, read a sign encouraging the young sprinter Adriano Baffi. "Viva Fondriest," countered another, referring to the coming Italian star, Maurizio Fondriest. The Giuseppe Saronni Club of Buscate had parked a bus just where the race was to turn out of the piazza and into the Via Guglielmo Marconi.

Spring was officially a day away. Milan–San Remo is nicknamed the Primavera, or spring, which Botticelli painted in his Primavera allegory as Venus blessing a nymph dressed in flowers while the three graces danced under fruit trees. Botticelli's spirit lives not in Milan but southwest on the Italian Riviera. Around Milan it was not yet spring: The sky had closed down, the air had turned cold and held a taste of rain. Where thousands of fans stood, leafless trees lined the road and the fields were barren.

For the first 64 of the 294 kilometers, it was *gruppo compatto* all the way. Then suddenly four riders decided to flee the winter—Domenico Cavallo of Isoglass, John Carlsen of Fagor, Alberto Elli of Fanini and Henri Manders of Weinmann, *domestiques* all. Off they went as the pack failed to respond, knowing that a long race lay ahead. What the race radio called the *quattro fuggitivi* (lovely word!) did not relay willingly at the start, as if they assumed they were going to be hauled back soon. Why waste their effort? By kilometer 102, as they sped through the town of musical Bassaluzzo and past Via Rossini, Via Toscanini and Via Donizetti, they were more than six minutes up. Elli, who had been dithering, went into a tuck and the four began to pull together, each taking a turn at the front of their trim formation. Now they were riding a team time trial.

Still the sky glowered and the only touch of color alongside the road was the occasional yellow sign announcing in red letters 200, then 175, then 150 kilometers to go. At kilometer 144, as the lead riders ended the only long climb and entered the Turchino tunnel, the race radio reported sun on the other side of the mountain—light at the end of the tunnel. Down the road was the Italian Riviera, the Mediterranean and, sure enough, the sun. Palm trees stood tall, pink almond trees glowed on the hillsides. Primavera!

Down the slick and long descent from the Turchino and into the southwestern leg, into Arenzano, where pots of red geraniums marked balconies and the sun glinted on the placid sea. In Varazzo, nuns in white habits clapped in delight as the breakaway sped along the coast. In Savona, a line of sailboats capered offshore and the radio announced that Moreno Argentin's Bianchi team had taken the initiative in chasing. Argentin, the 1986 world champion, needed a big victory at home, where he has never been popular. Alfa Lum of Italy pitched in, carefully relaying Fondriest, saving his power for the end. ("Milan–San Remo is difficult because it's really so easy and everybody is around near the end," Fondriest felt.) The gap began to close.

Later, the *fuggitivo* Manders admitted that he knew all along the break was doomed. Asked if he had ever thought he would get away, he replied, "No, never. With four you can't make it, it's just not possible with four. They can go only as long as the peloton lets them go. To really get away, you need eight or 10 riders." Then why did he keep going? "Yeah, why? I was there. What do I do, stop racing? Besides, the television exposure was good for the team and it was a nice day to ride."

Nice? In Sportono, green buds began appearing on trees. In Borghetto San Spirito, orange trees were sighted, and forsythia. Again the radio announced Bianchi stepping up the chase, assisted now by Carrera. In Alassio, magnolias flowered and lemon trees lined the streets. In Cervo, tubs of marigolds decorated the town square. Primavera!

By Imperia, where the signs proclaimed 35 kilometers to go, the breakaway was falling apart. "I was really exhausted," Manders said. One by one the leaders were picked up, with Carlsen the last to go. Up the Cipressa hill the race went in segments, stirred by a crash on the descent that threw Thierry Marie of Système U over a guardrail and into a ravine.

Argentin flatted and fell hopelessly behind. Then came the Poggio, four kilometers of ascending switchbacks and a tricky descent that for decades have been the race's Boot Hill. "There's only one rule for Milan–San Remo," said Cyrille Guimard, *directeur sportif* for Système U. "You've got to get up the Poggio among the first five. The way everybody careens around in the descent, if you've got too many riders ahead of you, you're blocked."

Guimard's strategy was not lost on his star rider, Laurent Fignon, the winner of the Tour de France in 1983 and 1984 and nothing major since. Ten riders paced the Poggio climb until Fignon stood on his pedals and zipped away a kilometer short of the peak. The others hesitated, Fondriest said later. "I held back for a moment," the Italian remembered, "waiting for Van der Poel or Kelly to go after him. When I realized they weren't going to do it, I went myself." Kelly and Adri Van der Poel were cooked, they admitted. "Fignon just shot off," Kelly said. "When Fondriest went after him I wanted to go, too, but it all happened too quickly. I just couldn't do it."

Fignon and Fondriest went through the descent together before turning into San Remo's Corso Cavallotti. Until recently, Milan–San Remo finished on the Via Roma, a four-kilometer straightaway that allowed the sprinters time to make up lost ground. Now the finish from the Poggio is only one kilometer along the Corso Cavallotti and the sprinters cannot overtake. The two leaders dueled with each other, first Fondriest on Fignon's wheel, then the other way around. On form, Fondriest should have won, but 294 kilometers leave a young rider weary and sometimes in the wrong gear as the final line approaches.

With 300 meters left, Fignon went around his rival and easily drew away. Triumphant, he nearly shot from the saddle with joy. Eight seconds behind them were the sprinters. Of the 198 starters, 111 finished.

Yes, Fignon said a few minutes later as he accepted a huge trophy and a bouquet of tulips, roses, mimosa and poinciana, it promised to be a fine spring. His drought was over, his hunger to win was back. "It's the end of a long period of doubt. Let's say that I've finally worked things out in my head and all the rest will follow. Under the sun," he explained, "I've bloomed again."

A Day in the Country

1985

LAURENT BIONDI ARRIVED in a Hitachi team station wagon, yellow and orange with bicycle racks on the roof, and Philippe Delaurier rolled up in a La Redoute team car with wheels bolted to the top and a team official driving. Rudy Dhaenens of Hitachi pulled up in his Mercedes, leaving it in the middle of the street even though there was plenty of room at the curb; fifth in the grueling Paris-Roubaix race a few weeks before, he was still strutting.

Johannes Habets of the Skil team drove with his fiancée from Maastricht in the Netherlands, two hours distant even with the superhighway from Brussels. Habets needed this race badly, he said, because he had been out of competition 14 days already. The Skil team was a French one and the French bicycling rules then insisted that two-thirds of a team be composed of Frenchmen. Habets is a Dutchman and so, to keep him, Skil would have had to sign two more Frenchmen. Instead the team dropped Habets from its official roster, although it continued to pay him, and announced its intention to sue the French Cycling Federation for violating Common Market rules guaranteeing freedom of employment.

Not to worry, Skil officials told Habets, but he was worrying nevertheless. A second-year professional, he needed some good results after an uneventful first year: His contract came up for renewal at the end of the season. After some mediocre showings in Spanish and Dutch races, he was barred from Milan–San Remo when French officials warned that he was ineligible for Skil's roster and risked sanctions if he participated.

And so he was furloughed, shunted off to the world of what he described as semi-classics, a euphemism for minor races in backwater towns. Habets had a better term for these races: "Where was it?"—as in his description of his best result the year before: "I had a 12th place in where was it in the Ardennes."

Now he was in Nokere, a Belgian village of 600 inhabitants where chickens peck in front yards on the main street and sheep and cows graze between houses, for the 23rd annual Nokere village race, or *kermesse.* In France such races are called criteriums and they used to sprout everywhere in August, just after the Tour de France, where a good result guaranteed a promoter's attention.

Even the dubious distinction of having been the Tour's *lanterne rouge*—the red lantern, the last man in the pack—could mean a few thousand francs in appearance fees. The top rate was the 35,000 francs (then $6,000) that Francesco Moser commanded for each appearance in 1984 after he broke Eddy Merckx's record for the hour ride against the clock.

These days criteriums are disappearing in France. Part of the problem is that the level of competition is often suspect. The races tend to be exhibitions, with the winner sometimes decided beforehand, rather than the straightforward competition of the *kermesse.* Another part was that star riders killed the golden goose by demanding more money.

Thirty years ago, before television was anything but a rarity in France and when people had little money to spend on summer vacations, criteriums were at their peak. Three a day, five on Sunday, were scheduled in various parts of the country. A top rider would compete in 50 to 60 criteriums after the Tour de France; now a top rider may pick up a dozen engagements.

In Belgium and the Netherlands, *kermesses* continue to flourish, probably because they have commercial sponsors and are thus usually free to the public, unlike the criteriums in France, which charge admission fees. They are not held only in August, as in France, but all season, and professional riders barely known to the public make a decent living by scooping up prizes and appearance money on these circuits. The pot in Nokere came to 100,000 Belgian francs (about $1,800) divided down to 30th place and put up by such local sponsors as the RaesTijtgat bakery, Jules Boonaert & Son country furniture, the Kredietbank and the *Nieuwsblad* newspaper. It was surely not a fortune and the race is just a local affair, but not much happens in Nokere, deep in the countryside about 80 kilometers from Brussels, and so race day is a holiday.

The village had done its best to merit the attention it would get today. Steel barriers were set up for 400 meters along Nokersdorp Straat, the main and almost only street, policemen who had been sent over from the town of Kruishoutem blocked traffic along the two roads flanking the village and, down at the Café Schuttershof, some of the farmers were even wearing neckties.

One wall of the café was covered with newspaper clippings about past Nokere races. Out peered the faces of such well-known winners as Gerrie Knetemann in 1981 and Freddy Maertens in 1974, plus such lesser lights as Frans De Looy in 1977 and Henrik de Vos in 1979. De Looy won in the biggest field ever, 174 riders, but since then the race has been drawing less attention and often attracts fewer than 100 riders.

The best explanation was the crowded racing calendar. Nokere was sandwiched between two major classics, the Flèche Wallonne two days before and Liège-Bastogne-Liège two days after. These drew the big names, a step or two above most of the entries in Nokere. Mostly Belgian, mostly Flemish, the Nokere riders belonged to minor teams or ranked 12th to 15th on major teams, which are restricted to no more than 10 riders in races. The major teams, therefore, use *kermesses* to give race experience to lesser riders.

The field filed into the Café Schuttershof, showed their licenses and paid a 200 Belgian franc deposit for their numbered bibs, and then filed out to find a place to change into racing clothes. Outside, hoping for autographs, youngsters waited with photographs and posters torn from bicycling magazines. They jostled to see Lucien van Impe, then 38 years but the winner of the Tour de France in 1976, or Eddy Planckaert, the sprinter with the Panasonic team who had won the Het Volk race, or Franck Hoste, the points champion in the 1984 Tour de France.

Or even Jan van Est, a Dutch rider and one of the few in the Nokere race not affiliated with a professional team. He raced instead for what he described only as "a private sponsor" but what his jersey identified as Henk van Rossum, a contractor in the Dutch town of Tricht.

At age 32, van Est realized that his best results were behind him. "This year it's not going so good," he admitted. "Last year was better." While he talked, he pulled the frame and wheels of his bicycle from the trunk of his car, a rather large sedan by European standards. Most riders have big cars, not only because it is the quickest way to demonstrate their prosperity but also because they need the extra trunk room for their equipment.

As his wife watched, van Est fitted the bicycle together and then pumped up the tires on two wheels and two spares. The car would not follow him on the course, as team cars do in major races, so if he had a puncture he would either have to quit or limp back to where the car was parked in front of Snoeck's general store. This choice had hampered him the year before in the Nokere race, he said.

"I did very well but the bike didn't." Something broke up front and van Est was lucky, he continued, to finish as well as he did, in the low 20s. "There's not much money beyond that." He rolled out a set of tools, did some last-minute tightening and then returned to sit in the car, drink some water and chat.

Up the street, near the French fry stand in front of the 12th-century St. Ursmarus Catholic Church and the booths selling hamburgers, simmered snails and stacks of salted herring, the crowd was gathering. Belgium is beer country and competing breweries had underwritten what seemed to be an abnormal number of cafés in such a small place: four, including the Schuttershof, De Ster and the Gemeentehuis, the Community House, with the year 1781 marked on its chimney. Business was brisk.

Then it was time to race, 147 kilometers in 13 circuits, 11 toward the town of Kruishoutem, 2 toward Wortegem. The course went past resolutely flat farms with modern split-level homes where two world wars had destroyed most of the traditional buildings, alongside a muddy pasture converted for the afternoon into a parking lot, past an old man walking through a freshly plowed field and broadcasting seed in the ancient way. Two men with jackets announcing that they represented Studio The Disc Brothers had rigged up loudspeakers on the roof of their car and they pulled out first, alerting the countryside to the passage of the race. Behind them came a car with blinking lights, then a police car and then the pack of riders.

All through the mild afternoon the riders traveled these back roads. Planckaert bolted away a few times and was quickly brought back; van Est labored mightily but was unable to move up from the far end of the line. On the distant reaches of the road the crowds were thin, but in Nokere the street was jammed and cheers rang from one end to the other whenever the pack appeared.

After 3 hours 35 minutes the race ended in a sprint finish with 10 riders charging up a slight incline. Didi Foubert of the Safir team crossed the line first, just nipping Patrick Versluys of Splendor and Jan Bogaert of Verandalux. Because Foubert is a Walloon, a French speaker, he was ineligible for the bonus title of Champion of the Five Provinces of East Flanders. That went instead to Versluys, a Fleming, or Dutch speaker. Habets finished seventh, his best "where was it?" result. Van Est was unsighted at the end.

The villagers gathered later at their cafés and agreed that it had been a wonderful time, the best since the Nokere *kermesse* the year before but probably not so good as the one to come next year.

King of the Walloons

1991

CLAUDE CRIQUIELION REALIZES that though he may be king of the Walloons, his fellow French-speaking Belgians, he will never become king of Wallonia, their territory. The difference is enormous.

Ask Moreno Argentin, an Italian and the reigning king of Wallonia, a title bestowed by the Liège-Bastogne-Liège race. Argentin has won it four times since 1985. Criquielion needed to win it only once to ascend to the throne, but in 13 years of trying he never finished better than second.

"My fans have been hoping for a long time that I'll win this race," Criquielion admitted. "They're hoping again. Nothing new there."

He was speaking at his hotel before the 77th running of Liège-Bastogne-Liège in 1991. First staged for professionals in 1894, it is the oldest and one of the most distinguished of the classics of the spring season. Twinned with the Flèche Wallonne, which is held four days earlier, Liège-Bastogne-Liège is the heart of the sport in the Walloon part of the country.

But no Walloon has won the race since 1978, when Joseph Bruyère did it. Until 1990, in fact, no Belgian had won Liège-Bastogne-Liège since Bruyère. Then Eric Van Lancker, a Dutch speaker from Flanders, came in an easy first, offering some balm to Belgium, a country scorched by two world wars, haunted by colonial ghosts and everlastingly divided by language. Of the 9.8 million Belgians, nearly 60 percent primarily speak Flemish, a form of Dutch, and 40 percent French.

This balance does not hold in bicycle racing. Few of the great Belgian riders have been Walloons and the current generation abounds with Flemish names: Van Hooydonck, Bruyneel, Museuuw, Vanderaerden, Dhaenens, de Wolf. These Dutch speakers have their own classic, the Tour of Flanders, the northern half of the country; Liège-Bastogne-Liège is for the south. For 13 years Criquielion (Criq or Claudy in the vernacular) was reminded of this every Apri,l and for 13 years he tried to oblige.

"I'm in good shape, and this is the time of the year that I'm usually at my best," he said before the race. "One more chance."

The finest of the Walloon riders, Criquielion won his share of races, including the

Flèche Wallonne twice and the world championship in 1984. (He lost another chance at the title in 1988 when he and Steve Bauer, a Canadian, bumped as they led the final sprint and the Belgian crashed.) In 1991, at the age of 34 and in his last season before retirement, Criquielion wore the black, yellow and red jersey of Belgium's champion. When he won that title, he postponed his plan to retire at the end of 1990.

Now, he said, only a victory in the 1991 world championship in Stuttgart could force him to continue for another season. "And I honestly don't expect to win there," he continued. "It's too tough a course for me."

He also did not expect to fulfill his ambition of winning a stage in the Tour de France. A consummate "man of the Tour"—by which people mean a rider who gives full effort, suffers through and completes the world's greatest bicycle race—Criquielion had finished as high as fifth twice without ever winning a stage. He describes this as his greatest disappointment in the sport. Second, surely, was his failure in Liège-Bastogne-Liège. He came close so many times: seventh in 1984, second in 1985, fourth in 1986, third in 1987.

Three times he was frustrated directly by Argentin. In 1985, Criquielion seemed to have broken away on the race's major hill, the Redoute, but was blocked by a flotilla of photographers' motorcycles just long enough for Stephen Roche, an Irishman, and Argentin to catch up. In the sprint finish, the Italian has few peers and won easily. In 1986, Argentin won a sprint again, this time against six riders, including Criquielion.

Worse was to come in 1987, when Criquielion and Roche broke away but slowly spent the final kilometers watching each other, wondering who was to be first to try to make the decisive move and forgetting that they were being chased by the pack. With 400 meters remaining, Argentin caught, and beat, them both.

The next three years Argentin was no factor but neither was Criquielion, who finished 26th, 32nd and 14th. Wallonia mourned. "There's a lot of pressure, yes," Criquielion said at his hotel. His thick eyebrows tightened.

Was he confident? "I hope to be at least as good as I was in the Flèche Wallonne." He finished second in that race, beaten by—who else?—Argentin. The Italian had been in splendid form, going on a 70-kilometer breakaway and winning by 2 minutes 20 seconds. Nobody could doubt his strength after he held off all pursuers for such a distance over short and steep hills similar to those in Liège-Bastogne-Liège. Argentin's message had reached Criquielion. "If I don't win tomorrow," he said, "I hope at least to be in the front."

On the day of the race, Criquielion stayed discreetly in the huge field of riders as they passed the spruce forests of the Ardennes, climbed the first of 10 hills, moved into Bastogne and swung right, on the return leg to Liège, at Patton Tank USA 380152, a memorial to the World War II siege of the town.

A brisk snow began falling as the pack approached the Haussire hill, at 4.6 kilometers, the longest of the day. This was familiar territory for Criquielion, who often trained over the hill and who lends his name to a cycling contest there: Beat his best time and win a gold medal. "Everybody here is a fan of his," said Hubert Goffinet, an organizer of the contest. "Criq is the king of the Walloons."

The king and his court of 195 riders were chasing a solitary breakaway, Thierry Bourguignon of the Toshiba team, who was reeled in after 181 kilometers of the 267 in the race. At kilometer 193, with the pack strung out on the Haute Levée hill, Criquielion made his move.

As he accelerated, he kept glancing backward over his left shoulder, wondering who would be able to stay with him. For a few seconds there was nobody there and then, suddenly, there was Argentin right on the Belgian's rear wheel. Eight other riders joined them, leaving the pack a minute behind.

The 10 breakaways began to dwindle over the next 70 kilometers and 5 remaining hills. By the time they reached the Redoute, three hills from home, the group was down to Criquielion, Argentin, his teammate Rolf Sørensen and Miguel Indurain. On the Hornay hill, the next to last, Criquielion tried to speed away but Argentin was right on him, and then so were Sørensen and Indurain.

Sixteen kilometers from the end, on the Forges hill, Criquielion had his last chance to leave the others behind, but couldn't. It had been a demanding seven hours and, at age 34, Criquielion was feeling the ride in his legs.

Once over the crest and onto the plain leading into Liège, Argentin and Sørensen, the Ariostea teammates, began playing cat and mouse with the Belgian. Argentin attacked, Criquielion caught him; Sørensen attacked, Criquielion caught him; Sørensen attacked again, Criquielion caught him again. The one time Criquielion attacked, Argentin and Sørensen caught him easily.

"Over the last 30 kilometers I came to terms with the idea that I would lose," Criquielion confessed later. "Against Argentin, all I could do was try to finish second."

The four swept along the Meuse River into Liège and the decisive sprint. With 600 meters to go, Sørensen surged ahead. Criquielion and Argentin were side by side as they passed him and side by side until the final 50 meters, when the Italian displayed his power. He is, after all, one of the sport's top sprinters.

Argentin crossed the line with his arms raised in victory, coasting as Criquielion still bore down, the length of a bicycle behind. Minutes later, Criquielion was wiping his dirt-streaked face, removing his helmet and adjusting a clean cloth cap to give his Lotto team maximum publicity before the photographers.

Second in the Flèche Wallonne and second in Liège-Bastogne-Liège. He shook his head wearily, the king of the Walloons but not Wallonia.

Occupational Hazards

1991

NEARLY EVERYBODY IN THE SMALL WORLD of bicycle racing remembers the photograph, and Davis Phinney remembers it best. It shows him sitting on the ground behind a car, his right hand up to his face, his body limp and blood everywhere.

"I just center-punched that car," Phinney said. Traveling at high speed and with his head down in the 1988 Liège-Bastogne-Liège race, he rammed the stopped car from the rear and went head-first into the window, which shattered. "I just had time to get my left arm up to my face," the American rider said, repeating the motion and showing a long scar on the underside of his arm. "I lost the use of my little finger. It just hangs there, limp."

His nose was broken and his face so badly ripped that he needed 150 stitches to repair the damage. The scars have faded now. When he laughs, which is often, the scars around his eyes blend into a worldly crinkle. "People say they add character to my face," Phinney boasted.

Liège-Bastogne-Liège is even older than the Tour de France. Begun in 1890 as a race for amateurs, it is generally regarded as the oldest of bicycle racing's classics by one year over Bordeaux-Paris. Some historians of the sport point out, however, that it did not become a race for professionals—the usual yardstick for measuring a race's longevity—until 1894 and then resumed its amateur status until 1912.

That amateur tradition lingers. Until 1990, Liège-Bastogne-Liège was organized by the "Royal Cyclist's Pesant Club Liègeois," which proudly listed on its stationery such local sponsors as a furniture manufacturer and a pinball-machine supplier. In a way it was charming to have a mom-and-pop organization running such an important race in an era when marketing studies and computer printouts are beginning to dominate the sport. Sometimes Liège-Bastogne-Liège seemed more like an overgrown *kermesse,* one of the lots-of-fun-for-the-family races that nearly every town in Belgium holds annually. Sometimes, though, because it was all so casual and the weather often rainy and even snowy, Liège-Bastogne-Liège was unsafe. Roads up and down some of its hills were narrow and clogged with spectators, making it difficult for the racers to get through. Press photographers on motorcycles were allowed to shadow the riders so closely that they could block a breakaway.

In 1988, before Phinney was hurt, dozens of riders spilled into a drainage ditch that had been dug across the course. In major races, the organizers monitor the roads beforehand to prevent unexpected obstacles or they post sentries with yellow flags to warn the riders, but in Liège-Bastogne-Liège nobody seemed to know about the trench. "I was in that crash," Phinney said, "and I wrecked both wheels. By the time I got going again, I was five minutes down and ready to quit." Mike Neel, then the director of the 7-Eleven team, drove up and told Phinney and a teammate, Alex Stieda, to stay in the race.

"'Come on, let's go,' he said," Phinney remembered. "I was feeling so good that we just took off. Because of the crash, there were riders all strung out ahead and I was raging and went by these groups. I was going, going, going. Team cars were all along the road and I tried to ride in the center, passing between the cars. I was leapfrogging cars but getting tired because I had been chasing for about 10 kilometers. I could see the pack and they were about 200 meters away, so I just put my head down and rode.

"I heard horns honking behind me and I thought it was just team cars wanting riders to move over and I put my head up and a car had just stopped in the middle of the road."

The car belonged to the Isoglass team and had stopped to replace a punctured tire for one of its riders. At the time, Phinney estimated, he was racing at 50 kilometers an hour and the car was about 5 feet ahead of him.

"It was a pretty narrow road," the American continued, "but he didn't stop on the side, the way you're supposed to. He stopped in the middle and I plowed into him. It was my fault. You assume there'll be nothing there, that the race is ongoing, but ultimately everything is pretty much your fault in bike racing."

He was rushed by ambulance to Liège for a two-hour operation. Two days later he was back on his bicycle, riding it on rollers, as racers do to warm up. "Mostly it was to sweat and clean out the anesthetics from my body," he said. A few days more and he was riding through the streets, careful about a cast on his left arm. "Like a batter who has been hit by a pitch, the trick is to get going right away, not brood about it." Ten days after he left the hospital he entered his first race, a *kermesse* in Belgium. Four weeks to the day after the crash, Phinney outsprinted the pack to win a stage of the Tour of Romandie, a Swiss race.

Phinney returned to Liège-Bastogne-Liège in 1989.

"I was really uptight and the closer I got to where I had crashed, I started to get this block in my mind. I couldn't ride in the field with everybody else. I was so tense that I was riding last guy. Once we went past the point, I started to relax."

Because he had been riding in Europe since the earliest races in February and because he was still recovering from a tendon operation on his left knee months before, the 7-Eleven team sent him home to Boulder, Colorado, a week before the 1990 Liège-Bastogne-Liège. "I'm really glad to miss that," he said.

The race is now one of the 12 classics that compose the prestigious World Cup. As such, its organizers were persuaded to bring in outside advisers and they asked the Société du Tour de France to help map a safer course and control the crowds and media motorcycles. The Tour de France people recommended eliminating one hill as too dangerous and adding three, for a total of 10.

As black clouds scudded across the sky, 196 riders started the 256-kilometer race south into the Ardennes and back to Liège. "It's very difficult and very hilly, quite a change from the first classics," explained Steve Bauer, a Canadian and Phinney's teammate with 7-Eleven. "The Tour of Flanders has hills, but they're short. In Liège-Bastogne-Liège, you need more stamina, more endurance. You need good climbing ability. You've been riding flat and riding cobblestones and you're not really prepared to be riding up and down. That's a tough transition."

This was a typical Liège-Bastogne-Liège. The hills were as long as ever and the weather—frequently hard and cold rain as the riders passed the spruce forests of southeastern Belgium—as bad as ever. With 22 kilometers to go, Eric Van Lancker of Panasonic broke away before the final climb. Of the 136 riders who finished, only two—Jean-Claude Leclercq of Helvetia and Steven Rooks of Panasonic—had the strength to go after him and Rooks was doing it as a piece of strategy, to put Leclercq in a nutcracker between two teammates.

Van Lancker crossed the finish line 34 seconds clear to give Belgium its first victory in the classic since 1978. The two others began to sprint for second place, with Leclercq coming straight down the middle and Rooks out to his left. The road should have been clear for Rooks, but just behind the finish a long line of photographers, reporters, officials and simple onlookers jutted directly into his path. Luckily, Rooks was racing with his head up and spotted them. He swerved away, losing ground as Leclercq crossed the line ahead of him. Nobody was hurt.

It was difficult not to think then about Phinney, an acclaimed sprinter, the best in America and one of the best in the world. With a big laugh, he tells about the attendant at a ski lift who did a double-take when he saw his scarred face.

"He asked, 'What happened? A cat scratch you?'

"'Yeah,' I said. 'And you know what kind of cat it was? A jaguar.'"

Another Crash

2000

UPBEAT AS ALWAYS, SCOTT SUNDERLAND sat in his home in Belgium with a leg in a cast and insisted that the 20 stitches in his right knee and a few more in his left arm should not be described as an example of continuing bad luck.

"I never try to look at it as bad luck," the 33-year-old Australian said on the phone. "It is bad luck but I try to look at it as, I'm lucky I got out of it with nothing worse. You've got to," he insisted, "or else you say, 'What the hell, I'm giving this up.'"

Which is exactly the way he felt the day before when he crashed in the Kuurne-Brussels-Kuurne race—"Bang and over, and we were going 60 ks an hour."

Afterward, he said, "I just wanted to stop racing, I didn't want to see the bike again. But today it's different. I'm sitting here with my chiropractor and we're talking about it like it's just a little injury and how I'm going to get out of it.

"I can't believe it, can't believe it," he said of the minimum of two weeks lost in what he hopes will be his comeback year. Then Sunderland brightened, as he always does. "But it just means a couple more weeks' delay in trying to get there."

"There" has filled his thoughts for nearly two years. It represents a return to the high level of racing that Sunderland enjoyed until he was nearly killed in a crash and had to spend more than 16 months out of competition.

Riding in the Amstel Gold Race in the Netherlands in April 1998, he was clipped on the rear wheel of his bicycle and hurtled onto the road. "All of a sudden, my bike was out of control," he said. "My wheel buckled and the brakes gripped, so I tried to fight it. The impact spun me around and I ended up falling on my back and banging my head."

The car that hit him was driven by Cees Priem, then the director of the TVM team from the Netherlands, one of those Sunderland has ridden for in his 11-year professional career. Priem did not stop to help the rider but continued to follow the race.

The unconscious Sunderland was taken by helicopter from the race to a hospital in Maastricht, close to the finish, where doctors diagnosed a concussion but failed to administer a scan to check for brain damage despite his complaints of blinding headaches and blurred vision. A lump the size of an orange was developing at the nape of his neck. Luckily, his wife, Sabine, had come from Belgium to watch the race. She ordered an ambulance to take him to Belgium and Ghent University Hospital, where neurologists performed the scan and ordered immediate surgery. "It was a life-and-death situation," he said of the buildup of blood at the base of his brain.

Five hours later, he was regaining consciousness and beginning a long recuperation, including five days in intensive care. His 1998 season was over.

Early in 1999, he tried to race again in Australia, but "I wasn't really ready. My body wasn't ready, and I ended up doing myself more harm than good.

"I returned to Europe having to take 12 weeks off the bike with problems with my knee and my foot. Then all of a sudden, things started to go my way."

In a midseason race in Spain he won the first stage.

"To win the first day and take the leader's jersey, what a feeling," he said. "I had some other good placings, too, and the world championships didn't go too bad."

Late last year he won the King of the Mountains jersey as the best climber in the Commonwealth Bank Classic in Australia, finishing fourth overall. Then in January he won the silver medal in the Australian road race championship.

But in between, he was reminded of the accident. "Constant little niggles," he calls the reminders. "In November, I had a serious problem with my back again, the muscles kept going into spasms. I've got ongoing health problems, including the loss of 20 percent of the vision in my right eye."

Still, he remains confident and, before his new crash, hoped to hit a peak in April for the classics. The new crash, he said, "puts a big hole in my preparation period. Even though I might not be riding at my best now, this is important base work for the classics.

"The classics," he repeated. "I'll be there."

Playing Through Pain

1999

AT FIRST, MARION CLIGNET tried to play through her pain, the old-fashioned way. That didn't work. The pain was too constant and too severe—"awful, agonizing" is how she remembers it.

The pain began in her lower back about a year after she won a gold medal in pursuit at the world championship in 1996, setting a time record for the ride. After an operation, "the pain kind of went away," she said, "but then it started again in my right knee, then the balls of my feet and then the arches of my feet."

That was bad for a racer. "It was a nightmare," she agreed. "I couldn't even sleep—the pain woke me up. I didn't know what it was, only that it was something I couldn't control and it got worse and worse."

With her career threatened, she retired from racing for 11 months late in 1997. Finally she received the correct diagnosis. "It's genetic," she explained, "a gene that can provoke inflammatory arthritis."

Once again her genes had betrayed her: She is also an epileptic.

Thirteen years ago, when she was a 22-year-old resident of suburban Maryland, she had her first seizure and has campaigned for years as a spokesperson for an epileptic foundation, proving that neurologic disorders and sports can cohabit.

For all her troublesome genes, obviously she also has many positive ones. At the world championships on the bicycle track in Berlin last month, Clignet won two gold medals, one in the pursuit and the other in the points race. That made a total of five gold medals for her in the world championships since she moved in 1990 from the United States, where she was born in Hyde Park, Illinois, to France, the home of her parents. (Her father, Rémy, taught sociology first at Northwestern and then at the University of Maryland in College Park.)

Comeback now accomplished, she said that she had only one goal left in racing, to win a gold medal in the 2000 Olympics in Sydney, Australia, to go with the silver one she won in pursuit at the 1996 Games in Atlanta.

Clignet sounded happy over the phone from her home just outside Toulouse in the southwest of France. "First time I've been home in four months," she said. "You wouldn't believe how much mail is piled up. And the phone's been ringing off the hook."

The letters and calls are congratulatory, of course, with an undertone of curiosity. Clignet has not talked publicly about her affliction or how she brought it under control.

At the beginning, she said, the proper treatment remained a mystery. "I went to a whole bunch of different doctors—we'll try this, we'll try that, no, let's do this, no, let's do that, this treatment, that treatment. Cortisone, anti-inflammatory—I tried everything.

"Finally I took 11 months off completely and I stopped everything. I was being given pretty heavy medication and it sparked my epileptic seizures, so I was having seizures along with my arthritis—that was really great. Lots of fun.

"When I figured all that out, I said I'll stop and see what happens. If I can ride again, I'll ride again and I'll ride to the top. And if I can't ride again, then I'll just have to figure out something else to do."

During part of her time off, she worked at finding sponsors for women's races and traveled to Paris one week a month to earn a coaching diploma in an accelerated program for athletes. She also talked to other riders about possible cures for her arthritis and two of them gave her the same name—"Brian Welsby, an Englishman who makes drinks out of plants, totally natural. The idea is to strengthen my immune system and help me protect myself from my own pain.

"I said, 'Let's give it a try' and wrote to him. It's an orange-flavored powder and I drink it every morning and at night, too.

"And this did it. I tried everything—acupuncture, homeopathic stuff, doctors, anything I could think and nothing worked. And this did it.

"It started to work almost immediately and I began to get back on track." But not the bicycle track. "No, I stayed off the bike for a while to let everything get back in sync and the program seemed to work. That's when I got back on the bike. I started racing again in January of this year, very slowly. I couldn't get out of my own way and I had to be very patient."

In March she won her first race since 1996, a time trial in a small race in France. By the summer she was near top form, winning the first stage in the women's Tour of Italy in June—"a big surprise," she called it, "a pretty wicked race and I hadn't done a long race like that in two years." She rode there for her professional team, Acca Due O, based in Italy.

Then she finished second in the French national pursuit championship and gained a ticket to the world championships, where pleasure replaced pain.

"I'm going to stay with Acca Due O and train my butt off for the Olympics," Clignet said. "And then I'll retire.

"I've been talking to people about coaching possibilities for various teams, some in France, some not. Wherever I can have the most impact and the best conditions to improve a group, that's where I'll go.

"If I stay in France I'd also like to work on improving conditions for women athletes. They're not up to par at all. But I'm not sure the French are ready for that. I've been working years at this and I just don't see any improvement."

A spokesperson for epileptics and a champion of women athletes, Clignet tried to make a joke about her social consciousness. "Maybe it's because my dad's a sociologist," she said.

Then her voice became serious. "I have been taken through so many tough turns that I try to react to people the way that I'd like them to react to me. In the last two years, a lot of people turned their backs on me, especially when I started riding again.

"I asked for help left and right, and a lot of people weren't there for me. I wouldn't want to see that happen to someone else."

More Woes for Indonesia

2000

INDONESIA HAS BEEN HAVING GEAR PROBLEMS.

Granted, the panoply of other Indonesian problems—financial meltdown, intercommunal butchery, the ousting of a strongman, secessionist pressures—might seem more important than getting the gears on the country's bicycle team to mesh properly.

Don't tell that, however, to Wawan Setyobudi, rider No. 182 in Le Tour de Langkawi.

He was sprawled on a sidewalk in the Malaysian resort island of Langkawi this week, taking deep gulps from a bottle of mineral water while explaining to his teammates how his gears had failed him on the first climb in the race. Barely a minute into the 12-day race and—whiz, spin, clank—his gears failed to connect as he shifted and began trying to move uphill.

Jutas Turisna, the team's masseur, looked on morosely.

"Three bikes already with gear problems," he said wistfully.

Then he brightened. Setyobudi brightened. The rest of the six-man team brightened. The Indonesians, an extremely likable racing club from East Java with matching jerseys and unmatching shorts, socks, shoes and bicycles, are not going to win any races here but they are having a swell time.

Whoever would have expected that the Polygon Sweetnice Racing Team—Setyobudi, Joni Suryo Agung, the brothers Herry Janto Setiawan and Hengky Setiawan and two riders who go by one name only, Sulistiono and Suyitno—would be moving up from the local Tour de Java to the international Tour de Langkawi? Tomorrow the world.

"Three months ago, the East Java team finished first in team and individual events in the Tour de Java," the masseur explained between drags on a clove-scented Indonesian cigarette with heavenly secondary smoke.

"That and the fact that the cycling federation has no money for a true national team got them into this race."

But, he added, four of the six riders have been members of the national team. "This is the best in Indonesia," he said firmly.

Hengky Setiawan, for example, has raced five times previously in smaller races in Malaysia and twice was a member of Indonesia's pre-Olympic squad, in 1992 and 1996. His brother raced on the track at the Olympic Games in Barcelona in 1992.

Both Setiawans are fans of the sport. Herry Janto's big moment here was a meeting with the Colombian climber Chepe Gonzalez, now of the Aguardiente Nectar team from Italy, whom he watched on television a few years back as Gonzalez won a stage in the Tour de France. "Nice guy," the Indonesian said in English. "Great rider."

Hengky Setiawan begged to differ. When it comes to great riders, who can top Eddy Merckx? When Hengky spent six months in the Netherlands in 1992, training to make the Olympic team that he didn't, he traveled one day to Belgium to visit the bicycle factory run by the five-time winner of the Tour de France. "Great rider, best ever," he decided.

Smiling as usual, the other Indonesians listened with awe to these judgments of heroes. Usually, they said, they traveled with smaller fish: Of their country's 170 million people, barely 120 rate as top-line competitors and of those 120, many are over 40 or under 18. Members of the Polygon Sweetnice team are in their 20s.

Their sponsors back home produce bicycles and components (Polygon) and what seems to be a jamlike spread for bread (Sweetnice). As they explained it, they are neither amateurs nor professionals—not amateurs because they are paid, not professionals because they are not paid much. "About $500 a year, small even for Indonesia," one said.

So Le Tour de Langkawi offers them several opportunities. "We're here for the experience, to learn to ride better," Herry Janto Setiawan said. "And the money, too. Oh yes, we hope so."

Time for Something

2000

BECAUSE THE FILIPINO TEAM in Le Tour de Langkawi did so poorly in the individual time trial that opened the race, its support car in the long caravan was No. 25—dead last among the teams and just ahead of the police cars and ambulance that bring up the rear.

"That's not where we belong," said Ric Rodriguez, the team's *directeur sportif.* "We deserve better. It's too difficult to help the riders that far back. So we had a meeting and decided to try to do something today to win some points and move up in the race."

"Something" began at kilometer 20 of the 173-kilometer second stage from the city of Alor Setar, where the starting line faced an imposing state mosque, Masjid Zahir, to the seaside resort of Batu Feringgi on the Malaysian island of Penang.

"Something" was two Filipino riders, Arnel Quirimit, 24, and Marculio Ramos, 21, off on a breakaway.

"We're aggressive," Rodriguez said at the finish. "We know that if we just ride with the pack, we don't have a chance. A lot of the other riders are European professionals, after all, and we're just a young team from the Philippines. So we try to break things up. Those were our tactics today."

Past crowds of schoolchildren massed along the roads, past rice paddies and rubber plantations, past the Restoran Mei Mei Yin and the Klinik Dr. Quak, past quarries and steel mills, Quirimit and Ramos rode a stage as good as any in most European races. For hours they held off their opponents and the weather: The temperature mounted, in occasional winds, to near 30 degrees centigrade (86 degrees Fahrenheit), as the lack of shade and the heavy humidity made it feel even hotter.

With Quirimit ("he's a veteran," Rodriguez explained) doing most of the work and Ramos ("a rookie") riding in his slipstream and saving energy, they opened a quick lead after their attack and then were left unhindered by the 147 other riders. Through the first bonus sprint they went, alone together, picking up points for themselves and their team, and then through the second at Petani, where throngs at roadside food stalls put down their lunches to applaud.

The road was still flat as the pair raced through the village of Bumbong Lima, kilometer 93, with a lead approaching 10 minutes. But by the final bonus sprint, at the middle of the long bridge that connects Penang to the mainland, the pack began to respond. When the two Filipinos crossed the bridge and turned right at the sign to the Snake Temple, their lead was under seven minutes.

The first hill of the day shattered them. "We ran out of gas in the mountains," Rodriguez admitted. It was a bad hill, and Ramos fell back, pushing his pedals in slow motion. Quirimit beckoned him to catch up, then continued alone. The pack was barely four minutes behind.

On the long descent, the pair were reunited, but the second and last hill ended their breakaway. First Ramos and then Quirimit were caught barely a kilometer from the top. Caught and discarded—Ramos finished 56th, Quirimit 58th.

"Too bad," Rodriguez said, "but we got the points at the sprints and on the climbs. Tomorrow, no more No. 25."

Quirimit arrived then and began toweling his face. "Happy?" he was asked.

"Happy," he responded. "But I could be happier."

Hold the Meat

2000

ENOUGH JOKES, PLEASE, about the Linda McCartney bicycle team, the only one in the sport that adheres to a strictly vegetarian diet.

No, when the team replaced eight of its 10 riders, it did not "beef up" the roster.

No, after a season during which Linda McCartney riders were usually left behind in races, the team did not feel as if it had gone through "a meat grinder" or been turned into "mincemeat."

And no, the addition of two such strong riders as Max Sciandri and Pascal Richard this year is not an attempt to move up in class from "hamburger" to "prime rib."

The vegetarian flapdoodle is limited to the media, said Sean Yates, a 39-year-old Briton, a former star descender and splendid time trialer for the Motorola team, among others, and now director of the Linda McCartney team. Rival riders, he added, are either unaware of his team's eating habits or indifferent.

Yates made it clear, in an interview during the six-day Tour Down Under in Adelaide, Australia, that the eating habits also had nothing to do with the team's dismal results after the first two years of a three-year contract with the sponsor.

The company, founded by the late photographer who was the wife of the Beatle Paul McCartney, is now owned by the Heinz food company, which produces a wide variety of frozen vegetarian dishes.

"Since we had an English sponsor," he said, "we wanted to have an English team. But it wasn't possible. We couldn't progress with just English riders. They have no background and the competition is so high.

"It's very hard to get results if you don't have the riders. The English guys just weren't used to it at that level. They were out of their depth."

The new team includes riders from Italy, Denmark, Norway and Switzerland.

"We weren't disgraced," he said about last season, "but we lacked that one person to get results. We wanted to progress and, in order to do that, we had to invest in better riders. We wanted a couple of people to attract organizers, a rider like Pascal Richard, whose name will open doors to us."

Richard, 35, a Swiss, is the reigning Olympic road race champion.

Nevertheless in this young season, the team knows about only its next two races after the Tour Down Under. "At the moment," Yates said, "our program is all up in the air. We know we're riding the Tour de Langkawi and the Rapport Race in South Africa.

"We're in a similar situation to last year, where we found it very difficult to get into big races and were settling for smaller races. There are so many teams out there. We're trying to get into the Spanish races this winter—Majorca, the Ruta del Sol, the Tour of Valencia—but there are 40 teams wanting to ride."

Sitting behind a lunch of sauceless spaghetti, stir-fried vegetables and three slices of bread, Yates said the vegetarian diet posed few problems for his riders at their different race hotels.

"We rarely eat anything special, just not the meat." Fish, also banned, is never served to cyclists for many reasons, including freshness.

"There's plenty of food to eat without the meat," he added. "If there isn't, we'll ask them to make something different. Sometimes they're accommodating, sometimes they're not. If they're not, we just have to lump it.

"A rider's diet is mostly carbohydrates and there's always pasta and bread. For the protein, there are protein supplements and we bring them with us, pills or some powder."

Yates grew up a vegetarian, he said, "because my family didn't eat meat, I don't know why, and we ate fish once in a blue moon."

He sometimes ate meat as a Tour de France rider but not since his retirement a few years back.

He can be somewhat whimsical on the subject: "So you don't eat meat but then somebody kills a cow anyway to make the shoes or the belt you wear."

He is straightforward, however, about the demands on his riders.

"They know those are the conditions when they come to the team," he said. "Their contract calls for them to promote a vegetarian image whenever and wherever possible. If they don't like it, they can go somewhere else."

Sciandri, 33 next month and a stage winner in the Tour de France, chose to come to Linda McCartney after a career with Italian, American and most recently French teams. He is a dual national, born in England to Italian parents who were running a restaurant there and now operate the acclaimed Ago and Toscano restaurants in Los Angeles.

A carnivore all his life, Sciandri dismissed the deprivations of his new lifestyle.

"Not eating meat is not a big problem," he said. "You take away pasta, that's a big problem. A nice piece of cake, that could be a problem.

"Besides, I'm curious to taste the food" that the sponsor provides monthly for the riders at home. "I hear the vegetarian burgers are great."

A Bunch of No-Shows

1997

THE DRIVER WARNED EVERYBODY ABOARD to remember the number of the bus—something like BXA 9235794 and lots of luck—because there would be many buses in the parking lot after the official dinner and they were going to different hotels.

But when the bus arrived in a central square in the city of X in the state of Y in Malaysia, the parking lot was empty. Although we were 20 minutes late, time was somewhat flexible in Le Tour de Langkawi bicycle race (Malaysian Rubber Time, it came to be called) and probably the rest of the guests were right behind us.

Not the 150 riders in the race, however. They were back in the dining room at the hotel. This dinner was for journalists only, we had been told. Attendance was recommended but not more or less mandatory as it had been at the dinner the night before that was given by the state of Y's minister for tourism or at the lunch that day that was visited by the prime minister. The riders attended both those meals.

Of the 35 or so international and Malaysian reporters, less than a third turned out for this dinner. It was sponsored by the state minister for Z, who was, to judge from the restaurant, considerably lower in rank than the minister for tourism. Still, the minister for Z had enough clout and budget to offer what kept being referred to as a banquet.

We went inside and were led to a huge dining room. Groups of Malaysians sat at four or five of the 30 tables, all of them set for dinner for eight. In the center of the floor, a larger table was occupied by official-looking men who could only be the minister for Z and his entourage. Just behind them was a stage and a banner: "Welcome to the Riders and Press of Le Tour de Langkawi." The minister's name and title were printed underneath.

What riders?

After we were seated, we waited. Ten minutes later, when nobody else had arrived, a man arose from the central table and motioned for those sitting in the far reaches of the room to move toward the middle. The wagons gathered, we waited again.

Finally waiters offered fruit drinks and somebody signaled to a woman, who went to a microphone and promised that there would be an exhibition of native dance during the banquet. First, however, a word from the sponsor.

Not the minister for Z himself. The speaker, who said he was the deputy chairman of the organizing committee in the state of Y, carried the pages of what looked to be a long speech. He cleared his throat, looked around dolefully and began.

He thanked the minister for sponsoring this banquet and offered a sincere welcome to . . . He coughed. He resumed. A sincere welcome to those present. "There seems to have been some miscommunication," he said, looking up from his text. "Miscommunication," he echoed. "I accept full responsibility for this miscommunication," he said. "Miscommunication," he repeated more quietly.

"However," he said, launching into his speech. It was really quite a good one. He noted that bicycle racers from 25 countries were gathered here—not physically present, no, unfortunately, because of a miscommunication—but here in the minister's state and that you . . . those . . . athletes had an opportunity to set an example for young people.

Although bicycle racing was a little-known sport in the state of Y, the presence of so many of you . . . them . . . the riders . . . could only inspire the young to seek glory themselves, to look to the stars. He spoke of the stars, the ones in the heavens, not you . . . those . . . present . . . if not actually here, in this state, and how they could beckon to young people or not.

He brought off the metaphor. Turning a page of his speech, he ran his eyes over it and turned immediately to the next page. In conclusion, welcome. In the name of the minister, welcome. And now to the banquet.

We few rose and began moving toward the buffet. The deputy chairman of the organizing committee lined up the pages of his speech, tucked it under his arm and headed for the central table and the minister for Z.

IN THE BROOM WAGON

1988

DRIVING IN THE PYRENEES, Philippe Pietrowski heard on the Tour de France's internal radio that two riders had fallen far behind. "I think we have customers," he said. "Maybe not," answered Raymond Guilmin, sounding hopeful. "Maybe not."

Pietrowski and Guilmin spend their days with the race in the *voiture balai,* trailing the field to pick up riders who have quit. The symbol of their work is the 15-foot-long broom—in French, a *balai*—mounted atop their blue 12-seat van.

"We sweep up after the race," Pietrowski explained before the 163-kilometer stage from Blagnac to the mountain resort of Guzet Neige. The stage, the first in the Pyrenees, was expected to generate business for the *voiture balai,* or broom wagon in English. It travels third from the end of the nearly 1,000 cars, trucks, motorcycles and, of course, bicycles in the race. Behind it come only a flatbed truck for wrecked cars and a police van marked *fin de course,* or end of the race.

So far back does the broom wagon roll that neither Pietrowski nor Guilmin had come within 15 minutes of seeing the finish of a stage in the Tour de France. When Massimo Ghirotto, an Italian with the Carrera team, won the day's climb, for example, the men in the broom wagon learned about it only by listening to a commercial radio station that broadcast the finish live.

The men in the van only heard how, in the sprint finish, Philippe Bouvatier of the BH team and Robert Millar of Fagor misunderstood a policeman's signal, began to take a wrong turn down a detour and were barely beaten by Ghirotto after they swerved back onto the course.

It was a rare and exciting finish but neither of the Frenchmen in the van minded not being there. "We don't miss much—just seeing it happen," remarked Guilmin as the radio reported that although Pedro Delgado had finished 14th, he had outdistanced his closest rivals and strengthened his hold on the yellow jersey. The Spaniard was now ahead of Steven Rooks by 3 minutes 28 seconds and Steve Bauer by 3:54. Delgado could virtually seal his victory the next day by doing well in the final stage in the Pyrenees, which would include five of the most demanding climbs in the race.

"Tomorrow we'll be busy," predicted Pietrowski.

When a rider quits the race, he usually stops on the side of the road and waits for the broom wagon to arrive, although a star rider sometimes is allowed to enter one of his team's two cars. In either case, Pietrowski helps hang the rider's bicycle on an accompanying truck and Guilmin performs the symbolic act of removing the two sets of numbers each rider wears for identification.

"I try to comfort them when they get into the van," Guilmin said. "I tell them what a hard race the Tour de France is, and I always say that a lot of other riders have quit, too." At that point, of the 198 riders who set out in Brittany, 176 remained. "I also tell them to think of next year, when they'll have another chance.

"Sometimes I help, sometimes not. I've seen riders weeping while they sit in the van and I've seen some laughing with relief that it's over. Most just sit there, quiet and exhausted."

If the van becomes too crowded, the overflow is moved to the flatbed truck carrying their bicycles. Or riders may be let out at a feeding station, where team cars are waiting to take them to their hotel.

Pietrowski, 26 years old, had been driving the van for two years and Guilmin, 67, had been a passenger for four years. He was a commissaire, or a race official, and spent 18 years riding second seat on a motorcycle, looking for infractions. "Then I got too old and they put me here," he said.

He is a soft-spoken, grandfatherly man who gave the impression that he might be willing to overlook mild transgressions. As he said while the van rolled past fields green with corn and golden with sunflowers, "No bicycle race in the world is as hard as this one. And a commissaire's job is hard, too. He must use his judgment."

The van never moves up the long parade to seek out a lagging rider but, if the last rider drops to the very rear, the van will remain a few feet behind him. To some, that might suggest a shark trailing a shipwreck survivor on a raft, but that impression is false, Guilmin said. "They recognize that we're not looking for business," he said. "It doesn't please us to have to pick somebody up."

He made his point when the Tour radio announced about 2 P.M. that No. 127, Atle Kvalsvoll, a 26-year-old Norwegian with the Z team, had fallen far behind on the climb to the Agnès pass. A few minutes later, Kvalsvoll came into sight as he labored up the mountain, 1,595 meters high and rated first category in difficulty. A first-year professional who was far down in the overall time standings, Kvalsvoll was struggling at a rate that registered less than 5 kilometers an hour on the van's speedometer.

For a few minutes, his team car rode alongside him to offer encouragement while a mechanic poured water on his head to help on the sunny and blazingly hot climb, but still Kvalsvoll wobbled. Even the cheers of the spectators did not help him push the pedals faster.

"Is he the last rider?" a spectator shouted at Guilmin. He looked away and quickly nodded yes, as if he were afraid of embarrassing the rider with an answer he might hear.

When a panel announced that the Norwegian still had 10 kilometers of climbing before the finish, the radio in the van was reporting Ghirotto's victory high atop the mountain. Kvalsvoll was fighting not only to finish but also to finish within the specified time differential with the winner. Beyond that point, which is determined by a complicated formula, he could be eliminated even if he did finish.

"I'm worrying about the time delay," Guilmin said to Pietrowski.

Then spectators began to take turns pushing the rider up the long series of switchbacks as Guilmin looked on. For a commissaire, pushes—even unsolicited—are exactly the sort of infraction to be on guard against, and indeed Kvalsvoll was later penalized 300 francs and 40 seconds for four unsolicited pushes.

Whatever the official number, Kvalsvoll must have broken the Tour de France record. One at a time, two at a time and sometimes even three at a time, fans planted their hands on his back and shoulders and on his bicycle seat and sped him up the mountain.

Finally he crossed the finish, in last place, 32 minutes 21 seconds behind the winner. From 67th place, he had fallen in the overall standings to 100th.

"Was he within the time limit?" Guilmin anxiously asked a finish-line judge who climbed into the parked van at the end. Assured that he had been, Guilmin smiled: No riders had entered the van on this stage.

But, he said gloomily, "Tomorrow we'll be busier."

JUST ANOTHER VILLAGE

2000

DOWN UNDER OR UP ABOVE, bicycle races seem to bring the same pleasures to small towns. This could have been a village in France, Belgium, Spain or Italy, but instead it was Urailda, Australia, population about 300, too small to be described in the press guide to the Tour Down Under.

Or perhaps there was nothing to say about Urailda, where the road took a sharp right 74.5 kilometers into the 136-kilometer stage.

Nothing to say? The guide found this much to say about Echunga, before Urailda: "The next township is Echunga, the site of a popular gold mining area in the 1880s." And this much to say about Lenswood, after Urailda: "Heading through the Onkaparinga Valley, the race will pass through the town of Lenswood—famous for its apple and pear orchards."

So no gold and no fruit. But Urailda did have, on its short main street, a social hall, a gas station, a butcher shop, a sports field, two groceries, a small building labeled a squash club, with a "For Lease" sign out front, and a hotel.

The hotel, the Urailda Hotel and Steak House, was hung with a big banner: "Party on till late / Xmas and New Year's Eve / Music Prizes Fun Guaranteed." This was mid-January but things move slowly in town and that banner will be coming down sooner or later. Things keep interfering, like the bike race.

According to residents, most everybody in Urailda turned out to watch at the spot where the road took its bend to the right. There were parents and, since this is summer school vacation, a lot of children, most of whom had stopped outside the butcher shop. A man behind a grill there was offering a tasty Sausage Sizzle for an Australian dollar (66 cents). Mustard is "mustard" here, but ketchup is "tomato sauce." And, yes, everybody is "mate."

Also in the crowd were a dozen bicycle riders, fans who follow the race but cut across and around the course so that they can see the proceedings at several points. Again, it could have been any small town in Europe.

Most of the fans' jerseys were labeled Gan, Buckler, PDM and MG, all defunct professional teams. Where the fan had no big stomach bulging under his jersey, the name on the shirt was a local amateur team.

The road signs pointed to Basket Range, Forest Range, Camelot Castle and, mysteriously, Aristologist. The best local explanation for the last was "Well, it's a, you know, aristologist."

Just before 1 P.M., some police motorcyclists with the race passed by, waving to the crowd. Perhaps because this was only the second running of the Tour Down Under, not the 91st edition of Paris-Roubaix, the South Australian police were remarkably friendly. Even the five men in the police patrol who rode bicycles as they kept spectators off the road at critical points refused to be blasé. Whenever they crossed a finish line or sprint point, the first one over raised his hands in echo of a Tour Down Under victor.

Soon, behind more motorcycles and cars, the riders arrived. No. 36, Ludovic Turpin of France and the AG2R team, was first to take the bend uphill, followed by No. 46, Nicolas Vogondy of France and the La Française des Jeux team. Both won loud applause. So did the rest of the pack a few seconds later. Even the ambulance that trails the race and completes the caravan was applauded.

"That was fun, wasn't it?" a mother asked her child as they began to leave.

But it was not over yet. Two minutes behind everybody else, including the ambulance that should have been behind him, came No. 94, Brett Lancaster, an Australian with the United Water–AIS team. He was laboring head down and, with nobody to follow, did not realize that the course turned to the right.

Instead he veered to the left, past the bankrupt squash club and the first of the two groceries. Another 30 seconds and he would have cleared town, going the wrong way. People started shouting and waving. Others jumped into Lancaster's path and held up their hands, then pointed up the hill. The rider stopped and turned around, leaving Urailda to tremendous applause.

"Now that was really fun, wasn't it?" the mother asked her child. "You know, different."

Sunday Outing

1984

WHEN THE 1984 TOUR DE FRANCE FINALLY BROKE FREE of its start in Seine-Saint-Denis, it was Sunday, and so everybody went for a ride in the country, as the French do on Sunday.

The day's stage, the Tour's second, was to cover 249 kilometers northeast to Louvroil in the beginning of a two-day penetration of what is now the Nord Department, the North, formerly Flanders. For about the first 20 kilometers, the road passed through anonymous suburbs until the fields on either side turned green and brown, no longer filled with gray stone houses in need of upkeep.

The crowds were larger than might have been expected of such sparse country, but it was Sunday and the first day of July besides, the start of the four-week French vacation, which, despite folklore, not all the French take in August. That alone could not explain the crowds, since the Tour was heading north and the French swarm south on vacation, accompanied by Belgians, Dutch, Danes, Swedes and Germans yearning for sun and heat. But there they stood, lining each turn and rise, many of the men in cycling jerseys.

Bicycling is practiced on a club level throughout France, with riders passing up the ranks based on age until they catch the eye of a top-flight amateur team, many of them affiliated with a professional team. At age 20, a rider may turn professional, but if he is any good, he will long since have signed a letter of intent with a professional team. If he does not attract one, he can continue to race with the amateurs until he begins to feel uncomfortable competing against boys or, worse, losing to them. Then he decides he is not breaking training if he has a few beers with his friends, because he is no longer really in training. At lunch with the gang from his factory or garage, he will eat sandwiches or French fries, and soon he is barely able to squeeze into his racing jersey. Luckily it is sold in an extra-large size in most cycling shops. By the time he is 30, the rider who was a great hope in his local cycling club when he was 17 is now the man at the side of the road in black shorts and striped jersey as the Tour comes by. The professionals carry fruit in the pockets of their jersey, but he will have stuffed his with a chunk of sausage, a piece of cheese and some bread, and his water bottle is filled with red wine. While the race passes, he and his buddies, similarly dressed and leaning on their bicycles, compliment this rider's style or criticize that rider's bearing. Afterward they lay their bicycles in the grass and enjoy their picnic; it is, after all, a Sunday in the country.

The Tour itself was only slightly more animated. The day before, Franck Hoste of the Europ Decor team had won the sprint finish of the first stage and picked up enough bonus seconds—actually a deduction from his overall time—touring the Seine-Saint-Denis towns to take the yellow jersey from Bernard Hinault, who was less than a minute behind.

Hinault would have ample opportunity to regain the 30 seconds Hoste had won by finishing first. Two types of time bonuses were available: reductions of up to 30 seconds from the times of the first three finishers of each stage, plus up to 12 minus seconds for the first three at specified bonus sprints, or "hot spots," along the way. Besides time reductions and financial prizes, points were awarded, ranging up to 35 on the flat and 12 in the mountains, to determine the wearer of the green jersey, the points leader.

Nothing stirred until the first bonus sprint, when Eddy Planckaert, a sprint specialist with the Panasonic team, found himself dueling with Greg LeMond, the world champion, for a 12-second bonus. Planckaert should have won but did not, overcome with amazement, like somebody at a country auction suddenly realizing that the other bidder for an old brass bed is the Getty Museum.

The day passed quietly, hot but not oppressively so because of a head wind that was strong enough to cool down the passion for breakaways.

"Everybody watched everybody else," LeMond later explained. "There was no chance of an exploit." There was also no daily prize for combativeness. Every once in a while somebody made a desultory attempt to escape, but it was obvious that he didn't mean it, and the pack turned up its pace a hair and quickly brought him back.

Strategy dictated a breakaway attempt by one of the weaker teams, those that had no strong mountain climber, because the first 10 days were all the race they had. But the road was narrow, allowing no more than three men abreast, and they blocked escape. For now the riders seemed most concerned with staying out of one another's way in such a big field, avoiding the accidental grazing of wheels that can cause a crash.

Still it happened: At kilometer 78, a tight left-hand turn through the village of Faverolles, Jean-René Bernaudeau of the Système U team fell, scraping a knee. Everybody managed to ride around him.

Sunday in the country. Dumas père grew up near Faverolles, and it was there that Victor Hugo had Jean Valjean steal the loaf of bread in *Les Miserables.* Asked for a cheese sandwich, the owner of a small café in Neufchelles proudly produced a cheese board with five or six varieties, and invited his customer to make his own sandwich. Near Condé-sur-Aisne, a young pheasant flapped across the road. Potatoes, it seems, do not simply grow like lumps of coal in the earth but put out a large and delicate green leaf. The rolling fields were broken by thickets of trees in which who knows how many soldiers died in World War I.

At kilometer 198, Giovanni Battaglin of the Carrera-Inoxpran team, Claude Criquielion of Splendor and Edgar Corredor of Teka all fell and quickly remounted. The crowds were especially large in Laon, where the road leading up to the ancient fortress was jammed. Some spectators carried signs for Hinault and some for Laurent Fignon; one boy stood on his lawn with a hand-lettered sign that said, "Que le meilleur gagne"—may the best man win.

This is farming country, not so rich as in the Loire Valley but still fertile enough to impress an Irish visitor who marveled that so much of the land could be given over to grain. For miles on the right the fields are planted in wheat and barley; on the left they are planted in potatoes.

Sunday in the country. The pack was still under control. Near Crécy-sur-Serre, across a field patchworked with brown barley and dark green kale, the riders descended a hill in what looked, from a distance, like slow motion. A multicolored column of ants was on the move. The sun was still hot, the head wind cool.

The fields gave out long before Louvroil, where the race was eagerly awaited. As a local newspaper put it: "What a pretty picture the Tour de France made sweeping into Louvroil, through the heart of red and gray houses, those houses of the North that go so well with bicycling. Through the heart, also, of an enormous crowd, excited and vibrant. Louvroil, a workers' city, a city stunned like its neighbors in the Sambre Basin by its industrial difficulties, Louvroil became suddenly the most-watched city in Europe. By the magic of a pack of cyclists, by the magic of the Tour de France. From now on no sports-minded Belgian, Dutchman, German, Swiss, Spaniard, Italian or even Colombian will no longer not know of our existence. They'll also know that hidden in this place are treasures of dynamism that allowed a welcome with flawless efficiency for the greatest cycling race in the world."

As the riders passed the finish line for the first time and began a five-kilometer circuit, they were still bunched. With half a kilometer to go, Marc Madiot of the Renault team fought clear and finished first by two seconds. The yellow jersey was taken over by Jacques Hanegraaf of the Kwantum team because of bonus time won en route.

The medical bulletin said Bernaudeau and Philippe Leleu of the Vie Claire team had been treated for skinned left knees, Francis Castaing of Peugeot for conjunctivitis, Corredor for a bruised left shoulder, Marc Sergeant of Europ Decor for an injured left thumb and Alfonso Florez of the Colombian team for a superficial scalp cut and scraped left knee and elbow after a fall. Florez was streaming blood down his face when he finished and looked a sight, but was chipper the next morning.

Jaime Vilamajo of the Reynolds team was fined 75 francs and penalized 10 seconds for receiving a bag of food from his team manager at kilometer 158, or 16 kilometers beyond the feeding zone, where the riders whiz through and grab a light sack of food. His manager was fined 375 francs. Claude Vinçendeau of the Système U team was fined 50 francs for stopping on the left side of the road, instead of the regulation right, after he had a flat. His manager was fined 100 francs for replacing the tire while his rider was on the wrong side of the road.

The crowd continued celebrating in Louvroil for some hours after the riders left for their hotels. For them, the race would continue tomorrow, and Sunday in the country was over.

Far from Home

2000

NEARLY EVERYTHING IS DIFFERENT. The flowers are not the anemones or irises of France but oleander, frangipani and bougainvillea. The birds are not alouettes or hirondelles but golden orioles. Even the pasta that Denis Leproux eats in large quantities is not the durum semolina that bicycle racers are always fed in Europe but bee hon, thin noodles made of rice flour.

"It's different, yes," Leproux says. "Exotic."

This is the first trip to Asia for Leproux, 35, a Frenchman who is racing in Le Tour de Langkawi in Malaysia with the Big Mat–Auber team from his native land. "Homesick?" he says, repeating a question. "A little, but it's good to see other parts of the world. Also, it's very cold in France now. This weather is much better for training."

He was leaning on his bicycle in the port town of Lumut, looking out at hills shrouded in heat haze even at 10 in the morning. Nearby were open-air shops selling dried cuttlefish and squid, star fruit and coconuts. Most of the female shoppers wore Muslim head scarves, a politicized issue in France but normal in a country where every hotel room has an arrow pointing worshippers to Mecca.

Some things were familiar: He could piece together the meaning of a sign that advertised the Akademie Muzik Kreatif, putting the adjective where the French do. As often happens at home, a brass band heralded the riders' arrival to sign in for the daily stage. But what did Leproux make of the dancers in ancient Malaysian costume and the men who followed them, bearing staffs with stylized flowers made of multicolored tinfoil?

"Different, yes." But then, so is Denis Leproux.

In 1986, as a 22-year-old amateur, he won a stage in the Tour du Limousin, a French race in which professionals also participated, and caught the eye of the Z team. Signed to a two-year professional contract, Leproux had some good results in 1987 but tailed off in 1988. When his contract was not renewed by Z and he could not find another employer, he rejoined the amateur ranks in 1989.

For nearly 10 years he continued to ride as an amateur for various clubs, having his finest year in 1997, when he won five multiday races and nearly a dozen small one-day races. He was named the top amateur rider in France by the sports newspaper *l'Equipe* and, at the end of that season, Leproux decided to turn professional again.

"I think I've missed something," he said then. "Now I've got this desire to see what kind of a professional I can be. Maybe when I left Z, they weren't patient enough with me. Or maybe I wasn't ready then to be a pro."

Committing himself to a new team that failed to find enough sponsorship money and folded before it opened, Leproux signed again with an amateur team. Then, in April 1998, three months into the season, the Big Mat second-division team lost its leader, Pascal Lino, to injury and looked around for a good climber.

Leproux is a good climber, he says honestly. Signed by Big Mat, he made its team for the Tour de France that year.

Last year he was one of two riders contesting the ninth and final spot on Big Mat's Tour team, which finally went to the other rider. Leproux rode well enough all year, however, to be signed for another season.

"This is just training," he said before Le Tour de Langkawi pushed into the Cameron Highlands and its first big climb, a 50-kilometer slope that is rated as the longest ascent on the international racing calendar.

"We'll see how it goes," he said. "I'm just testing my legs." He finished the stage 63rd among the 147 riders, nearly six minutes behind the winner, Wong Kam Po, a Hong Kong native with the Telekom Malaysia All-Star team. The next day, Leproux rode well and finished in the middle of the main pack after it passed over the one major climb on the way from Tapah to Bentong in the fifth stage of the 12-day race.

Many hills remain, including a testing climb in the Genting Highlands. "Maybe I can do something there," Leproux said over the music of a native band, heavy on the drums and gong.

Leap of Faith

1999

WHAT HELPED, OF COURSE, was that the sun came out. The same village that can look so forlorn in the rain will glow when the sun comes out.

In any case, this was a special village, neat and tidy, picturesque in a quiet way: the houses made of fieldstone and stucco, a town hall, school, firehouse and post office designed to be set together, a long lawn leading to a pond with a saltbox building at the far end.

While it looked like Vermont, it was *la France profonde,* the heartland, on a small road in Brittany. The sign along route D81 pointed to the nearby town of Vigneux de Bretagne and the distant attractions of Nantes.

The village is called Fay de Bretagne and it is too small a place for any of the prefab shopping centers, each building a small aircraft hangar, that have been rising just outside French towns for a decade, offering parking space while underpricing the local baker and grocer.

Fay de Bretagne is too small even to have a municipal swimming pool; a notice at a bus stop gave the hours for the trip to the pool in bigger Blain up the road.

On the Rue de Solferino, named for one of Napoleon's greatest victories, a few hundred people were waiting near a banner marking the spot for a bonus sprint in the Tour de France. There were many children in the crowd, lured there by the advertising caravan that precedes the riders by an hour and flings to the spectators caps, pieces of candy, leaflets, plastic bags, little bags of sausage, giant paper hands and supermarket flags.

Adults often grapple with a child for the junk. Not in this village, though. The same decorum that marked the architecture governed the spectators.

A man at the curb explained that this was dairy country, gesturing at pastures that spread flat to the horizon. Black-and-white cows moved under a sky full of puffball clouds.

Where the road turns gently right and the street name becomes the Rue de la Mairie stands the Résidence St. Joseph, an old folks' home.

About 20 residents were ranged in wheelchairs on the front lawn, facing toward the sprint banner. More than half of them were wearing either the red-and-yellow gas company caps or the yellow mobile phone caps that the hucksters had thrown from their cars. A few residents wore straw hats obviously their own. Behind the line of wheelchairs, attendants in white chatted with each other.

Four old men stood on the steps leading to the residence's door.

You like the Tour de France? a visitor asked one of them. Never miss one, he said. (The bicycle race may have passed this way once before in the decade and then again may not have.) Got any favorite riders? All of them. What are you going to do after the race passes? Wait for dinner.

The noise of beeping cars and motorcycles heralded the Tour. Ten minutes later the wave of color down the road came close enough to be identified as individual riders surging toward the bonus sprint banner. The first man across the invisible line was, appropriately, the man in the yellow jersey of the overall leader. Behind him the pack formed a long unbroken line.

The riders made the soft right turn in front of the Résidence St. Joseph and began heading out of the village, past St. Martin's church and homes with vegetable gardens at their sides.

Already the crowd by the sprint banner had begun leaving. For them, the Tour de France had come and gone.

The four old men swiveled slowly, carefully, and watched the race pass. Like the village, the many colors of the riders' jerseys glowed in the sunlight. A mother and father came down the street and their two small boys shrieked with joy at the disappearing riders. In that moment, it became possible to believe again in the race's purity.

Native Son

1998

IF ANDREI TCHMIL, EX-RUSSIAN, EX-UKRAINIAN and freshly minted Belgian, had been given a choice of where to win his first bicycle race before his new countrymen, he might not have chosen Kuurne.

Certainly victory in the celebrated Tour of Flanders or Liège-Bastogne-Liège races would have been far more prestigious than victory in Kuurne-Brussels-Kuurne. The first two are World Cup classics while Kuurne-Brussels-Kuurne is just a tune-up race, a chance to put some kilometers in the riders' legs for the season—and the major races—ahead. The competition is minor, mainly second-division Belgian teams, the weather almost always dreadful and the race itself not overly demanding.

But Kuurne, a village in Flanders, is a bicycle-mad hot spot in a bicycle-mad country. They know how to put on a race here: the thousands who show up early at the staging area outside the hippodrome to look the riders over and offer a word of advice, the thousands who pack the main streets and stand, as they probably have stood for all 51 runnings of the race, in the inevitable cold, hard rain (who can forget the battering sleet of 1995?) to cheer at the finish.

On Sunday, they had a chance to cheer Tchmil, ranked sixth in the world and now one of their own. Since 1994 the leader of the Lotto team based in Belgium, he has ridden Kuurne-Brussels-Kuurne before, of course, and usually finished in the top 10 over its 200 kilometers. But then he was licensed in Ukraine, where he was born in 1963 to Russian parents.

For the last few months, he has been a Belgian. The reason, he explained after his victory last fall in the Paris-Tours classic, was security for himself and his family. As one of the first eastern European riders to come West a decade ago, he settled in Italy and was given a visa that will be withdrawn once he stops racing. Now 35, he expects the finish to come in 2000.

The decision to apply for Belgian citizenship wasn't easy, he said, especially for somebody who speaks several languages but finds Flemish, in his own word, incomprehensible. As an example, his name is sometimes being written this season as Tsjmil, probably no problem for somebody who started life in Cyrillic.

So there was Tchmil, one Belgian among many. Older men rode clunker bicycles and wore the jerseys of nearly forgotten Belgian teams: Isoglass, Hitachi, Histor-Sigma, Tonton Tapis; boys showed up in the jerseys of their local sponsors: Garage Johan, Atlas, Sani Perfect.

The bar in the grandstand of the hippodrome, where the riders signed in, began to attract beer drinkers about 10:30 A.M., more than an hour and a half before the race start. The Tiercé café outside was packed, as was the Paddock café down the street. After all—Belgium.

It was cold but, in the quickly changeable Belgian weather, sunny all morning. People circulated. Two pretty girls passed out posters of the Spar team. The organizers of the Cholet-Pays de Loire race later this month in France wooed team officials to compete there. Small boys distributed start lists of the names and numbers of the 178 riders for 25 teams. The sun cheered everybody up.

The rain began a few hours later, when the pack was moving at high speed past fields speckled with crows eating freshly sown seeds. On and off, it rained most of the afternoon and the wind and cold increased. By the time the muddy riders came down the Kluisberg hill, 70 kilometers from the finish, the pack was down to about 60 men.

On the descent, three riders attacked. They were Frank Vandenbroucke, a Belgian with the Mapei team, Emmanuel Magnien, a Frenchman with La Française des Jeux, and Tchmil. From 10 seconds on the Kluisberg, their lead rose to a minute and a half when they reached Kuurne and began the first of three long laps around the village. The rain was steady. Vandenbroucke tried to escape on the final lap but Tchmil caught him and then attacked himself. Magnien was unable to hold the pace and Tchmil had no real difficulty in pulling alone away to win by five seconds.

Jammed behind the barriers along the narrow main street, the people of Kuurne applauded the one-two finish by local boys. Vandenbroucke hails from Mouscron, just down the road, near the border with France, and Tchmil—he now comes from Belgium itself, doesn't he?

THE LAST LEGENDARY RACE

1984

MOST OF THE YEAR, Maurice Le Guilloux thought only of others: his wife, his two young daughters, his employer, the Vie Claire bicycle team. At work, he continued to be selfless. He was not a star but an *équipier*, literally "teammate," but actually a support rider, one of the men who earn their living by sacrificing their ambitions in the service of a leader.

At the lowest level, that of *domestique*, the *équipier* fetches and distributes water bottles and raincoats during a race; when the team manager's car is blocked in race traffic, the *équipier* will relay instructions to the leader; if the leader has a flat, the *équipier* will give him the wheel from his own bicycle.

At a higher level, the *équipier* will be sent after a rival on a breakaway, wearing him down with pursuit, increasing the pace for the riders left behind. At the highest level, the *équipier* rides with his leader, helping him set his rhythm, preceding him up hills so that the leader can save strength by riding in the slipstream of the *équipier's* bicycle.

Le Guilloux had done all these tasks, and done them well. At the age of 34 and after 11 years as a professional, by 1984 he was regarded as a model *équipier.*

"He's a team rider, really fantastic in his loyalty, always doing his job," said Greg LeMond, a former teammate of Le Guilloux's. "He's a devoted team rider, and there's never a problem with him," said Bernard Hinault, a longtime friend and leader to Le Guilloux. "For as long as I can remember, since I've ridden for Bernard I've never started a race with the hope of winning," Le Guilloux said in corroboration.

Sometimes Le Guilloux thought about how he had never won a major race, how he rarely had the opportunity or strength to shine at the end of the day. "I wanted to do something in front of my public," he said a few years ago after a stage of the Tour de France in his native Brittany, "but I didn't have anything left. I have to do an *équipier's* job, and people don't always understand an *équipier's* job."

When he thought about this, he also realized that he had become one of the elders of professional racing. How many seasons could be left? He thought especially about the race he had consistently come closest to winning—the 586-kilometer one-day race in May from Bordeaux to Paris.

Run partly during the night, Bordeaux-Paris is one of the most demanding of all races. He finished fifth in 1978, third in 1981 and second in 1982. At these times, Le Guilloux, who thought only of others most of the year, allowed himself to think of Le Guilloux. "It's the one race where I can work for myself," he said. "There's no strategy in Bordeaux-Paris, no tactics. It's simply every man for himself." He sat back in his chair and appeared to enjoy the thought during a chat that spring.

Le Guilloux was at his training camp, a hotel in forests west of Bordeaux, just beyond the fields and châteaus of the wine country. In its isolation the hotel was perfect as a bus stop for group tours heading to the Atlantic beaches, for businessmen holding weekend seminars and for a cyclist preparing for an ordeal.

Businesslike, he ticked off the many hours of training he had spent in his week at the hotel before the race. "I did 200 kilometers on Monday, 380 on Tuesday, 100 on Thursday, and just 60 today"—about 12 hours before the race started at 2:30 A.M. The training was divided between riding alone and following a motor bicycle; for 358 of its 586 kilometers, Bordeaux-Paris is run behind a motor bicycle, called a *burdin*.

"It's not only long, but hard, and goes so fast," Le Guilloux said. "Behind the *burdin* you can reach 65 kilometers an hour, and there's no stopping, never. You just concentrate and pedal," he continued, screwing up his face and hunching his back as his hands reached for imaginary handlebars. "Your feet begin to hurt terribly, and it's impossible to relax. You can't look around or breathe deeply for even 50 meters. The wind changes constantly and you really get buffeted. A house by the side of the road, some trees, they change the wind. And then there's the traffic, the cars and trucks—that's very dangerous.

"And the tedium gets to you. Even eating is difficult. You're sitting down and you need the kind of food that takes two hours to get from here"—he sliced at his throat—"to here"—he jabbed at his stomach. "I'll tell you, it's so difficult that all you want to do is win.

"I've spent three months preparing for the race, I've sacrificed so many chances to win small races in Brittany and make some money. The team has spent so much money on me. But if I knew that I would finish third in this Bordeaux-Paris, I'd leave right now and go straight home.

"So why do I want to do it?" he repeated the question. "For the glory. More for the glory than for the sport or the money. What does the winner make? Ten thousand francs" (actually 17,000 francs, or about $3,400).

"It's the last great race," Le Guilloux said. "It's an inhuman race—the distance, the hardship, the danger. People love to watch it. It's the last legendary race, and a chance for me to become part of the legend."

Le Guilloux didn't mention it, but he was also seeking revenge. After his second place Bordeaux-Paris in 1982, he had no doubt that his team, then Renault, would enter him in 1983. Instead, while he was riding in the Tour of Spain, he learned that he had been passed over for a younger rider.

"I have no illusions left," Le Guilloux said then. "This was the chance of my career. I have to avoid thinking too much about it because I'm in Spain to help Bernard Hinault and I don't have the right to waste my energy. If I give in to the blues, I'd have to believe my career has just ended."

At the end of the season, Le Guilloux joined Hinault in leaving Renault and moving to a new team, La Vie Claire. When Hinault called a press conference to announce the team, Le Guilloux was present, bursting to talk about another chance at Bordeaux-Paris.

Intensive training began in March. Le Guilloux was set back by an attack of nephritis that put him in the hospital for a week in April and took 11 pounds off his 6-foot, 165-pound frame.

"Despite all this, he's in good shape," said Paul Köchli, Le Guilloux's trainer with *La Vie Claire.* Basing his method on "the physiology of the body," Köchli is a *directeur sportif* of the new school in cycling. Nevertheless, he uses the old-school definition in talking about the Bordeaux-Paris race. "It's a test of perseverance," he said, "a rider knowing his limits and pushing himself right up to that line."

In final preparation, Le Guilloux planned a late lunch, then a massage, and then he hoped to nap. "It's difficult to sleep the evening before this race," he said. "I always try, but I haven't succeeded yet. Instead, I pack my things, concentrate my thoughts and pray for good weather."

He went in to lunch, sitting with his masseur, his mechanic and Köchli next to a long table with 20 businessmen discussing that morning's sales seminar and *le marketing.* When his steak arrived, Le Guilloux—just a country boy—startled the businessmen by noisily stropping his knife against his fork.

So much for Le Guilloux's prayers: It was raining hard when the 20 riders gathered at 2 A.M. to get ready for the race. Nor had he managed to nap. He was intense as he adjusted his heavy uniform for the nightlong ride in the rain.

A few hundred fans stood in the street, mostly jammed against the windows of the Maison du Vin de Bordeaux with its casual display of great bottles of Pauillacs, St. Emilions and Médocs. This was the 81st running of Bordeaux-Paris, which began in 1891 and was interrupted by the two world wars and, in 1971–1972, by lack of interest. The race was held then in October, at the end of the season, and nobody had the strength to ride all the way to Paris overnight. Once the date was shifted to the late spring, it regained popularity.

At 2:30 the riders moved out in the ceremonial start, and at 3 A.M., at a supermarket outside Bordeaux, they left officially. Despite the hour, there were people waiting to cheer them in nearly every small town along the route, a secondary road often paralleling the Paris-Bordeaux superhighway. Most of the fans stood under umbrellas, a few here at a crossroads, which the police had blocked until the riders passed, a few there outside a cluster of houses or a late-night *brasserie.* In many villages the only spectators were bakers, standing at the curb in their white uniforms, the open doors behind them showing their ovens.

The pace for the first hour, with the riders bunched in the light of trailing cars, was steady at 36 kilometers. It was cold and wet, and soon Köchli's car pulled alongside Le Guilloux to pass him food—rice pudding, chicken ("things that are good for him and that he likes," the trainer explained), bread, cheese ("in a long race you need some fats, not just sugar"), even some baby food ("Why not? It's easy to digest").

To wash it down, Le Guilloux had mineral water or tea. As he finished his snack, a signboard announced that Paris was 513 kilometers away.

Rain was still falling as it began to turn light at 5:20. The empty green fields of Chevançeaux, Barbezieux and Roullet-Saint-Estèphe rolled by. In the village of La Chignole, a farmer stood in his driveway next to two milk cans. By 6:30 the rain had stopped, and by 7:30 the sun was up and the riders were too hot in their plastic raincoats. One by one, their team cars moved alongside and the riders pulled off clothes and gloves and passed them to hands reaching out the car windows. The UNCP team took advantage of the transfer; a hand reached out a window and settled in the small of a rider's back to push him along. It is a well-practiced trick, and was quickly spotted in the main official's car, if not by the judge riding in each team car. "Stop that, please, the UNCP car," crackled a message on the radio linking all cars. After a few moments, the hand moved out again and settled on the rider. "This is the last warning," the radio announced. The team car dropped back.

Small-town France was awake by this time. In Ruffec, just opening for the day, the butcher stopped loading his small truck with meat for a nearby market day and went to summon his family; two daughters appeared in bathrobes and waved as the cyclists sped by. In the local bar, two men put down their 8 A.M. Scotch and soda and came outside to cheer. Villagers love bicycle racing, the only sport they can watch free.

At Vivonne, the riders had a 45-minute rest stop, the only one of the race. Sitting in a manor house converted for the day to a training center, the cyclists changed from their bulky night clothing to the shorts and short-sleeved jerseys they would wear the rest of the way.

It was time to eat again, and some were content with a yogurt, some with thick sandwiches. Many were rubbing lanolin into the padded crotch of their racing shorts: A long ride lay ahead, and cyclists dread boils.

Outside, their bicycles were being tightened and washed, to reduce the chance of grit in the chains and brakes. Inside, the smell of wintergreen was heavy. Le Guilloux, looking concerned, was massaging his feet as the masseur kneaded his thighs.

The crowds were out now along the route, with whole classes of schoolchildren cheering anything that moved, including police cars and television motorcyclists. A great cheer was heard at Poitiers, when the riders, at full speed, fell in behind their pacers on motor bicycles.

The trick is to stay close enough to take full advantage of the slipstream and the windbreak, and yet never let the bicycle's front wheel touch the machine; at that high speed the bicycle would spin away, out of control. Bicyclist and pacesetter have practiced together for long hours, and the best-coordinated teams looked as if they were attached. A reserve motor bicyclist trailed each tandem as protection for mechanical failure.

Up through the Loire Valley the race continued. It is accepted wisdom that the race does not really start until Orléans—150 kilometers short of Paris—when fatigue begins to separate the riders, but the first sustained breakaway came at Montbazon, 130 kilometers before Orléans.

Marcel Tinazzi of the UNCP team accelerated and quickly built up a five-minute lead. The winner of this race in 1982, Tinazzi was outspoken as head of the French cyclists' labor union and considered to be a bit of a troublemaker. Whatever the reason, he had not found an employer for the 1984 season and, on France's welfare rolls, had formed his own team—all five riders on relief. He spent his own money to keep the team going, finding a sponsor only two days before the race. As he said later, he had something to prove in Bordeaux-Paris.

Through Orléans and Pithiviers and Milly-la-Forêt, through the departments of Loiret and Seine-et-Marne and Essonne and finally into the last leg, Val-de-Marne—for 275 kilometers Tinazzi kept his lead, the longest breakaway in memory.

With Tinazzi nine minutes ahead, Le Guilloux began to move up in a counterattack. He was racing well when, at Malesherbes, 87 kilometers from Paris, his back wheel began to crumple. In the few minutes before his bicycle could be repaired by the mechanic in his team car, he had lost his chance to catch Tinazzi. "After that," he said, "I rode without hope."

Close to 4:30 P.M., 14 hours after he left Bordeaux, Tinazzi cruised alone into the Paris suburb of Fontenay-sous-Bois, the winner by 4 minutes 27 seconds. Hubert Linard of the Peugeot team was second, and Le Guilloux outlasted three rivals for third place. Of the 20 riders who began the race, 16 finished.

Wan, his face covered with grime, Le Guilloux admitted he was disappointed. "It was an easy race," he said, "except for the rain. I thought I had a good chance until the wheel broke."

Did Le Guilloux remember saying beforehand that if he knew he would finish third he would go straight home? Mercifully, nobody asked that question. Instead, he was asked if he would be back next year to try again. Looking past his questioner, Maurice Le Guilloux chose not to reply.

In Philly

1997

A BIG TREE, A SYCAMORE by the dessicated look of it, uprooted itself and tumbled onto the course during the bicycle race in Philadelphia on Sunday. With about a third of the 156-mile race still to be run, there the tree lay on the road below the Art Museum in Fairmount Park.

"About 800 people attacked that tree and moved it right off the road," said a race official. "They were like ants, pulling the branches and manhandling the trunk back onto the grass."

When what was left of the 150-man pack swept through minutes later, coming down Lemon Hill off the Schuylkill River, the road was clear.

"Those people came to see this bicycle race and they weren't about to let a tree get in the way," the official said.

That sums up the spirit of the CoreStates USPRO Championship, which has been staged in Philadelphia once a year since 1985 and which has sponsorship from the CoreStates Bank until 2005. In a time of dwindling financial support for bicycle road racing, the race appears to be a model of how a sponsor and a municipality—American, European or Asian—can work together to produce what the 1960s called a people's festival.

In the suburb of Manayunk, for example. Along Main Street, which the race traversed 10 times, the yuppie crowds were as thick as the cream in their cappuccinos at outdoor tables near Le Bus café, Ma Jolie Atelier and such secondhand clothes stores as Wear It Again Sam and Worn Yesterday. At least one of the $4,000 bicycles leaning against a storefront had a crooked, and therefore inefficient, saddle but hey, whatever.

Take a right off Main Street into another world, that of the Manayunk Wall, the town's 21st Ward, a kilometer-long uphill past blue-collar houses.

"There's a bicycle race, grab a beer and watch for six hours," somebody said. "There isn't a bicycle race, grab a beer and don't watch for six hours."

A lot of beers were grabbed Sunday. A lot of food, too. Despite the 80-degree heat, people worked over grills to make and sell cheese steaks, a Philadelphia staple that takes some getting used to, sausage-and-pepper-and-optional-onion sandwiches, barbecue and barbecued ribs, soft pretzels, Italian ices, hot dogs, crab cakes and hoagie sandwiches, whose name seems to be as obscure as the luncheon meat within.

People also throw private parties, as a first-time visitor learned when he followed his nose down an alley between houses and found a man making omelets on an outdoor stove. "It's my own party," he said, "for my neighbors and friends." He looked the visitor over. "Always nice to make new friends," he said.

Manayunk knows how to make the day a festival. At O'Brien's Watering Hole, a small series of pierced pipes extended over the road and sprayed water onto any rider who didn't—or didn't want to—get out of the way. "Been doing it since the race started," O'Brien said. "The riders appreciate it on a hot day."

The championship always has been run on a hot day, officials said. Never a drop of rain yet. That helps draw the crowds, which are estimated between 200,000 and 750,000; the higher ranking the official, the higher the estimate.

It also helps that the race is shown in its six-hour entirety on local television and broadcast on an otherwise rock 'n' roll radio station.

"People see or hear the race and decide to come on down for the last few hours," a Philadelphian said. "The crowds are always biggest at the finish.

"Of course," he admitted, "it's free. And there isn't all that much else to do in Philadelphia on a Sunday."

Dreaming Big Dreams

2000

"WELCOME TO THE BIG LEAGUES," John Wordin grumbled as loudspeakers announced the imminent start of the bicycle race.

While he inched along the car from which he advises, browbeats, cajoles and inspires the riders of his Mercury team, Wordin kept grumbling. Finally he came out with it: The day before, at the customary meeting of team directors to discuss the race, the head of the Telekom team from Germany had leaned over and politely asked Wordin, "Do you know the rules?"

"'Do you know the rules?'" Wordin repeated. "Well, we did win 83 races last year, so I guess we know the rules."

This race was the Critérium International in France and the Telekom official had no reason to know Wordin or his team. Telekom is a First Division team and rides in all the big races on the European circuit, where its men have won two of the last four Tours de France; Mercury is a Second Division team and rides almost exclusively in North America, where the races are less prestigious.

Wordin, a 38-year-old Californian, is striving to upgrade his team's rank, which is why he brought eight riders to France and Belgium this spring for four races. Mercury did well. It won a stage in the two-day Critérium International and placed first, second and first again in the three other races, all one-day competitions.

Now Wordin and Mercury have returned for the second part of their European campaign: they will be competing for the next two weeks in three races in Spain. The visit started triumphantly as Mercury's Henk Vogels won the first stage of the Tour of Rioja.

"We're trying to get into the Tour of Sweden, the Tour of Luxembourg, the Tour of Catalonia, but our big goal is to try to get into the Tour of Spain this year," Wordin explained as he joined the long automotive caravan behind the riders in the Critérium International. "If we ride well in the spring races in Spain, we'll probably get in."

The Tour of Spain, more formally the Vuelta a España, is not his highest goal, however. That one is the Tour de France. "If you're in cycling, that's the Super Bowl of cycling," he feels. "That's the biggest showcase, the biggest spotlight, the biggest event there is. If you're in cycling, that's your dream."

To fulfill that dream he will have to talk his sponsor, a division of the Ford Motor Company, into vastly increasing his budget, a figure he will not divulge. With the extra money, Wordin could hire riders with many International Cycling Union points, which determine, in total, whether a team is in the First Division, with its automatic invitations to major races, or the Second.

Thinking about it, Wordin broke into a grin. "I get calls, asking about jobs, from better riders now than I used to," he said. "This winter I suspect I'll get a lot of calls. In the beginning, it was guys you never heard of, they're probably good regional riders and they want to try to get that opportunity. But now I get calls from guys you know."

While he was dreaming about the Tour de France, the Telekom team car passed on the left and the official driving it waved hello to Wordin. "Just trying to be helpful, I guess, when he asked that question," he decided.

The flag went down, the race radio linking all cars said "Top," as the French do to signify the start, and Wordin had other worries than perceived slights.

"One reminder, guys," he said over another radio, which broadcast through earpieces to each of his riders. "If you flat, call out your name on the radio and say, 'Chris flatted' or 'Floyd flatted.' Keep riding till I get there. Everybody copy?"

Wordin admitted that he and the team were under some pressure in the race, which was run by the organizers of the Tour de France—good people for an upwardly mobile team to have on its side. If Mercury does not make it to the First Division, many races, including the Tour, hold a few wild-card spots for Second Division teams.

"The riders know what the stakes are as far as making a good result here," Wordin said. "We've talked about it."

As for himself, he continued, "I put pressure on myself. I have my own expectations of how I want things to go." Those expectations have sometimes been criticized in the United States as overly aggressive.

David Clinger, a Californian who rode for Wordin last year and now is with the Festina team based in France, put it this way: "If you're not riding for him, he's probably the worst guy you can have against you."

Jonathan Vaughters, a Coloradoan and another Wordin alumnus, who now is with the Crédit Agricole team in France, said: "Basically he doesn't say, 'This is the way it's been done before so this is the way we're going to do it.' He says, 'We'll try this and see if it works. If it doesn't, we'll try something else.'

"For American cycling to grow, there are going to have to be more people like him. You need people who will take an offbeat approach and do things a little bit out there in order to get sponsors involved. Overall, he's a really positive influence.

"But he definitely doesn't fit into the mold of a European director," Vaughters concluded. "He's a football coach, you know."

"Football coach" is not a metaphor. A former defensive lineman at California State University–Northridge, the 6-foot-5-inch Wordin coached high school football for years while he competed himself and began forming his first teams in 1992. His riders, present and past, report affectionately that he belongs to the "My way or the highway" school of coaching.

As if on cue, he snapped to his riders: "Let's go guys, who's tail-gunning it back there? Get your butt up there. Come on Jamie Drew, let's go. Steve Zampieri, let's go, get up there. Come on Jan, join the party. Get up there, Jan, come on, Jan, move up."

At other times he was more informational. "Six riders off, small gap, small gap," Wordin said about a breakaway that the race radio was detailing for him. When he heard the composition of the breakaway, he told the Mercury riders to relax. "Unless there are some pretty big guys in the group, it's not going to stay away."

Later: "Okay guys, we're at 16.7 kilometers, 16.7 ks." Why that piece of data? "Just to keep them focused. They were just meandering along. They were probably talking with their buddies." Wordin can be so focused that he says he rarely notices scenery along a race route.

Still later: "It's a very dangerous descent coming up" after a small hill. "One of the guys in the breakaway has crashed. Be careful on the descent." Whether because of the warning or not, no Mercury rider was involved in a mass crash on the descent.

And finally, with the day's stage nearing its end: "Move up, Jan. See where everybody else is up there?" Wordin was shouting now. "Come on Jan, get up there." His voice went back to normal. "The race takes a sharp left before the last 200 hundred meters. Jan, Henk, I want you to take Gord into that corner. Gord, you go after that."

Wordin's car was diverted off the route for the final few hundred meters and he could not see the finish but heard about it on the radio from a staff member at the line. In the final kilometer, Vogels set a strong pace for the team's sprinter, Gord Fraser. Then Jan Bratkowski towed him to within 200 meters of the line and Fraser sped to an easy victory.

Told that Wordin had let out a loud couple of whoops at the news, Fraser later said, "Normal. John likes to win more than we do."

The next day, because of the victory, the Mercury car was first in the caravan. As he set off for the stage, Wordin was exulting in the No. 1 sticker on the car and telling his mechanic to peel it off afterward. "I want it for my suitcase," he explained. "It says Critérium International, Car No. 1.

"Hey that's a nice souvenir. If we can get one from the Tour de France, then we're really doing well."

A Bleak Forecast

2001

FOR SOMEBODY WHO HAS SPENT a quarter of a century enthralled by the sport of bicycle racing, the news from the Giro d'Italia is heartbreaking. What was for so long a love affair increasingly feels now like the tag end of a bad marriage.

Not that the reports that 200 Italian police officers conducted a late-night swoop on riders' hotels and seized banned drugs, syringes and unlabeled medicine bottles really came as a surprise.

A memory: Two years ago this weekend, a reporter sat in a hotel garden in the French city of Aix les Bains, the lake a blue slur at the bottom of the hill, and chatted with Lance Armstrong, who was then in the early stages of his comeback from cancer. The first of his two consecutive victories in the Tour de France was nearly two months away.

Their talk was midway between an interview and a conversation by two old friends. The tape recorder was running except when Armstrong asked that it be turned off as the talk turned to drugs in the sport. He didn't want to say anything controversial on the record, the Texan explained. Nor off the record either, as it turned out.

Simply put, Armstrong believed the drug scandal of the 1998 Tour de France had played itself out. Most of the Festina team had confessed to systematically using illegal performance-enhancers; the police, while overreacting—the accepted wisdom among the riders—had made their point, and anybody who continued to rely on banned drugs had been warned off.

Finito, he said. Not so, the reporter said, not at all. Drugs are entrenched in the sport, he said. There will be scandals to come, he predicted.

Armstrong scoffed. *Finito*, he repeated.

The next day, as the riders were preparing to set off in the one-day Classique des Alpes from Aix les Bains to Chambéry, word swept through that Marco Pantani, winner of the 1998 Tour de France and Giro d'Italia, had been dismissed from the Italian race after he failed a blood test that indicated the use of the forbidden EPO drug. Pantani had been one day away from his second victory in the Giro.

The riders were already rolling away from the starting line and there was no chance to talk with them. That would have to wait, six or seven hours later, for the finish line.

There, at a school gym, the riders swerved along a potholed road, heading for the showers. Watching the road carefully for hazards, Armstrong changed course, gliding over to the reporter.

How did you know? he asked. What did you know?

It had been a tough day, many hills and a few mountains to climb, and the road dust powdered his face. His eyes were wide and, rarely for him, he sounded uncertain, puzzled, almost beseeching.

Nobody knew, he was told, but nearly everybody suspected.

That was June 1999. In the two years since, the suspicions have not abated.

Armstrong's first victory in the Tour de France was riddled with so many questions about drugs that he had to call a news conference to deny that he was using any. The fact that he later remembered he was using a cortisone cream, for which he had a medical waiver, did not resolve doubts.

After his second victory, the French media charged that his U.S. Postal Service team had used a product so obscure that it was not on the list of banned substances. The official results of tests of the riders' blood and urine are pending.

These tests have been refined and enlarged. Already this season, four riders have been suspended for using EPO. Two more retired from the Giro on Wednesday after tests showed, in the escapist term of the sport, that they had proven "non-negative."

Then the Italian police moved in, searching hotel rooms, suitcases and team cars. The rest of the script was a replay of the 1998 Tour de France: The riders met for hours in protest, the daily stage was first shortened, then canceled; the race was threatened with a mass walkout before everybody decided that the show must go on.

Just as familiar was the blather from bicycle racing officials.

Dieter Schellenberg of the International Cycling Union, which governs the sport, was quoted as having said: "In a way, this is a positive sign, it shows that everyone is against doping, but the manner is exaggerated. Nothing much will come out of this, but the prosecutor's name will be known by everyone.

"Doping is not particularly worse in cycling than in other sports, but it is more public," he added. "In the Tour de France in 1998, we found organized dealing and doping. But that doesn't exist anymore."

More sensibly, Giancarlo Ceruti, president of the Italian Cycling Federation, said the police raids were the price that must be paid if riders did not yet understand the need to clean up their sport.

Will it ever be cleaned up? At this point, can it be? How much further into the gloom can bicycle racing plunge before it becomes irrelevant?

There will be scandals to come, Armstrong was told two years ago. How did you know? he asked. Some things you just know.

The Heart of the Country

1989

THE OBLIGATION TO BE MODERN fuels the disappearance of the old France. "Chic" and "new," the buzzwords of advertising, are used to sell soap, groceries and fashions. In Paris, this is true especially. Paris is a sharp-elbowed city, a city strangled by cars and their insistent horns, a city teeming with people with thin lips and thinner eyes. This great city finds little room in its heart for that which is not chic or new. The *vélo*—the French word for bicycle—is neither in Paris.

A small article in the sports newspaper *l'Equipe* carries the headline "A New Bicycle Club in Paris." The Paris Cycliste Olympique club will start soon, the article reports, putting the proper spin on the fact that the club will incorporate the Athletic Club of the 20th arrondissement, the Vélo Club of the 12th arrondissement, the Vélo Club of Paris and the Vélo Club Lion of Denfert-Rochereau. "These will cease to exist," *l'Equipe* adds offhandedly.

There is Paris and, outside it, there is France.

Not so far outside Paris (2.2 kilometers, or a little over a mile) lies Puteaux, one of many towns where the capital's day laborers spend their nights. On the Rue de Verdun, a hotel advertises rooms by the season: 1,000 francs for the six months of spring and summer, 1,300 francs for the six months of fall and winter, when the cost of heating sends the bill up. The hotel appears to be crowded, with three or four men sharing a room and sending most of the rest of their wages back to their families in Algeria, Tunisia or Morocco. Half the town's restaurants seem to be named The Star of Tunis and a good couscous is available everywhere.

Portuguese live here, too, and some Africans and Spaniards. It is not a very large place, Puteaux, with its rundown charm and low prices and some cobblestoned streets with leaning houses that might have served as models for the paintings of Utrillo.

The town also has an amateur *vélo* club, CSM Puteaux, and one spring evening a couple of years ago it organized the eighth annual Grand Prix of Puteaux, leaving at 8:15 P.M. precisely from the covered market (open Thursdays and Sundays) on the Rue Chantecoq. In a sweet touch, the club invited cyclists from two of the European towns that Puteaux has twinned itself with, Offenbach, Germany, and Moedling, Austria. Also in the field of 105 riders were some from the premier French amateur clubs, including CSM Persan, VC Fontainebleau, US Creteil, CC Wasquehal and the vaunted ACBB of Boulogne-Billancourt.

The average foreign tourist has never heard of most of these towns, which offer nothing to see or do compared with the attractions of Paris. They are all much like Puteaux, which, for those interested in history, has little to show besides the 16th-century Notre Dame de Pitié church. The Seine does roll along an edge of town but its waters carry working barges instead of sightseeing boats. Signs posted along some of the major streets announce blips in the town's routine: School prizes will be distributed on June 17 and 24, a fair will be held in primary schools on June 10 and 17, a photography show will run from June 5 to July 13 at a cultural hall.

Puteaux is a slow town really, which is why the Grand Prix drew a good crowd on a chilly evening. The route was short, a circuit of 2.3 kilometers, covered 40 times for a total of 92 kilometers including one tough climb and many sharp corners lined with bales of hay. Almost from the start the field was splintered and a group of eight opened a lead of more than a minute. As hundreds standing near the finish line on the Rue Roque de Fillol cheered, Hervé Lepinay, a rider for CSM Puteaux, held off his only challenger, Bruno Lebras of CSM Persan. For Lepinay, this was sweet revenge. "I did to Lebras what he did to me in Paris-Vailly," Lepinay said as he accepted a trophy from the deputy mayor of Puteaux, who arrived just in time to present it and make a dull speech about the virtues of bicycling. Lepinay, who had been riding as an amateur for years and, in his late 20s, no longer had any hopes of turning professional, knew all about these virtues but smiled anyway.

Nobody there knew it but in another year Puteaux would be discovered by real estate speculators, who began knocking down some of the worst houses on the Rue de Verdun and replacing them with high-rise apartment blocks. The gentrification of Puteaux began. Two bakeries were face-lifted during the August vacation. Scaffolding began growing all over town and the piano store was scheduled to become a realty office. A vacant lot given over to lilac bushes turned into an office building. Banks opened branches. An appliance store that was selling cylinders of natural gas to the town's North Africans just a year ago now filled its windows with raclette machines. And hibachis. And electric knives to open oysters.

Suddenly a Beaujolais nouveau party was staged in the town hall. Next came a tour of Puteaux's historic homes and gardens, if any. Paris had arrived at the gates of Puteaux.

Coincidentally the CSM Puteaux bicycle club announced a few months later that, because it had lost sponsors in a time of ever-increasing costs, it would withdraw from competition. Presumably this doomed the Grand Prix. In vanishing France, in hoping-to-be-chic Puteaux, there was no protest.

But bicycle racing has roots deep into the French soil. In Paris the preference in sports has moved upmarket to tennis from bicycle racing, which, with its emphasis on struggle and sacrifice, was an ideal sport for a country rebuilding after World War II. Now the mood—in Paris—has turned against sacrifice and suffering. Despite their names, Paris-Roubaix, Paris-Nice, Paris-Camembert and a handful of other races prefixed with "Paris" start far outside the capital. Traffic problems, officials explain, but the true reason is indifference.

Only in the countryside, in vanishing France, where the old prejudices live on, is bicycle racing still a major sport. Boulogne sur Gesse in the French southwest is one of those places.

Boulogne is a small town (1,600 residents by generous count) founded by an order of monks in the 13th century. Between then and now not much appears to have happened in Boulogne, according to tourist literature. The biggest day ever arrived on March 23, 1814, when the English army under the Duke of Wellington camped there overnight on its way to fight Napoleon. In seven centuries, Boulogne sur Gesse has produced only two persons judged noteworthy by the same tourist literature: Emmanuel Perès de la Gesse, a minor figure in the French Revolution who advanced to become a baron of the empire, and Jacques Moujica, who won the marathon Bordeaux-Paris bicycle race in 1949. That same year he finished third in Paris-Brussels and fourth in Paris-Roubaix. A year later, at the age of 24, he was killed in a car crash while traveling to a bicycle critérium after the Tour de France.

Moujica is buried in Boulogne sur Gesse, which mourns him still. When the Tour de France whizzed through the town a few years ago on a stage from Blagnac to Luz Ardiden in the Pyrenees, journalists with the race were invited to a late breakfast/early lunch—"brunch" is a Paris word—in Boulogne and served bowls of hearty stew and beakers of heartier wine. The reception hall, a market most other days, was decorated with posters celebrating Moujica and his feats. Scrapbooks covered display cases, as did some of his Mercier team jerseys. Townspeople sat on wooden benches with the journalists and talked about Moujica and that glorious Bordeaux-Paris as if he had won it earlier in the season.

The mayor spoke, too. He discussed the decline of rural France, where agriculture is imperiled by rising costs and falling subsidies, and quoted Talleyrand as having said that "Industry can only weaken the national morality; France must remain agricultural." Everybody applauded, even the farmers who mainly wanted to talk bicycle racing, that elegant and humble sport.

Outside Paris, where there is little obligation to be modern, where chic and new are distrusted, fans still flock to races to play their own small roles: If the day is hot and a climb long and tiring, people will hold out a bottle of water to a cyclist or pour it over his head. Pushes, even unsolicited ones, may be illegal and yet officials will often look away when a fan helps a faltering climber by shoving him uphill. In the time before a race starts, fans will circulate among the pack, seeking autographs from their favorites, posing for photographs alongside this rider or that, wishing good luck to all. Their grandparents did it, their parents did it and now they do it, bringing their own children. Sacrifice and struggle are still part of this world.

So who could have really been surprised when, last spring, posters announced the next Grand Prix of Puteaux? Any observant eye noticed that the pace of the town's modernization had slowed. The new apartment houses were only partly filled, an attempt at a trendy restaurant opened and closed twice before it became a sandwich shop, vacant stores remained vacant despite their signs promising a bank or boutique. The invasion by Paris had been repulsed and Puteaux was returning to its roots.

One evening last June, the Rue Chantecoq was filled by more than 100 riders from such clubs as AS Corbeil Essonne, VC Levallois and CM Aubervilliers, all towns that no tourist to France ever visits. The field included nine riders from CSM Puteaux, the host club. Had it been resurrected? Or had it never gone away?

Following two motorcycle policemen whose blinking yellow lights announced that the riders were right behind them, the Grand Prix of Puteaux turned a corner and was quickly under way. Long after the riders were out of sight, shouts of "*allez, allez,*" chased them on the evening breeze. Go, go. Go forever.

Index

About the Author

SAMUEL ABT, an associate editor of the *International Herald Tribune*, has covered bicycle racing for 25 years. He has written 10 books about the sport, including the acclaimed *Breakaway: On the Road With the Tour de France* and *LeMond*. He is the only American to have been awarded the medal of the Tour de France for distinguished service to the race.

A graduate of Brown University, where he studied American literature, he has also been a Professional Journalism Fellow at Stanford University, where he studied history. Before he moved to France, he was an editor for several newspapers in New England, for the *Baltimore Sun* and for *The New York Times*.

After being based in Paris for three decades, he has been working in Asia since 2000, first as founding editor of an English-language daily newspaper in South Korea and more recently in Hong Kong as Asia/Pacific News Editor for the *International Herald Tribune*.